Reading Philosophy of Religion

Reading Philosophy

Reading Philosophy is a series of textbooks offering interactive commentaries on selected readings, and covering the major sub-disciplines of the field. Each volume contains a number of topical chapters each containing primary readings, accompanied by an introduction to the topic, introductions to the readings as well as the commentary. Edited by leading scholars, the aim of the books is to encourage the practice of philosophy in the process of engagement with philosophical texts.

Reading Philosophy
Samuel Guttenplan, Jennifer Hornsby and Christopher Janaway

Reading Philosophy of Language
Jennifer Hornsby and Guy Longworth

Reading Aesthetics and Philosophy of Art
Christopher Janaway

Reading Epistemology
Sven Bernecker

Reading Metaphysics
Helen Beebee and Julian Dodd

Reading Ethics
Miranda Fricker and Samuel Guttenplan

Reading Philosophy of Religion
Graham Oppy and Michael Scott

Forthcoming

Reading Philosophy of Mind
Louise Antony

Reading Philosophy of Religion

Selected Texts with Interactive Commentary

Graham Oppy
and
Michael Scott

A John Wiley & Sons, Ltd., Publication

This edition first published 2010

Blackwell Publishing was acquired by John Wiley & Sons in February 2007. Blackwell's publishing program has been merged with Wiley's global Scientific, Technical and Medical business to form Wiley-Blackwell.

Registered office
John Wiley & Sons Ltd, The Atrium, Southern Gate, Chichester, West Sussex, PO19 8SQ, United Kingdom

Editorial offices
350 Main Street, Malden, MA 02148-5020, USA
9600 Garsington Road, Oxford, OX4 2DQ, UK
The Atrium, Southern Gate, Chichester, West Sussex, PO19 8SQ, UK

For details of our global editorial offices, for customer services, and for information about how to apply for permission to reuse the copyright material in this book, please see our website at www.wiley.com/wiley-blackwell

Library of Congress cataloging-in-publication data
Reading philosophy of religion : selected texts with interactive commentary / [compiled by] Graham Oppy and Michael Scott.
p. cm. – (Reading philosophy)
Includes bibliographical references and index.
ISBN 978-1-4051-7082-6 (hardcover : alk. paper) – ISBN 978-1-4051-7081-9 (pbk. : alk. paper)
1. Religion–Philosophy–Textbooks. I. Oppy, Graham Robert. II. Scott, Michael, 1970–
BL51.R322 2010
210–dc22

2009050990

A catalogue record for this book is available from the British Library.

Set in 10/12pt Sabon by Graphicraft Limited, Hong Kong
Printed and bound in Malaysia by Vivar Printing Sdn Bhd

1 2010

Contents

Sources and Acknowledgements

The editors and the publisher gratefully acknowledge the permission granted to reproduce the copyright material in this book:

William Alston, 'Irreducible Metaphors in Theology', from *From Experience, Reason, and God*, ed. Eugene T. Long (Catholic University of America Press, 1980). Text taken from a reprint in *Divine Nature and Human Language: Essays in Philosophical Theology* (Cornell University Press, 1989), pp. 17–38.

Anselm, 'Chapter II', pp. 7–8 from *Proslogium; Monologium; an Appendix in Behalf of the Fool by Gaunilon; and Cur Deus Homo*, trans. Norton Deane (Open Court, 1903).

Aquinas, 'Whether There Is a God', p. 15 from *Summa Theologiae*, Volume 2, *Existence and Nature of God*, trans. T. McDermott (Eyre & Spottiswoode, 1964). © Blackfriars, 1964. Reprinted with permission from Cambridge University Press.

A. J. Ayer, 'Language, Truth and Logic', pp. 151–5 from *Language, Truth and Logic* (Penguin, 1986). © 1936, 1946 by A. J. Ayer. Reprinted with permission from Victor Gollancz, an imprint of The Orion Publishing Group, London.

George Berkeley, 'The Seventh Dialogue', pp. 286–93, 296–7, 301–3 from *Alciphron* (Thomas Nelson & Sons, 1950).

Boethius, 'Free Will and Foreknowledge', pp. 197–204 from *The Consolation of Philosophy of Boethius*, trans. H. R. James (Routledge, 1900).

William Clifford, 'The Ethics of Belief', pp. 177–87 from *Lectures and Essays*, ed. Stephen Pollock (Macmillan, 1879).

Nicholas Everitt, 'Arguments from Scale', pp. 213–18 from *The Non-Existence of God* (Routledge, 2003). © 2004 by Nicholas Everitt. Reproduced by permission of Taylor & Francis Books.

John Hick, 'The Pluralistic Hypothesis', pp. 233–49 from *An Interpretation of Religion: Human Responses to the Transcendent* (Macmillan, 1989). © 1989 by John Hick. Reprinted with permission from the author and Palgrave Macmillan.

David Hume, 'Dialogues Concerning Natural Religion', pp. 467–80 from *The Philosophical Works of David Hume*, Volume II (Adam Black and William Tate, 1828).

William James, 'The Will to Believe', pp. 2–30 from *The Will to Believe and Other Essays in Popular Philosophy* (Longmans, Green and Co., 1912).

Norman J. Kretzmann, 'Abraham, Isaac and Euthyphro: God and the Basis of Morality', pp. 35–46 from *Harmartia: The Concept of Error in the Western Tradition*, ed. D. Stump (The Edwin Mellen Press, 1983). © 1983 by The Edwin Mellen Press.

John Leslie Mackie, 'Evil and Omnipotence', pp. 200–4, 206–9, 212 from *Mind*, 64 (1955). © 2006 by the Mind Association. Reprinted with permission from Oxford University Press.

Christopher New, 'Antitheism: A Reflection', pp. 36–43 from *Ratio* (New Series), 6 (Blackwell Publishing, 1993). © 1993 by Blackwell Publishing. Reprinted with permission from Blackwell Publishing Ltd.

William Paley, 'State of the Argument', pp. 9–20 from *Natural Theology* (American Tract Society, 1881).

Blaise Pascal, 'Pascal's Thoughts of the Necessity of the Wager', pp. 84–7 from *Blaise Pascal Thoughts, Letters, Minor Works*, trans. W. F. Trotter, M. L. Booth and O. W. Wight (P. F. Collier & Son, 1910).

Nelson Pike, 'Divine Omniscience and Voluntary Action', pp. 31–5 from *The Philosophical Review*, 74 (1) (Duke University Press, 1965). © 1965, Sage School of Philosophy at Cornell University. All rights reserved. Used by permission of the publisher, Duke University Press.

Alvin Plantinga, 'Is Belief in God Properly Basic?', pp. 41–51 from *Nous*, 15 (1) (Blackwell Publishing, 1981).

Alvin Plantinga, 'Pluralism: A Defense of Religious Exclusivism', pp. 191–215 from *The Rationality of Belief and the Plurality of Faith*, ed. T. D. Senor (Cornell University Press, 1995). © 1995 by Cornell University. Reprinted with permission from the publisher, Cornell University Press.

Hilary Putnam, 'Wittgenstein on Religious Belief' and 'Wittgenstein on Reference and Relativism', pp. 142–56, 158, 167–8 from *Renewing Philosophy* (Harvard University Press, 1992). © 1992 by the President and Fellows of Harvard College. Reprinted with permission from Harvard University Press.

Georges Rey, 'Meta-atheism: Religious Avowal as Self-Deception', pp. 252–8, 259–60, 261 from *Philosophers without Gods: Meditations on Atheism and the Secular Life*, ed. Louise M. Antony (Oxford University Press, 2007). © 2007 by Oxford University Press, Inc. Reprinted by permission of Oxford University Press, Inc.

William Leonard Rowe, 'The Problem of Evil and Some Varieties of Atheism', pp. 335–8 from *American Philosophical Quarterly*, 16 (4) (University of Illinois Press, 1979). © 1979 by American Philosophical Quarterly. Reprinted with permission from the journal.

C. Wade Savage, 'The Paradox of the Stone', pp. 74–9 from *The Philosophical Review*, 76 (1967). © 1967, Sage School of Philosophy at Cornell University. All rights reserved. Used by permission of the publisher, Duke University Press.

Every effort has been made to trace copyright-holders and to obtain their permission for the use of copyright material. The publisher apologises for any errors or omissions in the above list and would be grateful if notified of any corrections that should be incorporated in future reprints or editions of this book.

Introduction

Religion is a ubiquitous feature of human life. Most human beings self-identify as members of one of the world's long-established major religions: Christianity, Islam, Hinduism, Judaism, Buddhism, Taoism, Confucianism, Shinto, Jainism, Sikhism, and traditional indigenous religions. Many other human beings self-identify as members of religions or religious sects of more recent provenance: Rastafarianism, Unificationism, Jehovah's Witnesses, Santeria, Voodoo, Christian Science, Radhasoami, Wicca, neo-Paganism, New Age spiritualism, Theosophism, Baha'i, Aum Shinrikyo, Order of the Solar Temple, Branch Davidians, Falun Gong, and countless others. Moreover, this is not merely a fact about *contemporary* human life: it seems that it has *always* been the case that religion is a ubiquitous feature of human life.

Religion is not merely a ubiquitous feature of human life; it is also an extremely powerful force in human life. Most who self-identify as religious believers claim to found their life, their hopes and their values in their religion. Moreover, for many who self-identify as religious believers, religious observances are seamlessly integrated into the very fabric of their life: the lives of such people are structured by their religions and their religious beliefs. In many cases, religious organisations and religious traditions have enormous influence on the behaviour and beliefs of religious believers; and the positive effects of religion and religious belief can be recognised in almost all fields of human endeavour, including music, painting, literature, politics, business, sport, and so forth. On the other hand, much of the discord in human affairs can also be traced to religion and religious belief: many wars have been fought on the grounds of religious differences, and much of what is worst in human behaviour is exhibited in religious disputes. One reflection of the widespread recognition of the controversial nature of religion and religious belief is that religion has often been regarded as a *taboo* topic: sex, politics and religion are simply not proper matters for polite conversation.

Given the position that religion occupies in human life, it is not surprising that religion has been a perennial topic of philosophical inquiry. In the face of *disagreement* about religion and religious beliefs, there are a number of possible responses.

It might be that there is a single correct or true religion, and that every other religion is simply mistaken; and it might be that there are arguments that can demonstrate to all reasonable people which is the single correct or true religion. In particular, it might be that there is a single correct conception of the divine; and it might be that there are arguments that can demonstrate to all reasonable people that this particular conception of the divine is unique in being actually instantiated. If so, it might be hoped that the bad consequences of religious disagreement will ultimately be defeated because there will be convergence of opinion under the force of reason.

It might be that there is a single correct or true religion, and that every other religion is simply mistaken, even though there are no arguments that can demonstrate to all reasonable people which is the single correct or true religion. In that case, it might be that there can be reasonable disagreement amongst reasonable people about at least some religious questions; and it might be that there is no reasonable expectation that reasonable people will reasonably converge on any particular view – let alone the true view – on those religious questions. If so, it might be hoped that the bad consequences of religious disagreement will ultimately be defeated because it will become universally recognised that the only reasonable option is to live and let live when it comes to questions of religious belief.

It might be that there is no single correct or true religion, and that there are many religions that do equally well in approximating to the truth at which all genuine religions aim. In that case, it might be that reasonable people will reasonably agree that religious disagreements are not worth fighting over, since – despite appearances – it turns out that religious believers agree on what really matters. And, if so, there is again good reason to hope that the bad consequences of religious disagreement can ultimately be defeated, when the truth of the situation is universally recognised.

It might be that there is no single correct or true religion because it is simply inappropriate to assess religious claims in terms of 'truth' and 'correctness'. If religious claims are properly understood on analogy with, say, expressions of taste, it will turn out that there is no genuine disagreement between the proponents of the 'claims' of different religions. If you prefer chocolate to strawberry, and I prefer strawberry to chocolate, there is no factual dispute between us: it does not even make sense to suppose that I could mount a successful argument for the conclusion that you ought to prefer strawberry to chocolate. But, if so, there is good reason to hope that the bad consequences of 'religious disagreement' can ultimately be defeated, when the truth of the matter is properly understood.

It might be that there is no single correct or true religion because there is nothing that is divine, or transcendent, or ultimately meaningful, or the like. In this case, it might be that there are arguments that can demonstrate to all reasonable people that there is nothing that is divine, or transcendent, or ultimately meaningful, or the like; or it might be that there can be reasonable disagreement amongst reasonable people about whether there is something that is divine, or transcendent, or ultimately meaningful, or the like. Either way, there might be good reason to hope that the bad consequences of religious disagreement can ultimately be defeated – on similar grounds to cases discussed earlier – though, in this instance, one might worry about what would be lost if there were universal agreement that there is nothing that is divine, or transcendent, or ultimately meaningful, or the like.

The material in our book roughly covers the range of positions that we have just set out. In the first part of the book, we consider questions about the interpretation of religious language, and, in particular, questions about whether religious claims are properly assessed in terms of 'truth' and 'correctness'. In the second part of the book, we look at a range of arguments about the existence of God, and ask whether these arguments ought to be taken to settle certain religious questions once and for all. In the third part of the book, we examine questions about the range of reasonable disagreement in questions of religion: is it true that there can be *reasonable* disagreement between reasonable, reflective and well-informed people on matters of religion? In the fourth part of the book, we investigate some of the properties that are commonly attributed to God in monotheistic religions, and consider rguments for the view that it is impossible for anything to have these properties. In the fifth part of the book, we take up questions about religious diversity: is it reasonable to hold, given widespread disagreement among religious believers, that just one religious tradition is true?

Our book is an introduction to philosophy of religion: the aim of the book is to encourage readers to engage in the intellectual activities that are proper to philosophy of religion. To this end, our treatment of each of the topics that we have identified begins with excerpts from classic and contemporary philosophical texts that take particular positions on these topics. These excerpts are followed with commentaries that are intended to help you to engage with those texts: the commentaries provide suggestions about *how* to read the texts, and about how to engage with the ideas and arguments that are developed in the texts. You will note, in particular, that we have divided some of the longer excerpts into sections and introduced markers in the margin to indicate short pieces of text that are referred to in the commentary: these are used to assist in understanding the structure and argument of the text. Our commentary is interspersed with questions and with suggestions about activities that one should undertake as part of one's engagement with our selected texts.

In some cases, there is further pedagogical design behind the choice of texts and the kind of commentary that is provided. Thus, for example, in Part 2 ('Arguments about the Existence of God'), we begin with very brief excerpts from Anselm and Aquinas, each of which presents a single philosophical argument. Here our commentary is designed to bring out the way in which very short pieces of text of this kind can be subjected to *very* detailed philosophical examination. The next two excerpts – from Pascal and Paley – are longer, and more complex. Here our commentary is designed to bring out ways in which longer pieces of philosophical text can be subjected to probing philosophical examination. For some of the later excerpts – e.g. from Everitt and from Rowe – the commentaries are designed to lead to the asking of *some* significant critical questions about the arguments in these texts, but analysis of much of the material is left to the reader. And for other of the later excerpts – e.g. from Mackie – the commentaries are designed to illustrate the process of *extracting* a philosophical argument that is not fully explicit in a given text.

1

Religious Language

Introduction

Here is a preliminary sketch of the aim of research on religious language. Our principal objective is to give a general account of the meaning of religious sentences. Religious sentences are sentences with a religious subject matter: they concern, for example, supernatural agents (God, other deities, angels, etc.), their properties and their actions. A general account of the meaning of religious sentences includes the following: determining their truth-conditions, showing whether they express beliefs or non-propositional attitudes, giving an account of the meaning of religious terms and how they combine to form meaningful sentences. We also need to consider whether there are distinctive features of religious language that have implications for theories of truth and reference.

Most contemporary work on religious language is concerned with one or more of these issues; and, although answers to some of them may appear straightforward, they are all matters of substantial debate. Even the question of whether we should be concerned with religious *language* is contentious. Let us consider some of the main points of discussion:

1. Should we be concerned with the meaning of the *sentences* and constitutive terms that make up religious language, or the *utterances* and expressions that make up religious speech or discourse? An utterance is the production of a token sentence, usually in verbal or written form. William Alston argues that language is not religious by virtue of its having a religious subject matter: 'religious language' is an inapt title for this field of philosophical research. Rather, we should be concerned with the use of language in religious contexts.

> What is erroneously called religious language is the use of language (any language) in connection with the practice of religion – in prayer, worship, praise, thanksgiving, confession, ritual, preaching, instruction, exhortation, theological reflection, and so on.
> ('Religious Language' 220)

There are, therefore, two views about our topic: that we should be concerned with sentences with a religious subject matter, or with utterances in a religious context. Note that Alston's theory has some surprising implications. For example, the utterance of a sentence in a religious context will count as religious even if the sentence has no religious subject matter (consider, for instance, all of the sentences uttered on non-religious topics in a discursive sermon). We shall touch on this topic in the chapter on Alston and metaphor.

2. What are the truth-conditions for religious sentences? The correct account of this might seem pretty obvious – 'God is omnipotent' is true just in case God is omnipotent – and, in general, we should be able to work out the truth-conditions of an indicative religious sentence from what is said. This is disputed, however, by reductionists. Reductionists propose that the truth-conditions of the sentences under discussion are given by some *other* class of sentences. To take some non-religious examples, phenomenalists contend that statements about the external world can be analysed in terms of statements about our actual or possible experiences, while some behaviourists take sentences about mental states to be reducible to sentences about behaviour and dispositions. Naturalistic reductions of theistic religious language have been proposed by, among many others, Julian Huxley and Henry Wieman. The prospects for religious reductionism are considered by Ayer, and we shall look at this issue further in the chapter on Ayer.

3. Are religious sentences truth-apt and do religious assertions express religious beliefs? Here, again, it may seem that the correct theory is obvious: religious sentences represent the world as being a certain way, and when sincerely uttered they convey the speakers' beliefs. However, this is denied in non-cognitivist – also called 'expressivist' or 'emotivist' – theories of religious language. According to expressivists, religious utterances do not express religious beliefs but rather stances, plans, emotions and other non-propositional attitudes. Religious expressivism has frequently been defended in philosophy (and in theology) but has never received widespread acceptance. As we shall see in the three chapters that follow, the theory is held by some as a response to Ayer's critique of religion, it is sometimes (contentiously) associated with Ludwig Wittgenstein, and can be seen (in a *very* restricted way) to form part of Berkeley's account of religious language.

4. We saw above that there are different views about whether an utterance is religious by virtue of its context or by the subject matter of the sentence that it expresses. But to what extent does context play a part in determining the meaning of what is said? Clearly, there are some expressions that are context-sensitive: 'I', 'you', 'here' or 'now' are fixed by the person uttering them or the time or place in which they are uttered. When one of these 'indexical' expressions occurs in a sentence, its meaning has to be filled in with details from the context in which the sentence is used. But does context intrude in other ways on what is said in religious discourse? According to Wittgenstein, a religious believer who asserts

'There will be a Last Judgement' is not contradicted by a non-believer who denies it (*Lectures and Conversations* 55). However, the sentence 'There will not be a Last Judgement' is the negation of the sentence 'There will be a Last Judgement', and neither sentence contains any obvious indexical. So presumably, on Wittgenstein's view, the meaning of these sentences must be changed in some way in the course of utterance: the meaning of religious utterances is in part determined by (non-standard) contextual factors. We shall return to this issue when looking at Putnam's discussion of Wittgenstein, and also consider Putnam's contention that even our concepts of reference and truth take on distinctive features when used in the context of religious discourse.

5. Early writers on religious language – notably the church fathers – were concerned with whether a predicate used of God such as 'good' has the same sense when it is used in a non-religious context (is 'univocal'), in a different but related sense ('analogical'), or in an entirely different sense ('equivocal'). More recent attention has focused on the role of metaphor in religious discourse. We can distinguish literal utterances like 'God created the world', where the speaker means what is said, from metaphorical utterances like

God is my rock,
The Lord is my shepherd,
God is our Father

where a speaker seems to use a (false) sentence to convey something else. Metaphors like these are commonplace in religious discourse. One line of inquiry about religious metaphor, pursued recently by Janet Soskice, considers the relationship between metaphors in religion and in science. A second issue, explored by William Alston in his paper on metaphor, is whether *all true* utterances about God are metaphorical. This position, one recent exponent of which is Anthony Kenny, is primarily motivated by metaphysics: because God is 'transcendent', nothing can be literally predicated of Him. Alston rejects this argument: all metaphors posit some kind of comparison that can at least in part be literally specified.

Through much of the twentieth century, research on religious language was extensively occupied by the problem, raised most effectively by A. J. Ayer, of whether religious claims can be verified by evidence – and, if not, whether they can be held to be meaningful. However, as we shall see in the chapter on Ayer, the verification challenge – at least as far as it is supposed to present a problem to the meaningfulness of religious claims – is without substance. The concern with the verifiability of religious claims has tended to obscure the central role played by questions about religious language in the philosophy of religion. Specifically, certain facts about the truth and content of religious sentences and utterances have to be in place for familiar questions about metaphysics and epistemology – the topics that we shall explore in subsequent sections – to come into play. For example, work on issues such as divine properties or the existence of God, and on epistemological issues such as the rationality of religious belief, require the rejection of non-cognitivist and metaphorical interpretations of religious language.

If you are interested in pursuing questions about religious language further, the following are useful:

Alston, W., *Divine Nature and Human Language*, Ithaca, NY: Cornell University Press, 1989.
Alston, W., 'Religious Language', in W. Wainwright (ed.), *The Oxford Handbook of Philosophy of Religion*, Oxford: Oxford University Press, 2005.
Moore, A. and Scott, M (eds), *Realism and Religion*, Aldershot: Ashgate, 2007.
Scott, M., 'Religious Language', *Philosophy Compass*, 2009.
Stiver, D., *The Philosophy of Religious Language: Sign, Symbol and Story*, Oxford: Blackwell, 1996.

Introduction to Ayer

A. J. Ayer (1910–89) made his name philosophically with the publication of *Language, Truth and Logic* (1936), written while he was only 24. The book is a popular exposition of 'logical positivism', a theory developed from some of the ideas of an early-twentieth-century grouping of philosophers called the Vienna Circle. A guiding motivation of Ayer's book was the defence of a strong form of *empiricism*, the theory that all of our knowledge and significant ideas about the world derive from experience. Chief among the stated aims of Ayer's book is the elimination of metaphysics, that is, inquiry into issues that transcend matters of science and the observable world. Philosophy should instead be concerned with the analysis of the meaning of key concepts such as freedom, causation, knowledge, etc. To this end, Ayer proposed the notorious *verification principle*, according to which 'a statement is held to be literally meaningful if and only if it is either analytic or empirically verifiable' (p. 12). That is, unless a statement is verifiable (can be rendered probable or conclusively established by experience) or is analytic (true only by virtue of the meanings of the words that make it up), it is literally meaningless. Since ethics, aesthetics and religion all appear to involve metaphysical commitments that are neither analytically true nor verifiable, the upshot of the verification principle seems to be to render these areas of language largely meaningless. In the following piece, taken from the penultimate chapter of his book, Ayer draws out the dramatic implications of logical positivism for religious language.

A. J. Ayer, 'Critique of Theology' (selection from *Language, Truth and Logic*, ch. 6)

[a]→ It is now generally admitted, at any rate by philosophers, that the existence of a being having the attributes which define the god of any non-animalistic religion cannot be demonstratively proved. To see that this is

so, we have only to ask ourselves what are the premises from which the existence of such a god could be deduced. If the conclusion that a god exists is to be demonstratively certain, then the premises must be certain; for, as the conclusion of a deductive argument is already contained in the premises, any uncertainty there may be about the truth of the premises is necessarily shared by it. But we know that no empirical proposition can ever be anything more than probable. It is only *a priori* propositions that are logically certain. But we cannot deduce the existence of a god from an *a priori* proposition. For we know that the reason why *a priori* propositions are certain is that they are tautologies. And from a set of tautologies nothing but a further tautology can be validly deduced. It follows that there is no possibility of demonstrating the existence of a god.

b→ What is not so generally recognized is that there can be no way of proving that the existence of a god, such as the God of Christianity, is even probable. Yet this also is easily shown. For if the existence of such a god were probable, then the proposition that he existed would be an empirical hypothesis. And in that case it would be possible to deduce from it, and other empirical hypotheses, certain experiential propositions which were not deducible from those other hypotheses alone. But in fact this is not possible. It is sometimes claimed, indeed, that the existence of a certain sort of regularity in nature constitutes sufficient evidence for the existence of a god. But if the sentence 'God exists' entails no more than that certain types of phenomena occur in certain sequences, then to assert the existence of a god will simply be equivalent to asserting that there is the requisite regularity in nature; and no religious man would admit that this was all he intended to assert in asserting the existence of a god. He would say that in talking about God he was talking about a transcendent being who might be known through certain empirical manifestations, but certainly could not be defined in terms of those manifestations. But in that case the term 'god' is a metaphysical term. And if 'god' is a metaphysical term, then it cannot be even probable that a god exists. For to say that 'God exists' is to make a metaphysical utterance which cannot be either true or false. And by the same criterion, no sentence which purports to describe the nature of a transcendent god can possess any literal significance.

 It is important not to confuse this view of religious assertions with the view adopted by atheists, or agnostics.[1] For it is characteristic of an agnostic to hold that the existence of a god is a possibility in which there is no good reason either to believe or disbelieve; and it is characteristic of an atheist to hold that it is at least probable that no god exists. And our view that all utterances about the nature of God are nonsensical, so far from being identical with, or even lending any support to, either of these familiar contentions, is actually incompatible with them. For if the assertion that there is a god is nonsensical, then the atheist's assertion that there is no god is

[1] This point was suggested to me by Professor H. H. Price.

equally nonsensical, since it is only a significant proposition that can be significantly contradicted. As for the agnostic, although he refrains from saying either that there is or that there is not a god, he does not deny that the question of whether a transcendent god exists is a genuine question. He does not deny that the two sentences 'There is a transcendent god' and 'There is no transcendent god' express propositions one of which is actually true and the other false. All he says is that we have no means of telling which of them is true, and therefore ought not to commit ourselves to either. But we have seen that the sentences in question do not express propositions at all. And this means that agnosticism is also ruled out.

Thus we offer the theist the same comfort as we gave to the moralist. His assertions cannot possibly be valid, but they cannot be invalid either. As he says nothing at all about the world, he cannot justly be accused of saying anything false, or anything for which he has insufficient grounds. It is only when the theist claims that in asserting the existence of a transcendent god he is expressing a genuine proposition that we are entitled to disagree with him.

d → It is to be remarked that in cases where deities are identified with natural objects, assertions concerning them may be allowed to be significant. If, for example, a man tells me that the occurrence of thunder is alone both necessary and sufficient to establish the truth of the proposition that Jehovah is angry, I may conclude that, in his usage of words, the sentence 'Jehovah is angry' is equivalent to 'It is thundering'. But in sophisticated religions, though they may be to some extent based on men's awe of natural processes which they cannot sufficiently understand, the 'person' who is supposed to control the empirical world is not himself located in it; he is held to be superior to the empirical world, and so outside it; and he is endowed with super-empirical attributes. But the notion of a person whose essential attributes are non-empirical is not an intelligible notion at all. We may have a word which is used as if it named this 'person', but, unless the sentences in which it occurs express propositions which are empirically verifiable, it cannot be said to symbolize anything. And this is the case with regard to the word 'god', in the usage in which it is intended to refer to a transcendent object. The mere existence of the noun is enough to foster the illusion that there is a real, or at any rate a possible entity corresponding to it. It is only when we inquire what God's attributes are that we discover that 'God', in this usage, is not a genuine name.

It is common to find belief in a transcendent god conjoined with belief in an after-life. But, in the form which it usually takes, the content of this belief is not a genuine hypothesis. To say that men do not ever die, or that the state of death is merely a state of prolonged insensibility, is indeed to express a significant proposition, though all the available evidence goes to show that it is false. But to say that there is something imperceptible inside a man, which is his soul or his real self, and that it goes on living after he is dead, is to make a metaphysical assertion which has no more factual content than the assertion that there is a transcendent god.

It is worth mentioning that, according to the account which we have given of religious assertions, there is no logical ground for antagonism between religion and natural science. As far as the question of truth or falsehood is concerned, there is no opposition between the natural scientist and the theist who believes in a transcendent god. For since the religious utterances of the theist are not genuine propositions at all, they cannot stand in any logical relation to the propositions of science. Such antagonism as there is between religion and science appears to consist in the fact that science takes away one of the motives which make men religious. For it is acknowledged that one of the ultimate sources of religious feeling lies in the inability of men to determine their own destiny; and science tends to destroy the feeling of awe with which men regard an alien world, by making them believe that they can understand and anticipate the course of natural phenomena, and even to some extent control it. The fact that it has recently become fashionable for physicists themselves to be sympathetic towards religion is a point in favour of this hypothesis. For this sympathy towards religion marks the physicists' own lack of confidence in the validity of their hypotheses, which is a reaction on their part to the anti-religious dogmatism of the nineteenth-century scientists, and a natural outcome of the crisis through which physics has just passed.

It is not within the scope of this inquiry to enter more deeply into the causes of religious feeling, or to discuss the probability of the continuance of religious belief. We are concerned only to answer those questions which arise out of our discussion of the possibility of religious knowledge. The point which we wish to establish is that there cannot be any transcendent truths of religion. For the sentences which the theist uses to express such 'truths' are not literally significant.

Commentary on Ayer

Ayer's strategy is to argue that religious beliefs and statements are metaphysical. That is, they address a subject matter that transcends science and our experience. As such, they fall foul of the verification principle: since they are neither (i) verifiable nor (ii) analytically true, they are literally meaningless. However, for this strategy to work, Ayer needs to show that there is no plausible non-metaphysical reading of religious language, according to which religious statements are verifiable. He also needs to show that the central claims of religion could not be necessarily true. He begins by attempting to show the latter in [a]↦.

Ayer quickly dismisses the idea that there could be a successful deductive proof for the existence of a god. The first part of Ayer's argument runs as follows. The conclusion of a deductive argument is contained in its premises, and therefore the conclusion is only as certain as the premises. It follows that, if a deductive argument for the existence of a god is to prove that a god exists with certainty, we shall also need to be certain about the premises on which it relies. Consider, for example, the following argument:

1. If I passed my exams, there is a loving God.
2. I passed my exams.
3. There is a loving God.

A deductive argument is called *valid* if it satisfies the following condition: if the premises are true, then the conclusion cannot be false. The argument above is deductively valid, since the truth of the two premises of the argument – (1) and (2) – guarantees the truth of the conclusion (3) (it has the form of a *modus ponens*: $p \rightarrow q$, p therefore q). Now, while Ayer's point that the conclusion of the argument is 'contained' in premise (1) appears correct, it only appears as the consequent of a conditional. Neither premise actually states that there is a loving God – premise (1) only says that there is a loving God *if* I passed my exams. However, Ayer's more general point seems plausible: a deductive argument can only guarantee the truth of its conclusions if it does not introduce any new information that could possibly be false. So we should not expect the conclusion delivered by a deductive argument to be any more reliable than information given in premises on which it depends. In this case, even if we grant the truth of (2), premise (1) is clearly unreliable.

1. Consider the following argument: 2 + 2 = 4 ***therefore*** *either 2 + 2 = 4 or a concept which contains a synthesis is to be regarded as empty and as not related to any object if this synthesis does not belong to experience either as being derived from it or as being an a priori condition upon which experience in general in its formal aspect rests.* Do you think that this argument is valid? Can you explain why – perhaps despite appearances – the conclusion of the argument introduces no new information?

This leaves the question of whether there could be a deductively valid argument for the existence of a god that relies on premises about which we are certain. Ayer's response comes in two parts. First, Ayer briefly makes the point that an empirical proposition – one that describes the external world – cannot serve as the premise to a deductive argument for the existence of a god, because while empirical claims may be more or less probable they cannot be certain. Second, Ayer rejects the idea that a deductive argument that proves the existence of a god could depend on *a priori* premises, i.e. premises that are known to be certain independent of our experience of the external world. All *a priori* necessary claims, Ayer contends, are just analytic (or 'tautologies'): they are made true just by the meanings of their constituent terms. And we cannot arrive at the conclusion that there is a god from merely analytic truths.

Why does Ayer maintain that all *a priori* truths are analytic? Consider the empiricist motivation of Ayer's book mentioned in the introduction to this chapter. One problem for empiricism is that there seem to be propositions, most notably some mathematical propositions, that appear to be not only informative about the world but also knowable by reflection without recourse to experience (i.e. *a priori*). Ayer cannot concede that we can have *a priori* knowledge of reality without giving up on empiricism. His solution is to argue that, while there can be true *a priori* claims, including mathematical and logical truths, they are all analytic. For example, Ayer takes the truth of '7 + 5 = 12' to arise from the fact that '7 + 5' means the same as '12', just as 'An eye-doctor is an oculist' follows from the fact that 'eye-doctor' is synonymous with 'oculist'. The truth of these claims is in no way informative about the nature of reality but is the result of the meanings of their constituent terms. As such, *a priori* truths do not provide counter-examples to Ayer's empiricism.

There are a number of points at which Ayer's argument that all *a priori* truths are analytic can be challenged. Ayer himself raises the problem (in chapter 4) that, if a mathematical claim is true simply by virtue of the meanings of the symbols it contains, how can there be any place for discovery and invention in mathematics? If a mathematical equation merely conveys that the meaning of one statement is synonymous with another, why are some equations surprising? However, there are other difficulties. One is that there are non-mathematical propositions that we can know *a priori*: 'No object can be red and green all over at the same time', 'No object can wholly be in two different places at the same time' or (more debatably) 'Backwards causation is impossible'. It is not clear how Ayer could explain the truth of any of these claims from the meanings of their constituent terms. For example, it does not seem to follow from the meanings of 'object', 'red', 'green', 'all over', 'same time', etc., that no object can be red and green all over at the same time. Another difficulty for Ayer is that there is the ontological argument for the existence of God that has been presented as doing exactly what Ayer contends is impossible: providing a deductively valid proof based on *a priori* true premises. For more details on this, turn to the chapter on Anselm.

2. Do you think that it is true that no object can be red all over and green all over at the same time? If so, do you think that you can explain, just given the meanings of the terms 'object', 'red', 'green', 'all over', 'same time', etc., why no object can be red all over and green all over at the same time? (What, exactly, does it *mean* to say that something is 'red all over' or 'green all over'?)

Let us grant Ayer's contention that the existence of a god cannot be deductively proved, and look at his more surprising claim that the existence of a god cannot be shown to be probable, either. In reading [b]→, it is important to recall that Ayer's aim here is to show that religious beliefs have an ineliminable metaphysical component, and so (in so far as they are metaphysical) can be shown by the verification principle to be factually meaningless. With this in mind, his central line of argument is straightforward. A proposition can only be judged probable if it offers some factually contentful hypothesis about the world. But what is the content of the claim 'God exists'? One idea is that God accounts for the law-like character of the world and, in so far as the hypothesis that the behaviour of the world is law-like forms the content of the claim that God exists, it is factually significant. But this is clearly not *all* that a religious believer means by 'God exists'. It also means that there exists a transcendent deity. Ayer's position is as follows. If 'God exists' posits the existence of a transcendent deity, it is a metaphysical claim. But if 'God exists' is a metaphysical claim – it is not verifiable and, as Ayer has argued, it is not analytically true – then it follows from the verification principle that it is literally meaningless.

As Ayer makes clear in [C]→, his view that religious claims are literally meaningless is different from denying or doubting the existence of a god. The atheist denies the existence of God, or any other religious agent, and consequently believes that the statements of religious discourse involve systematic error. Although sincerely uttered religious statements aim accurately to describe the world, they are, on the atheist view, unsuccessful in doing so because the facts in question do not obtain: none of the religious agents and properties that religious statements describe actually exists. The atheist, the religious believer and the agnostic disagree with each other in their assessment of the truth of religious claims. But they agree that religious claims are either true or false and at least in the business of representing reality, even though they may not be successful in doing so. In contrast, Ayer denies that religious claims are representational. They are never descriptive, factual, true or false. Rather, they are literally meaningless. Now, it may seem that Ayer's position implies – or, perhaps, must collapse into – atheism. For, in arguing that religious claims do not represent or describe a religious reality, is not Ayer in effect *denying that there is* such a reality? Not exactly. The important distinction here is between denying that a claim is true, meaning that it is not true, and denying that a claim is true, meaning that it lacks a truth-value. Ayer's view is that religious claims lack truth-values, not that they are untrue.

3. Suppose that someone says: 'I am an atheist: I hold that it is not the case that God exists *because* I hold that it is not even meaningful to claim that God exists.' Does Ayer have to dispute what this person says? On his own principles, can Ayer assert that it is not even meaningful to claim that God exists?

We shall evaluate the verification principle shortly. It is worth pausing to consider at this point what exactly Ayer has established, allowing that the verification principle is correct. Ayer claims to have shown that religious claims are 'literally meaningless', that they are 'nonsense', that they 'cannot be true or false', and that they lack 'factual content'. These points certainly sound intimidating, and make matters look pretty bad not only for religious believers but also for any positive account of religious discourse. But Ayer more than somewhat overstates his position: he has not shown that religious claims are meaningless, nor has he shown that people should not be religious. What he establishes – and this is on the (very big) assumption that the verification principle is true – is that religious claims do not represent a metaphysical subject matter. That is, they do not successfully describe anything that goes beyond what can in principle be verified by our experiences. This is certainly a radical conclusion, but not the same as saying that religious claims are meaningless. Notably, Ayer effectively concedes this point in the preceding discussion of ethics. As with religious claims, Ayer argues that ethical claims are unverifiable and are not analytic, and therefore lack factual content. But Ayer also has a positive story to tell about what ethical claims mean. Although they do not serve to represent features of the world or to impart knowledge about the world, they do have a different non-cognitive function. Ayer proposes an *emotivist* theory of ethics, according to which an ethical claim such as 'stealing money is wrong' does not say anything that is true or false, but rather functions primarily to evince a feeling of disapproval, and to arouse a similar feeling in others. On this theory, calling something good or bad is meaningful but non-cognitive: it expresses an attitude rather than a belief about the action or event that one is evaluating. Ethical emotivism, in a substantially modified form now called expressivism, remains a topic of extensive debate in ethics. Is there a viable non-cognitivist theory of religion? Ayer is silent on the matter, though such a theory has been proposed by R. B. Braithwaite (1955) and R. M. Hare (1992). Although non-cognitivism in religion has received occasional support by philosophers and theologians, supporters have struggled to find a plausible formulation of the theory. Braithwaite's formulation, in particular, appears to face formidable problems (Swinburne 1993). We shall consider the non-cognitive aspects of religious language in the section on Berkeley that follows.

4. How plausible would it be to claim that religious assertions express attitudes towards life, or towards the universe? If it were true that religious assertions express attitudes towards life or the universe, do you think that the expressed attitudes would be positive (or would they rather be negative or neutral)?

In [d]→ Ayer rejects *naturalistic reductionism* about religious language. Reductionists typically propose a relationship between two classes of statement – the *given* class of statements, which are part of the field of discourse under discussion, and the *reduced* class of statements, which are the statements that specify the truth-conditions of statements of the given class. Typically, the reductionist proposes that what makes a statement of the given class true is that some statement or collection of statements of the reduced class is true. The particular form of reductionism that Ayer rejects is one in which religious statements constitute the given class, and naturalistic statements – those concerning scientifically detectable features of the natural world – constitute the reduced class. If a naturalistic reduction of religious statements were successful, their truth would be determined by statements which are non-metaphysical and verifiable, and consequently they would be literally meaningful.

Reductionist theses abound in philosophy. One example is phenomenalism, the view that statements about the external world can be analysed in terms of statements about our actual or possible experiences. So a phenomenalist might analyse 'There is a chair in the next room' as 'Were one to go into the next room, one would see a chair', reducing a statement about the external world in the given class to a statement from the reduced class about what one would perceive under certain circumstances. Scientific positivists analyse statements about unobservable entities, such as electrons, in terms of regularities in our experience. Behaviourists reduce statements about mental states to statements about behaviour and dispositions. A reductionist about the past analyses statements about the past in terms of our present memories, historical records, archaeological evidence, etc. Reductionist theories have also been proposed for religious discourse. Troubled by the implausibilities and metaphysical excesses posed by the family of Olympian gods, an interpretation of ancient Greek literature that treats statements about gods as representing natural forces and human temperament offers an appealing reductionist reading. Julian Huxley suggests a naturalistic reduction of monotheistic belief along with other central Christian beliefs: religious statements are ways of talking about phenomena for which we cannot find ordinary explanations. God, for instance, is identified with the forces of nature. However, there seems little prospect of a thoroughgoing reductionist account of religious statements. The limits of a reduction like Huxley's are apparent. It may be possible to give an analysis of the content of some basic claims about God in naturalistic terms; some of God's actions in the world, for example, might be taken as referring to unexplained natural phenomena. But it is not clear how this approach could be extended further. What reductionist interpretation should we give to 'Jesus is risen' or 'There will be a Last Judgement', or most statements of theology and doctrine? Those statements for which no plausible reductionist analysis is available will presumably have to be regarded by the reductionist as in error. But, if the reductionist believes that most religious statements are false, why continue to maintain a reductionist analysis for a small sub-class of them? If metaphysical error so permeates religious discourse, there seems little motivation to retain a partial reduction in preference to accepting atheism.

5. The above examples of reductionist claims – phenomenalism, behaviourism, antirealism about the past – are all cases that seem *prima facie* pretty implausible (or so it seems to us!). Can you think of examples of reductionist claims that are true, or at any rate more plausible than the examples given above?

To get a clearer idea of the range of available theories of religious language, it is useful to make a brief detour at this point to consider religious subjectivism, a noteworthy variety of religious reductionism. The subjectivist maintains that religious claims report or describe the states of mind of religious believers. The reduced class of statements in this case are statements about human psychological states. A subjectivist account of the statement 'God loves you' might be that the statement reports the speaker's feeling of benevolence towards those being addressed. Subjectivist theses have also been advanced for ethics and aesthetics. An ethical subjectivist might argue that statements of approbation or disapprobation should be taken to represent the speaker's feelings of approval or disapproval. So 'Breaking promises is wrong' would report the speaker's feeling of disapproval towards breaking promises; the claim is true, therefore, if it accurately represents the believer's feelings. For a brief period after his return to philosophy in the late 1920s, Wittgenstein seems to have adopted a subjectivist theory of religious claims, though there is little hint of it in any of his subsequent or preceding work. In 'A Lecture on Ethics' from 1929, Wittgenstein distinguishes two states: a 'wonder at the existence of the world' and 'the experience of feeling absolutely safe'. He then proceeds:

> the first of [these experiences] is, I believe, exactly what people were referring to when they said that God had created the world; and the experience of absolute safety has been described by saying that we feel safe in the hands of God. A third experience of the same kind is that of feeling guilty and again this was described by the phrase that God disapproves of our conduct.
>
> (*Philosophical Occasions* 42)

Wittgenstein presents us with some surprisingly crude subjectivist equations: to say that God created the world is to report one's sense of amazement at the world; to say that the world is safe in the hands of God is to report one's feeling of absolute security; to say that God disapproves of our conduct is to report one's feelings of guilt. On this analysis, it follows that what makes these statements true is that one has the appropriate feelings that they report.

Two final points about subjectivism. The first is that, despite its superficial similarity to non-cognitivism, subjectivism is a cognitivist theory: religious statements have truth-apt content, and their truth or falsity depends on the truth or falsity of the relevant statements about our psychologies to which they are reduced. According to the non-cognitivist, in contrast, religious statements in question express attitudes, but do not say anything about one's state of mind. In saying 'God created the world' one gives voice to attitudes that one has; one does not report that one has certain attitudes. Second, most cognitivists will also be unsympathetic to subjectivism. Whereas the subjectivist takes the truth of a religious assertion to be determined by the mental states of religious believers, most other cognitivists take their truth to be determined by the religious facts that they represent. Moreover, there is a very good reason for thinking that the subjectivist is wrong. Modifying one of Wittgenstein's examples, suppose that 'God disapproves of sloth' is true just in case 'I feel guilty when I act slothfully'. It seems to follow that Rachel, who feels guilty about bouts of laziness, when she says 'God disapproves of sloth' will not disagree with Jim, who is unrepentantly lazy, when he says 'God does not disapprove of sloth'. And Rachel will not be correct when she says that Jim is wrong (nor will Jim be correct when he says that Rachel is mistaken). Subjectivism seems to undermine disagreement between religious believers.

6. Suppose we accept that subjectivism about religious statements is discredited because it undermines the possibility of genuine disagreement between religious believers. Should we think that subjectivism about other classes of statements – e.g. ethical or political claims – is discredited on the same grounds? If not, why not?

The verification principle is now largely discredited. That something is seriously awry with the principle is shown when we apply to it its own standards. The verification principle is *itself* neither empirically verifiable nor a tautology, so literally meaningless according to its own criteria. The central reason for the theory's collapse, however, was the spectacular failure to come up with a workable version of the principle. Suppose we say that a statement is factually meaningful if it can be conclusively verified. Then universal generalisations such as 'Copper expands when heated', which cover an unlimited number of instances, will fail the test. This is because any finite number of observations of copper expanding when heated will at most establish the high probability of the generalisation; since we are only in a position to observe a limited number of copper–heat interactions that have or will occur, the statement cannot be conclusively verified. Similarly, while it may be possible to show that statements about the distant past are highly probable, they cannot be conclusively verified.

In response to this difficulty, Ayer proposed a less demanding criterion according to which a statement S is weakly verifiable, and thereby meaningful, if observation statements can be deduced from it in conjunction with certain additional premises which cannot be deduced from the premises alone. An observation statement is one that reports an actual or possible observation. So from the generalisation 'Copper expands when heated' and the additional premise 'There is a piece of copper on the table' we can deduce the observation statement 'If the piece of copper on the table is heated, it will expand', and the generalisation is meaningful because weakly verifiable. Unfortunately for Ayer, the upshot of weakening the verification principle is to allow *any* statement to be (weakly) verifiable. For, if we combine a statement S and an observation statement O with the additional premise 'If S, then O', we can deduce O from S. For instance, take the statement 'God is merciful' and an observation statement 'This ticket will win the lottery': the observation statement can be deduced from 'God is merciful' using the additional premise 'If God is merciful, then this ticket will win the lottery'. We do not, of course, need to believe that this gerrymandered premise is true. Ayer is seeking to give us a criterion for the meaningfulness of statements; the truth or falsity of the additional premises is not at issue. Clearly, we shall be able to use the same strategy to deduce observation statements from any religious statement (or any statement at all), with the upshot that religious statements will satisfy the weaker verification condition.

In the estimation of most contemporary philosophers, the verification principle is dead; none the less, it is interesting to consider what relationship, if any, there should be between the meaning of religious statements and their verifiability. Here are three different responses. (1) The sharp distinction between the 'empirical' subject matter of science and the 'metaphysical' subject matter of religion, on which Ayer's critique relies, might be rejected. John Hick (1960), for example, has argued that religious statements could be verified by post-mortem experiences (should belief in the afterlife actually be true); William Alston (1991) has proposed that we can perceive or have 'experiential encounters' with God. Richard Swinburne argues that some religious statements might be considered akin to scientific theories. 'God exists', according to Swinburne, can be shown to be probable by virtue of its role in explaining (among other things) various orderly features of the universe. (2) A different line of response, associated with the Wittgensteinian tradition in philosophy of religion, is that the verificationists' mistake was to connect meaning so closely with *empirical* verification. Empirical verification may be a suitable standard for observational discourse, but religious discourse is characterised by distinct standards that can be identified by looking at the way in which religious statements are in practice justified and used. We shall explore this option in more detail in the chapter on Putnam and Wittgenstein. (3) Another response, shared by many who are sympathetic to option (1), is that Ayer's critique confuses separate issues. There is an epistemological question about whether we can *know*, even in principle, that a religious assertion is true, and a distinct question as to whether a religious assertion is true. The truth of a religious assertion, on this view, is determined by whether it corresponds with reality. Ayer's critique conflates the knowability of a religious claim with its being truth-apt.

7. Consider the claim: *Every raven is the same colour as some other raven.* Do you think that this claim is meaningful? Do you think that there is some decisive test that could actually be performed to determine whether this claim is true (or false)? Do you think that you can give informative characterisations of possible states of the world in which this claim is true (or false)?

Ayer's theory of meaning is no longer defended, but useful contemporary discussions of his theory and its impact can be found in the reading given in the introduction to this section. For more on expressivism in ethics and religion, the work by Simon Blackburn cited below is a good starting point.

Alston, W., *Perceiving God: The Epistemology of Religious Experience*, Ithaca, NY: Cornell University Press, 1991.

Blackburn, S., 'Religion and Ontology', in A. Moore and M. Scott (eds), *Realism and Religion*, Aldershot: Ashgate, 2007.

Blackburn, S., *Spreading the Word*, Oxford: Oxford University Press, 1984.

Braithwaite, R. B. 'An Empiricist's View of the Nature of Religious Belief', in B. Mitchell (ed.), *The Philosophy of Religion*, Oxford: Oxford University Press, 1955.

Hare, R. M., *Essays on Religion and Education*, Oxford: Oxford University Press, 1992.

Hick, J., 'Theology and Verification', *Theology Today*, 17, 1 (1960), 12–31.

Huxley, J., *Religion without Revelation*, London: Benn, 1927.

Swinburne, R., *The Coherence of Theism*, Oxford: Oxford University Press, 1933.

Wittgenstein, L., *Philosophical Occasions*, ed. J. Klagge and A. Nordmann, Indianapolis, Ind.: Hackett, 1993.

Introduction to Berkeley

George Berkeley (1685–1753) is widely known for his defence of idealism, the theory that the world is constituted by ideas rather than by physical matter, but the following selection from his *Alciphron* (1732) addresses the distinct issue of his theory of ideas and language as it applies to religion. *Alciphron* was written by Berkeley during a visit to Rhode Island and published nearly two decades after his two most famous philosophical works, *Principles* (1710) and *Three Dialogues* (1713). The *Alciphron* is a Christian apologetic, a defence of Christian belief against its sceptical critics, consisting in seven dialogues. Chief among the dramatis personae are: Euphranor and Crito, who speak for Berkeley and Christianity, and Alciphron, a critic of religious belief described by Berkeley as 'freethinker' or 'minute philosopher'. The dialogues are wide-ranging and can move rapidly between topics. The following selection, taken from the seventh dialogue, extracts material that most directly concerns religious language; omitted are digressions on free will and personal identity. The discussion picks up at a point at which Alciphron has been persuaded by Euphranor and Crito that a strong case can be made in support of Christian belief. Alciphron remains sceptical, however, as to whether we have a clear understanding of what many central Christian claims mean.

George Berkeley, *Alciphron* (selection from the seventh dialogue)

1. The philosophers having resolved to set out for London next morning, we assembled at break of day in the library.

Alciphron began with a declaration of his sincerity, assuring us he had very maturely and with a most unbiased mind considered all that had been said the day before. He added that upon the whole he could not deny several probable reasons were produced for embracing the Christian faith. But, said he, those reasons being only probable, can never prevail against absolute certainty and demonstration. If, therefore, I can demonstrate your religion to be a thing altogether absurd and inconsistent, your probable arguments in its defence do from that moment lose their force, and with it all right to be answered or considered. . . . Things obscure and unaccountable in human affairs or in the operations of nature may yet be possible, and, if well attested, may be assented to; but religious assent or faith can be evidently shewn in its own nature to be impracticable, impossible, and absurd. This is the primary motive to infidelity. This is our citadel and fortress, which may, indeed, be graced with outworks of various erudition, but, if those are demolished, remains in itself and its own proper strength impregnable.

EUPHRANOR. This, it must be owned, reduceth our inquiry within a narrow compass: do but make out this, and I shall have nothing more to say.

ALCIPHRON. Know, then, that the shallow mind of the vulgar, as it dwells only on the outward surface of things, and considers them in the gross, may be easily imposed on. Hence a blind reverence for religious faith and mystery. But when an acute philosopher comes to dissect and analyse these points, the imposture plainly appears; and as he has no blindness, so he has no reverence for empty notions, or, to speak more properly, for mere forms of speech, which mean nothing, and are of no use to mankind.

2. Words are signs: they do or should stand for ideas, which so far as they suggest they are significant. But words that suggest no ideas are

insignificant. He who annexeth a clear idea to every word he makes use of speaks sense; but where such ideas are wanting, the speaker utters nonsense. In order therefore to know whether any man's speech be senseless and insignificant, we have nothing to do but lay aside the words, and consider the ideas suggested by them. Men, not being able immediately to communicate their ideas one to another, are obliged to make use of sensible signs or words; the use of which is to raise those ideas in the hearer which are in the mind of the speaker; and if they fail of this end they serve to no purpose. He who really thinks hath a train of ideas succeeding each other and connected in his mind; and when he expresseth himself by discourse each word suggests a distinct idea to the hearer or reader; who by that means hath the same train of ideas in his which was in the mind of the speaker or writer. As far as this effect is produced, so far the discourse in intelligible, hath sense and meaning. Hence it follows that whoever can be supposed to understand what he reads or hears must have a train of ideas raised in his mind, correspondent to the train of words read or heard. These plain truths, to which men readily assent in theory, are but little attended to in practice, and therefore deserve to be enlarged on and inculcated, however obvious and undeniable. Mankind are generally averse from thinking, though apt enough to entertain discourse either in themselves or others: the effect whereof is that their minds are rather stored with names than ideas, the husk of science rather than the thing. And yet these words without meaning do often make distinctions of parties, the subject-matter of their disputes, and the object of their zeal. This is the most general cause of error, which doth not influence ordinary minds alone, but even those who pass for acute and learned philosophers are often employed about names instead of things or ideas, and are supposed to know when they only pronounce hard words without a meaning.

3. . . . And now, for the particular application of what I have said, I shall not single out any nice disputed points of school divinity, or those that relate to the nature and essence of God, which, being allowed infinite, you might pretend to screen them under the general notion of difficulties attending the nature of Infinity.

4. *Grace* is the main point in the Christian dispensation; nothing is oftener mentioned or more considered throughout the New Testament, wherein it is represented as somewhat of a very particular kind, distinct from anything revealed to the Jews, or known by the light of nature. The same grace is spoken of as the gift of God, as coming by Jesus Christ, as reigning, as abounding, as operating. Men are said to speak through grace, to believe through grace. Mention is made of the glory of grace, the riches of grace, the stewards of grace. Christians are said to be heirs of grace, to receive grace, grow in grace, be strong in grace, to stand in grace, and to fall from grace. And lastly, grace is said to justify and to save them. Hence Christianity is styled the covenant or dispensation of grace. And it is well

known that no point hath created more controversy in the church than this doctrine of grace. What disputes about its nature, extent, and effects, about universal, efficacious, sufficient, preventing, irresistible grace, have employed the pens of Protestant as well as Popish divines, of Jansenists and Molinists, of Lutherans, Calvinists, and Arminians, as I have not the least curiosity to know, so I need not say. It sufficeth to observe that there have been and are still subsisting great contests upon these points. Only one thing I should desire to be informed of, to wit, What is the clear and distinct idea marked by the word *grace*? I presume that a man may know the bare meaning of a term, without going into the depth of all those learned inquiries. This surely is an easy matter, provided there is an idea annexed to such term. And if there is not, it can be neither the subject of a rational dispute, nor the object of real faith. Men may indeed impose upon themselves or others, and pretend to argue and believe, when at bottom there is no argument or belief, farther than mere verbal trifling. Grace taken in the vulgar sense, either for beauty, or favour, I can easily understand. But when it denotes an active, vital, ruling principle, influencing and operating on the mind of man, distinct from every natural power or motive, I profess myself altogether unable to understand it, or frame any distinct idea of it; and therefore I cannot assent to any proposition concerning it, nor, consequently have any faith about it: and it is a self-evident truth, that God obligeth no man to impossibilities. At the request of a philosophical friend, I did cast an eye on the writings he showed me of some divines, and talked with others on this subject, but after all I had read or heard could make nothing of it, having always found, whenever I laid aside the word grace, and looked into my own mind, a perfect vacuity or privation of all ideas. And, as I am apt to think men's minds and faculties are made much alike, I suspect that other men, if they examine what they call grace with the same exactness and indifference, would agree with me, that there was nothing in it but an empty name. This is not the only instance where a word often heard and pronounced is believed intelligible, for no other reason but because it is familiar. Of the same kind are many other points reputed necessary articles of faith. That which in the present case imposeth upon mankind I take to be partly this. Men speak of this holy principle as of something that acts, moves, and determines, taking their ideas from corporeal things, from motion and the force or *momentum* of bodies, which, being of an obvious and sensible nature, they substitute in place of a thing spiritual and incomprehensible, which is a manifest delusion. For, though the idea of corporeal force be never so clear and intelligible, it will not therefore follow that the idea of a grace, a thing perfectly incorporeal, must be so too. And though we may reason distinctly, perceive, assent, and form opinions about the one, it will by no means follow that we can do so of the other. . . .

5. Euphranor. Be the use of words or names what it will, I can never think it is to do things impossible. Let us then inquire what it is, and see

if we can make sense of our daily practice. Words, it is agreed, are signs: it may not therefore be amiss to examine the use of other signs, in order to know that of words. Counters, for instance, at a card-table are used, not for their own sake, but only as signs substituted for money, as words are for ideas. Say now, Alciphron, is it necessary every time these counters are used throughout the progress of a game, to frame an idea of the distinct sum or value that each represents?

ALCIPHRON. By no means: it is sufficient the players at first agree on their respective values, and at last substitute those values in their stead.

EUPHRANOR. And in casting up a sum, where the figures stand for pounds, shillings, and pence, do you think it necessary, throughout the whole progress of the operation, in each step to form ideas of pounds, shillings, and pence?

ALCIPHRON. I do not; it will suffice if in the conclusion those figures direct our actions with respect to things.

EUPHRANOR. From hence it seems to follow, that words may not be insignificant, although they should not, every time they are used, excite the ideas they signify in our minds; it being sufficient that we have it in our power to substitute things or ideas for their signs when there is occasion. It seems also to follow that there may be another use of words beside that of marking and suggesting distinct ideas, to wit, the influencing our conduct and actions, which may be done either by forming rules for us to act by, or by raising certain passions, dispositions, and emotions in our minds. A discourse, therefore, that directs how to act or excites to the doing or forbearance of an action may, it seems, be useful and significant, although the words whereof it is composed should not bring each a distinct idea into our minds.

ALCIPHRON. It seems so.

EUPHRANOR. Pray tell me, Alciphron, is not an idea altogether inactive?

ALCIPHRON. It is.

EUPHRANOR. An agent therefore, an active mind or spirit, cannot be an idea, or like an idea. Whence it should seem to follow that those words which denote an active principle, soul, or spirit do not, in a strict and proper sense, stand for ideas. And yet they are not insignificant neither; since I understand what is signified by the term *I*, or *myself*, or know what it means, although it be no idea, nor like an idea, but that which thinks, and wills, and apprehends ideas, and operates about them. Certainly it must be allowed that we have some notion that we understand, or know what is meant by, the terms *myself*, *will*, *memory*, *love*, *hate*, and so forth; although, to speak exactly, these words do not suggest so many distinct ideas.

ALCIPHRON. What would infer from this?

EUPHRANOR. What hath been inferred already – that words may be significant, although they do not stand for ideas. The contrary whereof having been presumed seems to have produced the doctrine of abstract ideas.

ALCIPHRON. Will you not allow that the mind can abstract?

EUPHRANOR. I do not deny it may abstract in a certain sense; inasmuch as those things that can really exist, or be really perceived asunder, may be conceived asunder, or abstracted one from the other; for instance, a man's head from his body, colour from motion, figure from weight. But it will not thence follow that the mind can frame abstract general ideas, which appear to be impossible.

ALCIPHRON. And yet it is a current opinion that every substantive name marks out and exhibits to the mind one distinct idea separate from all others.

EUPHRANOR. Pray, Alciphron, is not the word *number* such a substantive name?

ALCIPHRON. It is.

EUPHRANOR. Do but try now whether you can frame an idea of number in abstract, exclusive of all signs, words, and things numbered. I profess for my own part I cannot.

ALCIPHRON. Can it be so hard a matter to form a simple idea of number, the object of a most evident demonstrable science? Hold, let me see if I cannot abstract the idea of number from the numerical names and characters, and all particular numerical things. Upon which Alciphron paused awhile, and then said, To confess the truth I do not find that I can.

EUPHRANOR. But, though it seems neither you nor I can form distinct simple *ideas* of number, we can nevertheless make a very proper and significant use of numerical names. They direct us in the disposition and management of our affairs, and are of such necessary use, that we should not know how to do without them. And yet, if other men's faculties may be judged of by mine, to obtain a precise simple abstract idea of number, is as difficult as to comprehend any mystery in religion.

[8] But, although terms are signs, yet having granted that those signs may be significant, though they should not suggest ideas represented by them, provided they serve to regulate and influence our wills, passions, or conduct, you have consequently granted that the mind of man may assent to propositions containing such terms, when it is so directed or affected by them, notwithstanding it should not perceive distinct ideas marked by those terms. Whence it seems to follow that a man may believe the doctrine of the Trinity, if he finds it revealed in Holy Scripture that the Father, the Son, and the Holy Ghost, are God, and that there is but one God, although he doth not frame in his mind any abstract or distinct ideas of trinity, substance, or personality; provided that this doctrine of a Creator, Redeemer, and Sanctifier makes proper impressions on his mind, producing therein love, hope, gratitude, and obedience, and thereby becomes a lively operative principle, influencing his life and actions, agreeably to that

notion of saving faith which is required in a Christian. This, I say, whether right or wrong, seems to follow from your own principles and concessions. . . .

[10. CRITO.] It seems that what hath been now said may be applied to other mysteries of our religion. Original sin, for instance, a man may find it impossible to form an idea of in abstract, or of the manner of its transmission; and yet the belief thereof may produce in his mind a salutary sense of his own unworthiness, and the goodness of his Redeemer: from whence may follow good habits, and from them good actions, the genuine effects of faith; which, considered in its true light, is a thing neither repugnant nor incomprehensible, as some men would persuade us, but suited even to vulgar capacities, placed in the will and affections rather than in the understanding, and producing holy lives rather than subtle theories. Faith, I say, is not an indolent perception, but an operative persuasion of mind, which ever worketh some suitable action, disposition, or emotion in those who have it; as it were easy to prove and illustrate by innumerable instances taken from human affairs. . . .

But, to convince you by a plain instance of the efficacious necessary use of faith without ideas: we will suppose a man of the world, a minute philosopher, prodigal and rapacious, one of large appetites and narrow circumstances, who shall have it in his power at once to seize upon a great fortune by one villainous act, a single breach of trust, which he can commit with impunity and secrecy. Is it not natural to suppose him arguing in this manner? All mankind in their senses pursue their interest. The interests of this present life are either of mind, body, or fortune. If I commit this act my life will be easy (having nought to fear here or hereafter); my bodily pleasures will be multiplied; and my fortune enlarged. Suppose now, one of your refined theorists talks to him about the harmony of mind and affections, inward worth, truth of character, in one word, the beauty of virtue; which is the only interest he can propose to turn the scale against all other secular interest and sensual pleasures; would it not, think you, be a vain attempt? . . . And what effect can this have on a mind callous to all those things, and at the same time strongly affected with a sense of corporeal pleasures, and the outward interest, ornaments, and conveniences of life? Whereas that every man, do but produce in him a sincere belief of a Future State, although it be a mystery, although it be what eye hath not seen, nor ear heard, nor hath it entered into the heart of man to conceive, he shall, nevertheless, by virtue of such belief, be withheld from executing his wicked project: and that for reasons which all men can comprehend, though nobody can be the object of them. I will allow the points insisted on by your refined moralists to be as lovely and excellent as you please to a reasonable, reflecting, philosophical mind. But I will venture to say that, as the world goes, few, very few, would be influenced by them. We see, therefore, the necessary use, as well as the powerful effects of faith, even where we have not ideas.

Commentary on Berkeley

Alciphron, the religious sceptic, begins by conceding in [1] what he believes has been established in the preceding dialogues: that persuasive arguments can be given for Christian beliefs. In this dialogue he raises a distinct line of objection. An argument in favour of any belief, however persuasive it may appear, Alciphron contends, will be of no value in establishing the truth of that belief if we lack a cogent conception of what the belief is about. However, this is precisely the problem with Christian beliefs: they are 'impossible' and 'absurd'. Consequently, all of Euphranor's and Crito's arguments for religious belief must be rejected. Moreover, Alciphron claims, worries about the cogency of religious belief are the primary motive for religious scepticism.

Consider two different ways in which Alciphron's sceptical argument might be developed. Suppose you read the chapter on Paley's design argument and form the opinion that there is a version of the design argument (a better one than Paley's!) that – perhaps in combination with other arguments – provides good reasons to believe in the existence of an omnipotent deity. That is, they make it more likely than not that an omnipotent deity exists. However, suppose you then look at the chapter on Savage's omnipotence paradox and you conclude that the notion of an omnipotent deity requires *both* that the deity can do anything logically possible *and* that there is something logically possible that he cannot do (either lift or create a stone that is too heavy for him to lift). That is, you conclude that the concept of an omnipotent deity is internally inconsistent: it can be used to generate contradictions. It follows from this second conclusion that your first conclusion about there being good arguments for the existence of an omnipotent deity must have been mistaken. For, if the concept of an omnipotent deity is internally inconsistent, it is logically impossible for an omnipotent deity to exist. To this extent, a conceptual analysis of the claims for which we are arguing should be prior to determining their truth, since it can reveal unexpected inconsistencies which show that the claims at issue cannot be true. This is why Richard Swinburne begins his multi-volume defence of Christian belief with *The Coherence of Theism*, which aims to establish that the religious claims that he is defending are both internally consistent and consistent with each other. Finding an inconsistency, therefore, is one way in which arguments that seem to show a conclusion to be probable can be overturned.

Calling faith 'impossible' suggests that Alciphron might be aiming to show that religious beliefs are inconsistent. However, he pursues a related but different line of argument for the same sceptical conclusion. Rather than try to show that religious concepts yield contradictions, Alciphron contends that we lack any clear ideas corresponding to many religious expressions that are central to Christian faith. Interestingly, this is a potentially more robust argument for scepticism than the first one we looked at. Consider again those two conclusions: that there is a successful design argument for an omnipotent deity and that if an omnipotent deity can do anything logically possible, then it is impossible for such a being to exist. The latter conclusion will only undermine the first if the analysis of omnipotence as 'can do anything logically possible' is the only one available. There may be another way of capturing the concept of omnipotence that avoids paradox and presents no obstacle to the initial conclusion that an omnipotent deity exists. In contrast, suppose that the problem with omnipotence is not that conceptual analysis uncovers paradoxes but that we lack *any* credible analysis of what it means. That is, while we use the term 'omnipotent' and expressions like 'omnipotent deity', we lack even a rudimentary concept of what omnipotence is. Then, short of inventing a new meaning for 'omnipotence', conceptual analysis will not help against the sceptic's argument. As we shall see, however, Alciphron advances his objection to more Christian-specific concepts like 'grace' and 'Trinity'.

1. Could it be true that we have concepts for which we are simply unable to give analyses? It is clear that we don't obtain all of our concepts by way of analysis: we must already have some concepts in order to provide analyses for other concepts. But might it be the case that there are concepts that we do not obtain by way of analysis for which we are unable to give analyses? How plausible do you think it is that we can give credible analyses of the following concepts: *game*, *knowledge*, *cause*, *person*, *god*, *artwork*, *philosophy*?

In [2] Berkeley, via Alciphron, rolls out his theory of language and prepares the ground for the discussion of religious language. The background to Berkeley's account is the theory of communication developed by John Locke in book III of *An Essay Concerning Human Understanding*. Locke takes language to be an artificial construction of repeatable articulate sounds and that these sounds facilitate communication by being used to stand for ideas:

> Besides articulate Sounds, therefore, it was farther necessary, that [man] should be *able to use these Sounds as Signs of internal Conceptions*; and to make them stand as marks for the *Ideas* within his own Mind, whereby they might be made known to others, and the Thoughts of Men's Minds be conveyed from one to another.
>
> (3.1.2)

The connection between a particular word and the idea it stands for is 'arbitrary', established by choice and convention. However, once established, we can use words to record our ideas and the thoughts that they constitute, and convey them to other people. From this Locke concludes: '*Words in their primary or immediate Signification, stand for nothing, but the* Ideas *in the Mind of him that uses them*' (3.2.2).

One standard but unfounded objection to Locke is that his account commits him to an extreme form of subjectivism. If words stand only for ideas, and specifically for ideas in the mind of the person using them, the upshot seems to be that we can only talk about our own ideas. That is, all we shall be able to communicate with words are facts about our own states of mind. J. S. Mill puts the point as follows: 'When I say, "the sun is the cause of the day", I do not mean that my idea of the sun causes or excites in me the idea of day' (Mill 1973–4: 25). It is often the things in the world about which we have ideas that we are talking about, rather than the ideas that we have about those things – Locke's theory seems to make the former impossible. However, this objection is now held to be based on a misreading of Locke. First, Locke's claim that words primarily *signify* or *stand for* ideas should not be equated with the claim that words primarily are about or *refer to* our ideas. Signification is a looser notion that can mean reference but also representation, expression or making known. Second, while words may have as their primary signification ideas, they also (secondarily) signify things. So Locke can be understood as arguing that, while words must signify ideas to be meaningful, and that successful linguistic communication consists in conveying ideas with words, words can also refer to things, and what they refer to is determined by the signified idea.

Berkeley takes as a starting point Locke's theory that words stand for ideas, and then elaborates on this theory with three further related points. (1) Words are significant and facilitate communication in so far as they are associated with the same clear ideas in the speaker as they suggest in hearers. For example, my use of the word 'Berkeley' becomes significant by my associating it with an idea of Berkeley, and it can be successfully used in communicating with you the reader as it suggests to you the idea of Berkeley. Without the association with ideas words are nonsense, and without the suggestion of ideas words serve no purpose. Berkeley also claims that every word needs to have an idea associated with/suggested by it to be significant. This is implausible. Both you and I can understand the meaning of *this* sentence, for example, without having a distinct idea associated with each word. Moreover, there seem to be numerous words useful in communication for which we have no particular idea. Even Locke concedes that words like *and* or *but* 'are not truly, by themselves, the names of any *Ideas*' (3.7.2). However, as we shall see shortly, Berkeley allows that words have other purposes than standing for ideas. (2) Thinking consists in a train of ideas, and thought is communicated with a sequence of words suggesting a corollary sequence of ideas. (3) Our disinclination to think through what we are saying or hearing has the result that we sometimes use words that lack a suitable association with and suggestion of ideas. The use of these insignificant words to make distinctions or arguments is, according to Berkeley, the 'most general cause of error'.

2. It seems very implausible to say that 'and' and 'but' are words that lack meanings. Indeed, you might think that you can give a pretty good account of the meanings of these words. What, then, is the difficulty in the suggestion that 'and' and 'but' *are* the names of ideas, namely, those ideas that constitute the meanings of these terms?

The problem that Berkeley now addresses – through Alciphron – is to what extent this third point applies in religious discourse. The discussion proceeds as follows. First, Alciphron begins by setting out different uses of the term 'grace'. His aim here is twofold: to point up the centrality of grace to Christian faith and to show the variety of ways in which grace is talked about and the very different functions that grace is supposed to serve. Second, Alciphron notes that there is disagreement on almost every aspect of what grace actually is. So what, Alciphron asks, is the idea signified by the term *grace*? Clearly, Alciphron's conclusions are that no clear and distinct idea is signified by 'grace', that using the expression will be a 'cause of error' as described earlier, and that grace cannot be an object of faith. However, in arguing for this conclusion, Alciphron appeals, on the one hand, to the serious confusion in our thinking about grace and, on the other hand, to his inability to think of a clear and distinct idea when he considers what 'grace' means. These suggest two different lines of argument for his conclusions:

(A) Although I can form an idea of grace in its 'vulgar' sense as beauty or favour, the thing posited by Christian believers and discussed in theology denotes an 'active, vital, ruling principle, influencing and operating on the mind of man, distinct from every natural power or motive'. The latter applies ideas of motion and force drawn from physics to something incorporeal. But these physical ideas, which are clear in themselves, are essentially properties of corporeal objects and it is impossible to understand how they could be applied to incorporeal objects.

(B) It is possible to tell whether or not there is a clear and distinct idea associated with a word by introspection. However, when I consider what I mean by the word *grace* I find a 'perfect vacuity or privation of all ideas'. Since human introspective abilities are similar, I conclude that the same will be true if other people reflect on what they mean by grace. The upshot is that 'grace' is nonsense, and cannot be an object of faith.

Note also that the conclusions to (A) and (B) are slightly different. The point of (A) is that, while grace may suggest various ideas, they are so confused that we cannot identify any clear and distinct idea. The point of (B) is that, when we reflect on the meaning of grace, we find a complete absence of ideas. Whether or not Berkeley intends for Alciphron to present two distinct arguments, the main conclusion of [4] is clear: the word *grace* suggests no clear and distinct idea. The upshot, Alciphron argues, is that 'grace' is an insignificant term that does not suggest or convey clear and distinct ideas. As such, grace cannot be an object of faith.

Berkeley/Euphranor's response in [5] is to concede that, while Alciphron is correct that the word *grace* does not suggest a clear and distinct idea, it does not follow that the term is insignificant because the Lockean theory of language is incomplete: not all words are significant just by virtue of suggesting ideas. He offers three lines of argument.

First, consider the way in which counters can be substituted for money in a betting game, where the players agree to mark the counters to represent particular sums of money. The counters have a useful practical function both because it is easier to bet using counters than cash, and because it is quicker to see the standing of each player and determine the winnings. Evidently, however, it is possible to play the game and use the counters without framing ideas of what the counters represent, even though each counter signifies a sum of money. We can use words, Berkeley suggests, just as we use counters, as a practical way of signifying things without actually having ideas of what are signified. For instance, an arithmetical calculation may have a practical function in guiding our behaviour even though, while performing the calculation, we do not frame any ideas of the figures that constitute it. So, Berkeley concludes, words can have a practical function in 'influencing our conduct and action' that is distinct from their role in suggesting ideas. Note here that Berkeley's conclusion is suitably modest: he has only shown that some words can have both a practical and an idea-suggesting function, and can be significant even when only fulfilling the practical function. He has not yet established that there are significant words that have only a practical function.

3. Can you think of some examples of words that have uses as practical ways of signifying things even in the absence of ideas of that which is signified? Could it be, for example, that the word 'God' is such an expression?

Second, Berkeley contends that some words may be significant even though they suggest no clear and distinct ideas, such as *myself*, *will*, *memory*, *love*, *hate*. However, his argument for this is puzzling. It seems to go like this: (*a*) Ideas are inactive, (*b*) Some words – those referring to agents, action, emotions, etc. – stand for active things, (*c*) ideas do not resemble active things, (*d*) an idea resembles what it denotes; therefore, (*e*) words for active things do not stand for ideas. Putting aside what exactly Berkeley takes 'inactive' to mean, his argument seems to involve a faulty step at (*d*) which conflates an idea with what an idea refers to. An idea can be about something active without itself being an active thing. However, the inactivity of ideas plays a more interesting role in Berkeley's positive account of religious words that we shall come to shortly.

4. What is wrong with the suggestion that an idea resembles what it denotes? Pick an idea of a particular thing – say, your idea of Barack Obama – and draw up two lists, one of which gives the properties of Barack Obama, while the other gives the properties of your idea of Barack Obama. Be careful to distinguish between the properties that your idea *has*, and the properties that your idea *attributes* to Barack Obama. In order to help with the second part of this task, try to give an account of the nature of ideas: what, exactly, *is* an idea?

Third, Berkeley introduces abstract ideas and touches on a substantial area of dispute between himself and Locke. An apparent problem for the Lockean theory of language is that, in addition to naming expressions that pick out particular things, we also use general terms – 'horse', 'white', 'square', 'animal' – and can frame general statements about kinds of things. But what ideas are suggested by general terms? According to Locke, for each general term there is a corresponding general idea that is created by our faculty of abstraction. Beginning with the idea of a particular thing, and noticing ways in which it resembles other particular things, abstraction allows us to generate a new idea by extracting those respects in which the things resemble each other and filtering out their dissimilarities. For example, we can generate the concept 'number' by abstracting those respects in which one, two, three, etc., resemble each other, and leaving out those features where they differ. Berkeley, in contrast, while he allows that general terms are usable and useful, denies that we have any faculty of abstraction or that we can form an idea of number that is distinct from any particular number. The debate between Berkeley and Locke on abstract ideas is discussed in detail by Mackie (1976) and Lowe (1995). For the purposes of Berkeley's argument about religious language, it represents another respect in which he is prepared to break away from the theory that words must stand for ideas in order to be meaningful.

Berkeley's argument so far has been that there are words that do not suggest ideas but are still significant because of their practical function. They may play a role in guiding our behaviour, motivating us to act, or modifying our emotions or dispositions. A word may be significant, according to Berkeley, by having one or more of these functions even though they do not suggest any ideas. This is a position that Berkeley sketched out, but did not develop with much detail, in the introduction to his *Principles*:

> Besides, the communicating of ideas marked by words is not the chief and only end of language, as is commonly supposed. There are other ends, as the raising of some passion, the exciting to, or deterring from an action, the putting the mind in some particular disposition.
>
> (Introduction 20)

In [8]–[10], Berkeley uses this account of language to respond to Alciphron's sceptical objections and set out his positive account of the Christian mysteries. In effect, Berkeley – via his characters Euphranor and Crito – concedes to Alciphron that terms like 'Trinity', 'grace' and 'original sin' do not in their ordinary usage stand for any clear and distinct ideas. But these terms *are* nevertheless significant because of their desirable practical and motivational role for people with Christian faith. Berkeley gives three examples. Belief in the Trinity generates feelings of love and hope, and modifies behaviour towards gratitude and obedience in a way that is consistent with Christian principles. Belief in original sin, he proposes, produces an appropriate sense of unworthiness that promotes good habits. Belief in a 'future state' can motivate the believer to act morally.

5. Do you think that it is *plausible* that Christians can agree that terms like 'Trinity', 'grace', 'the afterlife' and 'original sin' do not stand for clear and distinct ideas on their ordinary usage? Do you think that it is plausible that Christians might suppose that terms like 'Trinity', 'grace', 'the afterlife' and 'original sin' have desirable practical and motivational roles *given* that they do not stand for clear and distinct ideas? How, exactly, could these terms play their motivational roles if they do not stand for clear and distinct ideas?

Berkeley supplements his proposal about the meaning of the Christian mysteries with two points about religious faith in [10]. The first is that faith is motivational:

it generates strong feelings and emotions, and causes the faithful to act in suitably Christian ways. Why does Berkeley draw this to our attention? His argument seems to be this. As we saw earlier, Berkeley believes that mere ideas do not motivate. If Christian beliefs suggested only ideas, that would not explain the motivational qualities of Christian faith. So, by giving some core religious beliefs a non-cognitive, practical function, it is also possible to explain motivational and affective qualities of faith. Berkeley's second point is that it is actually morally and religiously desirable that at least some core expressions of faith should be linked to our emotions and dispositions rather than to our ideas. Consider someone given to a life of indulgence. No new ideas or theories, however artfully expressed, are likely to effect a lifestyle change. Faith, in contrast, by introducing a change in the person's attitudes and dispositions can result in a change in the person's behaviour.

How should we evaluate Berkeley's account of religious language? There are no current defenders of the crude Lockean theory of language that largely informs Berkeley's argument, even with his modifications. As we have seen, the suggestion that there is a one-to-one relationship between words and ideas is clearly untenable. However, there are certainly current defenders of a related theory that, rather than focusing on particular words and their relationship with ideas, proposes that sentences aim to express states of mind. Moreover, it is possible to revise the main components of Berkeley's argument sympathetically with this theory. Alciphron's worries about the idea of grace, Trinity, original sin, etc., can be understood as questioning whether religious claims about the Christian mysteries genuinely express beliefs. That is, we lack any concept of grace, etc., and so cannot form beliefs about them. Berkeley's positive proposal stated by Euphranor and Crito can be seen as embracing the view that sentences can have other purposes than expressing thoughts or propositions, but may instead have the practical function of encouraging or implanting desires and other attitudes in ourselves and others. Claims about the Christian mysteries, on this view, play a non-cognitive role in religious faith. In the light of this sympathetic reconstruction, how should we assess Berkeley?

6. Unlike the kind of non-cognitivism looked at in the chapter on Ayer, Berkeley extends the non-cognitivist aspect of his theory to a very restricted range of religious statements – the Christian mysteries – but otherwise adopts a thoroughly cognitivist account of religious discourse. For example, he takes the various forms of behaviour that the non-cognitive uses of religious discourse promote to be in accordance with Christian thinking about proper belief and practice, which Berkeley believes is both cognitively contentful and rationally defensible. The preceding dialogues in *Alciphron* present such a defence, including arguments for the existence of God. To what extent therefore is it possible to combine a non-cognitive account of some religious claims with a cognitive account of others? Suppose, for example, we give a cognitivist account of 'God is good' and say that it expresses a belief, and we give a non-cognitivist account of 'Salvation is given by divine grace' and say that it has the practical function of encouraging moral behaviour. What, then, is meant by 'If God is good, then salvation is given by divine grace'?

7. Berkeley introduces a non-cognitivist account of the Christian mysteries as part of a *defence* of Christian faith against Alciphron's sceptical attack. But does he concede too much? It is not clear that Berkeley has a response to Alciphron's objection that claims about the Christian mysteries cannot be a matter of faith. If Berkeley agrees with Alciphron that assertions about the Christian mysteries do not express beliefs – his positive non-cognitive story about their meaning notwithstanding – then how is he to avoid the conclusion that they cannot be the subject of faith? So can Berkeley offer any positive account of what it is to have *faith* in matters to do with the Trinity, grace, etc.?

8. How plausible are Berkeley's specific proposals for a non-cognitive account of the Trinity, grace, the afterlife and original sin?

9. Alciphron's scepticism seems to be motivated in part by a kind of introspective experiment on religious terms: we reflect inwardly to see if we have any clear and distinct idea of what they mean. Is this a satisfactory way of determining what an expression means or whether it is meaningful?

10. Berkeley's discussion focuses on Christian beliefs. To what extent could the arguments that he considers be applied more widely to other religious beliefs?

For historical background to Berkeley's *Alciphron*, along with an abridged version of the text, see:

Berman, D., *George Berkeley – Alciphron in Focus*, London: Routledge, 1993.

References

Lowe, E. J., *Locke on Human Understanding*, London: Routledge, 1995.
Mackie, J. L., *Problems from Locke*, Oxford: Oxford University Press, 1976.
Mill, J. S., *A System of Logic, Ratiocinative and Inductive*, 2 vols (1843), ed. J. M. Robson, 2 vols, Toronto: University of Toronto Press, 1973–4.

Introduction to Putnam

Ludwig Wittgenstein (1889–1951), widely considered one of the greatest philosophers of the twentieth century, is one of the few major figures in recent analytic philosophy to have contributed to the philosophy of religion. His work in the area, which principally concerns religious language, has been influential and has generated a substantial literature. However, interpretation of Wittgenstein's views is seriously hampered by his most concentrated treatment of religious language surviving only in the form of lecture notes taken by his students. These were published as part of *Lectures and Conversations on Aesthetics, Psychology and Religious Belief* in 1966. Wittgenstein's other work in the field, published in *Culture and Value*, is made up of often interesting but only occasional remarks extracted from his extensive notebooks. Consequently, philosophers of religion sympathetic to Wittgenstein's views – D. Z. Phillips the most prominent among them – have tended to apply ideas and themes from Wittgenstein's extensive and more developed work on the philosophy of language to religion, rather than look in detail at the source material.

Hilary Putnam has been a leading figure in analytic philosophy since the 1960s and is best-known for his significant contributions to philosophy of language, mind and science. In his recent book *Renewing Philosophy*, Putnam aims to reassess a range of issues in contemporary philosophy and particularly in the philosophy of language. In the course of this, he provides us with one of the most accessible and philosophically well informed discussions of Wittgenstein's philosophy of religion in recent years.

Hilary Putnam, 'Wittgenstein on Religious Language' (selection from *Renewing Philosophy*, chs 7–8)

[1] I was first led to study the published notes on the Lectures on Religious Belief by their subject, of course, but as I studied them and though about them it came to seem to me more and more that besides the interest they have for anyone who has thought about the subject of religious language and religious belief, they also have great interest for anyone who is interested in understanding the work of the later Wittgenstein. They were given, in fact, in a transitional period, the summer of 1938, when Wittgenstein's later views were in development, and they by no means bear their meaning on their sleeve. Even if we had the full text of what Wittgenstein said in that room in Cambridge in 1938, I suspect we would be deeply puzzled by these lectures; as it is, we have only twenty-one printed pages of notes summarizing the three lectures.

[2] The first of the three lectures sets the interpretative problem before us. What Wittgenstein says in this first lecture is very much contrary to received opinion in linguistic philosophy, and there is an obvious problem as to how it is to be understood. In this lecture, Wittgenstein considers a number of religious utterances, not utterances about God, but about the afterlife, or the Last Judgement, such as 'an Austrian general said to someone, "I shall think of you after my death, if that should be possible"'. (Wittgenstein says, 'We can imagine one group would find this ludicrous, another who wouldn't.') Again, Wittgenstein imagines someone asking him if he believes

in the Last Judgement, and on the first page of the published notes Wittgenstein says, 'Suppose I say that the body will rot, and another says "No. Particles will rejoin in a thousand years, and there will be a Resurrection of you".' Wittgenstein's comment is 'If some said: "Wittgenstein, do you believe in this?" I'd say: "No." "Do you contradict the man?" I'd say: "No." . . . Would you say: "I believe the opposite," or "There is no reason to suppose such a thing"? I'd say neither.' In short – and perhaps this is the only thing that is absolutely clear about these lectures – Wittgenstein believes that the religious man and the atheist talk past one another.

I remember that the first time I had lunch with a great student of comparative religion, Wilfrid Cantwell Smith, Smith said to me that when the religious person says 'I believe that there is a God' and the atheist says 'I don't believe there is a God' they do not affirm and deny the same thing. We shall see that Wittgenstein makes the same point later in his lectures. Religious discourse is commonly viewed (by atheists) as pre-scientific or 'primitive' discourse which has somehow strangely – due to human folly and superstition – managed to survive into the age of the digital computer and the neutron bomb. Wittgenstein (and Smith) clearly believe no such thing. Wittgenstein's picture is not that the believer makes a claim and the atheist asserts its negation. It is as if religious discourse were somehow incommensurable, to employ a much-abused word. But there are many theories of incommensurability, and the problem is to decide in what way Wittgenstein means to deny the commensurability or homophony of religious and non-religious discourse.

[a]→ [3] The first lecture provides us with a number of clues. When a question is an ordinary empirical question, the appropriate attitude is often not to say 'I believe' or 'I don't believe', but to say, 'probably not' or 'probably yes' or possibly 'I'm not sure'. Wittgenstein uses the example of someone's saying 'There is a German aeroplane overhead'. If Wittgenstein were to reply, 'Possibly I'm not so sure', one would say that the two speakers were 'fairly near'. But what if someone says 'I believe in a Last Judgement' and Wittgenstein replies 'Well, I'm not so sure. Possibly'? Wittgenstein says, 'You would say that there is an enormous gulf between us'. For a typical non-believer, the Last Judgment isn't even a possibility.

[b]→ I don't think that Wittgenstein is denying that there is a state of mind in which someone on the verge of a religious conversion might suddenly stop and say, 'What if there is a Last Judgment?'. But I think that Wittgenstein would deny that this is at all like 'Possibly there is a German airplane overhead.'

[c]→ Wittgenstein distinguishes religious beliefs partly by what he calls their unshakeability. Speaking again of the man who believes in a Last Judgment, Wittgenstein says: 'But he has what you might call an unshakeable belief. It will show, not by reasoning or appeal to ordinary grounds for belief, but rather by regulating for in [*sic*] all his life. This is a very much stronger fact – foregoing pleasures, always appealing to this picture. This in one

sense must be called the firmest of all beliefs, because the man risks things on account of it which he would not do on things which are by far better established for him. Although he distinguishes between things well-established and not well-established'.

In understanding these remarks I think it is important to know that although Wittgenstein presents himself in these lectures as a non-believer, we know from the other posthumous writings published as *Culture and Value* that Wittgenstein had a deep respect for religious belief, that he thought a great deal about religious belief, especially about Christianity, and that in particular he paid a great deal of attention to the writings of Kierkegaard, and especially to the *Concluding Unscientific Postscript*. The man who has an unshakeable belief in the Last Judgment and lets it regulate for all his life, although he is very willing to admit that the Last Judgment is not an established fact, sounds like a Christian after Kierkegaard's own heart. Yet Kierkegaard himself wrote that faith 'has in every moment the infinite dialectic of uncertainty present with it'. It would be ludicrous to suppose that inner struggles with the issue of religious belief are something that Wittgenstein did not know. When he takes the unshakeableness of a religious belief as one of its characteristics, he does not mean that a genuine religious belief is always and at every moment free from doubt. Kierkegaard spoke of faith as a state to be repeatedly re-entered, and not as a state in which one can permanently stay. But I think that Kierkegaard would agree with Wittgenstein – and that Wittgenstein is here agreeing with Kierkegaard – that religious belief 'regulates for all' in the believer's life, even though his religious belief may alternate with doubt. If I confidently believe that a certain way is the right way to build a bridge, then I will set out building the bridge that way. If I come to have doubts, I will not go on building the bridge in that way (unless I am a crooked contractor); I will halt the construction and run further tests and make calculations.

Wittgenstein uses the following example:

Suppose you had two people, and one of them, when he had to decide which course to take, thought of retribution and the other did not. One person might, for instance, be inclined to take everything that happened to him as a reward or punishment, and another person doesn't think of this at all.

If he is ill, he may think: 'What have I done to deserve this?' This is one way of thinking about retribution. Another way is, he thinks in a general way whenever he is ashamed of himself: 'This will be punished.'

Take two people, one of whom talks of his behaviour and of what happens to him in terms of retribution, the other one does not. These people think entirely differently. Yet, so far, you can't say they believe different things.

[Wittgenstein adds] It is this way: if someone said: 'Wittgenstein, you don't take illness as a punishment, so what do you believe?' – I'd say: I don't have any thoughts of punishment.

> There are, for instance, these entirely different ways of thinking first of all – which needn't be expressed by one person saying one thing, another person saying another thing.

I think we take this example in the wrong way if we suppose that the person who thinks of his life in terms of retribution is supposed to be what we ordinarily call a religious believer. The example doesn't depend on whether he is or isn't. What Wittgenstein means to bring out by the example is that one's life may be organized by very different pictures. And he means to suggest that religion has more to do with the kind of picture that one allows to organize one's life than it does with expressions of belief. As Wittgenstein says, summing up this example, 'What we call believing in a Judgment Day – The expression of belief may play an absolutely minor role'.

d→ Wittgenstein also contrasts the basis upon which one forms empirical beliefs and the basis upon which one forms religious beliefs. 'Reasons look entirely different from normal reasons' in the religious case. 'They are, in a way, quite inconclusive'. He contrasts two cases: a person who believes that something that fits the description of the Last Judgment will in fact happen, years and years in the future, and who believes this on the basis of what we would call scientific evidence, and a person who has a religious belief which 'might in fact fly in the face of such a forecast and say "No. There it will break down."' Wittgenstein says that if a scientist told him that there would be a Last Judgment in a thousand years, and that he had to forgo all pleasures because of such a forecast, that he, Wittgenstein, 'wouldn't budge'. But the person whose belief in such a forecast was religious and not scientific 'would fight for his life not to be dragged into the fire. No induction. Terror. That is, as it were, part of the substance of the belief.'

The quoted passages give some sense to the texture of these notes. What seems most important in the first lecture is the repeated claim that the relation between Wittgenstein (who thoroughly conceals his own struggle with or against religious belief in these lectures) and the believer is not one of contradiction:

> If you ask me whether or not I believe in a Judgment Day, in the sense in which religious people have belief in it, I wouldn't say: 'No. I don't believe there will be such a thing.' It would seem to be utterly crazy to say this.
>
> And then I give an explanation: 'I don't believe in . . .', but then the religious person never believes what I describe.
>
> I can't say. I can't contradict that person.
>
> In one sense, I understand all he says – the English words 'God', 'separate', etc. I understand. I could say: 'I don't believe in this,' and this would be true, meaning I haven't got these thoughts or anything that hangs together with them. But not that I could contradict the thing.

e→ At this point, a number of possible interpretations of what Wittgenstein is saying might occur to one. (1) I already mentioned the Kuhnian idea of incommensurability. Perhaps Wittgenstein thinks that religious language and ordinary empirical language are incommensurable forms of discourse. The non-religious person simply can't understand the religious person. (2) The religious person and the non-religious person can understand one another, but the non-religious person is using language literally and the religious person is using it in some non-literal way, perhaps emotively, or to 'express an attitude'. (3) Ordinary discourse is 'cognitive' and the religious person is making some kind of 'non-cognitive' use of language. What I shall try to show in the light of these lectures, and especially the third and concluding lecture, is that Wittgenstein regards the first as a useless thing to say, and the second and third as simply wrong.

This will, of course, not solve the interpretative problem, but it will in a sense sharpen it, and make it interesting. If Wittgenstein is not saying one of the standard things about religious language – for example, that it expresses false pre-scientific theories, or that it is incommensurable – then what is he saying and how is it possible for him to avoid all of these standard alternatives? Still more important, how does he think we, including those of us who are not religious (and I don't think that Wittgenstein himself ever succeeded in recovering the Christian faith in which he was raised, although it was always a possibility for him that he might), are to think about religious language? What sort of a model is Wittgenstein offering us for reflection on what is always a very important, very difficult, and sometimes very divisive part of human life?

Superstition, Religious Belief, Incommensurability

In the second lecture Wittgenstein discusses the difference between the use of pictures to represent people, including biblical subjects, such as Noah and the ark, and the use of pictures to represent God. 'You might ask this question: "Did Michelangelo think that Noah in the ark looked like this, and that God creating Adam looked like this?" He wouldn't have said that God or Adam looked as they look in this picture.' Interestingly, Wittgenstein says: 'In general, there is nothing which explains the meanings of words so well as a picture, and I take it that Michelangelo was as good as anyone can be and did his best, and here is the picture of the Deity creating Adam. If we ever saw this, we certainly wouldn't think this the Deity. The picture has to be used in an entirely different way if we are to call the man in that queer blanket "God", and so on.'

[f]→ One concern of Wittgenstein's in the first two lectures is to contrast superstition and credulity – which often coexist with religion, to be sure – with religious belief in his sense. (Again, the parallelism with Kierkegaard is striking.) In the first lecture, the example of superstition is a Catholic priest who tries to offer scientific arguments for the truths of religion. Wittgenstein's comment is:

I would definitely call O'Hara unreasonable. I would say, if this is religious belief, then it's all superstition.

But I would ridicule it, not by saying it is based on insufficient evidence. I would say: here is a man who is cheating himself. You can say: this man is ridiculous because he believes, and bases it on weak reasons.

In the second lecture, Wittgenstein says:

Suppose I went to somewhere like Lourdes in France. Suppose I went with a very credulous person. There we see blood coming out of something. He says: 'There you are, Wittgenstein, how can you doubt?' I'd say: 'Can it only be explained one way? Can't it be this or that?' I'd try to convince him that he'd seen nothing of any consequence. I wonder whether I would do that under all circumstances. I certainly know that I would under normal circumstances.

'Oughtn't one after all to consider this?' I'd say: 'Come on. Come on.' I would treat the phenomenon in this case just as I would treat an experiment in a laboratory which I thought badly executed.

Wittgenstein is concerned to deny any continuity at all between what he considers religious belief and scientific beliefs. When there is a continuity, and only when there is a continuity, Wittgenstein is willing to use words like 'ridiculous', 'absurd', 'credulous', 'superstition'.

[4] To come back now to the question of incommensurability. An example might seem to be afforded by Wittgenstein's own thought experiment at the beginning of the first lecture, of imagining two people of whom the first one says 'I believe in a Last Judgment' and the second (whom Wittgenstein imagines to be himself) says 'Well, I'm not so sure. Possibly.' Here Wittgenstein does say 'It isn't a question of my being anywhere near him, but on an entirely different plane, which you could express by saying: "You mean something altogether different, Wittgenstein."' Now, at the beginning of the *Philosophical Investigation* (#43), Wittgenstein famously (or notoriously) wrote, 'For a *large* class of cases – though not for all – in which we employ the word "meaning" it can be defined thus: the meaning of a word is its use in the language.' If, as is too often done, one simply ignores the qualification 'though not for all', and ascribes to Wittgenstein the view that meaning can always be defined as use, then it is natural to read this 'theory of meaning' back into the statement I just quoted, from the first of the Lectures on Religious Belief, and to take it that when Wittgenstein insists again and again that the religious person and the non-religious person are using words in different ways, then he literally means that the words 'I believe in a Last Judgment' have a different meaning for someone who can speak of the Last Judgment as a matter of 'probability' and for a religious believer. But Wittgenstein doesn't say this. In the notes we have of the first lecture. Wittgenstein replies to his

imaginary interlocutor, 'The difference might not show up at all in any explanation of the meaning.'

Something lovely happens here. Wittgenstein is often charged with simple-mindedly equating use and meaning. Yet here he imagines an interlocutor who plays the role of the stock 'Wittgenstein' and proposes to say that the words 'I believe in a Last Judgment' have a different meaning in the two uses (one is, of course, completely imaginary), and the real Wittgenstein reminds the stock 'Wittgenstein' that we don't use the word 'meaning' that way, that is, that the difference in these two uses is not something that we would ordinarily call a difference in meaning.

Wittgenstein says something more about this towards the end of the same lecture. He points out that as an educated person who has read (and, as we know, has thought deeply about) the religious classics there is a very good sense in which he knows what the religious person means, although there is another sense in which Wittgenstein is inclined to say 'I don't know whether I understand him or not': 'If Mr. Lewy [Cassimir Lewy, one of the students present at these sessions] is religious and says he believes in a Judgment Day, I won't even know whether to say I understand him or not. I've read the same things as he's read. In a most important sense, I know what he means.' Wittgenstein immediately goes on to ask, 'If an atheist says: "There won't be a Judgment Day", and another person says there will, do they mean the same? – Not clear what the criterion of meaning the same is. They might describe the same things. You might say, this already shows that this means the same.'

So Wittgenstein is warning us against supposing that talk of 'meaning the same' and 'not meaning the same' will clarify anything here. In a perfectly ordinary sense of meaning the same, we might say that they do not mean the same (although Wittgenstein is still inclined to say 'I don't even know whether I should say that I understand him or not'); and to dismiss the question whether the words mean the same here, that is, whether the sentence means the same, as of no help here, is precisely to dismiss 'incommensurability' talk. That the two speakers aren't able to communicate *because* their words have different 'meanings' is precisely the doctrine of incommensurability.

[5] Another familiar move is to say that religious language is 'emotive', that is, that it is used to 'express attitudes'. It might seem possible (at least to some) to read these lectures as holding some version of this doctrine, if it were not for the very end of the third lecture. At that point Wittgenstein returns again to the question of whether he (as a non-believer) should say that he understands the sentences of the religious person or not.

Suppose someone, before going to China, when he might never see me again, said to me: 'We might see one another after death' – would I necessarily say that I didn't understand him? I might say [want to say] simply, 'Yes. I *understand* him entirely.'

Lewy: 'In this case, you might only mean that he expressed a certain attitude.'

I would say 'No, it isn't the same as saying "I'm very fond of you"' – and it may not be the same as saying anything else. It says what it says. Why should you be able to substitute something else?

Suppose I say: 'The man used a picture.'

I want to postpone discussion of the last suggestion for a few moments. The reply to Lewy is extremely interesting. What I take Wittgenstein to be pointing out is that there is a perfectly ordinary notion of expressing an attitude, and what he is doing is contrasting the kind of metaphysical emphasis that non-cognitivists (either about religious language or about ethical language) want to put on the notion of expressing an attitude with the ordinary unemphasized use of that notion. If I am fond of someone, I may express my fondness in a variety of ways, for example, by saying 'there's no one like you'. In such a case, we might say that I was expressing an attitude, and we can say what the attitude was, namely, I was expressing my fondness for the person. That attitude can be expressed explicitly, by saying 'I am very fond of So-and-so'. However, Wittgenstein is refusing to say that language is 'used to express an attitude' when there is no possibility of replacing the language in question by an explicit expression of the so-called attitude. The reason is not hard to guess. Wittgenstein refused to turn the distinction between saying something because that is, quite literally, what one means to say, and saying something to express an attitude, into a *metaphysical* distinction. As a metaphysical distinction it makes no sense at all without an appropriate metaphysical notion of a 'real fact' (the sort of fact that David Lewis can 'take at face value'); and that, evidently, is what Wittgenstein thinks we haven't got. . . . In *The Claim of Reason*, Stanley Cavell suggested that Charles Stevenson, the father of emotivism, wrote as if he had forgotten what ethical arguments sound like. Wittgenstein is saying that Lewy is talking as if he had forgotten what religious language sounds like. The philosophical doctrine of non-cognitivism does not help us to understand what religious discourse is really like any more than the philosophical doctrine of incommensurability does.

[6] What then is Wittgenstein saying? I believe that what Wittgenstein (in company with Kierkegaard) is saying is this: that religious discourse can be understood in any depth only by understanding the form of life to which it belongs. What characterizes that form of life is not the expressions of belief that accompany it, but a way – a way that includes words and pictures, but is far from consisting in just words and pictures – of living one's life, of regulating all of one's decisions. Here the believer, Kierkegaard, would add something that Wittgenstein does not say, but that I think he would agree with: namely, that a person may think and say all the right words and be living a thoroughly non-religious life. Indeed, Kierkegaard insists that a person may think he or she is worshipping God and really be worshipping an idol. (I suspect that this is one of the reasons that Kierkegaard is so much hated by fundamentalists. For Kierkegaard an authentically religious form of life is characterized by a constant concern that one not replace the

idea of God with a narcissistic creation of one's own; and this concern expresses itself in uncertainty as much as in certainty. For Kierkegaard, to be absolutely sure you are 'born again' is a sign that you are lost.) What Kierkegaard and Wittgenstein have in common is the idea that understanding the words of a religious person properly – whether you want to speak of understanding their 'meaning' or not – is inseparable from understanding a religious form of life, and this is not a matter of 'semantic theory', but a matter of understanding a human being.

The Religious Person 'Uses a Picture'

[7] Still, Wittgenstein himself does say that the religious person 'uses a picture'. Is this not a way of saying that religious language is non-cognitive? Indeed, Yorick Smythies seems to share this worry, since he objects towards the very end of the third lecture, 'This isn't all he does – associate a use with a picture.' Wittgenstein's initial reply is, 'Rubbish' – hardly an encouraging response. Wittgenstein goes on to explain that when he says the religious man is using a picture, he does not mean by that anything that the religious person himself would not say:

Smythies: 'This isn't all he does – associate a use with a picture.'

Wittgenstein: Rubbish. I meant: what conclusions are you going to draw? Etc. Are eyebrows going to be talked of, in connection with the Eye of God?

'He could just as well have said so and so' – this [remark] is foreshadowed by the word 'attitude'. He couldn't just as well have said something else.

If I say he used a picture, I don't want to say anything he himself wouldn't say. I want to say that he draws these conclusions.

Isn't it as important as anything else, what picture he does use?

Of certain pictures we say that they might just as well be replaced by another – e.g. we could, under certain circumstances, have one projection of an ellipse drawn instead of another.

[He *may* say]: 'I would have been prepared to use another picture, it would have had the same effect . . .'

The whole *weight* may be in the picture. . . .

When I say he's using a picture, I'm merely making a *grammatical* remark: [What I say] can only be verified by the consequences he does or does not draw.

If Smythies disagrees, I don't take notice of this disagreement.

All I wished to characterize was the conventions [*sic*] he wished to draw. If I wished to say anything more I was merely being philosophically arrogant.

'All I wished to characterize was the conventions [consequences] he wished to draw. If I wished to say anything more I was merely being philosophically arrogant.' One of the most impressive remarks a great philosopher has ever made in a discussion! Wittgenstein is saying here that to say the religious person is using a picture is simply to describe what we can in fact observe: that religious people do employ pictures, and that they draw certain consequences from them, but not the same consequences that we draw when we use similar pictures in other contexts. If I speak of my friend as having an eye, then normally I am prepared to say that he has an eyebrow, but when I speak of the Eye of God being upon me, I am not prepared to speak of the eyebrow of God. But the impressive thing here is not what Wittgenstein says, but the limit he places on his own observation. Pictures are important in life. The whole weight of a form of life may lie in the pictures that that form of life uses. In his own notes, some of which are republished in the collection *Culture and Value*, Wittgenstein says 'It is true that we can compare a picture that is firmly rooted in us to a superstition, but it is equally true that we *always* eventually have to reach some firm ground, either a picture or something else, so that a picture which is at the root of all our thinking is to be respected and not treated as superstition'.

. . . I have been discussing the suggestion that Wittgenstein thought that religious language is non-cognitive (even if he doesn't explicitly say so). But what can 'non-cognitive' come to when one suggests that 'religious language is non-cognitive'? The traditional realist way to spell out the suggestion that religious language is non-cognitive would be to say that ordinary descriptive terms like 'my brother' and 'America' and 'the Arc de Triomphe' all refer to something, but words used in the religious contexts Wittgenstein discusses do not. Isn't Wittgenstein hinting that when one speaks of the Eye of God or the Last Judgment one is *merely* using a picture, that is to say, one isn't referring to anything? . . .

[8] In *Philosophical Investigations* Wittgenstein attacks the idea that one can use a word only if one possesses a necessary and sufficient condition for its application. He uses the word 'game' as an example (the example has now become famous), and he says that in the case of that word we don't have a necessary and sufficient condition. We have some paradigms – paradigms of different kinds, in fact – and we extend the word 'game' to new cases because they strike us as similar to cases in which we have used it before (he describes this as our 'natural reaction'). He speaks of games as forming a family, as having a family resemblance, and he also uses the metaphor of a rope. The rope is made up of fibers, but there is no fiber running the length of the whole rope. There are similarities between one game and another, but there is no one similarity between all games.

While the notion of a family-resemblance word has become commonplace, many people miss Wittgenstein's point: as Rush Rhees emphasized a long time ago, Wittgenstein was not just making a low-level empirical observation to the effect that in addition to words like *scarlet*, which apply to things all of which are similar in a particular respect, there are words like *game* which apply to things which are not all similar in some one respect.

Wittgenstein was primarily thinking not of words like *game*, but of words like *language* and *reference*. It is precisely the big philosophical notions to which Wittgenstein wishes to apply the notion of a family resemblance. On Rush Rhees's reading (and I am convinced he is right), what Wittgenstein is telling us is that referring uses don't have an 'essence'; there isn't some one thing which can be called referring. There are overlapping similarities between one sort of referring and the next, that is all. That is why, for example, Wittgenstein is not puzzled, as many philosophers are, about how we can 'refer' to abstract entities. After all, we are not causally attached to the number three, so how can we refer to it? Indeed, do we know that there is such an object at all? For Wittgenstein the fact is that the use of number words is simply a different use from the use of words like *cow*. Stop calling three an 'object' or an 'abstract entity' and look at the way number words are used, is the advice.

Now, the relevance of this to a lecture on the philosophy of religion is as follows: just as I have suggested that Wittgenstein would not have regarded talk of incommensurability as helpful, and would not have regarded talk of certain discourses' being 'cognitive' and other discourses' being 'non-cognitive' as helpful, I suggest that he would not have regarded the question as to whether religious language *refers* as helpful either. (He speaks of a 'muddle'.) The use of religious language is both like and unlike ordinary cases of reference: but to ask whether it is 'really' reference or 'not really' reference is to be in a muddle. There is no essence of reference. Religious thinkers will be the first to tell you that when they refer to God, their 'referring use' is quite unlike the referring use of 'his brother in America'. In short, Wittgenstein is telling you what *isn't* the way to understand religious language. The way to understand religious language isn't to try to apply some metaphysical classification of possible forms of discourse.

Commentary on Putnam

After briefly introducing the topic in section 1, Putnam addresses in section 2 what he takes to be the central issue raised by Wittgenstein in his lectures: the incommensurability of religious and non-religious discourse. Section 3 draws on evidence from the lectures as to what Wittgenstein understands by incommensurability. Putnam looks at, and rejects, two possible interpretations: in section 4 that religious believers and non-believers mean something different when they use religious terms, and in section 5 that religious claims are non-cognitive. In section [7] Putnam discusses Wittgenstein's idea that religious believers use 'pictures'. In sections [6] and [8], Putnam explains the differences between religious and non-religious discourse in terms of the different – but resembling – conceptions of reference operating in them.

Putnam introduces in section [2] some examples from Wittgenstein's lectures on religious belief where the claims of someone who believes in an afterlife are contrasted with expressions of disbelief in the afterlife. In these cases, Wittgenstein proposes, the believer and non-believer do not 'contradict' or say the 'opposite' to one another. According to Putnam, Wittgenstein thinks that the religious believer and the atheist talk past one another and also that in general there is a failure to connect between religious and empirical claims. Understanding in what way religious and non-religious discourse are not commensurate is the *interpretative problem*.

1. Do you think there is any plausibility to the idea Wittgenstein seems to be hinting at in the quoted comments in section 2, that religious believers and atheists are talking past one another? In what way might they be failing to communicate?

Putnam follows up with three clues, in [a]→, [c]→ and [d]→ respectively, from Wittgenstein's lectures as to what he might mean. (1) Wittgenstein proposes that we tend to express either belief or disbelief in religious statements rather than tentative agreement or disagreement, whereas with empirical claims it is often appropriate to describe them as more or less probable. Putnam notes that Wittgenstein is not denying that someone could wonder whether there is, for example, a Last Judgement. But he thinks that Wittgenstein would deny that is 'at all like' speculating on whether an empirical claim might be true. (2) Wittgenstein takes religious beliefs to be characterised by their 'unshakeability', which Putnam sees as a point of contact between Wittgenstein and Kierkegaard. Although Putnam thinks that both of them would allow that a religious believer may experience moments of uncertainty, he understands them as proposing that religious beliefs typically have a regulative function in the life of a religious believer. Putnam develops this with Wittgenstein's comments comparing religious belief with the example of someone organising their life with a picture. (3) Wittgenstein contends that the reasons for religious beliefs often look different from the reasons given for empirical beliefs. A religious belief in the afterlife does not seem to depend on the strength of the empirical evidence for or against it. Even the possession of compelling evidence for the Last Judgement, Wittgenstein thinks, would not generate the life-changing commitments characteristic of religious belief.

2. Explain the point that Putnam makes at [b]→.

3. What does it mean to say that a religious belief is 'unshakeable'? What is the relationship between a belief being unshakeable and it 'regulating' or 'organising' one's life?

4. Carefully read through [d]→. What point do you think Wittgenstein is making here? Is it correct to say that someone who believed in the Last Judgement on the basis of evidence would not have a religious belief?

Before advancing his own solution to the interpretative problem, Putnam introduces in [e]→ two possible accounts of what Wittgenstein is proposing (options (2) and (3) cover similar ground), neither of which he thinks are successful: incommensurability and non-cognitivism.

The incommensurability thesis is associated with Thomas Kuhn's philosophy of science and in particular with his (1962/1970) book *The Structure of Scientific Reality*. According to Kuhn, the development of science is not a uniform progression of knowledge but has 'normal' and 'revolutionary' stages. During periods of normal science, scientists work on a range of problems and questions against a background of shared theoretical beliefs, scientific standards and techniques – what Kuhn sometimes calls a 'paradigm'. During periods of revolutionary science, this background consensus characteristic of normal science breaks down, and there are revisions to scientific belief and practice: there is a 'paradigm shift'. Kuhn went on to claim that science guided by one paradigm is 'incommensurable' with science guided by a different paradigm, i.e. that there is no common standard by which to assess the theories of different paradigms. Moreover, on the grounds that even one's observations are influenced by one's theories, Kuhn suggests that scientists operating with different paradigms will perceive the world differently.

One way of understanding the incommensurability thesis is that there is a change in the meaning of scientific terms when paradigms change. Kuhn gives the example of the term 'mass', which, he suggests, has a different meaning in Newtonian and in Einsteinian physics – a point that he extends to the entire repertoire of apparently common terms like 'space', 'time', 'matter', 'force', etc. (1962/1970: 149). The background to this view is meaning holism, the theory that the meanings of terms are extensively interconnected and that changing the meaning of one term results in changes in the meanings of all interconnected terms. A paradigm shift, on this theory, effects a systematic change in the meanings of scientific terms. This also seems to be what Putnam has in mind as a way of interpreting Wittgenstein, when he says that the atheist and the religious believer 'do not understand' each other. Wittgenstein's position would be something like this: the atheist and the religious believer work with different paradigms or 'worldviews' that result in them meaning something different when they talk about 'God', 'Last Judgement', etc. Despite appearances, they do not mean the same thing when they use these terms – and, moreover, lacking the other's paradigm, do not understand each other's meanings. This provides an answer to the interpretative problem, because it follows from the incommensurability of religious and non-religious discourse that the atheist and the religious believer do not (and are unable to) contradict one another. My denial of what you say will only contradict you if what I deny is the same as what you assert to be true.

We briefly considered the second option, non-cognitivism, in the first two chapters. For the non-cognitivist, a religious utterance like 'There will be a Last Judgement' does not express a religious belief that there will be a Last Judgement, but rather expresses an attitude. Which attitudes are in play (and which attitudes are being expressed by this particular utterance) will depend on the version of non-cognitivism in question, but they might include: hope, awe, guilt, approval/disapproval, solidarity. So, on the non-cognitivist view, religious statements are used to give voice to one's attitudes. How does this provide an answer to the interpretative problem? Putnam's point seems to be, in line with a position taken by David Hume, that attitudes do not contradict either with other attitudes or with other beliefs. My wish to play loud chant and drone music into the night, for example, may conflict with my neighbour's wish for a quiet life, and may need practical resolution, but my desires do not contradict my neighbour's beliefs or desires. So if religious non-cognitivism is right, then religious statements (which express attitudes) do not contradict with other statements (which express attitudes or beliefs).

5. Explain the distinction between superstition and religious belief introduced at [f]→. How do the following two examples illustrate the distinction? Why does Putnam introduce this distinction at this point in the discussion? Is the distinction useful?

Putnam rejects the incommensurability theory as a solution to the interpretative problem in section 4 on the grounds that Wittgenstein himself seems to reject this idea when he suggests that the difference between someone who asserts 'I believe in the Last Judgement' and someone with no religious convictions who doubts or denies it 'might not show up at all in any explanation of the meaning'. And Wittgenstein follows up by apparently giving the question of whether the religious believer and the atheist mean the same thing little importance. Putnam rejects the non-cognitivist solution to the interpretative problem in section 5 because Wittgenstein in conversation with Lewy seems to reject the idea that a statement expresses an attitude unless it could be replaced with a statement of the attitude being expressed. Since this does not seem possible for most religious claims (what statement of one's attitudes could replace 'I believe in the Last Judgement'?), Wittgenstein seems to be rejecting religious non-cognitivism.

Putnam seems right in rejecting incommensurability as a plausible answer to the interpretative problem. And Putnam is not alone in thinking that Wittgenstein's brief dialogue with Lewy also shows that he rejects non-cognitivism (see Clack 1999: 36). But there is a problem. Recall the distinction in the chapter on Ayer between religious non-cognitivism and subjectivism: the subjectivist thinks that religious claims can be reduced to claims about our mental states, whereas the non-cognitivist thinks that religious claims give voice to our mental states (and specifically our attitudes rather than our beliefs). Subjectivism, as we saw, is a form of cognitivism – albeit, not one that many religious cognitivists would endorse. Now, consider the dialogue between Lewy and Wittgenstein. Wittgenstein appears to take the student's question as asking whether religious claims *report* attitudes, and so could be replaced by a statement of how one feels; in this case, whether 'I will see you after death' means 'I am very fond of you'. But this is just a form of subjectivism. So there does not seem to be anything in Wittgenstein's exchange with Lewy, therefore, to suggest that he rejected non-cognitivism.

Putnam recognises the *prima facie* plausibility of the non-cognitivist reading of Wittgenstein in his discussion of pictures – could Wittgenstein be saying that the religious believer is *merely* using a picture to guide her life?

6. Examine the discussion in section 7. What does it mean to say that a religious believer 'uses a picture'? Is it true? Why does Wittgenstein say that some pictures should be 'respected and not treated as superstition'?

In section 8, Putnam gives his own answer to the interpretative problem. He begins with Wittgenstein's idea that for some words there are no necessary and sufficient conditions for their use, but rather an interconnected collection of related uses. These are 'family-resemblance' terms. According to Putnam, Wittgenstein thought that terms of central philosophical interest, like *reference* and *truth*, are also family-resemblance terms. In other words, there is no one set of necessary and sufficient conditions for the correct use of 'refer', and of the different sets of conditions that are used there is none that is uniquely privileged over the others. By implication, Putnam thinks that *different* standards of reference and truth are operative within religious discourse from those that are operative in scientific, mathematical or other kinds of discourse.

How does this help with the interpretative problem? Putnam's point seems to be that Wittgenstein's position is that the atheist and the religious believer do not contradict because they employ different (though possibly related) concepts of reference and truth in their talk of God. What are these different concepts? Putnam refers us to the 'forms of life' in which religious and other expressions are used. Unfortunately, he does not spell out the details. But possibly he has something like the following in mind. For a non-believer inquiring into whether some object has a property, the availability of publicly accessible evidence and the testability of the claim about that thing will be among the crucial standards that are used in finding the correct answer. In contrast, for a religious believer asking whether God has a certain property, the judgement of a respected figure in a religious community, the claims of an authoritative text, or personal religious experiences may play a role in determining the correct answer. This is not to say that a religious believer disregards empirical evidence when evaluating the truth of religious claims; but, as Wittgenstein seems to suggest in [d]↦, it is not a failing of the standards of *religious* discourse to believe where there is no supportive empirical evidence. So the reason that someone who asserts 'There will be a Last Judgement' is not contradicted by someone who denies it is that the non-believer and the believer are employing different criteria in the assessment of the truth of this claim.

We have noted that Putnam's rejection of the non-cognitivist interpretation of Wittgenstein is not entirely persuasive. But how does Putnam's version of Wittgenstein's views on religion stand up as an account of religious discourse? Here are a couple of problems.

The first problem concerns a seeming muddle between religious discourse and the use of religious discourse to express religious beliefs. Wittgenstein does not say what class of statements he takes to be religious and attempt to offer some general characterisation of them. Rather, he considers statements that we would usually agree express religious beliefs and contrasts them sometimes with statements that we would not take to be religious, for example, statements about physical objects in our environment, and at other times with statements that express disbelief about religious matters. For example, he contrasts the following two statements:

1. There is a German aeroplane overhead.
2. There will be a Last Judgement.

Putnam characterises these as an empirical and a religious statement. And Wittgenstein also contrasts

2. There will be a Last Judgement.
3. There will not be a Last Judgement.

But note that (2) and (3), unlike (1) and (2), are both religious claims in the sense that they employ religious terms and have a religious subject matter; where they differ is that (2) uses religious language to express a religious conviction, whereas (3) uses religious language to express disbelief. We have, in effect, *two* interpretative problems: why Wittgenstein thinks that religious believers and non-believers talk past one another, and why he thinks that religious and non-religious discourses are not commensurate. Now, Putnam proposes in [8] that we can resolve the interpretative problem on the basis that the concept of reference operating in religious discourse is different from – though presumably related to – the concept of reference operating in other fields of discourse. But how is a distinction between reference in religious discourse and reference in non-religious discourse going to solve the interpretative problem of why religious believers and non-believers – even when they are both using religious discourse – talk past one another? If, on the other hand, Putnam were to suggest that religious believers and non-believers use different standards of reference, how will that help with the apparently quite distinct issue of the relationship between religious and non-religious discourse?

7. Do you think that it is plausible to say either that religious discourse has different standards of reference and truth from non-religious (specifically scientific) discourse, or that religious believers employ different standards of reference and truth from non-believers?

The second problem concerns the family-resemblance account of reference, truth, and other concepts. Suppose that we accept that to understand the meaning of an expression we need to know about the 'form of life' of which it forms a part. Accordingly we look at religious and non-religious discourse and find, perhaps on the lines suggested above, that different standards are used (particularly with regard to empirical evidence and testability) to determine whether an expression refers or a statement is true. Why should it follow from this that there is any change in the necessary and sufficient conditions for 'truth' or 'reference'? The methods we use to establish the temperature of a room are different from those we use to establish the temperature of the surface of the sun, but it does not follow that 'It is true that this room is 22C' and 'It is true that the photosphere of the sun is about 6000C' involve different concepts of *truth*, or that if we say of each sentence that it is referring to temperature we are using different concepts of *reference*. In other words, while religious truths and scientific truths may be different, and there may be different ways of discovering them, it does not follow that we have more than one concept of truth. Moreover, if we accept Putnam–Wittgenstein's conclusion that the concepts of truth and reference vary in their meaning in different areas of discourse, then our talk of truth and reference will be ambiguous. The implications of this are drawn out by Timothy Williamson. Consider two discourses D1 and D2 in English, and two statements A1 and A2 which belong to D1 and D2 respectively. 'A1 or A2' will be a disjunction in English. It is a platitude about truth that a disjunction is true if either of its disjuncts is true. But if different truth-predicates apply in D1 and D2 this platitudinous inference will be invalid, because the claim that a disjunction is true if and only if one of its disjuncts is true will involve an equivocation. A similar problem arises for other platitudes about truth. The rule for conjunction is that 'A1 and A2' is true if and only if A1 is true and A2 is true. But this will only hold if a single concept of truth applies for both D1 and D2. So it must be the case that there is a single truth-predicate for both discourses, and for all discourses in English, unless we are to give up on elementary logical operations.

We have touched on just a few of the issues and problems that have been central to work on Wittgenstein and religion. For a lucid introduction to Wittgenstein's lectures and writings on religions, see:

Clack, B., *An Introduction to Wittgenstein's Philosophy of Religion*, Edinburgh: Edinburgh University Press, 1999.

D. Z. Phillips has written extensively on Wittgenstein and religion. For a useful collection of his work, see his *Wittgenstein and Religion*, Basingstoke: Palgrave Macmillan, 1994.

There are two principal sources for Wittgenstein's work on religion:

Lectures and Conversations on Aesthetics, Psychology and Religious Belief, Oxford: Blackwell, 1966.

Culture and Value, ed. G. H. von Wright, H. Nyman and A. Pichler, 2nd edn, Oxford: Blackwell, 1998.

In addition, a posthumously discovered notebook written in the 1930s that contains numerous comments on religion has been published as:

Public and Private Occasions, ed. J. Klagge and A. Nordmann, Lanham, Md: Rowman & Littlefield, 2003.

Introduction to Alston

William Alston (1921–2009) was professor emeritus at Syracuse University, New York. He was one of the most significant philosophers of religion of recent decades, and one of a small group of philosophers to help initiate the resurgence of interest in the topic in the late twentieth century. His work in philosophy of religion has focused primarily on issues in epistemology and language (though Alston would perhaps prefer the latter to be characterised as religious *speech*). His book *Divine Nature and Human Language*, from which the following chapter is taken, has become a seminal text in the field.

Metaphors are widespread and occur frequently in religious discourse. 'God is my rock', 'God is love', 'The Lord is my shepherd' are just three examples of metaphorical claims about God. However, motivated by the idea that God is transcendent, some philosophers (Anthony Kenny in *The Unknown God: Agnostic Essays*) and theologians (Sallie McFague in *Metaphorical Theology: Models of God in Religious Language*) have argued that it is impossible to speak any literal truth about God. In so far as one can say anything true about God, therefore, it must be metaphorical. Moreover, it must be irreducibly metaphorical – if there is any literal component to a metaphorical claim about God, then the claim will be false. Alston draws on some general considerations about the nature of metaphor and applies them to religious metaphors to show that this position is untenable.

William Alston, 'Irreducible Metaphors in Theology'

I

My primary concern in this essay is with the possibility of irreducible metaphor in talk about God, and with the kind of significance such talk would have if possible. But before tackling those problems head on I should indicate why it seems to many that theology needs irreducible metaphors.

The impossibility of literal talk about God has become almost an article of faith for theology in this century. Of course it is not denied that one can *make* a statement in which some term, used literally, is applied to God; that is not regarded as being beyond human powers. The impossibility alleged is, rather, an impossibility of saying anything *true* about God while using terms literally. Various reasons have been given for this sweeping proscription. Perhaps the most popular in our day is the *transcendence* of God, His 'wholly otherness'. This appears in various forms; Tillich, e.g., holds that (a) God is not *a* being, but Being Itself, since anything that is *a* being would not be an appropriate object of religious worship, and (b) only what is *a* being can be literally characterized. Those who identify themselves with the mystical tradition emphasize the principle that God is an ineffable, undifferentiated unity. Coming from another quarter is the infamous verifiability criterion of meaning, which has been used to argue the still more sweeping thesis that no theological predication has any truth value at all.

I myself do not regard any of these arguments as successful, but this is not the place to say why. The present point is that arguments like these have been convincing to many contemporary theologians and philosophers of religion. But many of them are not prepared to give up theological discourse. And so they must find some other way of construing what look like literal theological statements, such as,

God created the heavens and the earth.
God spoke to Jeremiah.
God brought the Israelites out of Egypt.
God sent His only begotten Son into the world.
God forgives the sins of those who are truly repentant.
God's purpose is that we shall all enjoy eternal life.

One popular move is to give them some non-cognitive interpretation, as expressive of attitudes, feelings, or commitments,[1] or evocative of mystical experience, 'insight', or 'seeing X as Y'.[2] But again a sizable proportion are unwilling to give up the idea that it is possible to make *true statements* about God, to articulate something that really does pertain to the divine nature, to convey in words some apprehension, however inadequate, of what God is like.

To those who find themselves in this position, metaphor can seem a promising way out. In many spheres of discourse we manage to make true statements without using terms literally. We can correctly describe what Russia did at the end of Word War II by saying that she dropped an iron curtain across Europe, even though no iron curtain was literally dropped. Why can't we analogously provide some insight into the divine nature and operations by saying things like 'God spoke to Jeremiah', even if none of these predicates are literally true of God? Just as the dropping of an iron curtain across a stage provides a useful 'model' for thinking about what Russia did just after Word War II, why can't human speech provide a useful model for thinking about God's relation to Jeremiah, and sending one's son to do a certain job provide a useful model for thinking of God's relation to the work of Jesus Christ? But of course if *no* term can be literally [a]→ applied to God, our metaphorical talk about God will be *irreducible*. A metaphor is *irreducible* if what is said in the metaphorical utterance cannot be said, *even in part*, in literal terms. Obviously, if no term can be literally applied to God, we cannot do *anything* to spell out in literal terms what is said metaphorically about God. Hence theologians who go the route we

[1] See, e.g., George Santayana, *Reason in Religion* (New York: Scribner, 1905), and R. B. Braithwaite, *An Empiricist's View of the Nature of Religious Belief* (Cambridge: Cambridge University Press, 1955).

[2] See, e.g., W. T. Stace, *Time and Eternity* (Princeton: Princeton University Press, 1952), J. H. Randall, Jr., *The Role of Knowledge in Western Religion*, (Boston: Starr King Press, 1958), chap. 4, and John Wisdom, 'Gods,' *Proceedings of the Aristotelian Society*, 45 (1944–45).

have been describing will wind up construing talk about God as made up of irreducible metaphors.[3]

II

We can effectively come to grips with our central question only if we have an explicit account of the nature of metaphor. To this I now turn.

Despite the frequent occurrence of terms like 'metaphorical *meaning*' and 'metaphorical *sense*' in discussions of the subject, I believe that they reflect a confused, or at least a loose, way of thinking about metaphor. To get straight about the matter we need to keep a firm grip on the Saussurian distinction between *language* and *speech*. A (natural) language is an abstract system, a system of abstract sound types or, in principle, types of other sorts of perceptible items. The systematicity involved is both 'internal' and 'external'. The phonology, morphology and syntax of a language constitute its 'internal' system – the ways in which its elements can be combined to form larger units. The 'external' system is revealed by the semantics of the language – the ways in which units of the language have the function of 'representing' things in, and features of, the world.[4] A language serves as a means of communication; that is its basic raison d'être. *Speech* is the *use* of language in communication (using speech in an extended sense to cover written as well as oral communication). It is what we *do* in the course of exploiting a linguistic system for purposes of communication.[5]

[3] I want to emphasize that in this essay we are not asking the (silly) question as to whether it is possible to have metaphors of any sort in talk about God, nor are we asking what status our metaphorical God-talk actually has. It is obvious that much talk about God is metaphorical. For example:

The Lord is my shepherd.
His hands prepared the dry land.
The Lord is my rock and my fortress.
In thy light do we see light.
The Lord looks down from heaven.

I believe that it is commonly supposed that metaphors like these are reducible, that it is possible to say in literal terms at least part of what is being said about God metaphorically in these utterances. In saying 'The Lord is my shepherd' I am saying that God will protect me and see to it that my needs are satisfied; and so on. But we are not concerned in this paper to determine whether this is so. We are concerned with a certain project – interpreting all talk about God, including the more literal-sounding statements just mentioned, as *irreducible* metaphors. We are dealing with a question that is fundamental to that project, viz., whether there can be irreducible metaphors, and if so what status they would have.

[4] This is a very crude way of characterizing semantics, but it will have to do for now. There is no general agreement on what an adequate characterization would look like.

[5] Language and speech may also be interrelated in other and more intimate ways. Thus, in my view, language *exists* only as a set of potentialities for speech; the fact that speech is patterned in certain ways *constitutes* the reality of a natural language; if there were no speech, there would be no *actual* languages. But that is quite compatible with the existence and fundamental importance of the distinction drawn in the text.

Now the fact that a given word or phrase has the meaning(s) or sense(s)[6] it has is a fact about the language; it is part of the semantic constitution of the language. Thus it is a (semantic) fact about the English language that 'knit' has among its meanings:

1. To form, as a fabric, by interlacing a single yarn or thread in loops, by means of long thin bluntly pointed rods.
2. To draw together; to contract into wrinkles; as he knit his brow in thought.[7]

The fact that a word has a certain meaning is (part of) what gives it its usability for communication; it constitutes part of the linguistic resources we draw on in saying what we have to say.

The term 'metaphor', on the other hand, stands for a certain way of *using* words, a mode of *speech* rather than a type of meaning or any other feature of *language*. More specifically, it belongs to the family of *figurative* uses of terms ('figures of *speech*', as they are appropriately called in the tradition) that stand in contrast with *literal* uses of terms. Let's make explicit the distinction between *literal* and *metaphorical* uses, restricting ourselves to the uses of predicates in subject–predicate statements, since that is the application with which we are especially concerned.

We may think of each meaning of a predicate term 'correlating' the term with some (possibly very complex) property.[8] Each of the definitions of 'knit' given above specifies a (relational) property with which 'knit' is 'correlated' in one of its meanings. Different theories of meaning provide different accounts of the nature of this correlation. Thus the 'ideational' theory of meaning found in, e.g., Locke's *Essay*, holds that a meaning of a predicate term 'correlates' it with a certain property, P, *iff* the term functions as a sign of the *idea* of P in communication. It will be convenient to speak of a predicate term 'signifying' or 'standing for' the correlated property.

Now when I make a literal use of a predicate term, in one of its meanings, in a subject-predicate sentence, I utter the sentence with the claim that the property signified by the predicate is possessed by the subject (the referent of the subject-term), or, if the predicate is a relational one, that the property holds between the subjects. Thus if I make a literal use of 'knit'

[6] We shall not distinguish between *meaning* and *sense*.

[7] *Webster's New Collegiate Dictionary* (Springfield, Mass.: Merriam, 1959). I am far from claiming that this is the best or most adequate way to specify these meanings. Indeed it is far from clear, at this stage of development of the art, what is the most adequate way to specify meanings. But it does seem clear that 'knit' has the two meanings thus specified, however lamely and haltingly, and that its having these two meanings is (a small) part of what makes the English language what it is at the current stage of its history.

[8] I would want this supposition to be compatible with the fact that most (all?) predicate terms have meanings that are vague, have 'open texture', or suffer from indeterminacy in other ways. This means that an adequate formulation would have to be considerably more complicated than the one given here.

in saying, e.g., 'My wife knitted that sweater', I would be claiming that the relation specified in the first of our two definitions holds between my wife and that sweater. And if my statement is true, if that relation does in fact hold between these terms, then we may say that 'knit' is *literally true* of these terms, or does *literally apply* to them.

But suppose I say, as Shakespeare has Macbeth say, 'Sleep knits up the ravelled sleeve of care'. It is clear that sleep cannot possibly do to care either of the things listed as meanings of 'knit'. Nor, if we surveyed all the meanings that 'knit' has in the language, would we find any relation that literally holds between sleep and care. Hence, if I am sensible, I will not be uttering that sentence with the claim that 'knit' literally applies to sleep. Instead I will be using the term *metaphorically*. But what is it to use the term metaphorically? In presenting a brief answer to that question I shall be more or less following the admirable account given by Paul Henle in chapter 7 of *Language, Thought, and Culture*.[9]

When I use a predicate term metaphorically, or in accordance with some other figure of speech (metonymy, synecdoche, irony, hyperbole, or whatever), I am not turning my back on the meaning(s) that term has in the language. Even though I am not claiming that the term is literally true of the subject in any of those senses, I am not ignoring those senses. On the contrary, I am using the term in one of those senses, though not in the same way as in literal speech. Instead of straightforwardly applying the term in that sense to the subject, I am engaged in the following multi-stage operation. First, I envisage, and 'invite' the hearer to envisage, something of the sort to which the term does literally apply. In the case under discussion this would be a person repairing a ravelled piece of fabric. Let's call something to which the predicate literally applies an *exemplar*. Needless to say, we will ordinarily be dealing with *envisaged*, rather than actual exemplars. In the metaphorical statement cited earlier, 'Russia has dropped an iron curtain across Europe', the exemplar is a person dropping a curtain (a rather unusual one, made of iron) in front of a stage. In 'Life's a walking shadow', the exemplar is a shadow cast by a walking man (among other possibilities). Now what the metaphorical statement most basically 'says' is that the exemplar can usefully be taken as a 'model' of the subject. The hearer is invited to consider the exemplar *as* a model of the subject, as a way of discovering, highlighting, or rendering salient, various features of the subject.

As so far characterized, a metaphorical 'statement' does not appear to be making any truth claim about the subject, other than the implicit claim that it is sufficiently like the exemplar to make the latter a useful model of

[9] Paul Henle, ed. (Ann Arbor: University of Michigan Press, 1958). The literature on metaphor bristles with controversy. Nevertheless, I believe that there is widespread agreement on the general lines of the following account; and the agreement would be much greater if everyone were to get straight on the language–speech distinction.

the former. So long as I am simply *presenting* a model to the hearer for him to use as he sees fit, I am not myself attributing any particular feature to the subject. Now this may sometimes be a complete account of what the speaker is doing; he is simply suggesting a model that has caught his fancy, that feels right to him. But more typically the speaker is concerned to exploit the model in a particular way; he will 'have in mind' one or more particular points of resemblance (between model and subject) that he intends to be attributing to the subject.[10] Thus when Churchill said 'Russia has dropped an iron curtain across Europe', he wasn't just throwing the image of an iron curtain up for grabs, leaving it to his auditors to make of it what they would. He meant to be exploiting the model in a certain way – to assert that Russia has made it almost impossible to exchange information, goods, and persons between her sphere of influence and Western Europe.

Thus in the typical metaphorical statement the speaker is 'building on' the relevant meaning of his predicate terms in two ways. First, he is presenting the sort of thing to which the term literally applies as a model of the subject. Second, he has in mind one or more resemblances between model and subject, and he extracts from these resemblances what he means to be attributing to the subject. In the Churchill quote, the resemblance is the inhibition of communication. In the 'knitting' lines from Macbeth the resemblance is that the agent is doing something to restore the patient to a sounder condition, one more nearly in accord with what it is 'supposed' to be. And these points of resemblance are just what are being attributed to the subject(s).

Note that the speaker is doing this 'on his own'. Of course the semantic content of the sentence plays certain constraints on him, because that is what he has to work with. But within that framework it is 'up to him' *whether* he uses the predicate term metaphorically, and, if so, what features of the model he selects for attribution to the subject. . . .

The sharp outlines of this idealized picture will have to be softened in various ways if it is to faithfully depict the often blurred reality of metaphorical speech. Let me mention the most important qualifications. (A) 'Speaker' will have to be taken in an extended sense to include 'hearers' as well. For a hearer may himself exploit the model in certain specific ways, and thus endow the statement with a propositional content not foreshadowed in the speaker's intentions; and do this without abandoning the communicative role of the hearer. We can handle this by thinking of the hearer as making a metaphorical statement himself. (B) . . . Speaker intention can be of all degrees of explicitness. The speaker need not rehearse to himself in so many words that he intends to be asserting that. . . . In certain cases he may not even be able to say, in literal terms, what it is that he is asserting, but be asserting that nonetheless. (This might be elicited by

[10] Of course, these 'havings in mind' and these intentions can be of all degrees of explicitness and articulateness, just as with other thoughts and communicative intentions.

skilful questioning.) What it finally comes down to is what the speaker would take as truth conditions of his utterance when they are presented to him. Of course, as with all such issues, questions can be raised as to whether his later responses to suggested truth conditions accurately reproduce his dispositions at the moment of utterance. But like practically all interesting concepts, the concept of *what a speaker asserted* does not come with fool-proof decision procedures attached. . . .

III

With this background we may turn to our central problem concerning the possibility and status of irreducible metaphors in theology. A metaphor is irreducible if what it says cannot be said, even in part, in literal terms. How we answer our central question will depend, inter alia, on how we pick out *what is said* in a metaphorical utterance. So a word on this is in order.

There are, no doubt, various ways of drawing a distinction between *what* is said, *how* it is said, and other aspects of what is *done* in a speech act. One way of drawing these distinctions is dictated by the fact that we are interested specifically in the use of metaphors to attribute properties to subjects, with an attached 'truth claim', the claim that the property in question does indeed belong to the subject in question. Hence the 'what-is-said' on which we will concentrate is the proposition(s) *asserted* in an
b→ utterance, those propositions the speaker is claiming to be true. When we ask whether what is said in a metaphor can be said in literal terms, we are asking whether the *propositional* content of the metaphorical statement can be literally expressed. This is by no means the whole story about a metaphorical statement. As we have seen, a speaker makes a metaphorical statement by using the literal meaning of his predicate to present a model of the subject. Now, by definition, that *way* of asserting a certain proposition cannot be reproduced in a literal utterance; any assertion done
c→ that way is, by definition, a metaphorical assertion. And any feature that attaches to a metaphorical statement by virtue of this distinctive mode of statement will likewise fail to survive transportation to the literal mode. Thus it is often pointed out that a metaphorical statement is characterized by a certain 'open-endedness'. However definite an attribution the speaker means to be making via his model, he is also *presenting* the model as a source of hitherto unnoticed insights into the nature of the subject. And so metaphorical statements have what might (metaphorically) be called a penumbra of inexplicit suggestions that surround whatever definite propositional content is presented. Again, this cannot be captured in a literal re-statement. Even if we explicitly assert in literal terms *that* the model may be indefinitely rich in insights into the subject, that is not the same as *presenting* the model with the implied suggestion of untapped resources. Thus we are not asking whether metaphors can receive exact

or exhaustive literal paraphrase, as that question has often been understood in the literature.

Moreover we are not even asking whether the propositional content can be exactly or exhaustively expressed in literal terms. It may be, e.g., that the 'open-endedness' alluded to in the last paragraph affects the propositional content of a metaphorical statement. It may be that in a metaphorical statement there is no sharp line between what is being asserted and what is only more or less explicitly suggested, so that propositions asserted metaphorically possess a kind of fuzzy boundary that is not shared by propositions expressed literally. But even if that is so it would not prevent the propositional content from being partially expressed in literal terms. Remember that our concern is with the idea that, since no predicates can be literally true of God, God can be spoken of only in metaphors that are wholly irreducible. Our question is, then, whether there can be a metaphorical statement the propositional content of which cannot be expressed, even in part, in literal terms.

In tackling this question it will be useful to consider separately the two strata of truth claims we have found to be contained in metaphors. First, there is the very *unspecific* claim that the exemplar is sufficiently similar to the subject, in some way(s) or other, to make the former a useful model of the latter. (Call this M-similarity.) Second, there is, normally, some more *specific* attribution that is derived from one or more particular points of resemblance.

The first level can be handled very quickly. There is obviously no difficulty in literally applying the predicate 'M-similar' to any pair of entities whatever. Moreover this predicate will be literally true of the exemplar and subject whenever the metaphorical statement is true, or, indeed, whenever the metaphor is successful or appropriate in any way.[11] Thus the literal expressibility of that much of the propositional content unquestionably holds for any metaphorical statement whatever. This gives us a 'floor' of guaranteed literal paraphrasability that cannot be gainsaid.

The additional, *specific* proposition content is a more complicated problem. Yet I believe there to be a simple argument that shows that the specific content must, in principle, be expressed in literal terms. Let's restrict ourselves to the predicative part of the propositional content, since we have

[11] If the basic truth claim were only that exemplar and subject are similar in some way or other, then we could say without qualification that it could never fail to succeed. It is a priori true that any pair of objects exhibit similarity in indefinitely many respects. Just for starters, each shared non-identity constitutes a point of similarity. But the basic presupposition has a bit more content than that; it stipulates similarity in such a way as to make the one a useful model for the other. It is not clear just what that takes. Presumably the fact that X and Y are both non-identical with Z would not suffice by itself. But since we are often surprised at what ingenious modellers can make of unpromising material, it is not clear that this presupposition cuts out anything that would be allowed by the more unqualified presupposition. Hence it may be that even this presupposition is satisfied by any pair of objects whatever. But I do not feel confident in pushing this point.

just been taking for granted the reference to the subject; and let's consider the statement 'God is my rock'. Let us say that when a speaker asserts this, the property he means to be attributing to God is P. What would it take to express P in literal terms? There must be some predicate term such that by a literal employment of that term in the frame 'God is ___' I can attribute P to God. That is, we need a term that signifies P, so that just by virtue of the term's meaning what it does one can use it to attribute to some subject. And what does it take for that to be possible? An adequate answer to that question would involve going into the mechanisms by which terms acquire meaning in natural languages – a very murky subject. But at least this much is clear. So long as it is possible for members of the linguistic community to form a concept of P, it will be possible for P to become the meaning of a predicate term in the language. For so long as I can form the concept of P, it will be possible for me to associate an element of the language with P in such a way as to use that element to attribute P to something. How could that be impossible for me to do, so long as I have 'cognitive access' to P? And if the property is cognitively accessible to me, then, unless this is by virtue of superhuman powers, it will be in principle, cognitively accessible to any other human being. But if it is conceptually accessible to the language community, there is no bar in principle to a word's signifying the property *in the language*.

And now we are ready for the final turn of the screw. The sufficient condition just uncovered is automatically satisfied whenever a certain property figures in the propositional content of a metaphorical utterance. For, as we have seen, it cannot so figure unless the speaker has that property in mind as what he means to be attributing to the subject. And he cannot have the property in mind without having a concept of that property. No matter in how inexplicit or inarticulate a fashion he 'has it in mind', he will be in possession of at least an equally inexplicit or inarticulate concept. Therefore a statement cannot possess a propositional content unless it is, in principle, possible that a language should contain words that have that have the meanings required for the literal expression of that content. . . .

IV

e → The argument against irreducibly metaphorical statements has been a completely general one. Let's now apply the results to theology. Of course the direct application is obvious; it is just universal instantiation. If there can be no irreducible metaphorical statements anywhere there can be none in theology. So this way out is unavailable for one who denies the possibility of literal predication. But let us not be too hasty. The distinction between two levels of propositional content may give our quarry some room for manoeuvre. In particular, we might imagine an opponent of literal predication attempting to construct the following halfway house.

'Let's grant that in order to have any metaphorical truth claim at all, one must at least be presupposing that the exemplar is like the subject in some significant way(s); and your point that at least this presupposition can be literally expressed is an undeniable one. Nor is this a trivial point; it does show that the unqualified denial of literal predication cannot be sustained, if we are to talk of God even metaphorically. But that denial never was (should have been) issued in so unqualified a form. What we anti-literalist are really concerned about is not those abstract, "structural" predicates like (*significantly*) *similar in some way or other*, but specific predicates like *wise*, *loving*, *makes*, *forgives*, *commands*, and so on. Therefore if we can make the denial of specific literal predictability stick, we will have gotten what we were after. For in that case it will be impossible to say, literally, what God is like, what He has planned, done, what He would have us do, and so on. We deniers of literal predication will be only minimally shaken by having to admit that God is, literally, *significantly like* f→ *a king in some way or other*. Again, we will admit that you have shown that if we issue a metaphor with some specific property "in mind" as the one we mean to be attributing to God, then it is, in principle, possible to make that attribution in literal terms. Since we are operating within these constraints, the way out is to construe theological statements as limited to the unspecific claim, as far as "propositional content" is concerned. So when one says "God gave me courage to face that situation", he is to be interpreted as simply putting forward the model of one human being encouraging another, with only the unspecific claim that this is sufficiently similar to God's relation to my being encouraged to be usefully employed as a model thereof. There is no further claim of some particular point of similarity, P. The speaker is simply suggesting that we think of the matter in terms of that model. And hence the assertion need be literally paraphrasable only so far as the totally unspecific claim is concerned.' . . .

Metaphorical statements about God that are restricted to the *unspecific* truth claim will suffer from a number of disabilities that render them unfit for theological duty.

(A) Since virtually any such statement will be true, the theological attributions we like will enjoy this status only at the price of sharing it with indefinitely many statements we do not like. Perhaps we can best appreciate this point by starting from the weaker but more clear-cut presupposition of *some similarity or other between exemplar and model*. As noted above, since it is a priori true that any two entities are similar in indefinitely many respects, if that were all that were being claimed in a statement about God, all such statements would be true alike; it would be just as true, true in the same way, that God is cruel as that God is merciful, just as true that God is a spider, or a mud-pie, or a thief as that God is the creator of heaven and earth and that he has reconciled us to Himself. To be sure, the presupposition with which we are working is not as empty as that; it involves the more specific claim that the exemplar is *M-similar* to God, similar in some way(s) that renders it suitable to be used as a model. But since the force of this further restriction is so difficult to assess, we are in a similar position. Though I cannot claim it is a priori true that God is M-similar to anything whatever, it is difficult to be confident, with respect to any proffered example, that it is not M-similar to God. . . .

(B) The theological relations in which a theological statement stands with other statements (theological and otherwise) are determined by their propositional contents, i.e., on this position, by the unspecific presupposition. And that content fails to stand in the desired logical relations. First consider contradictoriness. For the same reasons that led us to suppose that virtually any statement about God will turn out to be true, we will also be forced to recognize that a given statement about God will be logically incompatible with virtually no other statements about God. 'God is loving and merciful' does not logically exclude 'God is arbitrarily cruel and bloodthirsty'. For the fact that a loving and merciful human being is a suitable model for God certainly does not *logically* exclude the possibility that an arbitrarily cruel and bloodthirsty human being is a suitable model for God (in some respect or other). Not even straight contradiction works. The fact that human wisdom is a suitable model for God does not *logically* prevent the lack of wisdom (the holy fool) from being a suitable model. Thus 'God is wise' is logically compatible with 'God is not wise'.

(C) Nor does entailment fare better. Consider the following apparently unexceptionable argument.

1. A perfectly loving being will forgive the sins of the truly repentant.
2. God is perfectly loving.
3. Therefore God will forgive the sins of the truly repentant.

Surprisingly enough, on the position under consideration one does not fall into contradiction by affirming the premises and denying the conclusion. For even granting the literal truth of the first premise, it is certainly *logically* possible that both a perfectly loving human being and an unforgiving human being are useful models of God, in some respect(s) or other. Thus we must abandon all hope of inferring theological propositions from other propositions, theological or otherwise, or of rejecting some theological propositions because they contradict others; in short, any hope of logically systematizing theology in any way whatever.

. . . I take it that these consequences are radically unacceptable to the 'religious attitude' or, to speak less pretentiously, to the bulk of those in the mainstream of the Judeo-Christian tradition. A theology the propositions of which are logically compatible with anything else sayable of God, which can be true only in the same way virtually anything one might say of God is true, which have not determinate consequences either for theory or for practice, se eviscerated a theology is stripped of all its impact for human life.

Commentary on Alston

Alston's paper is divided into four sections. Section 1 introduces the idea of irreducible metaphors in talk about God. Section 2 explains the distinction between 'language' and 'speech', and sets out an account of metaphor.

1. Look at the examples of literal and metaphorical religious claims that Alston gives in section I and footnote 3. Give some examples of your own of metaphorical and literal religious claims. What is the difference between a metaphor and a simile?

Questions about the meanings of metaphors have become a major topic in philosophy of language over the last twenty years. To give some context to the following discussion of religious metaphor, and to see how it connects up with contemporary work on metaphor, we shall begin by briefly setting out two contrasting and standard theories of metaphor.

A simple and elegant theory of metaphor has been proposed by Donald Davidson. On Davidson's account, 'a metaphor doesn't say anything beyond its literal meaning (nor does its maker say anything, in using the metaphor, beyond the literal)' (2001: 246). Davidson rejects here two intuitively plausible theories of what metaphors mean. On the one hand, metaphorical claims are not distinguished by their having some metaphorical meaning that sets them apart from literal claims; for Davidson, what a metaphor says is exactly what it appears to say. Moreover, this is typically straightforwardly false: 'God is our father', 'God is my rock', etc., are literally false claims. According to Davidson, a metaphor means simply what it says: a false claim, and often glaringly so. However, Davidson is not proposing that metaphorical language is just a way of making false claims. Although in using a metaphor the speaker does not communicate a content or intention to us, we are presented with an image or a picture. For example, 'God is our father' presents an idea of God having the role of a father to us. This picture may prompt us to have further ideas – that God protects us, cares for us, etc. However, these further ideas are not what are communicated by the speaker's utterance. All that is communicated is the (false) claim that God is our father. The impact that a metaphor has on its audience is therefore a causal phenomenon: 'Joke or dream or metaphor can, like a picture or a bump on the head, make us appreciate some fact – but not by standing for, or expressing, the fact' (Davidson 1979: 262).

The second standard theory draws on work by H. P. Grice on 'conversational implicature'. Consider that metaphorical claims are marked out by their saying something that is (usually) plainly false – 'All the world's a stage', 'Tony is a bulldozer', etc. This fact about metaphorical claims can be taken to indicate that the speaker is not following conventional linguistic practice (where one typically does not make assertions that are patently false), and so intends something other than what is said. John Searle (1979: 85) argues

> In order to understand the metaphorical utterance, the hearer requires something more than his knowledge of the language. . . . He must have some other principles, or some other factual information, or some combination of principles and factual information that enables him to figure out that when the speaker says, 'S is P', he means 'S is R'.

Searle's theory of metaphor is modelled on Grice's account of irony. Someone who says 'That was charming', having just been insulted, is saying something the literal meaning of which is not intended. Anyone taking the claim non-ironically would miss out on what was meant. Attuned to the conventions of irony, we shall recognise that the sentence should not be taken at face value: the speaker is communicating just the opposite, that the experience was unpleasant. In a similar way, once we are in command of the principles governing metaphorical sentences, we can interpret 'Juliet is the sun' as communicating something other than what is literally said: Juliet has a range of properties, one example of which might be 'essential to my life'.

One point on which these theories differ is that, whereas Davidson thinks that the meaning of a metaphor is just what it literally says, Searle thinks that metaphors have secondary metaphorical meanings that can be extracted from contextual information and the speaker's intentions. A second important matter on which the theories differ is that, while Davidson takes the meaning of a metaphor to be determined by what it says, Searle takes a metaphor's meaning to be fixed (at least in part) by what the metaphor suggests or implies. The distinction between what an utterance says and what it implies is a traditional way of drawing the distinction between semantics and pragmatics. So Davidson's account of metaphor can be seen as a semantic theory, while Searle's is a pragmatic theory. (Note that a number of objections have been raised against each of these theories. For further reading on this topic, see the bibliography.)

2. Carefully read through section II and summarise in your own words Alston's position on metaphor. Explain what he means by 'exemplar'. Would you describe it as a semantic or a pragmatic account of metaphor?

3. We can distinguish between *theories* of metaphor that give us an account of what metaphors mean and how we understand them from *classifications* of metaphor which tell us how to identify metaphors and distinguish them from literal claims. Does Alston give us a theory or a classification of metaphor?

Alston gives us a succinct statement of the theory that he is attacking at [a]→. Let's call this the *irreducibility thesis* or *IT*. To refute IT, Alston aims to show that the content of a metaphor can, at least in part, be expressed literally. However, he begins by noting at [b]→ and [c]→ two respects in which the meaning of a metaphor might not be possible to capture in literal terms. First, only the propositional content of a metaphor could be conveyed in a literal utterance: we should not expect that the way in which the metaphor presents a model of the subject could be captured literally. Second, a metaphor involves a comparison between exemplar and subject that may be 'open-ended', and these 'inexplicit suggestions' cannot be captured literally.

Notwithstanding these two exceptions, Alston argues that the propositional content of a metaphor can be at least partially expressed in literal terms. He identifies at d↦ two sorts of literal truth-claim in the content of any metaphor. First, there is an unspecific part, that the exemplar is (literally) similar to the subject in a way that makes it a useful model for the subject. Alston calls this *M-similarity*. That a metaphor involves positing an M-similarity follows straightforwardly from Alston's account of metaphor given in section II. The posited M-similarity between the subject and the exemplar in a metaphor guarantees that it can be given a partial literal paraphrase. Second, there is the *specific* content. Suppose the speaker asserts 'God is my rock', intending to attribute to God some property P (this being the specific content). In so far as the speaker can form some concept of P, it should be possible to express it in language and use it as a predicate term. Consequently, it should be possible to express for any metaphor about God a corresponding literal sentence of the form 'God is P', where P can be substituted with the specific point of resemblance that the speaker intends. Alston is not suggesting, of course, that the speaker should be in a position to state this literal claim, but only that it is in principle expressible.

Since Alston's argument applies to all metaphors, it appears to follow – as Alston points out at e↦ – that it must also apply to religious metaphors and that therefore it is possible to express at least part of a metaphor's content literally and IT fails.

4. Supporters of IT argue that we cannot say anything literally true about God. But IT is itself a claim about God that is presumably intended by its supporters to be literally true. Does it follow that IT is self-defeating? How serious a problem is this for IT?

5. Alston notes at f↦ that the supporter of the irreducibility thesis could just concede that metaphorical talk of God involves literal predication but *only* of the unspecific sort. Summarise in your own words Alston's objection to this modified position in a↦, b↦ and c↦.

6. Alston claims that his objections to the modified version of IT in a↦ to c↦ show that the theory is religiously unacceptable. Is he right? Is the theory also philosophically unacceptable?

In one respect Alston is too generous to the irreducibility thesis. Although he argues that the content of metaphors is *in part* literally expressible, he seems prepared to concede that the content of metaphors is not wholly expressible in literal terms. Call the thesis that the content of a metaphor can in principle be wholly captured literally the *reducibility theory* or *RT*. Why does Alston concede RT? As we have seen, he argues at [c]↦ that metaphors are 'open-ended' in that they have any number of inexplicit implications, and these cannot be exhaustively captured literally. But the fact that a metaphor might suggest or imply further ideas is not really relevant to whether its content is literally expressible. However, Alston goes on to claim that there may be cases where the open-endedness 'affects the propositional content of a metaphorical statement'. What Alston seems to have in mind here is that the content of a metaphor could be inherently suggestive and difficult to pin down or specify its truth-conditions. This seems to be his main reason for conceding that metaphors may only be partially expressible literally. But, even supposing that a metaphor has open-ended content, why should not this be paraphrased literally? Literal statements, just as much as metaphorical ones, can be ambiguous, suggestive, elusive, insightful, baffling, etc. What is required for a literal expression of an open-ended metaphor, therefore, is a literal sentence or collection of sentences that are similarly suggestive. Alston's worry with RT seems to confuse a literal paraphrase of a metaphor with an attempt to make it fully explicit. Clearly, it may not always be possible literally to specify all of the inexplicit suggestions of a metaphor, since there may be an arbitrarily large number of them. But RT requires only that there are literal sentences that can convey a similar range of inexplicit suggestions. Alston gives no reason why this should not be possible.

Does Alston successfully refute IT? Here, too, we might wonder whether he has been too generous with the theory. Consider the two accounts of metaphor given at the beginning of this commentary. On the Davidsonian theory, IT looks unintelligible. If a metaphor is typically just a (patently) false literal sentence that is used to (causally) stimulate further ideas, then there is no metaphorical meaning to reduce or paraphrase in literal terms. The content of 'The Lord is my shepherd' will be (literally) <the Lord is my shepherd>, which (taken literally) is trivially false.

On the face of it, a similar problem is going to arise for Searle's theory. Here, too, it is the evident literal falsity of the metaphorical utterance that indicates that some secondary meaning – what it implies in this context, or what can be inferred about the speaker's intentions – should be looked for. So it appears that IT again fails from the outset, since metaphors have literally expressible content. However, perhaps the IT could be modified, while keeping to the spirit of the position, in the following way.

IT*: Statements about God have a primary meaning (a literal content) that is literally expressible, but a secondary meaning that is irreducible and cannot be literally paraphrased.

Unfortunately, IT* runs into a serious difficulty. Take the statement 'God is our father'. On Searle's theory, the evident falsity of the literal content of this claim leads us to look for a secondary component of the meaning (such as what the speaker intends), for example, that God cares for us, guides us, nurtures us, etc. But IT* requires that these latter claims are themselves non-literal. But suppose they are all metaphorical (which they don't appear to be). Then Searle's account requires that they must have false literal content that leads us to some secondary meaning or, in this case, to a tertiary meaning. But now the same problem will arise for the tertiary sentences. Are they literally expressible, in which case IT* fails, or are they metaphorical, in which case we shall have the same problem with quaternary claims? So it seems that a more pressing problem for the supporters of IT than the one that Alston presents is whether there is a version of the theory that makes sense on any standard.

7. Despite the problems with IT, the intuition that motivates the theory – that God's transcendence should present *some* kind of difficulty with saying anything literally true about him – does not seem entirely unreasonable. Is there a better way of developing this intuition into a theory about what we can literally say about God that avoids the pitfalls of IT? Is it coherent to argue, for example, that we can only make true *negative* claims about God – i.e. that for any property *x* we can truly say 'God is not *x*', but not 'God is *x*'?

For more discussion of metaphor in religious language, see:

Soskice, J. M., *Metaphor and Religious Language*, Oxford: Clarendon Press, 1985.

For other works on metaphor in philosophy of language, see:

Guttenplan, S., *Objects of Metaphor*, Oxford: Clarendon Press, 2005.
Davidson, D., 'What Metaphors Mean', in *Inquiries into Truth and Interpretation*, Oxford: Oxford University Press, 2001.
Searle, J., *Expression and Meaning: Studies in the Theory of Speech Acts*, Cambridge: Cambridge University Press, 1979.

2

Arguments about the Existence of God

Introduction

In this section, we consider some of the best-known arguments for the existence of God from the works of Anselm, Aquinas, Pascal and Paley; some of Hume's criticisms of the kind of argument that is defended by Paley; a relatively new argument against the existence of God by Everitt; and a member of the family of best-known arguments against the existence of God – the arguments from evil – by Rowe and Mackie. Before we turn to the texts, there are a few preliminary matters to address.

Because there are different views about the nature of God, the conclusions of arguments for the existence of God can be different. Some arguments try to establish the existence of the God of the Bible; some arguments try to establish the existence of a personal creator of the universe; some arguments try to establish the existence of a personal designer of the universe; some arguments try to establish the existence of a perfect being; and so on. If God exists, it may well be the case that these arguments are all arguments for the existence of God; but, if God does not exist, it is not at all obvious that these arguments are all arguments for the existence of the same being. (Suppose, for example, that the universe was made by a powerful, clever, but evil person. That being would be a personal designer of the universe, and it would be a personal creator of the universe; but it would not be the God of the Bible, and it would not be a perfect being.)

There are many different kinds of arguments for the existence of God. Famously, in his *Critique of Pure Reason*, Immanuel Kant divided theoretical arguments for the existence of God into three kinds: ontological, cosmological and teleological. We shall here examine what are perhaps the best-known examples of arguments of these three kinds: the ontological argument from Anselm's *Proslogion*, the second cosmological argument from Aquinas' Five Ways (in his *Summa theologica*), and the teleological argument from Paley's *Natural Theology*. We shall also consider a rather different practical argument for the existence of God, from Pascal's *Pensées*.

There have been many different kinds of critical discussions of arguments for the existence of God. Every argument that has been put forward for the existence of God has been subjected to careful scrutiny, and every argument has had many objections lodged against it. Here we shall examine part of the well-known critical discussion of teleological arguments in Hume's *Dialogues Concerning Natural Religion*.

There are also many different kinds of arguments against the existence of God. The best-known arguments of this kind are either members of the family of arguments from evil, or else arguments for the conclusion that there is some kind of incoherence in the very idea of God. Here, we shall examine Mackie's well-known formulation of a logical argument from evil, and Rowe's equally well-known formulation of an evidential argument from evil. We shall also look at a rather different argument against the existence of God in Everitt's recent book *The Non-existence of God*.

Any discussion of arguments for and against the existence of God should pay some attention to foundational questions about reason, reasoning and argumentation. In order to determine whether an argument is a good argument, we need to have a clear idea of what it is that makes for a good argument. In order to have a satisfactory conception of what makes for a good argument, we need to be clear about what it is that arguments are properly supposed to achieve.

Suppose that we *identify* arguments as collections of premises and conclusions. It is a consequence of this identification that, if we have an argument with premises $P_1, \ldots, P_n$ and conclusion Q, and we replace one of these premises with a claim R that is distinct from all of the premises $P_1, \ldots, P_n$, then we now have a different argument that may very well possess very different argumentative virtues. On this way of thinking about arguments, there are countless different arguments with the conclusion that God exists, and countless different arguments with the conclusion that God does not exist. Moreover, on this way of thinking about arguments, there are *many different* ontological arguments, cosmological arguments, teleological arguments, arguments from evil, and so forth.

In assessing the argumentative virtues of an argument $P_1, \ldots, P_n$ therefore Q, there are two main questions that we need to consider. The first question is whether the conclusion Q is *supported by* the premises $P_1, \ldots, P_n$. The second question is whether the premises of the argument are *acceptable*. If the conclusion of an argument is supported by the premises, and the premises of the argument are acceptable, then we have a good argument.

There are various ways in which the premises of an argument might support the conclusion of the argument. It could be, for example, that the conclusion of the argument is logically entailed by the premises. Or it could be that the conclusion of the argument is highly probable or, at any rate, more probable than not, given the premises. Amongst the arguments that we shall examine, the arguments of Aquinas and Anselm clearly purport to be cases in which the conclusion of the argument is logically entailed by the premises (though, in each case, we shall ask whether it is really the case that the conclusions of these arguments are entailed by their premises).

Perhaps the hardest question to address in thinking about the virtues of arguments is raised by the suggestion that the premises of a good argument are acceptable. *Acceptable to whom?* In order to address this question, we need to think about the purpose that arguments are supposed to serve. If we suppose that the purpose of arguments is to bring about changes in belief – i.e. to bring people who did not already accept a particular conclusion to accept that conclusion – then a plausible answer to the question is: *acceptable to those who do not already accept the conclusion of the argument*. By this standard, a good argument for the existence of God will only have premises that are acceptable to those who do not already believe that God exists; and a good argument against the existence of God will only have premises that are acceptable to those who do not already believe that God does not exist.

When we examine disputes about arguments for and against the existence of God, we find that, in practice, people do assume something like the standard mentioned in the previous paragraph. When theists look at arguments against the existence of God, they are satisfied if they can show that there is at least one premise in the argument that theists – typical theists, theists like themselves, thoughtful and well-informed and reflective theists, perhaps the majority of theists – have good reason not to accept. And, when atheists look at arguments for the existence of God, they are satisfied if they can show that there is at least one premise in the argument that atheists – typical atheists, atheists like themselves, thoughtful and well-informed and reflective atheists, perhaps the majority of atheists – have good reason not to accept. (Of course, in many cases, there are *other* kinds of objections that theists can make against arguments against the existence of God, and *other* kinds of objections that atheists can make against arguments for the existence of God: the point being made here is simply that application of the proposed standard of acceptance is taken on all sides to underwrite reasonable judgements about the failure of arguments.)

It would not perhaps be surprising to be told that, given the proposed standard of acceptance, there are no uncontroversially successful widely known arguments for the conclusion that God does not exist or for the conclusion that God exists. Since thoughtful and well-informed and reflective people disagree about whether or not God exists, it would be very surprising if there were a widely known argument for the conclusion that God exists, or for the conclusion that God does not exist, that meets the suggested standards for support and acceptability. True enough, there may be widely known arguments that count as good arguments given a very weak understanding of the notion of support – perhaps, for example, there are arguments the conclusions of which are more probable given the premises of the argument than they are given standard background assumptions that are independent of those premises – but it is hard to believe that those arguments could have a serious role in bringing about revisions in belief.

Given that it would also not be surprising to be told that, given the proposed standard of acceptance, there are very few uncontroversially successful widely known arguments *on any topics* about the conclusions of which thoughtful and well-informed and reflective people disagree, one might be inclined to think that there must be a problem with the proposed standard for acceptance. However, at the very least, it is hard to point to some other purpose that arguments might be supposed to have that better fits the actual practices that philosophers adopt when confronted with arguments with the conclusions of which they disagree.

Even if we do think that the proposed standard of acceptance is correct, we are still left with a range of questions about the connection between good argument and reason. If it is very hard to come up with good arguments in a particular domain, does it follow that we should suspend judgement about the claims in that domain? If it is true that there are no well-known arguments for the existence of God that are successful, and there are no well-known arguments against the existence of God that are successful, do we have here the makings of an argument for the conclusion that we should all suspend judgement on the question whether God exists? (Of course, the questions lead us on to some of the issues that will be taken up in our subsequent discussion of reason, argument and religious belief.)

From this very brief introductory sketch, it should be clear that we are not proposing to give a systematic treatment of arguments about the existence of God. Rather, we shall be introducing ourselves to a small part of what is a very much larger discussion. If you are interested in pursuing a wider survey of arguments about the existence of God – and a wider discussion of the issues that are raised in the course of scrutiny of arguments about the existence of God – you might be interested in having a look at some of the following books:

Everitt, N., *The Non-existence of God*, London: Routledge, 2004.

Gale, R., *On the Nature and Existence of God*, Cambridge: Cambridge University Press, 1991.

Mackie, J., *The Miracle of Theism*, Oxford: Clarendon Press, 1982.

Oppy, G., *Arguing about Gods*, Cambridge: Cambridge University Press, 2006.

Sobel, H., *Logic and Theism*, Cambridge: Cambridge University Press, 2004.

Swinburne, R., *The Existence of God*, Oxford: Clarendon Press, 1979.

Introduction to Anselm

Anselm of Canterbury (1033–1109) was Archbishop of Canterbury from 1093 until his death. Between 1060 and 1093, he lived in the Benedictine abbey at Bec in Normandy, where he was successively novice, prior and abbot. Just before his election as abbot, Anselm produced two works – the *Monologion* and the *Proslogion* – in which he sought to provide proofs of the existence and nature of God. In the *Proslogion* – from which our reading is taken – Anselm aimed to give a single simple argument that would establish the existence and nature of God to the satisfaction of any rational and moderately intelligent person.

The argument of chapter II of the *Proslogion* is short, but it is surely not simple. We shall endeavour to analyse the argument of this chapter, using the same method that we employ in our discussion of Aquinas' Second Way.

Anselm, *Proslogion*, ch. II

Truly there is a God, although the fool has said in his heart, There is no God.

a → AND so, Lord, do you, who do give understanding to faith, give me, so far as you knowest it to be profitable, to understand that you are as we

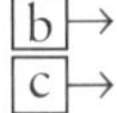 believe; and that you are that which we believe. And indeed, we believe that you are a being than which nothing greater can be conceived. Or is there no such nature, since the fool has said in his heart, there is no God? 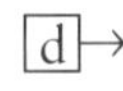 (Psalms xiv. 1). But, at any rate, this very fool, when he hears of this being of which I speak – a being than which nothing greater can be conceived – understands what be hears, and what he understands is in his understanding; although he does not understand it to exist.

For, it is one thing for an object to be in the understanding, and another to understand that the object exists. When a painter first conceives of what he will afterwards perform, he has it in his understanding, but be does not yet understand it to be, because he has not yet performed it. But after he has made the painting, he both has it in his understanding, and he understands that it exists, because he has made it.

Hence, even the fool is convinced that something exists in the understanding, at least, than which nothing greater can be conceived. For, when he hears of this, he understands it. And whatever is understood, exists in the understanding. e↦ And assuredly that, than which nothing greater can be conceived, cannot exist in the understanding alone. For, suppose it exists in the understanding alone: then it can be conceived to exist in reality; which is greater.

Therefore, if that, than which nothing greater can be conceived, exists in the understanding alone, the very being, than which nothing greater can be conceived, is one, than which a greater can be conceived. But obviously this is impossible. Hence, there is no doubt that there exists a being, than which nothing greater can be conceived, and it exists both in the understanding and in reality.

Commentary on Anselm

The text divides naturally into three main parts. At b↦ we get a statement of the conclusion of the overall argument of the chapter: there is a being than which nothing greater can be conceived. At d↦ we get an argument for the conclusion that a being than which nothing greater can be conceived exists in the understanding. And at e↦ we get an argument for the conclusion that a being than which nothing greater can be conceived cannot exist only in the understanding, and hence must also exist in reality – i.e. we get an argument for the conclusion that there is (both in the understanding and in reality) a being than which no greater can be conceived.

There are, of course, other things that happen in the various parts of this chapter. At a↦, by addressing his initial remarks to God, Anselm makes it clear that he is in no doubt that God exists. However, there are other people – such as the Fool of Psalms 14: 1 introduced at c↦ – who deny that God exists. The purpose of the rest of the chapter is to show that people such as the Biblical Fool are wrong.

Also, in the first part, Anselm forges a presumptive identification between God and a being than which nothing greater can be conceived: he says that '*we believe* that you are a being than which nothing greater can be conceived'. Depending upon what else Anselm believes about God, it is not obvious that this presumptive identification should be conceded. If, for example, Anselm supposes that *everything* that the Old Testament says about God is true, then, at the very least, it is not *obvious* that God is a being than which nothing greater can be conceived. However, we can set these kinds of worries aside, since the rest of the discussion is couched entirely in terms of the existence of a being than which no greater can be conceived. If Anselm succeeds in showing that there is a being than which no greater can be conceived – and if (as he argues in subsequent chapters of the *Proslogion*) it is plausible to suppose that this being is omnipotent, omniscient, perfectly good, and the like – then his argument is of great philosophical significance whether or not we can identify this being with the God of the *Bible*.

1. Explain what Anselm is praying for at [a]↦. What role, if any, does [a]↦ play in the following argument?

At [d]↦, Anselm gives an argument which is intended to establish that there is a well-founded distinction between having an object in your understanding, and understanding that that object exists (in reality). Although it is not entirely clear what role this sub-argument plays in the larger argument for the conclusion that a being than which nothing greater can be conceived exists both in the understanding and in reality, it is plausible to take Anselm to be establishing that, in general, we can make sense of the thought that a person has an idea of something ('has that thing in her understanding') even though that person does not suppose that the thing in question exists ('does not understand that the thing exists'). So the Fool is not open to criticism *merely* on the grounds that there is something that exists in his understanding even though he does not understand that thing to exist in reality.

2. Does Anselm's example of the painter in [d]↦ successfully illustrate the thought that one can have an idea of something without that thing existing? Describe its strengths and weaknesses as an example. Can you think of a better example?

The main argument at [d]↦ has as its conclusion the claim that a being than which no greater can be conceived exists in the understanding of anyone who has heard and understood the expression 'being than which no greater can be conceived'. On Anselm's account, even the Fool understands this expression when he hears it; the implicit intended generalisation is that anyone with minimal intelligence and competence in the language does understand the expression 'being than which no greater can be conceived'. Making use of this implicit intended generalisation, the vocabulary at [d]↦ makes a transition from talk about what is in 'the understanding of the Fool' to talk about what is in 'the understanding'. Taking account of this transition, we can give a standard-form representation of the argument as follows:

1. When the expression 'being than which no greater can be conceived' is heard, it is understood. (Premise)

2. Whatever is understood exists in the understanding. (Premise)
3. (Hence) there is in the understanding a being than which no greater can be conceived. (From 1, 2)

In order for it to be plausible that 3 follows from 1 and 2, it is clear that 2 must be understood in something like the following way: whenever an expression 'F' is understood, an F – i.e. at least one F – exists in the understanding. Moreover, there must be restrictions on the range of expressions to which this principle is supposed to apply: speaking rather loosely, it is only if 'F' is an understood *naming* expression that an F exists in the understanding. (Anselm would not want to say that, because you understand the expression 'not', it follows that *not* exists in your understanding; this doesn't even make sense!) Also note that, while the general principle says that, whenever an expression 'F' is understood, *at least one* F exists in the understanding, there will be cases in which, when an expression 'F' is understood, *exactly one* F exists in the understanding. Moreover, it is plausible to suppose that Anselm understands the expression 'being than which no greater can be conceived' in this way: it is, he thinks, a consequence of the meaning of this expression that there is at most one being than which no greater can be conceived.

At [e]↦, Anselm gives an argument which is intended to establish that it is not the case that a being than which no greater can be conceived exists only in the understanding: if a being than which no greater can be conceived exists in the understanding, then a being than which no greater can be conceived also exists in reality. Anselm's argument here is in the form of a *reductio ad absurdum*: we suppose, for the sake of argument, that a being than which no greater can be conceived exists only in the understanding, and we show that this supposition has absurd consequences. Whence we conclude that the supposition is false: it is not true that a being than which no greater can be conceived exists only in the understanding.

3. Construct *reductio ad absurdum* arguments to show that the following statements are false:

a. An omnipotent God can create a stone too heavy for him to lift.
b. 5 is less than 6 and more than 7.
c. Only statements that are necessarily true or empirically verifiable are meaningful.

Anselm's presentation of the *reductio* argument is very compressed. Setting it out in standard form, it seems to run like this:

1. A being than which no greater can be conceived exists only in the understanding. (Hypothesis for *reductio*)
2. A being than which no greater can be conceived can be conceived to exist in reality. (Premise)
3. It is greater [for a being than which no greater can be conceived] to exist in reality than it is [for a being than which no greater can be conceived] to exist merely in the understanding. (Premise)

4. Hence, we can conceive of a being which is greater than a being than which no greater can be conceived. (From 1, 2, 3)
5. It is impossible to conceive of a being which is greater than a being than which no greater can be conceived. (Premise)
6. It is impossible for a being than which no greater can be conceived to exist only in the understanding (1, 4 , 5 *reductio*)

While it would have been useful to have Anselm spell out in more detail why it is that he supposes that 4 follows from 1, 2 and 3, we have no more to work with than the text bequeathed to us. However, taking the materials that we have developed to this point, we can now set out the overall structure of what is standardly taken to be the central argument of chapter II of the *Proslogion*:

1. A being than which no greater can be conceived exists in the understanding. (Premise)
2. A being than which no greater can be conceived can be conceived to exist in reality. (Premise)
3. It is greater [for a being than which no greater can be conceived] to exist in reality than it is [for a being than which no greater can be conceived] to exist merely in the understanding. (Premise)
4. It is impossible to conceive of a being which is greater than a being than which no greater can be conceived. (Premise)
5. (Hence) a being than which no greater can be conceived exists in reality. (From 1–4)

This way of presenting the argument does not make it clear how the conclusion is supposed to follow from the premises; but it does show the premises that Anselm supposes are sufficient to establish the desired conclusion.

Given that we have now established what it is that Anselm argues in chapter II of the *Proslogion*, our next task is to assess the argument that he gives. In assessing the argument, there are various different kinds of questions we could ask. First, we could investigate the background assumptions that Anselm makes in framing his argument: can we really make sense of talk about 'existence in the understanding' and, if so, can we develop a theory of understanding and existence in the understanding that will help in the assessment of Anselm's argument? Second, we could try to determine whether the conclusion of Anselm's argument really does follow from his premises. Third, we could ask whether the premises that are employed in his argument are true. And, fourth, we could ask whether the Fool – someone who is not antecedently convinced that there is a being than which none greater can be conceived – ought to be persuaded to change his mind when presented with Anselm's argument.

To see why we might worry about the way in which Anselm talks about understanding and existence in the understanding, consider the expression 'prime number than which no greater prime number can be conceived'. Clearly, there is a sense in which we understand this expression: a prime number than which no greater prime number can be conceived would be a prime number that is bigger than every other prime number. However, it has been known since the time of Euclid that there is a simple *proof* that it is not the case that there is a largest prime number. Put differently, the supposition that something answers to the expression 'prime number than which no greater prime number can be conceived' leads to straight-out contradiction: it is *impossible* for there to be a greatest prime number. If Anselm supposes that, none the less, a prime number than which no greater prime number can be conceived exists in the understanding, then it seems that he will be committed to the attribution of contradictory properties to that thing in the understanding. For, on the one hand, by Euclid's proof, since it is impossible for anything to have the property of being a prime number that is greater than any other prime number, then, in particular, this thing in the understanding cannot have this property; and, on the other hand, of its very nature, this thing in the understanding does have the property of being a prime number that is greater than any other prime number.

If Anselm were to bite the bullet, and allow that things in the understanding can have contradictory properties, then, at the very least, it is not clear that he would still have entitlement to argue by *reductio ad absurdum*. (If some contradictions are acceptable, then how do you discriminate between the contradictions that are acceptable and the contradictions that are not acceptable?) But if Anselm does not have entitlement to argue by *reductio ad absurdum*, then the main part of his argument at C→ does not go through. So it seems that Anselm has to modify his initial position: at best, it is only if there is no contradiction or impossibility bound up in an expression 'F' that we are entitled to claim that there is at least one F in the understanding. And, of course, this modification puts pressure on the first premise in Anselm's argument: perhaps it is acceptable after all for the Fool to deny that a being than which no greater can be conceived exists in the understanding, because there is some contradiction or impossibility bound up in the expression 'being than which no greater can be conceived'.

4. Give two examples of reasons that 'the Fool' might use to deny Anselm's contention that a being than which no greater can be conceived exists in the understanding.

If we are to talk about 'existence in the understanding' seriously, then we need to be clear about the kinds of properties that are possessed 'in the understanding'. It is clear that Anselm supposes that there can be objects that exist both in the understanding and in reality (e.g. real objects with which people have cognitive interplay), that there can be objects that exist only in the understanding (e.g. fictional objects and, perhaps, entirely past or entirely future objects), and that there can be objects that exist only in reality (e.g. real objects that no one has ever thought about). However, Anselm does not give us an account of the properties that are possessed by objects in the different domains. We may suppose that there is nothing special to say about the properties that are possessed by objects in so far as those objects exist in reality. But what properties are possessed in the understanding by objects that also exist in reality? And what properties are possessed in the understanding by objects that exist only in the understanding?

Suppose, for example, that there is a brown chair in the next room, but I mistakenly think that that chair is blue. Since I am thinking about *that* chair, presumably Anselm would have to grant that the chair exists in my understanding. But what colour is the chair in my understanding? Is it only blue, or is it both brown and blue? Since the latter suggestion appears to lead into contradiction, or, at any rate, impossibility, it seems that we are required to suppose that the chair that exists in my understanding is blue (and not brown) even though it is the very same chair as the one that exists in reality, and which in reality is brown. Put differently, it seems that Anselm will be required to say that the chair has the property of being blue in my understanding, but that it also has the property of being brown in reality. Generalising, then, for objects that exist both in the understanding and in reality, Anselm will need to be very careful in distinguishing between the properties that these objects have in the understanding, and the properties that these objects have in reality. For, in general, on the scheme that we are here attributing to Anselm, objects have two different kinds of properties: properties in the understanding (of one, or many, or all people), and properties in reality.

Suppose that I have no views about the colour of the chair in the next room, even though I am thinking about it. In that case, what colour is the chair in my understanding? It seems that the correct answer is that there is no particular colour that the chair has in my understanding. While we can suppose that the chair is coloured in my understanding – since, of course, I do believe that the chair has some colour or other – it seems that we should also hold that there is no particular colour that the chair has in my understanding. Generalising from this example and the example discussed in the previous paragraph, it seems that Anselm should be committed to *something like* the following claim: I am thinking consistently about x and thinking that x has the property F if and only if x possesses the property F in my understanding.

While there is much more to be said in developing a theory of existence in the understanding, we already have enough to raise further difficulties for Anselm. Consider, again, the Fool, who, we may suppose, is thinking that a being than which no greater can be conceived does not exist in reality. If it is true that a being than which no greater can be conceived exists in the understanding of the Fool, then it seems that it must also be true that, in the understanding of the Fool, this being possesses the property of not existing in reality. But, if that's right, then it is not true that, as things stand, the Fool can consistently conceive or suppose that *this* being possesses the property of existing in reality: if a being than which no greater can be conceived exists in the understanding of the Fool, then, as things stand in the understanding of the Fool, *that* being cannot be consistently conceived to have the property of existing in reality.

5. Suppose that Anselm responded to the above argument by arguing that the Fool is required to change the way he thinks about this being than which no greater can be conceived: the Fool should think of this being as existing in reality. Is this a satisfactory response?

Perhaps Anselm can say that we went wrong in failing to distinguish between the properties that a thing has in the understanding and the properties that we attribute to that thing in the understanding. Returning to the example of the chair: perhaps Anselm can say that, even though we attribute colour properties to the chair in the understanding, still the chair does not have any colour properties in the understanding. More generally, we might suppose that Anselm rejects the claim that *x* possesses the property F in my understanding if and only if I'm thinking consistently about *x* and thinking that *x* has the property F. However, if Anselm does go that way, then, as things stand, it seems that we are completely at a loss about how to determine what are the properties that are possessed by objects in the understanding (and hence we are completely at a loss about how to understand the claim that there are things that exist in the understanding). Consequently, until we have a decent account of existence in the understanding, it seems that it must be reasonable to refrain from accepting the first premise in Anselm's argument: we do not really understand what we are being asked to accept when we are asked to accept that a being than which no greater can be conceived exists in the understanding.

6. Suppose that, rather than talking of F existing in the understanding, Anselm instead talked of F being the object of understanding, or of understanding F. Reconstruct Anselm's argument accordingly. Does it help or hinder the argument?

Suppose – contrary to the preceding argument – that we do think that we understand talk about 'existence in the understanding' in a way that suffices to make it reasonable for us to hold that the first premise in Anselm's argument is true. Are we then obliged to think that Anselm's argument is persuasive? There is a well-known line of argument – first devised by the monk Gaunilo, one of Anselm's contemporaries – which many have supposed furnishes grounds for a negative answer to this question. The argument that we are about to give is not quite the argument that Gaunilo originally gave, but it is in a very similar spirit.

Consider the expression 'island than which no greater island can be conceived'. It seems that we can rerun Anselm's argument, using this expression in place of the expression 'being than which no greater [being] can be conceived'. If we do this, we get the following argument:

1. An island than which no greater island can be conceived exists in the understanding. (Premise)
2. An island than which no greater island can be conceived can be conceived to exist in reality. (Premise)
3. It is greater [for an island than which no greater island can be conceived] to exist in reality than it is [for an island than which no greater island can be conceived] to exist merely in the understanding. (Premise)

4. It is impossible to conceive of an island which is greater than an island than which no greater island can be conceived. (Premise)
5. (Hence) an island than which no greater island can be conceived exists in reality. (From 1–4)

We can now imagine the Fool objecting to Anselm in the following way: When I look at the premises in this argument, it seems to me that each is no less plausible than the corresponding premise in your argument for the existence in reality of a being than which no greater can be conceived. Moreover, the logical form of the argument is exactly the same: that is, one of these arguments is logically valid just in case the other argument is, too. So I have no less reason to accept the existence in reality of an island than which no greater island can be conceived on the basis of this argument than I have reason to accept the existence of a being than which none greater can be conceived on the basis of your argument. But it would be absurd to think that there is, in reality, an island than which no greater island can be conceived. (And, of course, there is nothing special about islands: we could run similar arguments about any other kind of thing that admits of grades of excellence.) So we should agree that the argument for the existence of a being than which no greater can be conceived is unsuccessful: it plainly does not supply *me* with a good reason for thinking that there is such a being.

Since the logic of the two arguments is plainly identical, the only question about Gaunilo's argument is whether it is really true that it is reasonable for the Fool to suppose that the premises in this island-argument are no less plausible than the premises in Anselm's argument. Unless we are all required to think that the set of claims

1. An F than which no greater F can be conceived exists in the understanding. (Premise)
2. An F than which no greater F can be conceived can be conceived to exist in reality. (Premise)
3. It is greater [for an F than which no greater F can be conceived] to exist in reality than it is [for an F than which no greater F can be conceived] to exist merely in the understanding. (Premise)
4. It is impossible to conceive of an F which is greater than an F than which no greater F can be conceived. (Premise)

is uniquely most plausible when 'F' is replaced with 'being' rather than with some other term (such as 'island') for which we have good reasons for thinking that there is no 'F than which no greater F can be conceived', Gaunilo has a winning response to Anselm's argument.

Even if it is agreed that Gaunilo's objection shows that there is something wrong with Anselm's argument, it is clear that Gaunilo's objection does not pinpoint where, exactly, the argument goes wrong. Moreover, even supposing that we think that we understand talk about 'existence in the understanding' well enough to allow us to make an assessment of the argument, there are a number of possibilities that remain to be examined.

7. It is sometimes pointed out that it is *impossible* to conceive of a greatest island because it is always possible to conceive of a greater one: an island with nicer weather, more palm trees, tastier fruit, etc. In contrast, divine properties have an intrinsic maximum: no being can be more powerful than an omnipotent being, more good than a wholly benevolent being, etc. So claims (1) and (2) above, according to this argument, are true where 'F' is replaced with 'being', but incoherent where 'F' is replaced with 'island'. Evaluate this argument.

One key question to ask concerns the validity of the argument, i.e. the question whether the conclusion of the argument really follows from the premises. We have seen that, in developing the core *reductio*, Anselm argues in the following way:

1. A being than which no greater can be conceived exists only in the understanding. (Hypothesis for *reductio*)
2. A being than which no greater can be conceived can be conceived to exist in reality. (Premise)
3. It is greater [for a being than which no greater can be conceived] to exist in reality than it is [for a being than which no greater can be conceived] to exist merely in the understanding. (Premise)
4. Hence we can conceive of a being which is greater than a being than which no greater can be conceived. (From 1, 2, 3)

But, as we noted earlier, it is not clear that 4 follows from 1, 2 and 3. Indeed, we can press this issue in the following way. Suppose that it is true that G exists only in the understanding, and that G can be conceived to exist in reality, and that it is greater for G to exist in reality than it is for G to exist only in the understanding. How does it follow from this that we can conceive of a being that is greater than G? Is not the most that we can conclude from these assumptions merely that we can conceive of G being greater than it in fact is? From 2, we can conceive of G's existing in reality; and, from 3, we can draw the conclusion that, in conceiving of G's existing in reality, we are conceiving of G's being greater than G is if G only exists in the understanding. But this all appears to be consistent with its being true both that G exists only in the understanding and that it is impossible to conceive of a being that is greater than G. Of course, if G exists only in the understanding, then, when G is conceived to exist in reality, this is an incorrect or false conception of G. But surely that is fine: an incorrect or false conception of G need not also be a correct or true conception of something other than G. (At the very least, we see here that, without a developed theory of existence in the understanding and its relation to what can be conceived, we are very hard put to determine whether Anselm's argument is so much as valid.)

8. Carefully read through the above argument and restate in your own words.

Another key question concerns the third premise in Anselm's overall argument, viz. the claim that it is greater [for a being than which no greater can be conceived] to exist in reality than it is [for a being than which no greater can be conceived] to exist merely in the understanding. It is not easy to determine whether there is good reason to accept this claim. Famously, Kant argues that we should not suppose that existence is a predicate; from which it would seem to follow, pretty directly, that existence is not a great-making property. Even if we suppose that Kant is wrong in claiming that existence is not a predicate, it is not clear that we should accept that existence is a great-making property. Consider, for example, the comparison between me as I actually am and a merely possible being – let's call him 'George' – who is just like me in all respects other than being smarter than me. It seems to me that we are happy to say that, in virtue of his superior intelligence, George is greater than I am. Moreover, it seems to me that, no matter how small we make the increment in intelligence, we are still prepared to judge that George is greater than I am. But, if that is right, then it seems that we must think that actual existence – 'existing in reality' – makes no difference at all to greatness: if we thought that it did make a difference, then, at some point, we would judge that, despite George's [perhaps very small] superiority in intelligence, I am greater than George because I actually exist and he does not.

9. Kant's point is sometimes expressed as follows: when I say, for example, that a cake is square, covered in chocolate and has nuts in it, 'square', 'covered in chocolate' and 'has nuts' are predicate expressions that attribute properties to the cake. But, if I add that the cake *exists*, 'exists' does not pick out an additional property of the cake, but rather tells us that there is a cake that has those *other* properties of being square, etc. Suppose this is correct. (i) Specify at what point Anselm's argument would fail. (ii) What would a statement like 'The cake exists' mean?

Perhaps it might be objected that Anselm only needs to assume that existence is a great-making property for a being than which none greater can be conceived. While this objection seems wrong on other grounds – why should we think that existence is a great-making property for a being than which none greater can be conceived if we don't think that existence is a great-making property in all cases? – it also is not clear that it really meets the difficulty. Suppose, for the sake of argument, that there is an actually existing being – call it 'B' – that is very nearly, but not quite, a being than which no greater can be conceived, and compare B with another being – call it 'R' – which is merely possible, but which otherwise has all the attributes of a being than which no greater can be conceived. Given that R is greater than B in some respects – having to do, let us suppose, with power and intelligence – and on the same standing with B in all other respects (save, of course, for those pertaining to existence), it seems to me that we have no difficulty in judging that R is greater than B, even though, by hypothesis, B actually exists whereas R does not. Moreover, as before, the judgement persists even as we make the differences in power and intelligence smaller and smaller. But when we reduce the differences in power and intelligence to zero it seems to us that we simply judge that B and R are identical in respect of greatness; and this gives us the same conclusion that we reached in the previous case.

9. The ontological argument aims to give an *a priori* proof for the existence of God. Do you think that there could be a successful *a priori* argument for the existence of God? Give reasons for your answer.

While we have by no means exhausted the possible discussion of Anselm's *Proslogion II* argument, we have done enough to show that this argument is subject to some serious difficulties. However, of course, even if Anselm's *Proslogion II* argument fails, it does not follow that there is no similar argument that succeeds. Since Anselm produced his argument, there have been many philosophers who have defended other kinds of ontological arguments. However, the discussion of those other ontological arguments – in the work of, for example, Descartes, Hartshorne, Plantinga and Gödel – will need to wait for another occasion. If you are interested in learning more about ontological arguments, you might like to look at:

Barnes, J., *The Ontological Argument*, London: Macmillan, 1972.

Oppy, G., *Ontological Arguments and Belief in God*, Cambridge: Cambridge University Press, 1995.

Plantinga, A., *The Nature of Necessity*, Oxford: Oxford University Press, 1974.

Introduction to Aquinas

Thomas Aquinas (*c.*1225–74) is one of the greatest systematic theologians, perhaps best-known for his *Summa contra Gentiles* and his monumental *Summa theologica*. The latter work alone runs to about sixty volumes in one standard modern edition. Aquinas defended an 'Aristotelian' version of Christianity against both proponents of 'Neo-Platonic' versions of Christianity and the various kinds of opponents of Christianity. In the long term, Aquinas' efforts were so successful that his 'Aristotelian' version of Christianity became the cornerstone of the philosophical and theological teachings of the Roman Catholic Church. While Aquinas held that there are parts of the Christian faith that can only be known on the basis of divine – especially scriptural – revelation, and while he also held that there is much about God that we simply cannot know, Aquinas did set out, and endorse, a range of proofs of the existence of God. In particular, in the *Summa theologiae*, Aquinas says that there are 'five ways' in which one can prove that God exists.

Here we shall examine only the second of Aquinas' five 'proofs' of the existence of God. Aquinas' exposition of this argument is very brief and very clear. We begin with this argument in part because we do not need to battle very hard to work out how the argument is supposed to run. This is not to say that there is no dispute about exactly what Aquinas thought could be achieved by this argument. However, setting aside questions about what Aquinas thought could actually be established by the argument, we shall simply consider whether it is reasonable to suppose that the text does provide us with 'a proof of the existence of God'. In conducting our examination, we model the way in which philosophical assessment of the merits of an argument standardly proceeds.

Aquinas, *Summa theologica*, The Second Way

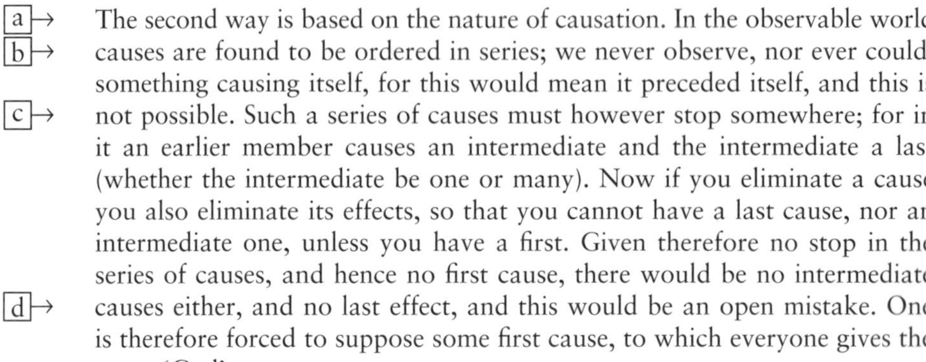

[a]→ The second way is based on the nature of causation. In the observable world [b]→ causes are found to be ordered in series; we never observe, nor ever could, something causing itself, for this would mean it preceded itself, and this is [c]→ not possible. Such a series of causes must however stop somewhere; for in it an earlier member causes an intermediate and the intermediate a last (whether the intermediate be one or many). Now if you eliminate a cause you also eliminate its effects, so that you cannot have a last cause, nor an intermediate one, unless you have a first. Given therefore no stop in the series of causes, and hence no first cause, there would be no intermediate [d]→ causes either, and no last effect, and this would be an open mistake. One is therefore forced to suppose some first cause, to which everyone gives the name 'God'.

Commentary on Aquinas

The text gives an orderly presentation of a single argument. At [a]→, Aquinas gives the first premise of the argument; [b]→ gives and justifies the second premise; [c]→ gives and justifies the third premise; and [d]→ gives the conclusion of the argument.

The first premise of the argument is that there are chains of causation. Aquinas provides no justification for this premise, presumably because he thinks that, in the context of the argument, this is so obvious that it does not require justification. It is worth noting that Aquinas does not tell us what kinds of things are the terms of causal relation: he does not say, for example, that there are chains of *events* in which a given event causes another event which in turn causes a further event, and so on. Moreover, since the conclusion of the argument is that there is a first cause which everyone calls 'God', there is at least *prima facie* reason to think that Aquinas must be supposing that the terms of the causal relation that he has in mind are *objects*: after all, it surely is not true that everyone supposes that 'God' is the proper name for an initial *event*. These considerations notwithstanding, we could take Aquinas to be supposing that events are the relata of causal relation if we are prepared to revise the wording of his conclusion. For we could say, instead, that the initial event that is the conclusion of the chain of reasoning is what everyone calls 'God's initial creative act' – and, while Aquinas himself would have been happy to *identify* God's initial creative act with God, taking this to be a consequence of his doctrine of divine simplicity, there are others who would want to reject this identification (as, indeed, there were at the time that Aquinas was writing).

It is also worth noting that, in the text of the Second Way, Aquinas does not tell us anything about the *kinds* of chains of causation to which his argument is supposed to apply. Many commentators have maintained that it is important to understand Aquinas to be talking, not about *temporal* causal chains – e.g. the cue strikes the cue ball, causing it to roll down the table and collide with the triangular arrangement of red balls, causing some of those red balls to move towards the cushions of the table, etc. – but rather about '*contemporaneous*' causal chains – e.g. the sun heats the earth, which causes the earth to nourish the apple tree, which causes the apple tree to produce apples, which causes hungry blackbirds to alight on the apple tree, etc. While the idea that there is 'contemporaneous' causation is controversial, we note (i) that it is important to this idea that the continuing existence of an effect requires the continuing existence of its contemporaneous cases; and (ii) that there is a close connection between the idea that there are contemporaneous causes and the idea that there are answers to what we might call contemporaneous Why-questions. (Why are there hungry blackbirds alighting on the tree? Because there are apples growing on the tree. Why are there apples growing on the tree? Because the earth is nourishing the tree. Why is the earth nourishing the tree? Because the sun is heating the earth. Etc.)

We shall conduct an initial investigation on the assumption – or, perhaps, pretence – that Aquinas means to be talking about temporal causal chains; and then we shall turn our attention to an assessment of the argument if it is taken instead to advert to 'contemporaneous' causal chains.

1. Give your own examples of: a contemporaneous causal chain of events, a contemporaneous chain of objects, a temporal chain of events, and a temporal chain of objects. Make sure that each chain has at least three components.

The second premise of the argument is that nothing causes itself (and, indeed, more strongly, that it is impossible for anything to cause itself). If we suppose that events are the relata of causal relation, then this premise becomes the claim that no event causes itself. Aquinas argues that it is impossible for anything to cause itself since it is impossible for anything to precede itself. Since it would be plainly question-begging to interpret the precedence invoked here as causal precedence, it seems that what Aquinas must have in mind is temporal precedence. Moreover, though he does not make this explicit in his argument, he must be supposing that it is necessarily the case that if x is causally prior to y, then x is temporally prior to y. Making use of this supposition, his argument is that, if x caused itself, i.e. if x were causally prior to itself, then x would be earlier than itself. But it is obviously impossible for anything to be earlier than itself. So it is impossible for anything to cause itself. More formally:

1. Necessarily, if something were to cause itself, then that thing would be earlier than itself. (Premise)

2. It is impossible for anything to be earlier than itself. (Premise)
3. Therefore it is impossible for something to cause itself. (From 1, 2)

It is not obvious that this is a compelling argument, since it is not obvious that 1 and 2 are true. In particular, if it is possible for time to be circular, then it seems that 2 is false: if time were circular, then each thing would be both earlier than itself and later than itself. Moreover, if it is possible for there to be simultaneous causation – i.e. cases in which the cause and the effect happen at the same time – then it is not obvious that we are required to admit that, if something were to cause itself, then it would be earlier than itself. It seems the merest truism, if a little odd, to say that a thing is at the same time as itself!

2. Imagine an iron ball is placed on a cushion: the ball presses down on the cushion and the cushion compresses. Is this an example of simultaneous causation? If it undermines (1), explain why; if not, why not?

Even if Aquinas' argument, for the conclusion that it is impossible for something to cause itself, is not compelling, that need not make difficulties for the argument of the Second Way. The claim that nothing causes itself does seem *prima facie* plausible; and, besides, there may well be some other way of defending the claim, if it is thought that further defence of the claim is required. On the other hand, the case that makes difficulty for the second premise in the above sub-argument – i.e. the case of circular time – would, it seems, make problems for the claim that nothing is the cause of itself if we were prepared to admit that the causal relation is transitive. To say that causation is transitive is to say that, whenever *a* causes *b* and *b* causes *c*, then *a* causes *c*. If causation is transitive, and time is circular, then it could be that there is a causal chain that commences from a particular thing and returns to that thing; whence, by transitivity, that thing causes itself. So, perhaps, we should conclude that there is a further premise implicit in Aquinas' argument: Aquinas should be taken to hold that it is not possible for time (and causation) to run in a circle.

3. Explain how the possibility of time travel could present a counter-example to Aquinas' argument at [b]→. Is it a persuasive counter-example?

The third premise of the argument at [c]→ is that there cannot be an infinite regress of causes: it cannot be that *a* is caused by *b*, which is in turn caused by *c*, which is in turn caused by *d*, . . . , and so on, without end (i.e. 'to infinity'). Aquinas gives an argument for the claim that it is impossible for there to be an infinite regress of causes, based essentially on the claim that 'if you eliminate a cause you also eliminate its effects, so that you cannot have a last cause, nor an intermediate one, unless you have a first'. Now, it seems reasonable to accept the observation that 'if you eliminate a cause you also eliminate its effects', at least in the context of Aquinas' argument. (You might think that there are possible cases in which, if a given cause were suppressed, the act of suppressing that cause would have brought about the effect by a different mechanism: e.g. a cricket ball causes a window to smash in circumstances in which, had I dived to catch the ball, I would have broken the window with my shoulder. This is called *overdetermination*: the effect has two or more independent causes any one of which is sufficient to bring it about. But, even if you accept that there are cases of this kind, you should also accept that the standard case in which *a* causes *b* is one in which, if *a* had not occurred, then *b* also would not have occurred.) However, it simply seems wrong to think that it *follows* from this observation that 'you cannot have a last cause, nor an intermediate one, unless you have a first'.

4. Write in your own words what you take to be Aquinas' argument at [c]→.

What we are supposing for the sake of Aquinas' argument to be plainly true is that, for any given effect, you would not get that effect if you 'eliminated' *all* of the earlier causal chain. If, on the one hand, the earlier causal chain is *finite*, then we can conclude that, unless you had the first element in that chain, you would not have obtained the effect in question. On the other hand, if the earlier causal chain is *infinite*, then all you can say is that, for each initial segment of the chain, if you had not had that initial segment of the chain, you would not have obtained the effect in question. Perhaps surprisingly, in the infinite case, *every* initial segment of the chain is itself infinite: there is no finite initial segment of the chain. This is undeniably weird; and it might form the grounds for some other kind of objection to the thought that it is possible for there to be an infinite regress of causes. None the less, we should certainly still conclude that it is quite clear that the argument that Aquinas actually gives against the possibility of an infinite regress of causes is simply question-begging.

5. It is sometimes argued that there cannot be an infinite regress of causes stretching back in time, since to reach the present time an infinite period of time would have had to elapse. Is this a sound argument?

The conclusion that Aquinas draws from the premises in his argument is that there is a first cause, i.e. something which itself does not have a cause, but which does have causal consequences. Moreover, he adds that this first cause is that to which 'everyone gives the name "God"'. One way to think of this final comment is as the addition of a further premise to the argument: if there is a first cause, then that first cause is God.

Given the preceding discussion, we can set out the overarching argument of the Second Way in the following form:

1. There are causal chains. (Premise)
2. Nothing can cause itself. (Premise)
3. A regress of causes is impossible. (Premise)

4. A circle of causes is impossible. (Premise)
5. (Hence) there is a first cause. (From 1, 2, 3 and 4)
6. If there is a first cause, then that first cause is God. (Premise)
7. (Hence) God exists. (From 5, 6)

As it stands, this argument has a curious mix of modal and non-modal premises. (Modal premises are premises that talk about what is 'necessarily' – or 'possibly', or 'actually', or 'contingently' – the case, as against non-modal premises which simply talk about what is the case. In this formulation of the argument, premises 2, 3 and 4 are all modal, whereas premises 1 and 5 are not.) In order to reach the conclusion of the argument, it would be sufficient to have non-modal versions of 2, 3 and 4. Since it is generally easier to show that something *isn't* the case than that it *can't* be the case, a stronger version of the argument would be:

1. There are causal chains. (Premise)
2. Nothing causes itself. (Premise)
3. There is no regress of causes. (Premise)
4. There are no circles of causes. (Premise)
5. (Hence) there is a first cause. (From 1, 2, 3 and 4)
6. If there is a first cause, then that first cause is God. (Premise)
7. (Hence) God exists (From 5, 6)

If support for the weaker versions of 2, 3 and 4 is required, then it could be sought in the modal claims in the original formulation (if something cannot be the case, it follows that it is not the case) – and this is why the revised version of the argument is stronger. Such support could also be sought elsewhere. In the subsequent discussion, we shall focus on this stronger version of the argument, since this is the version of the argument that has most chance of success.

Our first item of business is to consider the validity of this argument. We begin by asking whether 5 follows from 1, 2, 3 and 4. To answer this question, we need to ask how 5 is meant to be understood. If 5 is the claim that there is at least one first cause, then it is just true that 5 does follow from 1, 2, 3 and 4. (We can argue this as follows. Suppose that *b* causes *a*. If *b* has no cause, then it is a first cause, and we're done. If *b* has a cause, then (by 2 and 4) it has to be something other than *a* and *b* – say, *c*. If *c* has no cause, then it is a first cause, and we're done. If *c* has a cause, then (by 2 and 4) it has to be something other than *a*, *b* and *c* – say, *d*. . . . By 3, this pattern of reasoning does not regress infinitely, since, if it did, we would have a regress of causes. Thus, at some point, we do reach a thing that has no cause. And that is what we sought to establish.)

Now, clearly, if 5 is interpreted to be the claim that there is at least one first cause, then the rest of the argument makes no sense: the claim that, if there is *at least one* first cause, then *that first* cause is God is not so much as grammatically respectable. So, it seems, we are forced to the view that, when Aquinas draws the conclusion that there is a first cause from his premises 1–4, the conclusion that he means to draw is that there is *exactly one* first cause (concerning which it at least does make sense to suppose that *it* is what everyone calls 'God'). But the difficulty that arises here for Aquinas is that it is obviously not the case that 5 follows from 1–4, on this way of understanding the conclusion 5. For all that we are given in premises 1–4, it could be that there are many 'first causes', i.e. many things which are themselves uncaused but which are causes of other things.

One way to remedy this defect in Aquinas' argument would be to include a further premise to bridge the gap to the conclusion. If Aquinas is prepared to add to his argument the premise that, if there is at least one first cause, then there is exactly one first cause, then at least he will be able to get to the intermediate conclusion that there is exactly one first cause. For now, let's assume that Aquinas does this, so that the explicit argument of the Second Way runs as follows:

1. There are causal chains. (Premise)
2. Nothing causes itself. (Premise)
3. There is no regress of causes. (Premise)
4. There are no circles of causes. (Premise)
5. If there is a first cause, then there is exactly one first cause. (Premise)
6. (Hence) there is a first cause. (From 1, 2, 3, 4 and 5)
7. If there is a first cause, then that first cause is God. (Premise)
8. (Hence) God exists. (From 6, 7)

Since the inference of 8 from 6 and 7 is obviously secure, we now have an argument that is in good logical order. The next item of business is to consider whether the premises are false or, at any rate, rationally disputable or rejectable.

There are philosophers who have denied that there is any such thing as causation. Thus, for example, in his *Tractatus Logico-Philosophicus*, Wittgenstein writes: 'There is no causal nexus to justify . . . an inference [from the existence of one situation to the existence of another, entirely different situation]. . . . Superstition is nothing but belief in the causal nexus' (props 5.136–8). However, if we are not prepared to adopt this kind of scepticism about causation, then it seems unproblematic that premise 1 is true: if there is causation, then there are chains of things that stand in relationships of cause and effect. Moreover, while sceptics about causation can escape Aquinas' conclusion simply because of their causal scepticism, it seems implausible to suppose that such scepticism could be motivated simply by a desire to avoid the conclusion of Aquinas' argument. Since most people – and, indeed, most philosophers – are not causal sceptics, we have good reason to turn our attention to the other premises in Aquinas' argument.

Premises 2 and 4 in Aquinas' argument seem to be in good shape. It is, we think, impossible to make sense of the idea that something is the immediate cause of itself, even if we allow that we can make sense of the idea that there are immediate causes. Assuming that there can be immediate causes, when one thing *a* is the immediate cause of another thing *b*, then – as David Hume maintained – *a* and *b* must be entirely distinct, non-overlapping things. Moreover, while we can perhaps make sense of the idea that something is a non-immediate cause of itself – because, for example, we can make sense of the idea that time is circular – we do not currently have good reason to think that there are actually cases in which something is a non-immediate cause of itself. That is, we do not currently have good reason to think that time actually is circular; we do not currently have good reason to suppose that there are actual cases of time travel into the past; and so forth. Thus, even if we can make sense of circular time, time travel into the past, and other scenarios which would admit of cases in which something is a non-immediate cause of itself, we do not have good reason to deny premises 2 and 4.

6. Evaluate the following argument (sometimes called the *bilking* argument) and explain its implications and relevance to premise 4: Imagine an event *b* that occurs earlier than an event *a*, and suppose that *b* is alleged to be the effect of *a*. Now, it seems possible that after *b* has occurred, and before *a* has occurred, we could intervene to prevent the occurrence of *a*. But if this is correct, then *a* cannot be the cause of *b*.

Premise 3 in Aquinas' argument is, perhaps, less secure than premises 2 and 4. If we suppose that we can make sense of an infinite regress of causes, then it is not entirely clear that we have good reason to deny that we have been preceded by an infinite regress of causes. It is well known that current cosmological evidence suggests that our visible universe has a finite history: our visible universe has expanded from an initial cosmological explosion – 'The Big Bang' – that took place about 13 billion years ago. However, current cosmological evidence is mute on the question of what happened at the time of, or before, that cosmological explosion. Moreover, amongst current cosmological theories, there are some which posit infinite regresses of causes (back beyond the cosmological explosion from which our visible universe arose), and there are others which do not posit any such kind of infinite regress of causes. Unless we can be very confident that an infinite regress of causes is impossible, it seems doubtful that we can rule out the claim that there actually has been an infinite regress of causes. While there is much more to say about philosophical arguments about the possibility of infinite regresses (and, in particular, infinite regresses of causes and times), we shall not be able to take up any of those arguments here.

Premise 5 in Aquinas' argument is controversial, although, to some extent, the degree to which it is controversial depends upon how we understand the notion of efficient – i.e. temporal – causation. (We recall that this premise says that, if there are any things that have no efficient cause, then there is exactly one such thing.) In the broadest terms, there are two different ways of thinking about efficient causation. On the one hand, we might think that efficient causes are *sufficient* for their effects: very roughly, on this kind of approach, we suppose that it is impossible for the effect to fail to occur if the cause occurs. On the other hand, we might think that efficient causes are *necessary* for their effects: very roughly, on this kind of approach, we suppose that it is impossible for the effect to occur if the cause fails to occur. If we adopt the former approach, then we suppose that causes supply answers to all contrastive questions of the form 'Why did E occur rather than the possible alternative E'?' However, if we adopt the latter approach, then we suppose that causes only supply answers to some contrastive questions of the form 'Why did E occur rather than the possible alternative E'?', and we make provision for objective chances and merely probabilistic causation.

On approaches that suppose that efficient causes are *sufficient* for their effects, there are two main reasons that philosophers have had for supposing that there might be many things that lack efficient causes. On the one hand, many of the standard interpretations of quantum mechanics – one of the best theories that physicists have devised for describing the workings of the universe – tell us that there are lots of cases of things that lack efficient causes. Consider, for example, the case of radioactive decay. Given standard interpretations of quantum mechanics, it is a purely statistical – objectively chancy – matter whether a given radioactive atom will decay in a given period of time; if a particular radioactive atom does decay in a given period of time, then there may well be no efficient cause that brings it about that the atom decays at the time that it does. But if it is true that there are lots of cases in which radioactive atoms decay, and yet there is no efficient cause of this decay, then Aquinas' premise 5 is simply false: there are many things that have no efficient cause. On the other hand, many philosophers – and, in particular, many theistic philosophers – have supposed that when a free agent makes a free decision the making of that free decision is something that does not have an efficient cause. But, if those philosophers are right, and there are lots of cases in which people make free decisions, and yet there is no efficient cause of the making of those decisions, then, again, Aquinas' premise 5 is just false: there are many things that have no efficient cause. While it is undeniably controversial to hold either that quantum events lack efficient causes or that the free choices of free agents lack efficient causes, it is, we think, even more controversial to hold that quantum events and the free choices of free agents do *always* have efficient causes.

On approaches that suppose that efficient causes are *necessary* for their effects, it is less clear that there is good reason to suppose that there might be many things that lack efficient causes. While we can model the idea that efficient causal chains trace back to independent initial causes which themselves have no causes – as, for example, in general relativistic models of the universe in which there is an uncaused initial surface on which there is a contingent distribution of data, and in which different causal chains trace back to different parts of that initial surface – there are intuitions about the causal unity of the universe that might be thought to tell against these kinds of models. However, at the very least, it seems that this is not a matter to be decided on *a priori* grounds: if, for example, our best physical theories tell us that our universe had an initial surface with a contingent distribution of data, then that would be *some* reason to reject the fifth premise of Aquinas' argument even on the supposition that efficient causes are merely necessary for their effects. (Of course, if this objection were good, it would also tell against the fifth premise of Aquinas' argument on the supposition that efficient causes are sufficient for their effects. However, as we noted above, there are more serious objections to the fifth premise of Aquinas' argument on the supposition that efficient causes are sufficient for their effects.)

7. State in your own words the difference between a necessary cause and a sufficient cause. Give an example of: (i) a cause that is necessary (but not sufficient) for its effect, (ii) a cause that is sufficient (but not necessary) for its effect; (iii) a cause that is both sufficient and necessary for its effect.

It is beyond our present brief to try to address the question whether we should think that efficient causes are sufficient for their effects. We suspect that the view that efficient causes are sufficient for their effects was the more common view at least up until the middle decades of the twentieth century; hence, in particular, we suspect that the view that causes are sufficient for their effects was the more common view at the time that Aquinas was writing, and we suspect that it is the view that Aquinas himself actually held.

Premise 7 in Aquinas' argument is also controversial. Even if we suppose that there is exactly one first cause – i.e. just one thing that has no efficient cause, even though it is the efficient cause of other things – why should we suppose that this first cause is God? Of course, there are some people who will naturally think that, if there is a first cause, then that first cause is God. In particular, this is evidently true of the faithful from the Abrahamic religions: Judaism, Christianity and Islam. But what about those people who do not already believe that God exists? Why cannot they think, for example, that the first cause is just the uncaused initial state of the natural universe? Since, in the Second Way at least, Aquinas gives no argument against the suggestion that the first cause is the uncaused initial state of the natural universe, it is clear that the argument of the Second Way is importantly incomplete.

Some philosophers have supposed that no one could seriously suggest that the first cause is the uncaused initial state of the natural universe. Indeed, there are quite different cosmological arguments for the existence of God that are framed around the intuition that the natural universe requires a cause for its coming into existence. Perhaps, for example, the key causal premise might be that everything that comes into existence requires a cause of its coming into existence; or perhaps the key causal premise might be that every contingent thing – i.e. every thing that exists, or obtains, or holds, but which might not have existed, or obtained, or held – requires a cause. But, no matter how things stand with those further arguments and with the claim that the first cause is the uncaused initial state of the natural universe, it is worth noting that the case of those who suppose that the first cause is the uncaused initial state of the natural universe merely illustrates a more general problem that arises for premise 7 in Aquinas' argument.

For, given only the information that something satisfies the description 'the first cause', it is hard to see that there is very much that you can properly conclude about that thing. From whence could come the conclusion that it is omnipotent, or omniscient, or perfectly good, or triune, or . . .? But, if you cannot extract this information from the description, then there is clearly a difficulty for the claim that what you have is a proof of the existence of *God*. If, for example, there were a perfectly evil first cause, would we all say that the first cause is God? True enough, if there were no other problems with his argument for the existence of a unique first cause, then Aquinas would have demonstrated the existence of something which, on independent grounds, he believes to be God. But it is surely just an error in logic to suppose that, if you have demonstrated the existence of something which – on, say, grounds of scripture – you believe to be God, you have thereby proved that God exists. A pantheist cannot *prove* that God exists simply by demonstrating the existence of the natural universe – even though, of course, the pantheist does believe that the natural universe is God. Yet Aquinas begins the presentation of his Five Ways with the claim that 'there are five ways in which one can prove that there is a God'.

8. Suppose Aquinas added the premise: 'Anything that comes into existence has a cause that explains its existence'. Would this help secure the conclusion to the argument – and, if so, how? Is the premise plausible?

The upshot of our examination of the argument of the Second Way, given that we interpret the argument in terms of temporal causal chains, might be encapsulated as follows. While there is a valid argument in the vicinity of the argument that Aquinas presents, that argument has a number of premises which those who do not believe that God exists – and a good many of those who do believe that God exists – have adequate reason to refrain from accepting. Even if Aquinas' ambition was merely to produce an argument which all of those who believe that God exists should say is sound – i.e. valid and possessed of true premises – it seems that the Second Way does not succeed in meeting that ambition; and anything that deserved the label 'proof of the existence of God' would surely need to do much more than meet that limited ambition.

How do things stand if, instead, we interpret the argument in terms of contemporaneous causal chains? As we noted earlier, many commentators have insisted that the causation invoked in the Second Way should be interpreted in terms of answers to chains of 'Why'-questions. In particular, then, we can ask: what should we say about the premises in the argument of the Second Way, given this alternative understanding of the notion of causation that is invoked in the argument?

The first premise of the argument looks secure. There are cases in which we are prepared to accept a series of claims of the form 'A because B', 'B because C', 'C because D', and so on. While we might scruple at the idea that it is proper to use the expression 'causal chain' to describe a series of claims of this form, this is no objection to the argument that we are now attributing to Aquinas: he may have used the word 'cause' in a way that we now find odd, but we can perfectly well understand the argument that he developed using the word in that no longer current way.

The second premise of the argument looks secure: you cannot satisfactorily answer the question 'Why A?' with 'Because A!' Since 'A because A' is always an explanatory solecism, we have the best of reasons for granting the second premise of the argument.

The fourth premise of the argument is a little bit more questionable. It is not entirely clear that we are never prepared to accept a series of claims of the form 'A because B', 'B because C', . . . , 'D because A'. To give a very simple example of the kind of relationship that we have in mind, consider: 'The hawk is hovering in the sky because the rabbit is hiding in the bush' and 'The rabbit is hiding in the bush because the hawk is hovering in the sky'. There are many different kinds of interdependent relationships in the universe that might plausibly give rise to circular causal chains, given the concept of contemporaneous causal chain that is now in play. It may be that, given the kind of cosmological theory that Aquinas adopted, he believed that the causal structure of the universe is uniformly hierarchical, and consequently failed to recognise the many different kinds of interdependencies that are characteristic of the universe in which we live.

The third premise of the argument may also be a little more questionable. It is not *utterly* obvious that there cannot be an infinite series of acceptable claims of the form 'A because B', 'B because C', 'C because D', and so forth, in which 'A', 'B', 'C', 'D', and so on, are all distinct from one another. Of course, in practice, even in the company of very young children, we never see the production of an *infinite* chain of questions of the form 'But why?' Moreover, if we *are* confident that there cannot be an infinite series of acceptable claims of this form, that will surely be because we are confident that such chains of explanation always terminate in necessary truths that have no need of explanation. To illustrate the thought here, consider the following question: Why do electrons have a negative charge? An answer that one might think to give to the question is this: Having a negative charge is an essential and primitive characteristic of electrons; there is nothing further that explains why electrons have the nature that they do. Perhaps this answer is wrong in the case of the negative charge of the electron; but, even if that is so, the general point stands: these kinds of causal chains could just terminate in the primitive and essential properties of the fundamental constituents of the universe.

Given the remarks towards the end of the previous paragraph, it should be clear that the fifth and seventh premises of the argument are highly controversial. Perhaps theists can make sense of the idea that God is somehow responsible for bringing it about that the fundamental constituents of the universe have the primitive and essential properties that they in fact have; but, even if that is so, it seems clear that we have been given no reason at all to suppose that this view is compulsory. For all that has been argued so far, it could be one kind of brute fact that electrons have negative charge, and an entirely independent brute fact that neutrons have no charge. If that were so, then there would be many first causes. Moreover, even if all causal chains terminated in the same claim about the primitive essential constituents of the universe, that would still not give us a persuasive argument for the existence of God.

Given the above discussion, it seems plausible to conclude that the Second Way is no more compelling if it is taken to be couched in terms of 'contemporaneous' causal chains rather than in terms of temporal causal chains. Indeed, on either interpretation, the major difficulties that face the argument seem to be very, very similar in kind. Once a valid version of the argument has been constructed, that version of the argument is seen to have a number of premises of which it is plainly true that many reasonable people have good reason to fail to accept those premises.

9. It is sometimes objected to Aquinas' argument that it provides no answer to the question 'What made God?'. Is this a decisive criticism of the argument?

Of course, even if this assessment of the Second Way is correct, it could be that one of the other members of 'the five ways' is more successful; and, even if none of 'the five ways' is successful, it could be that there is a different cosmological argument for the existence of God that does succeed. If you are interested in further discussions of cosmological arguments for the existence of God, you might like to look at:

Craig, W., *The Kalam Cosmological Argument*, London: Macmillan, 1979.
Kenny, A., *The Five Ways: St Thomas Aquinas' Proofs of God's Existence*, New York: Schocken Books, 1969.
Rowe, W., *The Cosmological Argument*, Princeton, NJ: Princeton University Press, 1975.

Introduction to Pascal

Blaise Pascal (1623–62) made important theoretical contributions to mathematics, physics, philosophy and literature: the work he published on conic sections at the age of 16 was the most important contribution to this topic in more than a millennium; his correspondence with Pierre Fermat established the foundations for modern theories of probability; his foundational work on barometers led to the use of his surname as the unit of atmospheric pressure; and his *Lettres provinciales* and *Pensées* are major contributions to theological and devotional literature. Pascal also made important practical contributions: he invented the first useful calculating machine (in 1642) to help his father work out his tax return; and he also founded the first public bus service, donating the profits that were thereby generated to charity. Pascal had two profound religious experiences during his life, the first of which led him to give up his work on mathematics and physics, and the second of which provided the impetus for the production of the *Pensées*.

The modern text of the *Pensées* has been assembled from a large collection of notes that Pascal left at the time of his death. Pascal had written these notes with the intention of incorporating most of them in a projected 'Apology for the Christian Religion'. The text that we shall be examining here – 'Pascal's Wager' – is taken from a single, very messy handwritten page that has been reconstructed in rather different ways by different editors. While Pascal himself probably intended the Wager argument to be no more than a hook that would lure secular readers into reading the rest of his *Apology*, considerable interest attaches to pursuit of the question whether the Wager argument yields a convincing argument for belief in God. We shall be interested in searching for the strongest arguments that can be constructed from the materials with which we have been furnished by Pascal.

Blaise Pascal, *Pensées*, 'Pascal's Wager'

[a] If there is a God, He is infinitely incomprehensible, since, having neither parts nor limits, He has no affinity to us. We are then incapable of knowing either what He is or if He is. This being so, who will dare to undertake the decision of the question? Not we, who have no affinity to Him.

Who then will blame Christians for not being able to give a reason for their belief, since they profess a religion for which they cannot give a reason? They declare, in expounding it to the world, that it is a foolishness, *stultitiam*; (1 *Cor*. 1:21.) and then you complain that they do not prove it! If they proved it, they would not keep their word; it is in lacking proofs that they are not lacking in sense. 'Yes, but although this excuses those who offer it as such and takes away from them the blame of putting it for- [b] ward without reason, it does not excuse those who receive it.' Let us then examine this point, and say, 'God is, or He is not.' But to which side shall we incline? Reason can decide nothing here. There is an infinite chaos which separated us. A game is being played at the extremity of this infinite distance where heads or tails will turn up. What will you wager? According to reason, you can do neither the one thing nor the other; according to reason, you can defend neither of the propositions.

Do not, then, reprove for error those who have made a choice; for you [c] know nothing about it. 'No, but I blame them for having made, not this choice, but a choice; for again both he who chooses heads and he who chooses tails are equally at fault, they are both in the wrong. The true course is not to wager at all.'

Yes; but you must wager. It is not optional. You are embarked. Which [d] will you choose then? Let us see. Since you must choose, let us see which interests you least. You have two things to lose, the true and the good; and two things to stake, your reason and your will, your knowledge and your happiness; and your nature has two things to shun, error and misery. Your reason is no more shocked in choosing one rather than the other, [e] since you must of necessity choose. This is one point settled. But your happiness? Let us weigh the gain and the loss in wagering that God is. Let us estimate these two chances. If you gain, you gain all; if you lose, you [f] lose nothing. Wager, then, without hesitation that He is. 'That is very fine. Yes, I must wager; but I may perhaps wager too much.' Let us see. Since there is an equal risk of gain and of loss, if you had only to gain two lives, instead of one, you might still wager. But if there were three lives to gain, you would have to play (since you are under the necessity of playing), and you would be imprudent, when you are forced to play, not to chance your life to gain three at a game where there is an equal risk of loss and gain. [g] But there is an eternity of life and happiness. And this being so, if there were an infinity of chances, of which one only would be for you, you would still be right in wagering one to win two, and you would act stupidly, being obliged to play, by refusing to stake one life against three at a game in which out of an infinity of chances there is one for you, if there were an infinity of an infinitely happy life to gain. But there is here an infinity of an infinitely happy life to gain, a chance of gain against a finite number of chances of loss, and what you stake is finite. It is all divided; wherever the infinite is and there is not an infinity of chances of loss against that of gain, there is no time to hesitate, you must give all. And thus, when one is forced to play, he must renounce reason to preserve his life, rather than risk it for infinite gain, as likely to happen as the loss of nothingness.

h → For it is no use to say it is uncertain if we will gain, and it is certain that we risk, and that the infinite distance between the certainly of what is staked and the uncertainty of what will be gained, equals the finite good which is certainly staked against the uncertain infinite. It is not so, as every player stakes a certainty to gain an uncertainty, and yet he stakes a finite certainty to gain a finite uncertainty, without transgressing against reason. There is not an infinite distance between the certainty staked and the uncertainty of the gain; that is untrue. In truth, there is an infinity between the certainty of gain and the certainty of loss. But the uncertainty of the gain is proportioned to the certainty of the stake according to the proportion of the chances of gain and loss. Hence it comes that, if there are as many risks on one side as on the other, the course is to play even; and then the certainty of the stake is equal to the uncertainty of the gain, so far is it from fact that there is an infinite distance between them. And so our proposition is of infinite force, when there is the finite to stake in a game where there are equal risks of gain and of loss, and the infinite to gain. This is demonstrable; and if men are capable of any truths, this is one.

'I confess it, I admit it. But, still, is there no means of seeing the faces of the cards?' Yes, Scripture and the rest, etc. 'Yes, but I have my hands tied and my mouth closed; I am forced to wager, and am not free. I am not released, and am so made that I cannot believe. What, then, would you have me do?'

True. But at least learn your inability to believe, since reason brings you to this, and yet you cannot believe. Endeavour, then, to convince yourself, not by increase of proofs of God, but by the abatement of your passions. You would like to attain faith and do not know the way; you would like to cure yourself of unbelief and ask the remedy for it. Learn of those who have been bound like you, and who now stake all their possessions. These are people who know the way which you would follow, and who are cured of an ill of which you would be cured. Follow the way by which they began; by acting as if they believed, taking the holy water, having masses said,  etc. Even this will naturally make you believe, and deaden your acuteness. 'But this is what I am afraid of.' And why? What have you to lose?

But to show you that this leads you there, it is this which will lessen the passions, which are your stumbling-blocks.

The end of this discourse. – Now, what harm will befall you in taking this side? You will be faithful, humble, grateful, generous, a sincere friend, truthful. Certainly you will not have those poisonous pleasures, glory and luxury; but will you not have others? I will tell you that you will thereby gain in this life, and that, at each step you take on this road, you will see so great certainty of gain, so much nothingness in what you risk, that you will at last recognize that you have wagered for something certain and infinite, for which you have given nothing.

Commentary on Pascal

We begin with a reasonably slow and careful examination of the text from [b]→ to [h]→.

1. What point is Pascal making at [a]→. Explain his comment 'although this excuses those who offer it . . . it does not excuse those who receive it'.

At [b]→ Pascal asserts that reason is powerless to decide whether or not God exists. It is not clear how extensive the presumed scepticism about the power of reason should be taken to be: as we shall see, if we suppose that reason cannot ascribe *any* probability to the claim that God exists, then the subsequent line of reasoning that Pascal attempts to run will fall flat. But, if we suppose that reason can ascribe *some* probability to the claim that God exists, then it is not clear why we should agree that reason is powerless to decide whether or not God exists. If, for example, reason tells me that there is a 60 per cent chance that God exists, then reason is telling me that it is more likely than not that God exists – but to make that judgement is surely to make a decision about whether or not God exists.

At [c]→, Pascal considers the possibility that someone might 'refuse to wager': i.e. that someone might suspend judgement on the question whether God exists. While it seems that this is clearly a possible option, Pascal makes the point that to suspend judgement is to 'wager against God': for either one does believe that God exists, or one does not believe that God exists, and suspension of judgement is just one of the ways in which one might fail to believe that God exists.

At [d]→, Pascal claims that, since reason is 'powerless to decide' whether or not God exists, it can be no affront to reason to believe either way. 'Your reason is no more shocked in choosing one rather than the other, since you must of necessity choose.' It is not at all clear that this is so. One might well be tempted to object: if reason issues no verdict on the question whether God exists, then reason simply tells you not to believe that God exists – though, of course, in that case, reason also tells you not to believe that God does not exist. While Pascal is right to claim that you cannot opt out of the wager, it does not follow from this fact that 'impotent' reason recommends anything other than refraining from believing that God exists.

2. Explain Pascal's claim that refusing to wager is to wager against God. Compare Pascal's argument at [c]↦ and at [d]↦ with William James's argument, in section X of his paper, that religion is a 'forced option'.

At [e]↦, Pascal introduces a first argument based on the idea that one might invoke considerations about 'happiness' in determining whether or not to believe that God exists.  Pascal's presentation of this argument is very compressed; we may fill it out as follows. There are two things that you might do: either believe that God exists or fail to believe that God exists. And there are two ways that things might be: either God exists or God does not exist. If God exists, then you 'win everything' if you believe (and you do not 'win everything' if you fail to believe); and if God does not exist, then you 'lose nothing' if you believe (and you do not gain anything further if you fail to believe). So, depending upon whether God exists, you may do much better, and you cannot do worse, by believing that God exists than by failing to believe that God exists. Thus, you should believe that God exists. In subsequent discussion, we shall call this 'the argument from domination'.

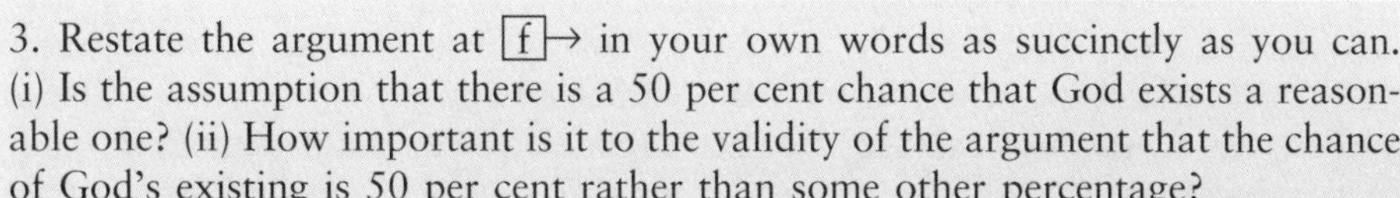

3. Restate the argument at [f]↦ in your own words as succinctly as you can. (i) Is the assumption that there is a 50 per cent chance that God exists a reasonable one? (ii) How important is it to the validity of the argument that the chance of God's existing is 50 per cent rather than some other percentage?

At [f]↦, Pascal introduces a new argument, based on the further assumption that 'there is an equal risk of gain and of loss'. While Pascal's presentation of the argument is not entirely transparent, we can set out the argument in the following way. As before, there are two things that you might do: either believe that God exists or fail to believe that God exists. And there are two ways that things might be: either God exists or God does not exist. However, we now assume that it is equally likely that God exists and that God does not exist: the probability of each of these states of affairs is 0.5. And we continue to assume that, if God exists and you believe that God exists, you make an infinite gain (and you fail to make this infinite gain if you do not believe that God exists); and if God does not exist, then, whether or not you believe that God exists, your gain or loss is merely finite. Given all of this information, we can compute the expected return to you of believing that God exists, and of failing to believe that God exists. If you believe that God exists, then there is a 50 per cent chance that you will make an infinite gain (because God exists), and there is a 50 per cent chance that you will make a merely finite gain or loss (because God does not exist). But $\frac{1}{2}$ × infinity + $\frac{1}{2}$ × finite value = infinity. So your expected return is infinite. On the other hand, if you fail to believe that God exists, there is a 50 per cent chance of a finite gain or loss, and another 50 per cent chance of a finite gain or loss. But $\frac{1}{2}$ × finite value + $\frac{1}{2}$ × finite value = finite value. So your expected return is greater – indeed, infinitely greater! – if you believe that God exists than if you fail to believe that God exists. So you should believe that God exists. In subsequent discussion, we shall call this 'the argument from expectation'.

4. Expectation can be used to determine whether you should take a risk. The expectation of an action is calculated as follows. For each possible result of the action, multiply the utility of that result by the probability that it has that result; then add up these numbers. Here's an easy example. We win or lose on the toss of a fair coin: heads, I pay you \$10; tails, you pay me \$10. What is your expectation if you play? There are two possible results: $1/2$ chance of winning \$10 = 5; $1/2$ chance of losing \$10 = –5. Adding the results gives 0: there is no expected advantage or disadvantage. Calculate the following:

(i) Two cards are drawn at random from a normal pack of fifty-two. If both are black, you win \$100, but with any other result you lose \$20. What should you expect to win from playing?

(ii) A thousand lottery tickets are issued. The winning ticket, selected at random, receives \$1000; second place receives \$500; third place receives £250. A lottery ticket costs \$10. What are your expected winnings/losses from playing with one ticket?

At [g]↦, Pascal introduces a third argument, based on the assumption that 'there is a chance of gain against a finite number of chances of loss'. Again, it can hardly be said that Pascal's presentation of this argument is entirely transparent – indeed, the presentation of this argument is really entangled with the presentation of the previous argument throughout the text from [f]↦ to [h]↦ – but perhaps we can set out the argument in the following way. As before, there are two things that you might do: either believe that God exists or fail to believe that God exists. And there are two ways that things might be: either God exists or God does not exist. However, we now assume that there is a non-zero finite probability that God exists and a non-zero finite probability that God does not exist. And we continue to assume that, if God exists and you believe that God exists, you make an infinite gain (and you fail to make this infinite gain if you do not believe that God exists); and if God does not exist, then, whether or not you believe that God exists, your gain or loss is merely finite. We can represent this information as follows:

	God exists	*God does not exist*
Bet that God exists	Infinite gain	Finite loss
Bet that God does not exist	Nothing gained	Nothing gained or lost

Given all of this information, we can compute the expected return to you of believing that God exists, and of failing to believe that God exists. If you believe that God exists, then there is a non-zero finite chance that you will make an infinite gain (if God does exist), and there is a non-zero finite chance that you will make a merely finite gain or loss (if God does not exist). But non-zero finite probability × infinity + non-zero finite probability × finite value = infinity. So your expected return is infinite. On the other hand, if you fail to believe that God exists, there is a non-zero finite chance of a finite gain or loss (because God exists), and another non-zero finite chance of a finite gain or loss (because God does not exist). But non-zero finite probability × finite value + non-zero finite probability × finite value = finite value. So your expected return is greater if you believe that God exists than if you fail to believe that God exists. So you should believe that God exists. In subsequent discussion, we shall call this 'the argument from dominating expectation'.

5. State precisely where the argument from expectation and the argument from dominating expectation differ.

Most contemporary discussions of Pascal's Wager focus only on the argument from dominating expectation, since this is clearly the strongest of the three arguments – and this because it makes the weakest set of assumptions. However, before we turn to a discussion of this argument, we should briefly consider the other two arguments that Pascal presents.

Perhaps the most obvious difficulty that uniquely confronts the argument from dominance is that it is simply not plausible to suppose that, if God does not exist, you 'lose nothing' if you believe and you do not gain anything further if you fail to believe. If God does not exist, then 'taking the holy water, having masses said, etc.' is *certainly* just a waste of your life. If you take the view that, if God does not exist, life is meaningless and it makes no difference what you do, then you might argue that it remains plausible to hold that, if God does not exist, you 'lose nothing' if you believe and you do not gain anything further if you fail to believe. We think, however, that it is near-impossible to take this view seriously.

Perhaps the most obvious difficulty that uniquely confronts the argument from expectation is that it is simply not plausible to suppose that reason endorses the claim that there is a 50 per cent chance that God exists. In particular, given Pascal's claim that reason is powerless to decide whether or not God exists, it would just be a mistake to think that reason endorses this further claim. As things stand, reason seems no less powerless to decide whether there is a planet inhabited by intelligent creatures within 10 billion light years of the Earth: should we conclude that there is a 50 per cent chance that there is a planet inhabited by intelligent creatures within 10 billion light years of the Earth? Worse, as things stand, reason seems no less powerless to decide whether there is a planet inhabited by intelligent creatures within 9 billion light years of the Earth: should we also conclude that there is a 50 per cent chance that there is a planet inhabited by intelligent creatures within 9 billion light years of the Earth? Alas, it seems that this way lies inconsistency: for surely we also think that, as we consider a larger volume of space centred on the Earth, the probability that there is a planet inhabited by intelligent creatures somewhere within that volume *increases*!

Returning to the argument from dominating expectation, we might set out the argument more formally in the following way:

1. There is a non-zero finite probability that God exists. (Premise)
2. If one believes that God exists, and God exists, one makes an infinite gain. (Premise)

3. If one believes that God exists, and God does not exist, one makes a finite loss or finite gain. (Premise)
4. If one does not believe that God exists, and God exists, one makes a finite loss or a finite gain. (Premise)
5. If one does not believe that God exists, and God does not exist, one makes a finite loss or a finite gain. (Premise)
6. If a calculation yields the result that the expected value of believing that God exists is greater than the expected value of not believing that God exists, then one should believe that God exists. (Premise)
7. (Hence) one should believe that God exists. (From 1–6)

Let us write the probability that some statement *x* is true as Pr(x). A calculation of expected value, which supports the claim that the conclusion of this argument does indeed follow from its premises, might look like this:

Expected value of believing that God exists = {Pr (God exists) × Value (Believing that God exists given that God exists)} + {Pr (God does not exist) × Value (Believing that God exists given that God does not exist)} = {non-zero finite × infinite} + {non-zero finite × finite} = infinite.

Expected value of not believing that God exists = {Pr (God exists) × Value (Not believing that God exists given that God exists)} + {Pr (God does not exist) × Value (Not believing that God exists given that God does not exist)} = {non-zero finite × finite} + {non-zero finite × finite} = finite.

There are questions that can be asked about the first two premises in this argument. Those who think that there are good *a priori* arguments against the existence of God will reject the first premise, as will any who think that the probability that God exists is merely infinitesimal; and those who think that there is no sense to be made of the idea that a human person might have an *infinite* gain will reject the second premise, as will those who think that there is no sense to be made of any calculations that involve infinite quantities.

However, perhaps the most interesting questions for this argument arise in connection with premise 6. We shall consider three different kinds of objections that have been lodged against this premise.

Perhaps the best-known objection to premise 6 is known more widely as the 'Many Gods' objection. We shall consider one variant of this objection here. Suppose we grant Pascal the first five premises of his argument. Consider the hypothesis that there is a Demon who infinitely rewards all and only those who do *not* believe that God exists. Suppose that there is non-zero finite probability that the Demon exists. Now redo the calculation of the expected value of believing that God exists.

The expected value of believing that God exists = Pr (God exists and the Demon exists) × Value (Believing that God exists given that God and the Demon exist) + Pr (God exists and the Demon does not exist) × Value (Believing that God exists given that God exists and the Demon does not exist) + Pr (God does not exist and the Demon exists) × Value (Believing that God exists given that God does not exist and the Demon exists) + Pr (neither God nor the Demon exists) × Value (Believing that God exists given that neither God nor the Demon exists)

The expected value of not believing that God exists = Pr (God exists and the Demon exists) × Value (Not believing that God exists given that God and the Demon exist) + Pr (God exists and the Demon does not exist) × Value (Not believing that God exists given that God exists and the Demon does not exist) + Pr (God does not exist and the Demon exists) × Value (Not believing that God exists given that God does not exist and the Demon exists) + Pr (neither God nor the Demon exists) × Value (Not believing that God exists given that neither God nor the Demon exists)

In order to evaluate these expected values, we need to decide the values of the probabilities Pr (God and the Demon both exist), Pr (only God exists), Pr (only the Demon exists), and Pr (neither God nor the Demon exists). Since we have supposed that Pr (Demon exists) is non-zero and finite, we have supposed that at least one of Pr (God and the Demon both exist) and Pr (only the Demon exists) is non-zero and finite. On the one hand, if Pr (God and the Demon both exist) is non-zero and finite, then Pr (God exists and the Demon exists) × Value (Not believing that God exists given that God and the Demon both exist) is infinite (since the Demon gives an infinite reward to all of those who do not believe that God exists). On the other hand, if Pr (only the Demon exists) is non-zero and finite, then Pr (Not believing that God exists) × Value (Not believing that God exists given that only the Demon exists) is infinite (for the same reason as in the previous case). Either way, then, the expected value of not believing that God exists is infinite. So, given only the assumption that Pr (Demon exists) is non-zero and finite, we find that the expected value of believing that God exists is the same as the expected value of believing that God does not exist.

So far, we have one calculation of the expected value of believing in God which yields the result that the expected value of believing in God is greater than the expected value of not believing in God; and we have a second calculation of the expected value of believing in God which yields the result that the expected value of believing in God is the same as the expected value of not believing in God. One might think that this is already enough to undermine premise 6: for why should one prefer the result of Pascal's calculation to the result of the calculation that we have just carried out? In particular, if one is sceptical about the power of reason in this domain, how could one possibly justify accepting the claim that there is a non-zero finite probability that God exists while simultaneously rejecting the claim that there is a non-zero finite probability that the Demon exists?

Of course, once we have widened the scope of our calculation to take the Demon into account, there is no evident reason why we should not widen the scope of our inquiry further. If we are prepared to attribute non-zero finite probability to any other hypotheses about sources of infinite value or infinite disvalue – e.g. other kinds of supernatural agents with the power to bestow infinite rewards on those who hold certain favoured beliefs – then surely we *ought* to redo our calculations of the expected value of belief in God taking those further hypotheses into account.

6. It is sometimes pointed out that Pascal's Wager overlooks the question of which religion one should wager on. Perhaps a deity exists that will only offer salvation to the adherents to a particular religion. Perhaps a deity exists that will inflict infinite punishment on anyone who does not believe in him. How do these possibilities affect Pascal's calculations?

A second objection to premise 6 turns on the observation that, if we grant that the expected value of believing in God is infinite on the basis of Pascal's calculation, we shall be obliged to concede that there are countless other actions the expected value of which can be shown to be infinite on the basis of analogous calculations. Suppose, for example, that I am considering whether or not to perform the following action: toss a fair coin and adopt the belief that God exists if and only if this toss comes up heads. What is the expected value of performing this action?

Making use of Pascal's prior calculation, we have it that the expected value of believing that God exists is infinite, and the expected value of not believing that God exists is finite. Possible outcomes of my performing the action currently under consideration are: (1) the coin comes up heads and I believe that God exists; (2) the coin comes up tails and I do not believe that God exists. Since the coin is fair, there is a 50 per cent chance that it comes up heads, and a 50 per cent chance that it comes up tails. So the expected value of performing the action is 50 per cent × infinite + 50 per cent × finite = infinite. So the expected value of tossing a fair coin and adopting the belief that God exists if and only if the coin comes up heads is infinite: it has the same expectation as forming the belief that God exists, given Pascal's assumptions. Thus – absent further considerations – it seems that Pascal has given us no more reason to adopt belief in God than he has given us reason to determine whether or not to adopt belief in God on the basis of the toss of a coin (or the results of next Saturday's Lotto draw).

Suppose I were to adopt the following policy: I shall take on the belief that God exists when and only when I become the richest man in the world. I take it that there is a non-zero finite (but vanishingly small) probability that I shall become the richest man in the world at some time before I die. Consequently, it seems that – by Pascal's lights – my continuation in this policy at any given stage in my life has infinite expected value: at any time, my continuing with the policy that I shall take on the belief that God exists when and only when I become the richest man in the world has infinite expected value. Pascal's secular friends – Antoine Gombaud (the chevalier de Méré) and Damien Mitton, the direct targets of the projected 'Apology for the Christian Religion' – would not have been particularly disconcerted by the recommendation that they should adopt *this* kind of policy.

A third commonly encountered objection to premise 6 in our reconstruction of Pascal's argument is that it is just plain *wrong* to think that it is permissible to adjust the *probabilities* that you ascribe to propositions in the light of your *preferences* about the truth of those propositions. If one starts out thinking that there is a 1 in 10^{1000} chance that God exists prior to one's exposure to the wager argument, how can one reasonably think that there is anything other than a 1 in 10^{1000} chance that God exists after one has run through the wager argument? In order to adjust one's credence, one needs new evidence, or new conclusions from old evidence, or the like – and yet the wager argument gives one nothing of the sort. To adjust up one's credence from 1 in 10^{1000} to better than 1 in 2 on the basis of the wager argument would be a disastrous case of wishful thinking, or some other kind of intellectual folly.

Pascal has a response to this objection: what is being recommended is not that one choose to believe in God, but rather that one choose to enter into a course of action that is most likely to lead eventually to your believing in God. While this proposal gets around the immediate problem, it is not clear that it ultimately succeeds. After all, if there is to be reasonable adjustment of your credence – something that is required in order for you to come to believe that God exists – then you are going to need new evidence, or new conclusions from old evidence, or the like; else, all that Pascal's proposal does is to postpone the time at which one engages in wishful thinking or some other kind of intellectual folly. No amount of 'taking the holy water, having masses said, etc.' can provide one with what is rationally required in order for one to adjust the credence that one gives to the claim that God exists – or so it seems to us.

7. Pascal recommends that the non-believer take the wager by pursuing a course of action that will lead to belief in God, but he concedes that this may 'deaden your acuteness'. Even if the wager is a good bet, is there a moral argument against accepting it?

We have not canvassed all of the objections that have been made against Pascal's Wager, and nor have we considered the full range of ways in which Pascal's argument might be interpreted. While we have found reasons for thinking that Pascal's argument does not give non-believers a good reason to believe in God, it might be that there is some modification to Pascal's argument that would yield a successful argument to that end. If you are interested in further examination of Pascal's Wager, you might consider:

Hájek, A., 'Waging War on Pascal's Wager', *Philosophical Review*, 112, 1 (2003): 27–56.
Jordan, J., *Pascal's Wager: Pragmatic Arguments and Belief in God*, Oxford: Oxford University Press, 2006.
Rescher, N., *Pascal's Wager: A Study of Practical Reasoning in Philosophical Theology*, Notre Dame, Ind.: University of Notre Dame Press, 1985.

Introduction to Paley

William Paley (1743–1805), an Anglican clergyman who rose to become Archdeacon of Carlisle and Sub-Dean of Lincoln Cathedral, is best-known for his exposition of an argument for design in *Natural Theology; or, Evidence of the Existence and Attributes of the Deity, Collected from the Appearances of Nature* (1802). Paley wrote a number of other books – his *A View of the Evidences of Christianity* (1794) was required reading for all undergraduates at Cambridge into the fourth decade of the twentieth century – but they mostly belong to a rather outdated tradition of biblical scholarship.

The argument of the initial chapters of Paley's *Natural Theology* is presented in a much less compact form than the arguments of Anselm and Aquinas. Reading and understanding Paley requires the deployment of a wider range of interpretative skills. None the less, we shall be using the same kinds of techniques for assessing the merit of this argument that we deployed in analysing those more compact arguments.

William Paley, *Natural Theology* (selection)

[1] In crossing a heath, suppose I pitched my foot against a *stone* and were asked how the stone came to be there, I might possibly answer that for anything I knew to the contrary it had lain there forever; nor would it, perhaps, be very easy to show the absurdity of this answer. But suppose I had found a *watch* upon the ground, and it should be inquired how the watch happened to be in that place, I should hardly think of the answer which I had before given, that for anything I knew the watch might have always been there. Yet why should not this answer serve for the watch as well as for the stone? Why is it not as admissible in the second case as in the first? For this reason, and for no other, namely, that when we come to inspect the watch, we perceive – what we could not discover in the stone – that its several parts are framed and put together for a purpose, e.g., that they are so formed and adjusted as to produce motion, and that motion so regulated as to point out the hour of the day; that if the different parts had been differently shaped from what they are, of a different size from what they are, or placed after any other manner or in any other order than that in which they are placed, either no motion at all would have been carried on in the machine, or none which would have answered the use that is now served by it. To reckon up a few of the plainest of these parts and of their offices, all tending to one result; we see a cylindrical box containing a coiled elastic spring, which, by its endeavor to relax itself, turns round the box. We next observe a flexible chain – artificially wrought for the sake of flexure – communicating the action of the spring from the box to the fusee. We then find a series of wheels, the teeth of which catch in and apply to each other, conducting the motion from the fusee to the balance and from the balance to the pointer, and at the same time, by the size and shape of those wheels, so regulating that motion as to terminate in causing an index, by an equable and measured progression, to pass over a given space in a given time. We take notice that the wheels are made of brass, in order to keep them from rust; the springs of steel, no other metal being so elastic; that over the face of the watch there is placed a glass, a material employed in no other part of the work, but in the room of which, if there

had been any other than a transparent substance, the hour could not be seen without opening the case. This mechanism being observed – it requires indeed an examination of the instrument, and perhaps some previous knowledge of the subject, to perceive and understand it; but being once, as we have said, observed and understood – the inference we think is inevitable, that the watch must have had a maker – that there must have existed, at some time and at some place or other, an artificer or artificers who formed it for the purpose which we find it actually to answer, who comprehended its construction and designed its use.

[2] I. Nor would it, I apprehend, weaken the conclusion, that we had never seen a watch made – that we had never known an artist capable of making one – that we were altogether incapable of executing such a piece of workmanship ourselves, or of understanding in what manner it was performed; all this being no more than what is true of some exquisite remains of ancient art, of some lost arts, and, to the generality of mankind, of the more curious productions of modern manufacture. Does one man in a million know how oval frames are turned? Ignorance of this kind exalts our opinion of the unseen and unknown artist's skill, if he be unseen and unknown, but raises no doubt in our minds of the existence and agency of such an artist, at some former time and in some place or other. Nor can I perceive that it varies at all the inference, whether the question arise concerning a human agent or concerning an agent of a different species, or an agent possessing in some respects a different nature.

II. Neither, secondly, would it invalidate our conclusion, that the watch sometimes went wrong or that it seldom went exactly right. The purpose of the machinery, the design, and the designer might be evident, and in the case supposed, would be evident, in whatever way we accounted for the irregularity of the movement, or whether we could account for it or not. It is not necessary that a machine be perfect in order to show with what design it was made: still less necessary, where the only question is whether it were made with any design at all.

III. Nor, thirdly, would it bring any uncertainty into the argument, if there were a few parts of the watch, concerning which we could not discover or had not yet discovered in what manner they conduced to the general effect; or even some parts, concerning which we could not ascertain whether they conduced to that effect in any manner whatever. For, as to the first branch of the case, if by the loss, or disorder, or decay of the parts in question, the movement of the watch were found in fact to be stopped, or disturbed, or retarded, no doubt would remain in our minds as to the utility or intention of these parts, although we should be unable to investigate the manner according to which, or the connection by which, the ultimate effect depended upon their action or assistance; and the more complex is the machine, the more likely is this obscurity to arise. Then, as to the second thing supposed, namely, that there were parts which might be spared without prejudice to the movement of the watch, and that we had proved this by experiment, these superfluous parts, even if we were completely assured that they were such, would not vacate the reasoning which we had instituted concerning other parts. The indication of contrivance remained, with respect to them, nearly as it was before.

IV. Nor, fourthly, would any man in his senses think the existence of the watch with its various machinery accounted for, by being told that it was one out of possible combinations of material forms; that whatever he had found in the place where he found the watch, must have contained some internal configuration or other; and that this configuration might be the structure now exhibited, namely, of the works of a watch, as well as a different structure.

V. Nor, fifthly, would it yield his inquiry more satisfaction, to be answered that there existed in things a principle of order, which had disposed the parts of the watch into their present form and situation. He never knew a watch made by the principle of order; nor can he even form to himself an idea of what is meant by a principle of order distinct from the intelligence of the watchmaker.

VI. Sixthly, he would be surprised to hear that the mechanism of the watch was no proof of contrivance, only a motive to induce the mind to think so:

VII. And not less surprised to be informed that the watch in his hand was nothing more than the result of the laws of *metallic* nature. It is a perversion of language to assign any law as the efficient, operative cause of any thing. A law presupposes an agent, for it is only the mode according to which an agent proceeds: it implies a power, for it is the order according to which that power acts. Without this agent, without this power, which are both distinct from itself, the *law* does nothing, is nothing. The expression, 'the law of metallic nature,' may sound strange and harsh to a philosophic ear; but it seems quite as justifiable as some others which are more familiar to him, such as 'the law of vegetable nature,' 'the law of animal nature,' or, indeed, as 'the law of nature' in general, when assigned as the cause of phenomena, in exclusion of agency and power, or when it is substituted into the place of these.

VIII. Neither, lastly, would our observer be driven out of his conclusion or from his confidence in its truth by being told that he knew nothing at all about the matter. He knows enough for his argument; he knows the utility of the end; he knows the subserviency and adaptation of the means to the end. These points being known, his ignorance of other points, his doubts concerning other points affect not the certainty of his reasoning. The consciousness of knowing little need not beget a distrust of that which he does know.

Chapter II: State of the Argument Continued

[3] Suppose, in the next place, that the person who found the watch should after some time discover that, in addition to all the properties which

he had hitherto observed in it, it possessed the unexpected property of producing in the course of its movement another watch like itself – the thing is conceivable; that it contained within it a mechanism, a system of parts – a mould, for instance, or a complex adjustment of lathes, baffles, and other tools – evidently and separately calculated for this purpose; let us inquire what effect ought such a discovery to have upon his former conclusion.

I. The first effect would be to increase his admiration of the contrivance, and his conviction of the consummate skill of the contriver. Whether he regarded the object of the contrivance, the distinct apparatus, the intricate, yet in many parts intelligible mechanism by which it was carried on, he would perceive in this new observation nothing but an additional reason for doing what he had already done – for referring the construction of the watch to design and to supreme art. If that construction *without* this property, or, which is the same thing, before this property had been noticed, proved intention and art to have been employed about it, still more strong would the proof appear when he came to the knowledge of this further property, the crown and perfection of all the rest.

II. He would reflect, that though the watch before him were, *in some sense*, the maker of the watch, which, was fabricated in the course of its movements, yet it was in a very different sense from that in which a carpenter, for instance, is the maker of a chair – the author of its contrivance, the cause of the relation of its parts to their use. With respect to these, the first watch was no cause at all to the second; in no such sense as this was it the author of the constitution and order, either of the arts which the new watch contained, or of the parts by the aid and instrumentality of which it was produced. We might possibly say, but with great latitude of expression, that a stream of water ground corn; but no latitude of expression would allow us to say, no stretch of conjecture could lead us to think that the stream of water built the mill, though it were too ancient for us to know who the builder was. What the stream of water does in the affair is neither more nor less than this: by the application of an unintelligent impulse to a mechanism previously arranged, arranged independently of it and arranged by intelligence, an effect is produced, namely, the corn is ground. But the effect results from the arrangement. The force of the stream cannot be said to be the cause or author of the effect, still less of the arrangement. Understanding and plan in the formation of the mill were not the less necessary for any share which the water has in grinding the corn; yet is this share the same as that which the watch would have contributed to the production of the new watch, upon the supposition assumed in the last section. Therefore,

III. Though it be now no longer probable that the individual watch which our observer had found was made immediately by the hand of an artificer, yet does not this alteration in anyway affect the inference that an artificer had been originally employed and concerned in the production. The argument from design remains as it was. Marks of design and contrivance are no more accounted for now than they were before. In the same thing, we may ask for the cause of different properties. We may ask for the cause of the colour of a body, of its hardness, of its heat; and these causes may be all different. We are now asking for the cause of that subserviency to a use, that relation to an end, which we have remarked in the watch before us. No answer is given to this question by telling us that a preceding watch produced it. There cannot be design without a designer; contrivance without a contriver; order without choice; arrangement without anything capable of arranging; subserviency and relation to a purpose without that which could intend a purpose; means suitable to an end, and executing their office in accomplishing that end, without the end ever having been contemplated or the means accommodated to it. Arrangement, disposition of parts, subserviency of means to an end, relation of instruments to a use imply the presence of intelligence and mind. No one, therefore, can rationally believe that the insensible, inanimate watch, from which the watch before us issued, was the proper cause of the mechanism we so much admire in it – could be truly said to have constructed the instrument, disposed its parts, assigned their office, determined their order, action, and mutual dependency, combined their several motions into one result, and that also a result connected with the utilities of other beings. All these properties, therefore, are as much unaccounted for as they were before.

IV. Nor is anything gained by running the difficulty farther back, that is, by supposing the watch before us to have been produced from another watch, that from a former, and so on indefinitely. Our going back ever so far brings us no nearer to the least degree of satisfaction upon the subject. Contrivance is still unaccounted for. We still want a contriver. A designing mind is neither supplied by this supposition nor dispensed with. If the difficulty were diminished the farther we went back, by going back indefinitely we might exhaust it. And this is the only case to which this sort of reasoning applies. Where there is a tendency, or, as we increase the number of terms, a continual approach toward a limit, *there*, by supposing the number of terms to be what is called infinite, we may conceive the limit to be attained; but where there is no such tendency or approach, nothing is effected by lengthening the series. There is no difference as to the point in question, whatever there may be as to many points, between one series and another – between a series which is finite and a series which is infinite. A chain composed of an infinite number of links, can no more support itself, than a chain composed of a finite number of links. And of this we are assured, though we never *can* have tried the experiment; because, by increasing the number of links, from ten, for instance, to a hundred, from a hundred to a thousand, etc., we make not the smallest approach, we observe not the smallest tendency toward self support. There is no difference in this respect – yet there may be a great difference in several respects – between a chain of a greater or less length, between one chain and another, between one that is finite and one that is infinite. This very much resembles the case before us.

The machine which we are inspecting demonstrates, by its construction, contrivance and design. Contrivance must have had a contriver, design a designer, whether the machine immediately proceeded from another machine or not. That circumstance alters not the case. That other machine may, in like manner, have proceeded from a former machine: nor does that alter the case; contrivance must have had a contriver. That former one from one preceding it: no alteration still; a contriver is still necessary. No tendency is perceived, no approach toward a diminution of this necessity. It is the same with any and every succession of these machines – a succession of ten, of a hundred, of a thousand; with one series, as with another – a series which is finite, as with a series which is infinite. In whatever other respects they may differ, in this they do not. In all equally, contrivance and design are unaccounted for.

The question is not simply, How came the first watch into existence? which question, it may be pretended, is done away by supposing the series of watches thus produced from one another to have been infinite, and consequently to have had no such *first* for which it was necessary to provide a cause. This, perhaps, would have been nearly the state of the question, if nothing had been before us but an unorganized, unmechanized substance, without mark or indication of contrivance. It might be difficult to show that such substance could not have existed from eternity, either in succession – if it were possible, which I think it is not, for unorganized bodies to spring from one another – or by individual perpetuity. But that is not the question now. To suppose it to be so is to suppose that it made no difference whether he had found a watch or a stone. As it is, the metaphysics of that question have no place; for, in the watch which we are examining are seen contrivance, design, an end, a purpose, means for the end, adaptation to the purpose. And the question which irresistibly presses upon our thoughts is, whence this contrivance and design? The thing required is the intending mind, the adapting hand, the intelligence by which that hand was directed. This question, this demand is not shaken off by increasing a number or succession of substances destitute of these properties; nor the more, by increasing that number to infinity. If it be said that, upon the supposition of one watch being produced from another in the course of that other's movements and by means of the mechanism within it, we have a cause for the watch in my hand, namely, the watch from which it proceeded; I deny that for the design, the contrivance, the suitableness of means to an end, the adaptation of instruments to a use, all of which we discover in the watch, we have any cause whatever. It is in vain, therefore, to assign a series of such causes or to allege that a series may be carried back to infinity; for I do not admit that we have yet any cause at all for the phenomena, still less any series of causes either finite or infinite. Here is contrivance but no contriver; proofs of design, but no designer.

V. Our observer would further also reflect that the maker of the watch before him was in truth and reality the maker of every watch produced from it: there being no difference, except that the latter manifests a more exquisite skill, between the making of another watch with his own hands, by the mediation of files, lathes, chisels, etc., and the disposing, fixing, and inserting of these instruments, or of others equivalent to them, in the body of the watch already made, in such a manner as to form a new watch in the course of the movements which he had given to the old one. It is only working by one set of tools instead of another.

[4] The conclusion which the *first* examination of the watch, of its works, construction, and movement, suggested, was that it must have had, for cause and author of that construction, an artificer who understood its mechanism and designed its use. This conclusion is invincible. A *second* examination presents us with a new discovery. The watch is found, in the course of its movement, to produce another watch similar to itself; and not only so, but we perceive in it a system of organization separately calculated for that purpose. What effect would this discovery have or ought it to have upon our former inference? What, as has already been said, but to increase beyond measure our admiration of the skill which had been employed in the formation of such a machine? Or shall it, instead of this, all at once turn us round to an opposite conclusion, namely, that no art or skill whatever has been concerned in the business, although all other evidences of art and skill remain as they were, and this last and supreme piece of art be now added to the rest? Can this be maintained without absurdity? Yet this is atheism.

Chapter III: Application of the Argument

This is atheism: for every indication of contrivance, every manifestation of design which existed in the watch, exists in the works of nature, with the difference on the side of nature of being greater and more, and that in a degree which exceeds all computation. I mean that the contrivances of nature surpass the contrivances of art in the complexity, subtlety, and curiosity of the mechanism; and still more, if possible, do they go beyond them in number and variety; yet, in a multitude of cases, are not less evidently mechanical, not less evidently contrivances, not less evidently accommodated to their end or suited to their office than are the most perfect productions of human ingenuity.

Commentary on Paley

We have divided the excerpted part of Paley's *Natural Theology* into four sections. Section [1] gives an argument about what we inevitably infer from the observable properties of watches. Section [2] considers various objections to the claim that the inference in question is strong. Section [3] considers what difference it would make to the inevitable inference if it were observed that watches produce baby watches. The final section sets out the argument for theism as it has been developed to this point.

In rough outline, it seems clear enough that the overall argument goes *something* like this. Careful observation of watches 'inevitably' reveals to us that they are products of intelligent design. Careful observation of plants and animals reveals the same features (to at least the same degree) that make it 'inevitable' that we infer that watches are the products of intelligent design. Of course, plants and animals differ from watches because of the facts about biological reproduction. But those facts would do nothing to threaten the 'inevitability' of the inference to intelligent design in the case of watches. Hence careful observation of plants and animals 'inevitably' reveals to us that they, too, are the products of intelligent design.

1. Consider the story in [1] with which Paley introduces his argument. Which parts of the story are essential for the ensuing argument and which parts of it are rhetorical?

2. Why does Paley begin his argument by comparing a stone with a *watch*? What would be lost from his argument if he had introduced it by comparing pitching his foot against a stone with meeting another human being?

Our first task is to fill out this rough outline in more detail.

The key idea that is developed in the section in [1] is that there are observable properties of a watch which make it 'inevitable' that we 'infer' from the observation of those properties that the watch is a product of intelligent design. It seems clear enough that this idea is well founded: across a large range of cases we are, in general, pretty good at using observation as a basis for distinguishing between objects that are uncontroversially products of intelligent design and objects that are not uncontroversially products of intelligent design. True enough, there are cases where expert training is required: for example, the untutored novice may make more errors in sorting rocks that have been shaped by denizens of the Stone Age for use in cutting and grinding from rocks that have not been thus shaped. But, if there is an objection to the line of argument that Paley develops in the section in [1], it is plainly not an objection to the general idea that we can and do identify objects as the products of intelligent design on the basis of observation.

Paley makes some detailed claims about the observable features of the watch that form the basis of the 'inevitable inference' that a watch is the product of intelligent design. He claims that, on the basis of a careful examination, we observe that: (i) the watch is composed of many parts all of which make an essential contribution to the functioning of the watch; (ii) these parts all have shapes and material constitutions that are well suited to the roles that they play; and (iii) relatively small changes in the shapes and arrangement of these parts would destroy the functioning of the watch. Moreover, and crucially, he claims that it is our observation of these listed features of the watch that prompts our 'inevitable inference' that the watch is the product of intelligent design.

3. Paley follows up these three observations about watches that show it is the product of intelligent design with a list of properties of a particular type of spring-powered watch. To which observation(s), (i) to (iii), does each property that Paley identifies lend support?

It may be true that, on the basis of a careful examination, one could make the observations (i)–(iii) that Paley claims can be made in connection with the watch. Someone who had no previous experience with watches might need to take the watch apart, experiment to see what happens when particular parts are removed, and so forth; but, at least given a sufficiently liberal construal of the notion of 'observation', it seems reasonable to grant to Paley that we *could* make these observations when we conduct a careful examination of the watch. However, even if this is so, we have not yet settled whether it is true (*a*) that one *needs* to make these observations in order to be justified in 'inferring' that the watch is a product of intelligent design, or (*b*) that someone who made *only* these observations would be justified in 'inferring' that the watch is a product of intelligent design.

We can, perhaps, test whether the second of these claims – i.e. (*b*) – is true by asking the following question. Suppose I tell you that there is something outside in the yard that has the following properties: (i) it has many parts which contribute to its overall functioning; (ii) these parts all have shapes and material constitutions that are well suited to the roles that they play; and (iii) relatively small changes in the shapes and arrangement of these parts would destroy the functioning of the thing. Given just this information, how confident are you – and how confident should you be – that this thing outside in the yard is the product of intelligent design?

We can also test whether the first of these claims – i.e. (*a*) – is true by asking the following question. Suppose I tell you that there is something outside in the yard that is made of brass (or plate glass, or steel). Given just this information, how confident are you – and how confident should you be – that this thing outside in the yard is the product of intelligent design?

We take it that all of us will be extremely confident in the second case that the thing outside in the yard is the product of intelligent design: we all know that brass, plate glass and steel are not naturally occurring items. On the other hand, most of us will not be at all confident in the first case that the thing outside in the yard is the product of intelligent design: for all the information that we have been given, the thing outside in the yard could be an animal or a plant. However, if this is right, then it seems that we should conclude (*a*) that Paley has not properly understood why it is that, when we make an observation of a watch, we *do* 'inevitably infer' that the watch is the product of intelligent design, and (*b*) that Paley's own proposal about how we *could* 'inevitably infer' that the watch is the product of intelligent design is bound to seem inadequate to those who are not already certain that plants and animals are the products of intelligent design.

4. Look again at Paley's observations about the spring-powered watch that you considered in question 3. Distinguish the properties that Paley observes that are singly sufficient to justify the inference to intelligent design from those which could be possessed by an object without its being intelligently designed. Are there any properties of the watch, *not* covered by Paley's observations (i), (ii) or (iii), that justify the intelligent design inference?

It is perhaps worth noting that this criticism of the argument that Paley develops in the section from [1] to [2] is not idle. When Paley comes to complete his argument in the section from [4] he tells us that '*every* indication of contrivance, every manifestation of design which existed in the watch, exists in the works of nature'. On the basis of the discussion that we have just completed, it seems to me that we should say that this claim is obviously false: when was the last time you saw a real live plant or animal made from brass, or glass, or steel?

As we have already noted, section [2] is devoted to an examination of some claims that might be thought to weaken the 'inevitable inference' to the conclusion that the watch is the product of intelligent design. In assessing the arguments that Paley gives at this point, we should think both about the bearing of these claims on the 'inevitable inference' that we *would* make in the case of a watch, and about the bearing of these claims on the 'inevitable inference' that Paley thinks that we *could* make by way of his observations (i)–(iii). Until we look into the matter, it remains a possibility that, while these claims will not weaken the 'inevitable inference' that we actually make in the presence of a watch, some of these claims *would* weaken the 'inevitable inference' given the grounds that Paley identifies for that 'inference'.

5. Consider the first four of the problems with his inference that Paley raises and responds to in section 3. Does any of these problems pose a more serious difficulty that Paley recognises if the inference is made *only* on the basis of observations (i)–(iii)?

As we have also already noted, section [3] is devoted to an examination of the bearing that the discovery that watches reproduce in something like the way that plants and animals reproduce would properly have on our 'inevitable inference'. Once again, in assessing the arguments that Paley gives at this point, we should think both about the bearing of these claims on the 'inevitable inference' that we *would* make in the case of a watch, and about the bearing of these claims on the 'inevitable inference' that Paley thinks that we *could* make by way of observations (i)–(iii).

There has been much recent discussion about self-replicating machines; some scientists predict that a time will come when we succeed in constructing self-replicating machines. The self-replicating machines that these scientists envisage will bear the kinds of marks that, in fact, make it 'inevitable' that we 'infer' that they are products of intelligent design: they will be made from brass, or glass, or steel, or the like, and so forth. So, quite apart from the arguments that Paley actually gives, it seems that we can grant him the point that he wants to argue for in section [3]:

if it is really true that we find it 'inevitable' to 'infer' that a given type of machine is the product of intelligent design, then the further discovery that that machine is a descendant of an ancestral machine should not make any difference to the 'inevitability' of our 'inference'.

6. In section 3-IV, Paley considers the possibility that the watch-making machine might have an infinite sequence of ancestors, each machine being made by its immediate ancestor. He maintains that 'by increasing the number of links . . . we observe not the smallest tendency towards self support'. However, if the sequence extends infinitely backwards in time, then it has no beginning, and no designer could initiate it. What is Paley's response to this? Is it satisfactory?

Given the above exposition of Paley's argument, it is pretty clear where that argument is most vulnerable to attack. While it is true that plants and animals exhibit the properties (i)–(iii) that Paley takes to be the drivers of our confident judgements about the presence of intelligent design, it is not true that plants and animals exhibit the properties that actually are the drivers of our confident judgements about the presence of intelligent design. In consequence, despite his confident claims to the contrary, Paley's argument does not establish that we should be even more confident that plants and animals are the product of intelligent design than we are that, say, Neolithic axe-heads are the products of intelligent design.

While we think that the above exposition is true to Paley's text, it should be pointed out that most contemporary interpreters of Paley's argument attribute a rather different argument to him. This argument is an instance of what is commonly called 'inference to the best explanation', and it might be set out in something like the following way:

1. Plants and animals are composed of many parts all of which make an essential contribution to the functioning of these organisms; and the parts of plants and animals all have shapes and material constitutions that are well suited to the roles that they play; and relatively small changes in the shapes and arrangement of these parts of plants and animals would destroy the functioning of these organisms. (Premise)
2. If things are composed of many parts all of which make an essential contribution to the functioning of these things; and the parts of things all have shapes and material constitutions that are well suited to the roles that they play; and relatively small changes in the shapes and arrangement of these parts of these things would destroy their functioning, then we should infer that these things are the product of intelligent design unless we have a serious alternative hypothesis that can also account for these various facts. (Premise)
3. There is no serious alternative hypothesis that accounts for the fact that plants and animals are composed of many parts all of which make an essential contribution to the functioning of these organisms; and the fact that parts of plants and animals all have shapes and material constitutions that are well suited to the roles that they play; and the fact that relatively small changes in the shapes

and arrangement of these parts of plants and animals would destroy the functioning of these organisms. (Premise)

4. (Hence) we should infer that animals and plants are the products of intelligent design. (From 1, 2 and 3)

Whether or not it is correct to suppose that something like this is the argument that Paley actually intended to set out in his *Natural Theology*, we can certainly subject this argument to critical analysis.

Perhaps the most obvious question to ask about this argument concerns the third premise. According to the theory of evolution, complex and apparently designed natural phenomena can be produced, given sufficient time and a suitable environment, by natural selection. Since evolutionary theory offers a serious alternative hypothesis which explains the various facts mentioned in the first premise of the argument, it seems that the third premise is straightforwardly false. Moreover, it is hardly controversial to claim that it is not merely that there is a competing explanation that does *about as well* as the hypothesis of intelligent design in accounting for the observed facts; there is actually a competing explanation that gives a *much better* explanation of these facts. After Darwin, it is just impossible for sufficiently well informed people to suppose that the third premise of this argument is true.

Apart from the evident difficulty that arises for the third premise of this argument, there are also questions to be asked about the second premise. In particular, there is this question: why should it be supposed that, whenever we make Paley's observations (i)–(iii), we *should* infer that we are in the presence of intelligent design? True enough, we know that there are *some* cases in which products of intelligent design do support observations of this kind. But why is it better, in other cases, to infer that we are in the presence of intelligent design rather than to allow that we *don't know* why it is that these objects support the observations that they do?

7. Paley's argument is sometimes interpreted as positing an analogy between (*a*) a watch (or a watch-making watch) and its watchmaker and (*b*) natural organisms and God. Describe in what ways Paley can argue that (*a*) and (*b*) are analogous. How persuasive is the analogical version of Paley's argument? Are there any points where the analogy breaks down?

8. Suppose that we allow that Paley's inference to an intelligent designer is valid. It seems that Paley's argument could be used to justify the inference to a designer of that designer, and a designer of *that* designer, and so on. Set out this argument in your own words. Can you think of a plausible counter-argument on Paley's behalf?

As in the case of our earlier discussions of Aquinas and Anselm, our discussion of Paley has been by no means exhaustive. And, even if there are reasons to be dissatisfied with Paley's argument for design, there are many other teleological arguments for the existence of God that, for all that has been argued here, may do better. If you are interested in further exploration of teleological arguments, you might like to look at:

Leslie, J., *Universes*, London: Routledge, 1989.
Manson, N. (ed.), *God and Design*, London: Routledge, 2003.

Introduction to Hume

David Hume (1711–76) was one of the leading figures of the Enlightenment. He was best-known in his own lifetime for his six-volume *History of England*, but he is now better-known for his major philosophical works – *A Treatise of Human Nature* (1739), *An Enquiry Concerning Human Understanding* (1748), *An Enquiry Concerning the Principles of Morals* (1751) and *Dialogues Concerning Natural Religion* (1779) – and for his essays, including the highly influential 'The Natural History of Religion' (1757). In the 1760s, Hume was Secretary to the Embassy and then chargé d'affaires in Paris; by the end of his life, he enjoyed a reputation as one of the world's leading intellectual figures.

The *Dialogues Concerning Natural Religion* were published posthumously in 1779; although written some time in the decade prior to 1761, publication was delayed because Hume was reluctant to endure the outrage that he expected would accompany this event. Even during his lifetime, Hume was known to reject all versions of received religion, to disbelieve in human immortality, to reject the possibility of reasonable belief in the occurrence of miracles, and to deny that religion could form a proper basis for morality and the regulation of human conduct – all views guaranteed not to conduce to popularity.

The dialogue format of the *Dialogues Concerning Natural Religion* makes it difficult to determine the nature of Hume's own views from the text alone. The three principal participants in the dialogues have very different attitudes towards religion and religious belief. *Demea* is an orthodox rationalist who thinks that the existence of God can be proved by the kinds of arguments given by Anselm and Aquinas. *Cleanthes* is a proponent of eighteenth-century teleological arguments for the existence of God: he thinks that the existence and nature of God can be inferred from a careful examination of the natural world. *Philo* is a more sceptical philosopher, strongly opposed to the arguments of both Demea and Cleanthes. It is a matter for contemporary debate whether Philo is a deist or an agnostic; and it is also a matter for contemporary debate how closely Hume's own views aligned with those of Philo.

In the excerpts that we shall be examining, Philo raises some difficulties for Cleanthes' attempt to infer the nature of God from a careful examination of the natural world. One question to keep in mind when reading these excerpts is how we should suppose that these points bear upon the argument from Paley's *Natural Theology* that we have already examined.

David Hume, *Dialogues Concerning Natural Religion* (selection)

Part V

[1] But to show you still more inconveniences, continued Philo, in your
a→ anthropomorphism; please to take a new survey of your principles. Like effects prove like causes. This is the experimental argument; and this, you say too, is the sole theological argument. Now it is certain, that the liker the effects are, which are seen, and the liker the causes, which are inferred, the stronger is the argument. Every departure on either side diminishes the probability, and renders the experiment less conclusive. You cannot doubt of the principle: neither ought you to reject its consequences.

All the new discoveries in astronomy, which prove the immense grandeur and magnificence of the works of Nature, are so many additional arguments for a Deity, according to the true system of Theism: but according to your hypothesis of experimental Theism, they become so many objections, by removing the effect still farther from all resemblance to the effects of human art and contrivance. . . . If this argument, I say, had any force in former ages; how much greater must it have at present; when the bounds of Nature are so infinitely enlarged, and such a magnificent scene is opened to us? It is still more unreasonable to form our idea of so unlimited a cause from our experience of the narrow productions of human design and invention.

The discoveries by microscopes, as they open a new universe in miniature, are still objections, according to you; arguments, according to me. The farther we push our researches of this kind, we are still led to infer the universal cause of all to be vastly different from mankind, or from any object of human experience and observation.

And what say you to the discoveries in anatomy, chemistry, botany? . . . These surely are no objections, replied Cleanthes: they only discover new instances of art and contrivance. It is still the image of mind reflected on us from innumerable objects. Add, a mind like the human, said Philo. I know of no other, replied Cleanthes. And the liker the better, insisted Philo. To be sure, said Cleanthes.

[2] Now, Cleanthes, said Philo, with an air of alacrity and triumph, mark
b→ the consequences. First, By this method of reasoning, you renounce all claim to infinity in any of the attributes of the Deity. For as the cause ought only to be proportioned to the effect, and the effect, so far as it falls under our cognisance, is not infinite; what pretensions have we, upon your suppositions, to ascribe that attribute to the divine Being? You will still insist, that, by removing him so much from all similarity to human creatures, we give

in to the most arbitrary hypothesis, and at the same time weaken all proofs of his existence.

c → Secondly, You have no reason, on your theory, for ascribing perfection to the Deity, even in his finite capacity; or for supposing him free from every error, mistake, or incoherence in his undertakings. There are many inexplicable difficulties in the works of Nature, which, if we allow a perfect Author to be proved *a priori*, are easily solved, and become only seeming difficulties, from the narrow capacity of man, who cannot trace infinite relations. But according to your method of reasoning, these difficulties become all real; and perhaps will be insisted on, as new instances of likeness to human art and contrivance. At least, you must acknowledge, that it is impossible for us to tell, from our limited views, whether this system contains any great faults, or deserves any considerable praise, if compared to other possible, and even real systems. Could a peasant, if the Aeneid were read to him, pronounce that poem to be absolutely faultless, or even assign to it its proper rank among the productions of human wit; he, who had never seen any other production?

But were this world ever so perfect a production, it must still remain uncertain, whether all the excellences of the work can justly be ascribed to the workman. If we survey a ship, what an exalted idea must we form of the ingenuity of the carpenter, who framed so complicated, useful, and beautiful a machine? And what surprise must we feel, when we find him a stupid mechanic, who imitated others, and copied an art, which, through a long succession of ages, after multiplied trials, mistakes, corrections, deliberations, and controversies, had been gradually improving? Many worlds might have been botched and bungled, throughout an eternity, ere this system was struck out: much labour lost: many fruitless trials made: and a slow, but continued improvement carried on during infinite ages in the art of world-making. In such subjects, who can determine, where the truth; nay, who can conjecture where the probability, lies; amidst a great number of hypotheses which may be proposed, and a still greater number which may be imagined?

d → And what shadow of an argument, continued Philo, can you produce, from your hypothesis, to prove the unity of the Deity? A great number of men join in building a house or ship, in rearing a city, in framing a commonwealth: why may not several Deities combine in contriving and framing a world? This is only so much greater similarity to human affairs. By sharing the work among several, we may so much further limit the attributes of each, and get rid of that extensive power and knowledge, which must be supposed in one deity, and which, according to you, can only serve to weaken the proof of his existence. And if such foolish, such vicious creatures as man can yet often unite in framing and executing one plan; how much more those deities or daemons, whom we may suppose several degrees more perfect?

e → To multiply causes, without necessity, is indeed contrary to true philosophy: but this principle applies not to the present case. Were one deity antecedently proved by your theory, who were possessed of every attribute, requisite to the production of the universe; it would be needless, I own (though not absurd) to suppose any other deity existent. But while it is still a question, Whether all these attributes are united in one subject, or dispersed among several independent beings: by what phenomena in nature can we pretend to decide the controversy? Where we see a body raised in a scale, we are sure that there is in the opposite scale, however concealed from sight, some counterpoising weight equal to it: but it is still allowed to doubt, whether that weight be an aggregate of several distinct bodies, or one uniform united mass. And if the weight requisite very much exceeds any thing which we have ever seen conjoined in any single body, the former supposition becomes still more probable and natural. An intelligent being of such vast power and capacity, as is necessary to produce the universe, or, to speak in the language of ancient philosophy, so prodigious an animal, exceeds all analogy, and even comprehension.

In a word, Cleanthes, a man, who follows your hypothesis, is able, perhaps, to assert, or conjecture, that the universe, sometime, arose from something like design: but beyond that position he cannot ascertain one single circumstance, and is left afterwards to fix every point of his theology, by the utmost licence of fancy and hypothesis. This world, for aught he knows, is very faulty and imperfect, compared to a superior standard; and was only the first rude essay of some infant Deity, who afterwards abandoned it, ashamed of his lame performance: it is the work only of some dependent, inferior deity; and is the object of derision to his superiors: it is the production of old age and dotage in some superannuated deity; and ever since his death, has run on at adventures, from the first impulse and active force, which it received from him. You justly give signs of horror, Demea, at these strange suppositions: but these, and a thousand more of the same kind, are Cleanthes's suppositions, not mine. From the moment the attributes of the Deity are supposed finite, all these have place. And I cannot, for my part, think, that so wild and unsettled a system of theology is, in any respect, preferable to none at all.

[3] These suppositions I absolutely disown, cried Cleanthes: they strike me, however, with no horror; especially, when proposed in that rambling
 way in which they drop from you. On the contrary, they give me pleasure, when I see, that, by the utmost indulgence of your imagination, you never get rid of the hypothesis of design in the universe; but are obliged, at every turn, to have recourse to it. To this concession I adhere steadily; and this I regard as a sufficient foundation for religion.

Part VI

It must be a slight fabric, indeed, said Demea, which can be erected on so tottering a foundation. While we are uncertain, whether there is one deity or many; whether the deity or deities, to whom we owe our existence, be perfect or imperfect, subordinate or supreme, dead or alive; what trust or confidence can we repose in them? What devotion or worship address to them? What veneration or obedience pay them? To all the purposes of life, the theory of religion becomes altogether useless: and even with regard to speculative consequences, its uncertainty, according to you, must render it totally precarious and unsatisfactory.

g→ To render it still more unsatisfactory, said Philo, there occurs to me another hypothesis, which must acquire an air of probability from the method of reasoning so much insisted on by Cleanthes. That like effects arise from like causes: this principle he supposes the foundation of all religion. But there is another principle of the same kind, no less certain, and derived from the same source of experience; That where several known circumstances are observed to be similar, the unknown will also be found similar. Thus, if we see the limbs of a human body, we conclude, that it is also attended with a human head, though hid from us. Thus, if we see, through a chink in a wall, a small part of the sun, we conclude, that, were the wall removed, we should see the whole body. In short, this method of reasoning is so obvious and familiar, that no scruple can ever be made with regard to its solidity.

Now if we survey the universe, so far as it falls under our knowledge, it bears a great resemblance to an animal or organized body, and seems actuated with a like principle of life and motion. A continual circulation of matter in it produces no disorder: a continual waste in every part is incessantly repaired: the closest sympathy is perceived throughout the entire system: and each part or member, in performing its proper offices, operates both to its own preservation and to that of the whole. The world, therefore, I infer, is an animal, and the Deity is the Soul of the world, actuating it, and actuated by it.

You have too much learning, Cleanthes, to be at all surprised at this opinion, which, you know, was maintained by almost all the Theists of antiquity, and chiefly prevails in their discourses and reasonings. For though sometimes the ancient philosophers reason from final causes, as if they thought the world the workmanship of God; yet it appears rather their favourite notion to consider it as his body, whose organization renders it subservient to him. And it must be confessed, that as the universe resembles more a human body than it does the works of human art and contrivance; if our limited analogy could ever, with any propriety, be extended to the whole of nature, the inference seems juster in favour of the ancient than the modern theory.

[4] Why then, replied Cleanthes, it seems to me, that, though the world does, in many circumstances, resemble an animal body; yet is the analogy also defective in many circumstances, the most material: no organs of sense; no seat of thought or reason; no one precise origin of motion and action. In short, it seems to bear a stronger resemblance to a vegetable than to an animal, and your inference would be so far inconclusive in favour of the soul of the world.

But, in the next place, your theory seems to imply the eternity of the world; and that is a principle which, I think, can be refuted by the strongest reasons and probabilities. I shall suggest an argument to this purpose, h→ which, I believe, has not been insisted on by any writer. Those, who reason from the late origin of arts and sciences, though their inference wants not force, may perhaps be refuted by considerations, derived from the nature of human society, which is in continual revolution between ignorance and knowledge, liberty and slavery, riches and poverty; so that it is impossible for us, from our limited experience, to foretell with assurance what events may or may not be expected. Ancient learning and history seem to have been in great danger of entirely perishing after the inundation of the barbarous nations; and had these convulsions continued a little longer, or been a little more violent, we should not probably have now known what passed in the world a few centuries before us. Nay, were it not for the superstition of the Popes, who preserved a little jargon of Latin, in order to support the appearance of an ancient and universal church, that tongue must have been utterly lost: in which case, the Western world, being totally barbarous, would not have been in a fit disposition for receiving the Greek language and learning, which was conveyed to them after the sacking of Constantinople. When learning and books had been extinguished, even the mechanical arts would have fallen considerably to decay; and it is easily imagined, that fable or tradition might ascribe to them a much later origin than the true one. This vulgar argument, therefore, against the eternity of the world, seems a little precarious.

But here appears to be the foundation of a better argument. Lucullus was the first that brought cherry-trees from Asia to Europe; though that tree thrives so well in many European climates, that it grows in the woods without any culture. Is it possible, that, throughout a whole eternity, no European had ever passed into Asia, and thought of transplanting so delicious a fruit into his own country? Or if the tree was once transplanted and propagated, how could it ever afterwards perish? Empires may rise and fall; liberty and slavery succeed alternately; ignorance and knowledge give place to each other; but the cherry-tree will still remain in the woods of Greece, Spain and Italy, and will never be affected by the revolutions of human society.

It is not two thousand years since vines were transplanted into France; though there is no climate in the world more favourable to them. It is not three centuries since horses, cows, sheep, swine, dogs, corn, were known in America. Is it possibly, that, during the revolutions of a whole eternity, there never arose a Columbus, who might open the communication between Europe and that continent? We may as well imagine, that all men would wear stockings for ten thousand years, and never have the sense to think of garters to tie them. All these seem convincing proofs of the youth, or rather infancy of the world; as being founded on the operation of principles more constant and steady, than those by which human society is governed and directed. Nothing less than a total convulsion of the elements will ever destroy all the European animals and vegetables, which are now to be found in the Western world.

[5] And what argument have you against such convulsions? replied Philo. Strong and almost incontestable proofs may be traced over the whole earth, that every part of this globe has continued for many ages entirely covered with water. And though order were supposed inseparable from matter, and inherent in it; yet may matter be susceptible of many and great revolutions, through the endless periods of eternal duration. The incessant changes, to which every part of it is subject, seem to intimate some such general transformations; though at the same time, it is observable, that all the changes and corruptions, of which we have ever had experience, are but passages from one state of order to another; nor can matter ever rest in total deformity and confusion. What we see in the parts, we may infer in the whole; at least, that is the method of reasoning on which you rest your whole theory. And were I obliged to defend any particular system of this nature (which I never willingly should do) I esteem none more plausible, than that which ascribes an eternal, inherent principle of order to the world; though attended with great and continual revolutions and alterations. This at once solves all difficulties; and if the solution, by being so general, is not entirely complete and satisfactory, it is, at least, a theory, that we must, sooner or later, have recourse to, whatever system we embrace. How could things have been as they are, were there not an original, inherent principle of order somewhere, in thought or in matter? And it is very indifferent to which of these we give the preference. Chance has no place, on any hypothesis, sceptical or religious. Every thing is surely governed, by steady, inviolable laws. And were the inmost essence of things laid open to us, we should then discover a scene, of which, at present, we can have no idea. Instead of admiring the order of natural beings, we should clearly see that it was absolutely impossible for them, in the smallest article, ever to admit of any other disposition.

Were any one inclined to revive the ancient Pagan Theology, which maintained, as we learned from Hesiod, that this globe was governed by 30,000 deities, who arose from the unknown powers of nature: you would naturally object, Cleanthes, that nothing is gained by this hypothesis; and that it is as easy to suppose all men animals, beings more numerous, but less perfect, to have sprung immediately from a like origin. Push the same inference a step farther; and you will find a numerous society of deities as explicable as one universal deity, who possesses, within himself, the powers and perfections of the whole society. All these systems, then, of Scepticism, Polytheism, and Theism, you must allow, on your principles, to be on a like footing, and that no one of them has any advantage over the others. You may thence learn the fallacy of your principles.

Commentary on Hume

The text divides reasonably naturally into parts following the allocation of lines to the participants in the dialogues. In section [1], we have a brief summary of the argument that Cleanthes espouses. In section [2], Philo presents a series of objections to the idea that Cleanthes' argument provides a good reason to believe that the world was created by something like the Christian God. In section [3], Philo proposes an alternative hypothesis about the origins of the world. In section [4], Cleanthes makes some objections to this alternative hypothesis. Finally, in section [5], Philo responds to the objections made by Cleanthes.

The formulation of the argument for design that Hume puts into the mouth of Cleanthes in section [1] is a species of argument from analogy. The basic principle, given at [a]→, is that we infer like causes from like effects, with the strength of the inference depending upon the degree of similarity of the effects. Applied to the case of the natural world, the argument runs in the following way: *The world and its parts are similar to the products of human intelligent design: watches, cities, and the like. Since watches, cities, and the like are the products of human intelligent design, we can draw the conclusion that the world and its parts are the products of something very much like human intelligent design, namely, divine intelligent design.*

As we noted in our earlier discussion of Paley's argument for design, this is not the standard way in which the traditional argument for design is now formulated. In current formulations, the analogical principle upon which Cleanthes relies is replaced by a principle of inference to the best explanation. The argument then develops in something like the following way: *The world and its parts exhibit features that give the world the appearance of intelligent design. The best explanation of why it is that the world and its parts exhibit these features is that world and its parts are the products of intelligent design. Hence, we can draw the conclusion that the world and its parts are the products of divine intelligent design.* As we consider the objections that are developed against the argument defended by Cleanthes, we should also consider whether these are strong objections against formulations of the argument for design that rely upon the principle of inference to the best explanation.

1. From your reading of the chapter on Paley, is Hume's version of the design argument a fair representation of Paley's argument?

2. Here are a couple of arguments from analogy:

(i) I know from my own experience that certain experiences generate feelings and emotions in me and result in my acting in various ways. I know that other people are anatomically similar, and I can observe them reacting to different stimuli as I do. So, by analogy, it follows that other people also have similar mental states.

(ii) The Yamaha MT03 is a well-designed middleweight motorbike. The Kawasaki Z750 is a middleweight motorbike in the same price range. So the Kawasaki is also a well-designed bike.

Specify the analogy posited in each argument. What are their strengths and weaknesses as arguments?

In section [2], Philo begins his assault on the idea that Cleanthes' argument for design might be 'the sole theological argument'. If you suppose that we should infer 'like causes from like effects', then what we should conclude about the nature of the designer depends upon the similarity of the effects – the world and its parts – to the products of human intelligent design. Given the assumption that the world and its parts are very similar to – though grander in scale than – the products of human intelligent design, it seems that Cleanthes' principle will license the conclusion that the designers of the world and its parts are very similar to – though grander in scale than – human intelligent designers. However – as Philo takes great delight in observing – there is no way that Cleanthes' principle can license the conclusion that there is just one designer of the world and its parts (at [d]↦), or that the designers of the world and its parts are perfect (at [c]↦), or that the designers of the world and its parts are infinite (at [b]↦), and so on. If Cleanthes' argument is 'the sole theological argument', then theological argument cannot establish the existence of the God of the major monotheistic religions. (It is worth noting that the same conclusion would seem to hold in the case of formulations of the argument for design that rely upon the principle of inference to the best explanation. How could we pretend that the best explanation *requires* the assumption that there is just one designer of the world and its parts, or that the designers of the world and its parts are perfect, or that the designers of the world and its parts are infinite, and so on?)

3. In the paragraph beginning with [c]↦, Hume expands on his point that the analogy does not warrant attributing perfection to God. Explain and evaluate the points he makes in this paragraph.

4. Explain and evaluate Hume's argument at [d]↦ that the analogy does not warrant the conclusion that there is just one deity. How does Hume respond in [e]↦ to the counter-argument that it is simpler to suppose that there is only one deity? Is his response persuasive?

In response to Philo's initial barrage of criticism, Cleanthes observes at [f]↦ that Philo's attack has done nothing to dislodge confidence in the claim that the world and its parts are the products of intelligent design: at best, Philo has undermined confidence in the claim that the world has been designed by the God of the major monotheistic religions. None the less, Cleanthes still continues to insist that his 'sole theological argument' does provide 'a sufficient foundation for religion'.

Philo responds to Cleanthes' observation by asking whether it is really true that the world and its parts are *most like* the products of human intelligent design: watches, cities, and the like. In the rest of section [3], Philo sets out and defends the claim that the world is rather more like an animal or a human being than it is like a watch – and infers from this claim that 'the Deity is the soul of the world, actuating it, and actuated by it'. And, in the following part of the *Dialogues* – not here included – Philo advances similar considerations in connection with the claim that the world is rather more like a vegetable than it is like a watch, and infers that the world is more likely a product of 'vegetative generation' than a product of intelligent design.

5. At [g]→, Philo introduces a second principle of analogy. Explain this principle and its role in the following argument. Is the principle plausible?

If it is granted that the world is more like an animal, or a vegetable, or something else that is clearly not the product of human intelligent design, then it does seem plausible to suppose that Cleanthes' argument is in serious trouble. In section [4], Cleanthes objects to the suggestion that the world is much like an animal; and he also objects to the claim – implicit in Philo's formulation of the hypothesis that the world is an animal – that the world is infinitely old. Against the hypothesis that the world is like an animal, Cleanthes observes that the world has 'no organs of sense, no seat of thought or reason, and no one precise origin of motion and action'. While these claims are clearly correct, it is not clear that they save the position that Cleanthes defends. After all, Philo is only arguing for the conclusion that the world is *more like* an animal than it is like a typical product of human intelligent design: and it is clearly no less true that there are respects in which the world is not much like a typical product of human intelligent design. For example, the machines that we make all have external energy inputs and external energy outputs, and, in the case where they involve motion and action, 'one precise origin of motion and action'.

Cleanthes spends much more time developing an interesting argument against the eternity of the world, ending with the observation that 'nothing less than a total convulsion of the elements will ever destroy all the European animals and vegetables which are now to be found in the Western world'. While (alas!) we could now reply to Cleanthes that it may well be that something much less than a total convulsion of the elements will destroy all the European animals and vegetables, Philo argues – in section [5] – that Cleanthes does not have good reason to reject the claim that there has been an endless succession of total convulsions of the elements, interspersed with periods of order, and all governed by steady, inviolable laws of nature. Even though Philo may have been right that Cleanthes did not have good reason to reject the claim that there has been an endless succession of total convulsions of the elements, it seems that modern cosmology does give us good reason to reject that claim – and, with it, to reject Philo's speculation that the world is an eternal animal.

6. Summarise in your own words the 'vulgar' argument that Cleanthes-Hume gives at [h]→. Why does he claim that the argument given in the rest of [4] makes for a better argument?

Even if it is true that Cleanthes is on the winning side in the battle over the view that the world is an eternal animal, it is not clear that Cleanthes is on the winning side in the war over the claim that the world and its parts are *most like* the products of human intelligent design: watches, cities, and the like. However, in order to see how Hume develops the further details of that war, you will need to have a look at other sections of the *Dialogues* that have not been included in the present work.

It is perhaps worth noting here that the war over the claim that the world and its parts are *most like* the products of human intelligent design – watches, cities, and the like – does not obviously touch 'inference to the best explanation' formulations of arguments for design. If the world and watches are alike only in exhibiting characteristics that are clear marks of intelligent design – e.g. Paley's composition by many parts all of which make an essential contribution to the functioning of the whole, possession of parts all having shapes and material constitutions well suited to the roles that the parts play, etc. – that will still suffice to underwrite a strong inference to intelligent design, even if there are many respects in which the world and watches are quite dissimilar.

7. Say, giving reasons, whether you think that the world exhibits the features that Paley takes to be distinctive marks of intelligent design. Specifically: (i) Is the world composed of many parts all of which make an essential contribution to the functioning of the whole? (ii) Does the world possess parts all having shapes and material constitutions well suited to the roles that the parts play? (iii) Would relatively small changes in the shapes and arrangement of the parts of the world destroy the functioning of the world?

For further discussion of Hume's views on religion, and assistance in further investigation of the *Dialogues Concerning Natural Religion*, you might like to look at:

Gaskin, J., *Hume's Philosophy of Religion*, 2nd edn, Atlantic Highlands, NJ: Humanities Press International, 1988.

O'Connor, D., *Hume on Religion*, New York: Routledge, 2001.

Yandell, K., *Hume's 'Inexplicable Mystery': His Views on Religion*, Philadelphia, Pa: Temple University Press, 1990.

Introduction to Everitt

Nicholas Everitt is the author of *The Non-existence of God* (2004). At the time of publication of this book, Everitt was a Senior Lecturer in Philosophy at the University of East Anglia. Everitt is also the co-author (with Alec Fisher) of *Modern Epistemology* (1995), as well as of a range of articles on divers topics in the philosophy of religion (including ontological arguments, the possibility of miracles, and ways of understanding the hypothesis of divine eternity).

We have selected an excerpt from his book which presents an 'argument from scale' against the existence of God. Everitt's 'argument from scale' bears some similarity to arguments about the existence of God that have been discussed in previous generations. Thus, for example, in 1817, in his *Discourses on the Christian Revelation Viewed in Connection with the Modern Astronomy*, Thomas Chambers undertook to criticise an argument which began with the 'assertion' that Christianity is set up for the exclusive benefit of our minute and solitary world, and then 'argued' that God would not lavish such a quantity of attention on so insignificant a field. However, the argument that Everitt defends is clearly different from the argument that Chambers attacks, and it is also plainly an argument that is worthy of further attention.

Everitt's presentation of the argument in his book is followed by a discussion of five possible responses that might be made to the argument from scale. Here we have not included Everitt's discussion of these possible objections; however, we shall include our own discussion of some of these objections. If you are interested in Everitt's own take on these five objections, you can follow this up in his book.

Nicholas Everitt, *The Non-existence of God*, ch. 5 (selection)

[1] The first argument against theism which we consider is a modest science-based argument, and it aims to show that the picture of the universe with which modern science presents us constitutes evidence against the truth of theism. The evidence by itself is not very strong, certainly not overwhelming, but it is nonetheless significant. Traditional theism presents us with a certain picture of God and of his intentions in creating the universe at large, and in creating human beings in particular. In general, if someone hypothesises that there is an agent with a certain nature and a certain set of intentions, then we can form some idea of what the agent is likely to do – in what respect things will be different just in virtue of the hypothesised agent's having that nature, those beliefs, and that intention. If we then discover that the world is not as we have predicted, then we have evidence that the initial hypothesis that there was such an agent is mistaken. The argument thus has the form:

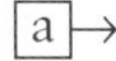

1. If there is an agent with nature N, beliefs B, and intention I, then he will produce change C in the world.
2. The world does not display C.
3. (So) There is evidence against the hypothesis that there is an agent with N and I and B.

[2] As an example of the argument at work in an uncontroversial context, consider an updated Robinson Crusoe. Suppose he considers the

hypothesis that elsewhere on the island with him is another survivor of the shipwreck similar to Crusoe himself in his physical and mental capacities, including his beliefs, and with the intention of making contact with any other survivors, such as Crusoe. Even given as vague and impoverished a hypothesis as this, Crusoe can make some predictions about what the hypothetical survivor will do. He can formulate in his mind a range of what he might call apt behaviour, and a range of inapt behaviour, which the survivor might display – apt and inapt relative to the intention with which Crusoe has tentatively credited him. It would be apt if, for example, the survivor left visible signs of his presence on the island (marks on trees, scratchings on rocks, carefully arranged pieces of wood or stone). It would be apt if he emitted characteristically human noises (whistling, singing, shouting, etc.). It would be apt if he lit a fire and tried to send smoke signals. These would be apt pieces of behaviour because they are just the sorts of things which a Crusoe-like survivor would do if he were trying to let other possible survivors know of his existence on the island. By contrast, it would not be apt if the hypothetical survivor, for example, found some deep undergrowth and lay in it, quiet and still, for the greater part of each day. It would not be apt if after being in any location on the island, he carefully removed all signs of his presence (footprints, ashes from fires, etc.). And so on. These are not apt ways of realising the intention of making your presence known to another human being who might be in the vicinity. They are not the kind of actions which it would be reasonable for Crusoe to expect another survivor to pursue, given the intentions and beliefs with which Crusoe is crediting him.

So, even before starting his empirical investigation of the island, Crusoe can formulate to himself a description of what evidence would help to confirm his initial hypothesis, and what evidence would help to disconfirm it. If he looks hard and carefully for evidence of what we have called apt behaviour, and finds none, that constitutes some evidence against his initial hypothesis that there is another survivor. It is evidence for saying that either there is no actual survivor, or if there is one, the initial hypothesis
[b]→ was wrong about either his capacities or his intentions. In saying that some kinds of behaviour by the hypothetical survivor would be 'inapt', we do not mean that it *absolutely disproves* the initial hypothesis about the survivor's capacities and intentions, but rather that it constitutes *evidence against* the hypothesis. The evidence is defeasible in that it is possible that there is some factor of which Crusoe is unaware which would explain away its initial anti-hypothesis import. (Perhaps the survivor is injured, or even unconscious.) But if he does not discover any such factor, he would be justified in concluding that the initial hypothesis is to some degree disconfirmed.

[3] Let us see now how considerations of this kind can be applied on a cosmic scale, and how the nature of the universe as revealed by modern science gives us reason to reject traditional theism.

Consider, first, the account of God's nature and purposes with which theism presents us. Theism tells us that God is a being who is omnipotent and omniscient, wholly self-sufficient, with no needs, or lacks, or deficiencies of any kind. For reasons that are not entirely clear, God decides to create a universe in which human beings will be the jewel. Although he will have a care for the whole of his creation, God will have an especial care for human beings. He will give these creatures the power of free choice. Exactly what this power is, no one can agree. Some think that it is a capacity the possession of which is incompatible with the truth of determinism; others think that it is a kind of freedom which is compatible with determinism, and which perhaps even requires determinism. Because humans are the jewel of creation, the rest of the universe will be at least not unremittingly hostile or even indifferent to human flourishing. Even if the universe will not make such flourishing immediately and easily and painlessly accessible, it will make it at least accessible in principle for humanity at large. The question then to ask is: what sort of universe would you expect to find? Which of all the possible worlds that God could create would you expect him to create, given this much knowledge of his nature and of his overall plan?

As with our example of Robinson Crusoe, it is difficult to answer this [c] question in any great detail. The description of God is so sketchy, and in particular the theistic hypothesis gives us so little information about his aims, that a large number of possible worlds are left equally likely. But among the more likely scenarios is a universe somewhat like the one [d] presented to us in the story of Genesis. In particular, traditional theism would lead you to expect human beings to appear fairly soon after the start of the universe. For, given the central role of humanity, what would be the point of a universe which came into existence and then existed for unimaginable aeons without the presence of the very species that supplied its [e] rationale? You would expect humans to appear after a great many animals, since the animals are subordinate species available for human utilisation, and there would be no point in having humans arrive on the scene needing animals (e.g. as a source of food, or clothing, or companionship) only [f] for them to discover that animals have not yet been created. But equally, you would not expect humans to arrive very long after the animals, for what would be the point of a universe existing for aeons full of animals [g] created for humanity's delectation, in the absence of any humans? Further, you would expect the earth to be fairly near the centre of the universe if it had one, or at some similarly significant location if it did not have an [h] actual centre. You would expect the total universe to be not many orders of magnitude greater than the size of the earth. The universe would be [i] on a *human* scale. You would expect that even if there are regions of the created world which are hostile to human life, and which perhaps are incompatible with it, the greater part of the universe would be accessible to human exploration. If this were not so, what would the point be of God creating it?

[4] These expectations are largely what we find in the Genesis story (or, strictly, stories) of creation. There is, then, a logic to the picture of the universe with which the Genesis story presents us: given the initial assumptions about God, his nature, and his intentions, the Genesis universe is pretty much how it would be reasonable for God to proceed. Given the hypothesis of theism and no scientific knowledge, and then asked to construct a picture of the universe and its creation, it is not surprising that the author(s) of Genesis came up with the account that they did. It is not that God would have had to proceed in the Genesis way (just as there is not just one kind of behaviour which a possible island survivor would need to produce to confirm Crusoe's initial hypothesis), and it is not that every non-Genesis way would be extremely puzzling. There is in fact a wide range of possible universes which God could have created and about which there would not be a puzzle of the form 'But how could a universe like [j→] that be an expression of a set of intentions like those?' Nevertheless, we can still draw a distinction between universes which would be apt, given the initial hypothesis, and universes which would be inapt. The Genesis universe is clearly an apt one, given the theistic hypothesis; but a universe in which (say) most humans could survive only by leading lives of great and endless pain would be a surprising one for God to choose, given the other assumptions that we make about him.

[5] The question now to raise is 'Is the universe as it is revealed to us by modern science roughly the sort of universe which we would antecedently expect a God of traditional theism to create? Is it an apt universe, given the admittedly sketchy conception we have of his nature and his intentions?'

The short answer to this is 'No'. In almost every respect, the universe as it is revealed to us by modern science is hugely unlike the sort of universe which the traditional thesis would lead us to expect. Although the bare quantitative facts will be familiar to many readers, it is worth repeating them. First, in terms of age: our best estimates are that the universe itself is very roughly 15 billion years, and the Earth is roughly 5 billion years old. How long humans have existed will depend partly on what we take a human to be. But if we take humans to be homo sapiens, and it we take them to be creatures with some sort of language and some sort of social culture, then realistic estimates would allow that they have existed for no more than 100,000 years. So if we imagine the history of the universe represented by a line which is roughly 24 miles long, human life would occupy only the last inch. Of it we imagine this history of the universe represented by a single year, humanity would emerge only in the last few seconds of the last minute of the last hour of the last day of the year. So for something more than 99.999 per cent of the history of the universe, the very creatures which are meant to be the jewel of creation have been absent from it. The question that at once arises is 'What, given the hypothesis of theism, was the point of this huge discrepancy between the age of the universe and the age of humanity?'. How very inapt a creation of that kind must strike us.

The same story recurs if we turn to the size of the universe. Suppose we take the size of our solar system to be within the expectable parameters of the theistic hypothesis. (This might seem over-generous to theism: why would God need a solar system as big as ours to achieve any of his purposes? Why does he need a sun that is 93 *million* miles from earth? Why wouldn't 93 thousand miles have been enough? Of course the laws of physics would then have had to be different if the sun were to make earth habitable – but as an omnipotent being, God could easily have adjusted the laws of physics. However, let us overlook this and allow that a distance of 93 million miles counts as intelligible – it is intelligible, that is, that God with the nature and intentions ascribed by traditional theism should create a universe that big.) But of course, we know now that the universe is staggeringly larger than any such intelligible size. The sun is about 8 light minutes from us, the next nearest star is about 4.3 light years, the next nearest galaxy to the Milky Way is scores of light years away. Current findings indicate that the furthest star visible from the earth is about 3 billion light years away. In other words, the most distant star is very roughly some 200, 000, 000, 000, 000, 000 times (two hundred million trillion times) as far from us as the sun. This sort of scale to the universe makes no conceivable sense on the theistic hypothesis. Nor should we assume that the most distant visible star is the most distant detectable entity. The furthest galaxy, detectable only by radio telescopes is reckoned to be about 3 times further away – 9 billion light years. The possible limits of the universe lie further away still. If the Big Bang occurred about 15 billion years ago, and if the expansion had occurred at the speed of light, the limits of the universe would be about 30 billion light years. Assuming that the expansion was at less than light speed, that still leaves the possibility of a universe whose overall size is between 10 and 30 billion light years across (i.e. up to two million trillion miles). Why would a God make it that big?

Further, astronomers tell us that there are about 100 trillion galaxies, each with a billion stars (giving us something of the order of 100, 000, 000, 000, 000, 000, 000, 000 stars) ([Sarah Woodward, 'Things to Come', *Cambridge Alumni Magazine*, 30 (2000): 25]). It could count as apt if a creator created a universe with one star or perhaps a few dozen or even a few hundred, so that the night sky were as beautiful as we now find it. But what could be the point of the huge superabundance of celestial matter, especially given the fact that the very great majority of humanity will never be aware of most of it? Again, given the theistic hypothesis, it is strikingly inapt.

If we confine our attention to the earth, the same extraordinary inaptness confronts us. The Genesis story presents God's actions as apt in relation to the non-human creatures who share the planet with humans: they all emerge at about the same time; and all the creatures which surround humanity in that story share a human scale – none are so tiny that it is impossible to detect them by the senses, and none are so huge (e.g. thousands or millions of times larger than humans) as to be recognisable as organisms at all. But again, modern science reveals this to be deeply wrong – not just in points of detail, but in almost every major respect. Life has existed on the planet for something like 3 to 3.5 billion years. For roughly half of that time, it has been solely bacterial in form. Given that humans have emerged only in the last 100,000 years, that means that for 99.99 per cent of the history of life on earth, there have been no humans. How very bizarre, given the theistic hypothesis. Further, from a biological point of view 'On any possible or reasonable or fair criterion, bacteria are – and always have been the dominant forms of life on earth' ([Stephen Jay Gould, *Life's Grandeur* (1996): 176]). In terms of their numbers, their longevity, their ability to exploit the widest variety of habitats, their degree of genetic variation, and even (amazingly, given how tiny they are individually) their total biomass, they outstrip every other kind of life. If God had intended any species to flourish, the obvious candidate for divine favour would be bacteria, not humans.

[6] In short, then, everything that modern science tells us about the size and scale and nature of the universe around us reveals it to be strikingly inapt as an expression of a set of divine intentions of the kind that theism postulates. Let us emphasise that the claim here is not that there is a logical incompatibility between these modern scientific findings and traditional theism. It is not that the findings disprove theism. The claim is weaker than that. The claim is only that the findings of modern science significantly reduce the probability that theism is true, because the universe is turning out to be very unlike the sort of universe which we would have expected, had theism been true.

Commentary on Everitt

We have divided Everitt's text into six sections. In section [1], Everitt enunciates a general form of argument. In section [2], Everitt illustrates this form of argument with a particular example. In section [3], Everitt explains how he proposes to argue against the existence of God using the general form of argument set out in section [1]. In section [4], Everitt argues that there would be no compelling argument from scale if the universe conformed roughly to the stories of creation to be found in Genesis. In section [5], Everitt sets out the cosmological data which he takes to underpin the argument from scale. Finally, in section [6], Everitt restates his conclusion: 'the findings of modern science significantly reduce the probability that theism is true, because the universe is turning out to be very unlike the sort of universe which we would have expected, had theism been true'.

1. Explain the distinction in [2] between apt and inapt behaviour.

While there might be room to quibble over the details of the general form of argument that Everitt presents, it does seem that something like the following general form of argument given at [a]→ is plausible:

1. If there were an agent with nature N who acted on beliefs B and intentions I, then the world would have feature C.
2. The world appears not to display feature C.
3. (So) there is evidence against the hypothesis that there is an agent with nature N who acts on beliefs B and intentions I.

Moreover, it seems right to say that the 'Robinson Crusoe' case that Everitt discusses in [2] does provide a plausible illustration of the intuitive attraction of this general argument form. If we see none of the signs that we would expect to observe if there were normal human survivors with standard human beliefs who wished to make their presence known to other survivors – marks on trees, scratchings on rocks, messages composed using sticks and stones, whistling, singing, shouting, smoke signals, campfires, etc. – then we clearly have defeasible reason for thinking that there are no normal human survivors with standard human beliefs who wish to make their presence known to other survivors. Furthermore, in the 'Robinson Crusoe' case, since it is very plausible to think that, if there were normal human survivors with standard human beliefs, they would wish to make their presence known to other survivors, we also have defeasible reason to conclude that there are no normal human survivors with standard human beliefs. That is, at least in the 'Robinson Crusoe' case, we can extend the general argument to arrive at the conclusion that there is no agent with nature N and beliefs B.

4. If there were an agent with nature N and beliefs B, then it would act on intentions I.
5. (So) there is evidence against the hypothesis that there is an agent with nature N and beliefs B.

Finally, in the 'Robinson Crusoe' case, since it is very plausible to suppose that, if there were normal human survivors, they would have standard human beliefs, we even have defeasible reason to conclude that there are no normal human survivors. That is, at least in the 'Robinson Crusoe' case, we can extend the general argument to arrive at the conclusion that there is no agent with nature N.

6. If there were an agent with nature N, then it would have beliefs B.
7. (So) there is evidence against the hypothesis that there is an agent with nature N.

2. At [b]→ Everitt distinguishes between absolutely disproving a hypothesis from having evidence against it. Explain this distinction. How strong should the evidence be against a hypothesis before the hypothesis is rejected? How strong do you think the evidence is against the hypothesis considered here?

3. Develop your own example, akin to the 'Robinson Crusoe' example, and fill out the details for the agent's nature N, beliefs B, interests I and the changes C. Are the arguments at [a]→ and the ones given above also valid for your example?

In order to construct an argument against the existence of God which conforms to the pattern of reasoning that is embodied in the 'Robinson Crusoe' case, we need to make some assumptions about God's nature, beliefs and intentions. Everitt claims that 'theism tells us that God is a being who is omnipotent and omniscient, wholly self-sufficient, with no needs, or lacks, or deficiencies of any kind' and who creates the universe. While there have been theists who have been prepared to deny that God has one or more of the properties that Everitt mentions here, it seems reasonable to say that the vast majority of theists have been prepared to accept this characterisation. But, if that is right, then we have our candidates for N and B in the schematic argument: the nature of God is to be 'an omnipotent, omniscient, and wholly self-sufficient creator of the universe', and – because God is omniscient – it is at least roughly correct to say that God believes exactly those things that are true.

The more controversial part of Everitt's assumptions concerns God's intentions: Everitt says that God 'decides to create a universe in which human beings will be the jewel' – i.e. in creating the universe, God acts on the intention to make a universe in which 'human beings are the jewel'. It is not exactly clear how we should interpret the claim that 'human beings are the jewel'. Everitt goes on to say that

> Because humans are the jewel of creation, the rest of the universe will be at least not unremittingly hostile or even indifferent to human flourishing. Even if the universe will not make such flourishing immediately and easily and painlessly accessible, it will make it at least accessible in principle for humanity at large.

This kind of remark seems to suggest that, if human beings are to be the jewel, then it should be possible for human beings to live in reasonable comfort more or less anywhere in the universe. Understood this way, the remark has the implication that human beings are not, in fact, the jewel (since, of course, it is not true that it is possible for human beings to live in relative comfort more or less anywhere in the universe); and so leads quickly to the conclusion that God does not exist. Moreover, Everitt's subsequent discussion confirms that this is how he understands the claim that human beings are the jewel: human beings have a 'central role' which leads one to expect that they will appear not too long after the start of the universe (at [d]→) and not too long after the appearance of the other living things over which they have dominion (at [f]→), and that the universe will have a human scale not too many orders of magnitude larger than the Earth (at [h]→).

4. Consider the point that Everitt makes at [c]→. In what way does this weaken his argument? Is it a fatal weakness?

Since it is not controversial that human beings have only been around for a tiny fraction of the time that the universe has existed, and it is not controversial that the universe is not on a human scale, and it is not controversial that it is impossible for human beings to live in relative comfort almost anywhere in the universe, if it is true that God would intend to create a universe in which human beings appear not too long after the start of the universe, and not too long after the other living things over which they have dominion, and it is true that God would intend to create a universe on a human scale not too many orders of magnitude larger than the Earth, and it is true that God would make a universe in which it is possible for human beings to live in relative comfort almost everywhere, then it surely follows that our universe was not created by God. But why should we suppose that, if God does exist, God intended to create a universe in which human beings appear not too long after the start of the universe and not too long after the other living things over which they have dominion, and God intended to create a universe on a human scale not too many orders of magnitude larger than the Earth, and God intended to make a universe in which is it possible for human beings to live in relative comfort almost everywhere? Indeed, given the assumption that God is omnipotent and omniscient, surely we can infer that, if God exists, God did not intend to create a universe in which human beings appear not too long after the start of the universe and not too long after the other living things over which they have dominion, and God did not intend to create a universe on a human scale not too many orders of magnitude larger than the Earth, and God did not intend to make a universe in which it is possible for human beings to live in relative comfort almost everywhere!

5. Consider Everitt's points [d]→ to [i]→ in turn. Giving reasons in each case, how confident should we be that [d]→ to [i]→ would occur were theism true?

6. Explain the distinction that Everitt makes at [j]→ between apt and inapt universes.

Against Everitt's claim that there is a mismatch between the kind of universe which one would expect, given the theistic conception of God and his purposes, and the kind of universe which modern science reveals to us, it seems that a theist might object that Everitt simply misunderstands the theistic conception of God and his purposes. For example, it might be true that, given the *full* range of God's creative intentions – including, for example, his intention to create a universe that is governed by physical laws whose workings can only be discovered by human beings at the cost of much investigative labour – there is an explanation for the fact that the universe does not have a human scale. Given the physical laws that our universe in fact obeys, and given the origins of our universe in a Big Bang, there is a very plausible argument to the conclusion that carbon-based life could not have appeared anywhere in the universe much earlier than life appeared on Earth. Given the physical laws that our universe in fact obeys, given the origins of our universe in a Big Bang, and given the observed expansion of the universe, there is a very plausible argument to the conclusion that a universe that contains carbon-based life could not be much smaller than the universe that we observe. Given the physical laws that our universe in fact obeys, given the origins of our universe in a Big

Bang, and given the observed expansion of the universe, there is a very plausible argument to the conclusion that it is bound to be the case that almost none of the universe is hospitable to the existence of carbon-based life. Provided that God has good reason to make a universe that obeys the physical laws that our universe in fact obeys, that originates in a Big Bang, and that expands in the way that our universe expands, then God has good reason to make a universe that is not on a human scale. Moreover, for all that Everitt argues, it seems that it could be the case that God's intention to make human beings the jewel in the crown is precisely what gives God reason to make a universe that obeys the physical laws that our universe in fact obeys, that originates in a Big Bang, and that expands in the way that our universe expands.

Perhaps Everitt might reply that it is surely possible for God to create a universe that is governed by physical laws the workings of which can only be discovered by human beings at the cost of much investigative labour *without* making a universe that obeys the physical laws that our universe in fact obeys, that originates in a Big Bang, and that expands in the way that our universe expands. While there is perhaps some force to this response, it has to be said that it is by no means obvious that there are other possible universes that meet God's creative demands. True enough, it seems that we can *imagine* or *conceive* that there are such universes; but it is not at all clear that this suffices to show that such universes are really *possible*. Moreover, even if it is true that there are other possible universes that meet the demand that they are governed by physical laws the workings of which can only be discovered by human beings at the cost of much investigative labour, we have still to consider the suggestion that there are yet more creative intentions which constrain the kind of universe that God is able to create. While we have considered in some detail the suggestion that God intended to create a universe that is governed by physical laws the workings of which can only be discovered by human beings at the cost of much investigative labour, this suggestion is merely one illustration of a more general point. Whether we should expect that God would create a universe on a human scale, even given the assumption that God wants human beings to be the jewel, depends upon the further assumptions that we make about the other intentions that God has for the universe.

7. Carefully read through the list of features of the universe given in section [5] that Everitt thinks would not have occurred were the theistic hypothesis true. Are there any non-theistic hypotheses that would lead us to expect these (or other) features of the universe?

As we mentioned in our introduction, the argument that Everitt advances bears superficial resemblance to the argument that Thomas Chambers criticises in his *Discourses on the Christian Revelation Viewed in Connection with Modern Astronomy*. The argument that Chambers criticises runs like this: *According to Christians, Christianity is set up for the exclusive benefit of our minute and solitary world. But God would not lavish such a quantity of attention on so insignificant a field. So Christian belief must be mistaken.* Against this argument, Chambers makes two major objections. On the one hand, it is not part of Christian doctrine to insist that Christianity – the resurrection and the atonement – have been set up exclusively for our benefit. For all that Christian doctrine says, there may be countless inhabited planets in the universe, each of which receives its own version of atonement. And, on the other hand, it is hard to see what reason there could be to hold that God would not 'lavish attention' on the inhabitants of the Earth. In particular, since God is omnipotent, it seems that the 'insignificance' of the Earth is entirely irrelevant to considerations about the actions that God takes in relation to human beings. While subsequent investigation has not (yet) given much support to Chambers's attack on the first premise of this argument – at the time of writing, we have discovered about 250 planets orbiting other stars, none showing any evidence of habitation by living creatures – there is good reason to accept the criticism that Chambers makes of the second premise of the argument that he attacks. However, even if it is accepted that an omnipotent and omniscient being would give perfect attention to every aspect of any universe that it creates, it should be clear that this point has no bearing at all on the argument that Everitt defends. As Everitt himself insists, the focus of his argument from scale has nothing to do with the comparative sizes of the human domain and the universe; rather, the focus of his argument is on the expected creative intentions of an omnipotent and omniscient creator.

We can set out the argument that Everitt *actually* defends as follows:

1. If there were an omnipotent, omniscient and wholly self-sufficient being who created the universe, and if that being acted on the intention to make human beings the jewel, then that being would make a universe on a human scale, such that it contains human beings at almost all times, and such that it is at least possible for human beings to exist in almost all places.
2. It is not the case that the universe is on a human scale, such that it contains human beings at almost all times, and such that it is at least possible for human beings to exist in almost all places.
3. (So) there is evidence against the hypothesis that there is an omnipotent, omniscient and wholly self-sufficient being who created the universe and who acted on the intention to make human beings the jewel of the universe.
4. (But) if there were an omnipotent, omniscient and wholly self-sufficient being who created the universe, then that being would have acted on the intention to make human beings the jewel of the universe.
5. (So) there is evidence against the hypothesis that there is an omnipotent, omniscient and wholly self-sufficient being who made the universe.

When we set out the argument in this way, it seems reasonably clear that both premise 1 and premise 4 are open to dispute. In our earlier discussion, we focused on objections to premise 1; however, it is worth noting that premise 4 is also highly questionable. Moreover, it is also worth observing that there may well be some overlap between objections that could reasonably be lodged against Everitt's premise 4 and objections that could reasonably be lodged against the first premise in the argument that Chambers attacks. While it is clearly central to Christian belief to hold that God loves human beings, and that God makes provision for human beings, it is not clear that it must be central to Christian belief to hold that human beings are the jewel of the universe (even if it is true that many earlier generations of Christians accepted this belief).

8. Everitt's argument has the following structure: he identifies features of the universe that we should expect to occur were theism true; he finds that these features do not occur, and presents these as evidence that theism is false. Compare Everitt's argument with the problem of evil. In what ways are these two arguments against theism similar or different?

Because Everitt's argument from scale is relatively new, there is not much else that has been written about it. For recent writings on the cosmological facts that support Everitt's argument – and on the historical development of the relevant cosmological theories – you might like to look at:

Dyson, F., *Infinite in All Directions*, London: Penguin, 1988.
Ferris, T., *Coming of Age in the Milky Way*, London: Vintage, 1988.
North, J., *The Fontana History of Astronomy and Cosmology*, London: HarperCollins, 1994.

Introduction to Mackie

John Leslie Mackie (1917–81) is one of the best-known atheistic philosophers of the second half of the twentieth century. After graduating from the University of Sydney – where he studied under John Anderson – and then completing further studies at Oriel College, Oxford, Mackie held various teaching appointments in the Antipodes: first at Sydney, then at Otago, and then a professorship at Sydney. After a brief sojourn at the University of York, Mackie spent highly productive years from 1967 to 1981 at Oxford.

Mackie is best-known in philosophy of religion for his 1955 paper 'Evil and Omnipotence' – reproduced below – and his posthumous 1982 book *The Miracle of Theism*. The book is almost universally acknowledged to be amongst the very best systematic defences of atheism, and contains penetrating discussions of a wide range of arguments for and against the existence of God. Mackie also wrote important books on other topics, including *Problems from Locke* (1974), *The Cement of the Universe: A Study of Causation* (1974), *Ethics: Inventing Right and Wrong* (1977) and *Hume's Moral Theory* (1980).

'Evil and Omnipotence' is one of the most-cited papers in philosophy of religion; it was responsible for initiating contemporary discussion of logical arguments from evil. While some philosophers of religion now think that Mackie's paper is merely a discredited remnant of the dark days when philosophy was dominated by logical positivism – see, for example, almost all of the contributions to Daniel Howard-Snyder's *The Evidential Argument from Evil* (1996) – we think that there is much to be learned from a close reading of Mackie's paper.

John Leslie Mackie, 'Evil and Omnipotence'

[1] The traditional arguments for the existence of God have been fairly thoroughly criticised by philosophers. But the theologian can, if he wishes, accept this criticism. He can admit that no rational proof of God's existence is possible. And he can still retain all that is essential to his position, by holding that God's existence is known in some other, non-rational way. I think, however, that a more telling criticism can be made by way of the traditional problem of evil. Here it can be shown, not that religious beliefs lack rational support, but that they are positively irrational, that the several parts of the essential theological doctrine are inconsistent with one another, so that the theologian can maintain his position as a whole only by a much more extreme rejection of reason than in the former case. He must now be prepared to believe, not merely what cannot be proved, but what can be *disproved* from other beliefs that he also holds.

The problem of evil, in the sense in which I shall be using the phrase, is a problem only for someone who believes that there is a God who is both omnipotent and wholly good. And it is a logical problem, the problem of clarifying and reconciling a number of beliefs: it is not a scientific problem that might be solved by further observations, or a practical problem that might be solved by a decision or an action. These points are obvious; I mention them only because they are sometimes ignored by theologians, who sometimes parry a statement of the problem with such remarks as 'Well, can you solve the problem yourself?' or 'This is a mystery which may be revealed to us later' or 'Evil is something to be faced and overcome, not to be merely discussed'.

[2] In its simplest form the problem is this: God is omnipotent; God is wholly good; and yet evil exists. There seems to be some contradiction between these three propositions, so that if any two of them were true the third would be false. But at the same time all three are essential parts of most theological positions: the theologian, it seems, at once *must* adhere and *cannot consistently* adhere to all three. (The problem does not arise only for theists, but I shall discuss it in the form in which it presents itself for ordinary theism.)

[3] However, the contradiction does not arise immediately; to show it we need some additional premises, or perhaps some quasi-logical rules connecting the terms 'good', 'evil', and 'omnipotent'. These additional principles are that good is opposed to evil, in such a way that a good thing always eliminates evil as far as it can, and that there are no limits to what an omnipotent thing can do. From these it follows that a good omnipotent thing eliminates evil completely, and then the propositions that a good omnipotent thing exists, and that evil exists, are incompatible.

A. Adequate Solutions

[4] Now once the problem is fully stated it is clear that it can be solved, in the sense that the problem will not arise if one gives up at least one of the propositions that constitute it. If you are prepared to say that God is not wholly good, or not quite omnipotent, or that evil does not exist, or that good is not opposed to the kind of evil that exists, or that there are limits to what an omnipotent thing can do, then the problem of evil will not arise for you.

There are, then, quite a number of adequate solutions of the problem of evil, and some of these have been adopted, or almost adopted, by various thinkers. For example, a few have been prepared to deny God's omnipotence, and rather more have been prepared to keep the term 'omnipotence' but severely to restrict its meaning, recording quite a number of things that an omnipotent being cannot do. Some have said that evil is an illusion, perhaps because they held that the whole world of temporal, changing things is an illusion, and that what we call evil belongs only to this world, or perhaps because they held that although temporal things *are* much as we see them, those that we call evil are not really evil. Some have said that what we call evil is merely the privation of good, that evil in a positive sense, evil that would really be opposed to good, does not exist. Many have agreed with Pope that disorder is harmony not understood, and that partial evil is universal good. Whether any of these views is *true* is, of course, another question. But each of them gives an adequate solution of the problem of evil in the sense that if you accept it this problem does not arise for you, though you may, of course, have *other* problems to face.

[5] But often enough these adequate solutions are only *almost* adopted. The thinkers who restrict God's power, but keep the term 'omnipotence', may reasonably be suspected of thinking, in other contexts, that his power is really unlimited. Those who say that evil is an illusion may also be thinking, inconsistently, that this illusion is itself an evil. Those who say that 'evil' is merely privation of good may also be thinking, inconsistently, that privation of good is an evil. (The fallacy here is akin to some forms of the 'naturalistic fallacy' in ethics, where some think, for example, that 'good' is just what contributes to evolutionary progress, and that evolutionary progress is itself good.) If Pope meant what he said in the first line of his couplet, that 'disorder' is only harmony not understood, the 'partial evil' of the second line must, for consistency, mean 'that which, taken in isolation, falsely appears to be evil', but it would more naturally mean 'that which, in isolation, really is evil'. The second line, in fact, hesitates between two views, that 'partial evil' isn't really evil, since only the universal quality is real, and that 'partial evil' is really an evil, but only a little one.

In addition, therefore, to adequate solutions, we must recognise unsatisfactory inconsistent solutions, in which there is only a half-hearted or temporary rejection of one of the propositions which together constitute the problem. In these, one of the constituent propositions is explicitly rejected, but it is covertly re-asserted or assumed elsewhere in the system.

B. Fallacious Solutions

[6] Besides these half-hearted solutions, which explicitly reject but implicitly assert one of the constituent propositions, there are definitely fallacious solutions which explicitly maintain all the constituent propositions, but implicitly reject at least one of them in the course of the argument that explains away the problem of evil.

There are, in fact, many so-called solutions which purport to remove the contradiction without abandoning any of its constituent propositions. These must be fallacious, as we can see from the very statement of the problem, but it is not so easy to see in each case precisely where the fallacy lies. I suggest that in all cases the fallacy has the general form suggested above: in order to solve the problem one (or perhaps more) of its constituent propositions is given up, but in such a way that it appears to have been retained, and can therefore be asserted without qualification in other contexts. Sometimes there is a further complication: the supposed solution moves to and fro between, say, two of the constituent propositions, at one point asserting the first of these but covertly abandoning the second, at another point asserting the second but covertly abandoning the first. These fallacious solutions often turn upon some equivocation with the words 'good' and 'evil', or upon some vagueness about the way in which good and evil are opposed to one another, or about how much is meant by 'omnipotence'. I propose to examine some of these so-called solutions, and to exhibit their fallacies in detail. Incidentally, I shall also be considering whether an adequate solution could be reached by a minor modification of one or more of the constituent propositions, which would, however, still satisfy all the essential requirements of ordinary theism.

1. 'Good cannot exist without evil' or 'Evil is necessary as a counterpart to good.'

[7] It is sometimes suggested that evil is necessary as a counterpart to good, that if there were no evil there could be no good either, and that this solves the problem of evil. It is true that it points to an answer to the question 'Why should there be evil?' But it does so only by qualifying some of the propositions that constitute the problem. First, it sets a limit to what God can do, saying that God *cannot* create good without simultaneously creating evil, and this means either that God is not omnipotent or that there
a→ are *some* limits to what an omnipotent thing can do. It may be replied that these limits are always presupposed, that omnipotence has never meant the power to do what is logically impossible, and on the present view the existence of good without evil would be a logical impossibility. This

interpretation of omnipotence may, indeed, be accepted as a modification of our original account which does not reject anything that is essential to theism, and I shall in general assume it in the subsequent discussion. It is, perhaps, the most common theistic view, but I think that some theists at least have maintained that God can do what is logically impossible. Many theists, at any rate, have held that logic itself is created or laid down by God, that logic is the way in which God arbitrarily chooses to think. (This is, of course, parallel to the ethical view that morally right actions are those which God arbitrarily chooses to command, and the two views encounter similar difficulties.) And *this* account of logic is clearly inconsistent with the view that God is bound by logical necessities – unless it is possible for an omnipotent being to bind himself, an issue which we shall consider later, when we come to the Paradox of Omnipotence. This solution of the problem of evil cannot, therefore, be consistently adopted along with the view that logic is itself created by God.

b→ But, secondly, this solution denies that evil is opposed to good in our original sense. If good and evil are counterparts, a good thing will not 'eliminate evil as far as it can'. Indeed, this view suggests that good and evil are not strictly qualities of things at all. Perhaps the suggestion is that good and evil are related in much the same way as great and small. Certainly, when the term 'great' is used relatively as a condensation of 'greater than so-and-so', and 'small' is used correspondingly, greatness and smallness are counterparts and cannot exist without each other. But in this sense greatness is not a quality, not an intrinsic feature of anything; and it would be absurd to think of a movement in favour of greatness and against smallness in this sense. Such a movement would be self-defeating, since relative greatness can be promoted only by a simultaneous promotion of relative smallness. I feel sure that no theists would be content to regard God's goodness as analogous to this-as if what he supports were not the good but the better, and as if he had the paradoxical aim that all things should be better than other things.

This point is obscured by the fact that 'great' and 'small' seem to have an absolute as well as a relative sense. I cannot discuss here whether there is absolute magnitude or not, but if there is, there could be an absolute sense for 'great', it could mean of at least a certain size, and it would make sense to speak of all things getting bigger, of a universe that was expanding all over, and therefore it would make sense to speak of promoting greatness. But in this sense great and small are not logically necessary counterparts: either quality could exist without the other. There would be no logical impossibility in everything's being small or in everything's being great.

3. 'The universe is better with some evil in it than it could be if there were no evil.'

[9] Much more important is a solution which at first seems to be a mere variant of the previous one, that evil may contribute to the goodness of a

whole in which it is found, so that the universe as a whole is better as it is, with some evil in it, than it would be if there were no evil. This solution may be developed in either of two ways. It may be supported by an aesthetic analogy, by the fact that contrasts heighten beauty, that in a musical work, for example, there may occur discords which somehow add to the beauty of the work as a whole. Alternatively, it may be worked out in connexion with the notion of progress, that the best possible organisation of the universe will not be static, but progressive, that the gradual overcoming of evil by good is really a finer thing than would be the eternal unchallenged supremacy of good.

In either case, this solution usually starts from the assumption that the evil whose existence gives rise to the problem of evil is primarily what is called physical evil, that is to say, pain. In Hume's rather half-hearted presentation of the problem of evil, the evils that he stresses are pain and disease. and those who reply to him argue that the existence of pain and disease makes possible the existence of sympathy, benevolence, heroism, and the gradually successful struggle of doctors and reformers to overcome these evils. In fact, theists often seize the opportunity to accuse those who stress the problem of evil of taking a low, materialistic view of good and evil, equating these with pleasure and pain, and of ignoring the more spiritual goods which can arise in the struggle against evils.

[10] But let us see exactly what is being done here. Let us call pain and misery 'first order evil' or 'evil (1)'. What contrasts with this, namely, pleasure and happiness, will be called 'first order good' or 'good (1)'. Distinct from this is 'second order good' or 'good (2)' which somehow emerges in a complex situation in which evil (1) is a necessary component – logically, not merely causally, necessary. (Exactly *how* it emerges does not matter: in the crudest version of this solution good (2) is simply the heightening of happiness by the contrast with misery, in other versions it includes sympathy with suffering, heroism in facing danger, and the gradual decrease of first order evil and increase of first order good.) It is also being assumed that second order good is more important than first order good or evil, in particular that it more than outweighs the first order evil it involves.

c → Now this is a particularly subtle attempt to solve the problem of evil. It defends God's goodness and omnipotence on the ground that (on a sufficiently long view) this is the best of all logically possible worlds, because it includes the important second order goods, and yet it admits that real evils, namely first order evils, exist. But does it still hold that good and evil are opposed? Not, clearly, in the sense that we set out originally: good does not tend to eliminate evil in general. Instead, we have a modified, a more complex pattern. First order good (e.g. happiness) contrasts with first order evil (e.g. misery): these two are opposed in a fairly mechanical way; some second order goods (e.g. benevolence) try to maximise first order good and minimise first order evil; but God's goodness is not this, it is rather the will to maximise second order good. We might, therefore, call God's goodness an example of a third order goodness, or good (3). While this account is different from our original one, it might well be held to be an improvement on it, to give a more accurate description of the way in which good is opposed to evil, and to be consistent with the essential theist position.

There might, however, be several objections to this solution.

First, some might argue that such qualities as benevolence – and a fortiori the third order goodness which promotes benevolence – have a merely derivative value, that they are not higher sorts of good, but merely means to good (1), that is, to happiness, so that it would be absurd for God to keep misery in existence in order to make possible the virtues of benevolence, heroism, etc. The theist who adopts the present solution must, of course, deny this, but he can do so with some plausibility, so I should not press this objection.

Secondly, it follows from this solution that God is not in our sense benevolent or sympathetic: he is not concerned to minimise evil (1), but only to promote good (2); and this might be a disturbing conclusion for some theists.

d → But, thirdly, the fatal objection is this. Our analysis shows clearly the possibility of the existence of a second order evil, an evil (2) contrasting with good (2) as evil (1) contrasts with good (1). This would include malevolence, cruelty, callousness, cowardice, and states in which good (1) is decreasing and evil (1) increasing. And just as good (2) is held to be the important kind of good, the kind that God is concerned to promote, so evil (2) will, by analogy, be the important kind of evil, the kind: which God, if he were wholly good and omnipotent, would eliminate. And yet evil (2) plainly exists, and indeed most theists (in other contexts) stress its existence more than that of evil (1). We should, therefore, state the problem of evil in terms of second order evil, and against this form of the problem the present solution is useless.

e → An attempt might be made to use this solution again, at a higher level, to explain the occurrence of evil (2): indeed the next main solution that we shall examine does just this, with the help of some new notions. Without any fresh notions, such a solution would have little plausibility: for example, we could hardly say that the really important good was a good (3), such as the increase of benevolence in proportion to cruelty, which logically required for its occurrence the occurrence of some second order evil. But even if evil (2) could be explained in this way, it is fairly clear that there would be third order evils contrasting with this third order good: and we should be well on the way to an infinite regress, where the solution of a problem of evil, stated in terms of evil (n), indicated the existence of an evil ($n + l$), and a further problem to be solved.

4. 'Evil is due to human freewill.'

[11] Perhaps the most important proposed solution of the problem of evil is that evil is not to be ascribed to God at all, but to the independent

actions of human beings, supposed to have been endowed by God with freedom of the will. This solution may be combined with the preceding one: first order evil (e.g. pain) may be justified as a logically necessary component in second order good (e.g. sympathy) while second order evil (e.g. cruelty) is not *justified*, but is so ascribed to human beings that God cannot be held responsible for it. This combination evades my third criticism of the preceding solution.

The freewill solution also involves the preceding solution at a higher level. To explain why a wholly good God gave men freewill although it would lead to some important evils, it must, be argued that it is better on the whole that men should act freely, and sometimes err, than that they should be innocent automata, acting rightly in a wholly determined way. Freedom, that is to say, is now treated as a third order good, and as being more valuable than second order goods (such as sympathy and heroism) would be if they were deterministically produced, and it is being assumed that second order evils, such as cruelty, are logically necessary accompaniments of freedom, just as pain is a logically necessary pre-condition of sympathy.

I think that this solution is unsatisfactory primarily because of the incoherence of the notion of freedom of the will: but I cannot discuss this topic adequately here, although some of my criticisms will touch upon it.

[12] First I should query the assumption that second order evils are logically necessary accompaniments of freedom. I should ask this: if God has made men such that in their free choices they sometimes prefer what is good and sometimes what is evil, why could he not have made men such that they always freely choose the good? If there is no logical impossibility in a man's freely choosing the good on one, or on several, occasions, there cannot be a logical impossibility in his freely choosing the good on every occasion. God was not, then, faced with a choice between making innocent automata and making beings who, in acting freely, would sometimes go wrong: there was open to him the obviously better possibility of making beings who would act freely but always go right. Clearly, his failure to avail himself of this possibility is inconsistent with his being both omnipotent and wholly good.

If it is replied that this objection is absurd, that the making of some wrong choices is logically necessary for freedom, it would seem that 'freedom' must here mean complete randomness or indeterminacy, including randomness with regard to the alternatives good and evil, in other words that men's choices and consequent actions can be 'free' only if they are not determined by their characters. Only on this assumption can God escape the responsibility for men's actions; for if he made them as they are, but did not determine their wrong choices, this can only be because the wrong choices are not determined by men as they are. But then if freedom is randomness, how can it be a characteristic of will? And, still more, how can it be the most important good? What value or merit would there be in free choices if these were random actions which were not determined by the nature of the agent?

I conclude that to make this solution plausible two different senses of 'freedom' must be confused, one sense which will justify the view that freedom is a third order good, more valuable than other goods would be without it, and another sense, sheer randomness, to prevent us from ascribing to God a decision to make men such that they sometimes go wrong when he might have made them such that they would always freely go right.

Conclusion

[14] Of the proposed solutions of the problem of evil which we have examined, none has stood up to criticism. There may be other solutions which require examination, but this study strongly suggests that there is no valid solution of the problem which does not modify at least one of the constituent propositions in a way which would seriously affect the essential core of the theistic position.

Commentary on Mackie

We divide the text more or less following the structure that Mackie imposes on it. Section [1] consists of introductory remarks. Section [2] gives a bald statement and section [3] a more careful statement of the argument. Section [4] discusses ways in which the argument can legitimately be defeated (but not without cost), while [5] discusses some unacceptable variants on these legitimate responses. Section [6] introduces the discussion of other unacceptable responses. Sections [7] to [11] discuss various responses: that evil is a logically necessary counterpart to good in [7]; that evil is a causally necessary means to good in [8]; that the world is overall better because it contains some evil in [9] and [10]; the claim that evil is justified by the goodness of freedom of choice and action in [11]. The 'free will defence' is criticised in section [12] on the grounds that an omnipotent being could make a world in which everyone always freely chooses the good, and in section [13] on the grounds that it is incoherent to suppose that an omnipotent being could make free creatures without giving up its omnipotence. Finally, section [14] concludes Mackie's discussion.

1. Explain Mackie's distinction in [1] between a logical and a scientific problem.

2. What does Mackie mean by an 'adequate solution' in [4]? Give an example of an 'adequate solution' different from those provided by Mackie.

Mackie's more careful statement of the argument in section [3] might be summarised like this:

1. If God exists, then God is omnipotent. (Premise)
2. If God exists, then God is perfectly good. (Premise)
3. A good thing always eliminates evil as far as it can. (Premise)
4. There are no limits to what an omnipotent being can do. (Premise)
5. Evil exists. (Premise)
6. (Therefore) God does not exist. (From 1, 2, 3, 4, 5)

3. What does Mackie mean by a 'half-hearted' solution in [5]? Why does he think, in [6], that purported solutions to the problem of evil are fallacious? Is he right to be so confident?

4. Explain Mackie's comparison of 'good' and 'great' at b↦. Does this show that 'good cannot exist without evil' is not a satisfactory solution to the problem of evil?

Mackie suggests that the 'additional premises' 3 and 4 are 'quasi-logical rules connecting the terms "good", "evil", and "omnipotent"'. However, far from being 'quasi-logical rules', these premises are highly contestable. On the one hand – as Mackie himself acknowledges, at least *inter alia*, at a↦ – it seems most reasonable to hold that there are at least *logical* limits to what an omnipotent being can do: not even an omnipotent being can do the logically impossible. And, on the other hand – as Mackie himself acknowledges, at least *inter alia*, at c↦ – it seems evidently false to claim that good things always eliminate evil as far as they can: for, in general, good things have projects aimed at things other than the elimination of evil – in particular, good things have projects aimed at achieving goods! – and good things can choose to pursue those other projects at the expense of some elimination of evil.

5. The argument beginning in section [9] is sometimes called the 'higher goods defence'. Explain this argument in your own words. Do you agree that Mackie's response at d↦ constitutes a fatal objection?

Can Mackie's argument be reformulated so that it avoids these objections? In order to address this question, we shall consider what Mackie says in connection with what he takes to be the two strongest objections to his argument.

In his discussion – in section [10] – of the idea that the world is overall better because it contains some evil, Mackie introduces the suggestion that we should discriminate between different 'orders' of good and evil between which there are logical connections. We might illustrate these thoughts in the following way:

First-order goods: Pleasure, Happiness
First-order evils: Pain, Misery
Second-order goods: Sympathy, Courage, Perseverance
Second-order evils: Malevolence, Cruelty, Callousness, Cowardice
. . .
N^{th}*-order goods:* [Logically dependent on obtaining of $(N - 1)^{th}$-order evils]
N^{th}*-order evils:* [Logically dependent on obtaining of $(N - 1)^{th}$-order goods]
. . .

Mackie suggests at [e]→ that, if we suppose that goods and evils are distributed across different orders in this way, then we are 'on the way to an infinite regress . . . where the solution of a problem of evil, stated in terms of evil (n), indicated the existence of an evil ($n + l$), and a further problem to be solved'. But this is not obviously correct. If we suppose that God wills to optimise *all* of the orders of good and evil in this infinite hierarchy – think of this as an ω-order good to which there corresponds no ω-order evil – then it seems that we actually have a proposal to which Mackie has given no serious objection. That is, for all that Mackie has argued in section [10], we could still maintain that our world exhibits the *optimal* distribution of amounts and kinds of goods and evils when all of the orders of good and evil in the infinite hierarchy are taken into account.

Given only the illustrative table above, it may not appear very *plausible* to suppose that our world really does exhibit the optimal distribution of amounts and kinds of goods and evils when all of the orders of good and evil in the infinite hierarchy are taken into account. Surely our world could have a better overall balance of goods over evils: more of the goods and less of the evils at some (or all) of the levels in the infinite hierarchy without more of the evils and less of the goods at some other levels in the infinite hierarchy. However, even if this is a plausible response that Mackie could make to rescue the discussion at [e]→, there is – as Mackie himself acknowledges, at least *inter alia*, in section [11] – a further move that the objector can make.

6. How does Mackie combine the free will defence with the higher goods defence? Why, precisely, does this combination argument evade the third objection to the higher goods defence at [d]→?

Suppose we think that, at each of the orders beyond the first, one of the goods at that order is freedom of choice and action with respect to the goods and evils at the immediately preceding level. That is, suppose we think that one of the nth-order goods is freedom of choice and action with respect to $(n - 1)^{th}$-order goods and $(n - 1)^{th}$-order evils. Moreover, suppose we think that it is true that the best kind of world is one that contains creatures who have freedom of choice and action with respect to all orders of goods and evils, or, at any rate, to some initial segment of the infinite hierarchy of goods and evils. Then we could say that, while it is true that our world does not exhibit the optimal distribution of amounts and kinds of goods and evils when all of the orders of good and evil in the infinite hierarchy are taken into account, none the less, our world might well be the best world that an omnipotent and perfectly good being could make, since departures from the optimal distribution of amounts and kinds of goods and evils in the world can all be accounted for in terms of the unfortunate choices made by creatures who have freedom of choice and action with respect to the various kinds of goods and evils that can be instantiated in the world.

In sections [11] and [12], Mackie gives two objections to the suggestion that we might appeal to considerations concerning freedom of choice and action in order to reconcile the claim that God created the world with the observation that the world does not exhibit the optimal distribution of amounts and kinds of goods and evils when all of the orders of good and evil in the infinite hierarchy are taken into account. We shall focus on the first of these objections here. (The second objection turns on the 'paradox of omnipotence', which we discuss in connection with an article by Savage in a subsequent section of this book.)

Mackie claims that, if God were able to make human beings 'such that in their free choices they sometimes prefer what is good and sometimes what is evil', then God would also be able to make human beings 'who would act freely but always go right'. But, if God were able to make human beings such that, in their free actions, they always prefer what is good, and never prefer what is evil, then considerations concerning freedom of choice and action are unable to reconcile the claim that God created the world with the observation that the world does not exhibit the optimal distribution of amounts and kinds of goods and evils when all of the orders of good and evil in the infinite hierarchy are taken into account.

Whether Mackie is right to claim that, if God exists, God could have made a world in which there are free agents who all always freely choose the good depends upon considerations about the nature of freedom. If one supposes that freedom is inconsistent with prior determination – i.e. that one can only choose freely in a given situation if the outcome of one's choice is not fixed prior to one's making of the choice – then it is plausible that one will deny that, if God exists, God could have made a world in which there are free agents who all always freely choose the good. However, if one supposes – as Mackie does – that freedom is consistent with prior determination – i.e. that one can choose freely in a given situation even if the outcome of one's choice is fixed prior to one's making of the choice, provided that the fixing is of the right kind – then it is less clear what it is plausible to think about the claim that, if God exists, God could have made a world in which there are free agents who all always freely choose the good. In particular, while, in general, we think that freedom of choice is undermined if we are forced to act in accordance with the wishes of another agent – e.g. one's freedom of choice is undermined when a gun is held to one's head, and one is directed to perform certain actions – it is not clear whether we should say that freedom of choice is undermined if our actions take place in accordance with the world-making choices of an omnipotent and perfectly good being. If we suppose that, if our world was not made by God, the causal determination of our actions is perfectly compatible with their freedom, why should we say that our world's being made by God – and all else remaining the same – is not compatible with our freedom of action?

7. The theory that free action is consistent with determinism is called *compatibilism*. The compatibilist holds that, *even if* all actions and events are caused by prior events (in accordance with natural laws), actions can *still* be free provided that they are unconstrained or voluntary. Explain in your own words how Mackie employs this compatibilist theory of freedom to argue in section [12] that God could create humans to choose freely to do good. Is his argument plausible?

8. Explain the distinction between freedom that is consistent with determinism and freedom that requires indeterminism. Which type of freedom do you think human beings possess? Which type of freedom do you think is needed for humans to be morally responsible for their actions?

Even if we think that, in the end, Mackie's argument is unconvincing, we are at least now in the position to give a formulation of his argument that is not vulnerable to the objections that could quite plainly be lodged against his initial formulation of his argument. We start with a definition. Say that an *A-universe* is one of a class of possible universes that are all *non-arbitrarily* better than any other universes that contain free agents. Perhaps there is only one A-universe: the unique A-universe that contains free agents in which there is *the* optimal distribution of amounts and kinds of goods and evils when all of the orders of good and evil in Mackie's infinite hierarchy are taken into account. Perhaps, however, there are many A-universes: many universes that contain free agents in which there is a distribution of amounts and kinds of goods and evils of such a kind that there is no non-arbitrary way of preferring one of these universes to the others on the grounds that it has a better distribution of amounts and kinds of goods and evils, even though any one of these universes can be non-arbitrarily preferred to any *other* universe – i.e. any universe that does not belong to the collection in question – on the grounds that it has a better distribution of amounts and kinds of goods and evils than that other universe has.

1. An omnipotent being can just choose to make an A-universe. (Premise)
2. A-universes are non-arbitrarily better than non-A-universes in which there are free agents. (Premise)
3. If a perfectly good being chooses between options, and some options are non-arbitrarily better than other options, then the perfect being chooses from amongst the non-arbitrarily better options. (Premise)
4. (Hence) if an omnipotent and perfectly good being makes a universe that contains free agents, then it makes an A-universe. (From 1–3)
5. Our universe contains free agents, but it is not an A-universe. (Premise)
6. (Hence) it is not the case that an omnipotent and perfectly good being made our universe. (From 4, 5)

Of course, our discussion of Mackie has barely scratched the surface of recent discussions of logical arguments from evil. If you are interested in pursuing this topic further, you might like to look at:

Peterson, M., *The Problem of Evil: Selected Readings*, Notre Dame, Ind.: University of Notre Dame Press, 1992.
Plantinga, A., *God and Other Minds*, Ithaca, NY: Cornell University Press, 1967.
Stump, E., 'The Problem of Evil', *Faith and Philosophy*, 2 (1985): 392–424.

Introduction to Rowe

William Leonard Rowe (b.1931) is professor emeritus at Purdue University. Rowe became an evangelical Christian during his teenage years, and planned to become a minister. During his study for a Master of Divinity at Chicago Theological Seminary, his views began to change. By the time that he completed his PhD – on the work of the theologian Paul Tillich – at Michigan University, Rowe had ceased to be a religious believer. Rowe is the author of four major books in the philosophy of religion: *The Cosmological Argument* (1975), *Philosophy of Religion: An Introduction* (1978), *Thomas Reid on Freedom and Morality* (1991) and *Can God Be Free?* (2004).

Rowe is perhaps best-known for his work defending evidential arguments from evil. Here we examine one of his most influential papers, in which he sets out what he takes to be a good argument against the existence of God, i.e. an argument that '[might] rationally justify someone in being an atheist'. One of the distinctive features of the position that Rowe defends is that, while he does claim that his argument '[can] justify someone in being an atheist', he also maintains that theists can quite reasonably refuse to be persuaded by the argument. Moreover, he goes on to claim that, despite the merits of his argument, atheists are not obliged to suppose that theists are irrational in virtue of their belief in God: atheists can be 'friendly' in their attitudes towards theistic religious believers and theistic religious belief.

Rowe's paper has three sections. Here we reproduce only the first section. While we think that the other sections of Rowe's paper also repay careful attention, they take up themes that are not our central focus here.

William Leonard Rowe, 'The Problem of Evil and Some Varieties of Atheism'

Before we consider the argument from evil, we need to distinguish a narrow and a broad sense of the terms 'theist,' 'atheist,' and 'agnostic.' By a 'theist' in the narrow sense I mean someone who believes in the existence of an omnipotent, omniscient, eternal, supremely good being who created the world. By a 'theist' in the broad sense I mean someone who believes in the existence of some sort of divine being or divine reality. To be a theist in the narrow sense is also to be a theist in the broad sense, but one may be a theist in the broad sense – as was Paul Tillich – without believing that there is a supremely good, omnipotent, omniscient, eternal being who created the world. Similar distinctions must be made between a narrow and a broad sense of the terms 'atheist' and 'agnostic.' To be an atheist in the broad sense is to deny the existence of any sort of divine being or divine reality. Tillich was not an atheist in the broad sense. But he was an atheist in the narrow sense, for he denied that there exists a divine being that is all-knowing, all-powerful and perfectly good. In this paper I will be using the terms 'theism,' 'theist,' 'atheism,' 'atheist,' 'agnosticism,' and 'agnostic' in the narrow sense, not in the broad sense.

1

In developing the argument for atheism based on the existence of evil, it will be useful to focus on some particular evil that our world contains in considerable abundance. Intense human and animal suffering, for example, occurs daily and in great plenitude in our world. Such intense suffering is a clear case of evil. Of course, if the intense suffering leads to some greater good, a good we could not have obtained without undergoing the suffering in question, we might conclude that the suffering is justified, but it remains an evil nevertheless. For we must not confuse the intense suffering in and of itself with the good things to which it sometimes leads or of which it may be a necessary part. Intense human or animal suffering is in itself bad, an evil, even though it may sometimes be justified by virtue of being a part of, or leading to, some good which is unobtainable without it. What is evil in itself may sometimes be good as a means because it leads to something that is good in itself. In such a case, while remaining an evil in itself, the intense human or animal suffering is, nevertheless, an evil which someone might be morally justified in permitting.

[1] Taking human and animal suffering as a clear instance of evil which occurs with great frequency in our world, the argument for atheism based on evil can be stated as follows:

a → 1. There exist instances of intense suffering which an omnipotent, omniscient being could have prevented without thereby losing some greater good or permitting some evil equally bad or worse.[1]

1 If there is some good, *G*, greater than any evil, (1) will be false for the trivial reason that no matter what evil, *E*, we pick, the conjunctive state of affairs consisting of *G* and *E* will outweigh *E* and be such that an omnipotent being could not obtain it without permitting *E*. (See Alvin Plantinga, *God and Other Minds*, Ithaca: Cornell University Press, 1967, 167.) To avoid this objection we may insert 'unreplaceable' into our premises (1) and (2) between 'some' and 'greater'. If *E* isn't required for *G*, and *G* is better than *G* plus *E*, then the good conjunctive state of affairs composed of *G* and *E* would be replaceable by the greater good of *G* alone. For the sake of simplicity, however, I will ignore this complication both in the formulation and discussion of premises (1) and (2).

2. An omniscient, wholly good being would prevent the occurrence of any intense suffering it could, unless it could not do so without thereby losing some greater good or permitting some evil equally bad or worse.
3. There does not exist an omnipotent, omniscient, wholly good being.

What are we to say about this argument for atheism, an argument based on the profusion of one sort of evil in our world? The argument is valid; therefore, if we have rational grounds for accepting its premises, to that extent we have rational grounds for accepting atheism. Do we, however, have rational grounds for accepting the premises of this argument?

Let's begin with the second premise. Let *sI* be an instance of intense human or animal suffering which an omniscient, wholly good being could prevent. We will also suppose that things are such that *sI* will occur unless prevented by the omniscient, wholly good (*OG*) being. We might be interested in determining what would be a sufficient condition of *OG* failing to prevent *sI*. But, for our purpose here, we need only try to state a necessary condition for *OG* failing to prevent *sI*. That condition, so it seems to me, is this:

b↦ *Either* (i) there is some greater good, *G*, such that *G* is obtainable by *OG* only if *OG* permits *sI*,[2]
or (ii) there is some greater good, *G*, such that *G* is obtainable by *OG* only if *OG* permits either *sI* or some evil equally bad or worse,
or (iii) *sI* is such that it is preventable by *OG* only if *OG* permits some evil equally bad or worse.

It is important to recognize that (iii) is not included in (i). For losing a good greater than *sI* is not the same as permitting an evil greater than *sI*. And this is because the absence of a good state of affairs need not itself be an evil state of affairs. It is also important to recognize that *sI* might be such that it is preventable by *OG* without losing *G* (so condition (i) is not satisfied) but also such that if *OG* did prevent it, *G* would be lost unless *OG* permitted some evil equal to or worse than *sI*. If this were so, it does not seem correct to require that *OG* prevent *sI*. Thus condition (ii) takes into account an important possibility not encompassed in condition (i).

[2] Is it true that if an omniscient, wholly good being permits the occurrence of some intense suffering it could have prevented, then either (i) or

[2] Three clarifying points need to be made in connection with (i). First, by 'good' I don't mean to exclude the fulfillment of certain moral principles. Perhaps preventing *sI* would preclude certain actions prescribed by the principles of justice. I shall allow that the satisfaction of certain principles of justice may be a good that outweighs the evil of *sI*. Second, even though (i) may suggest it, I don't mean to limit the good in question to something that would *follow in time* the occurrence of *sI*. And, finally, we should perhaps not fault *OG* if the good *G*, that would be lost were *sI* prevented, is not actually greater than *sI*, but merely such that allowing *sI* and *G*, as opposed to preventing *sI* and thereby losing *G*, would not alter the balance between good and evil. For reasons of simplicity, I have left this point out in stating (i), with the result that (i) is perhaps a bit stronger than it should be.

(ii) or (iii) obtains? It seems to me that it is true. But if it is true, then so is premise (2) of the argument for atheism. For that premise merely states in more compact form what we have suggested must be true if an omniscient, wholly good being fails to prevent some intense suffering it could [c]↦ prevent. Premise (2) says that an omniscient, wholly good being would prevent the occurrence of any intense suffering it could, unless it could not do so without thereby losing some greater good or permitting some evil equally bad or worse. This premise (or something not too distant from it) is, I think, held in common by many atheists and non-theists. Of course, there may be disagreement about whether something is good, and whether, if it is good, one would be morally justified in permitting some intense suffering to occur in order to obtain it. Someone might hold, for example, that no good is great enough to justify permitting an innocent child to suffer terribly.[3] Again, someone might hold that the mere fact that a given good outweighs some suffering and would be lost if the suffering were prevented, is not a morally sufficient reason for permitting that suffering. But to hold either of these views is not to deny (2). For (2) claims only that *if* an omniscient, wholly good being permits intense suffering, *then* either there is some greater good that would have been lost, or some equally bad or worse evil that would have occurred, had the intense suffering been prevented. (2) does not purport to describe what might be a *sufficient* condition for an omniscient, wholly good being to permit intense suffering, only what is a *necessary* condition. So stated, (2) seems to express a belief that accords with our basic moral principles, principles shared by both theists and non-theists. If we are to fault the argument for atheism, therefore, it seems we must find some fault with its first premise.

[3] Suppose in some distant forest lightning strikes a dead tree, resulting in a forest fire. In the fire a fawn is trapped, horribly burned, and lies in terrible agony for several days before death relieves its suffering. So far [d]↦ as we can see, the fawn's intense suffering is pointless. For there does not appear to be any greater good such that the prevention of the fawn's suffering would require either the loss of that good or the occurrence of an evil equally bad or worse. Nor does there seem to be any equally bad or worse evil so connected to the fawn's suffering that it would have had to occur had the fawn's suffering been prevented. Could an omnipotent, omniscient being have prevented the fawn's apparently pointless suffering? The answer is obvious, as even the theist will insist. An omnipotent, omniscient being could have easily prevented the fawn from being horribly burned, or, given the burning, could have spared the fawn the intense suffering by quickly ending its life, rather than allowing the fawn to lie in terrible agony for several days. Since the fawn's intense suffering was preventable and, so far as we can see, pointless, doesn't it appear that premise (1) of the argument is true, that there do exist instances of intense suffering which an

3 See Ivan's speech in Book V, Chapter IV of *The Brothers Karamazov*.

omnipotent, omniscient being could have prevented without thereby losing some greater good or permitting some evil equally bad or worse.

e → [4] It must be acknowledged that the case of the fawn's apparently pointless suffering does not *prove* that (1) is true. For even though we cannot see how the fawn's suffering is required to obtain some greater good (or to prevent some equally bad or worse evil), it hardly follows that it is not so required. After all, we are often surprised by how things we thought to be unconnected turn out to be intimately connected. Perhaps, for all we know, there is some familiar good outweighing the fawn's suffering to which that suffering is connected in a way we do not see. Furthermore, there may well be unfamiliar goods, goods we haven't dreamed of, to which the fawn's suffering is inextricably connected. Indeed, it would seem to require something like omniscience on our part before we could lay claim to knowing that there is no greater good connected to the fawn's suffering in such a manner than an omnipotent, omniscient being could not have achieved that good without permitting that suffering or some evil equally bad or worse. So the case of the fawn's suffering surely does not enable us to establish the truth of (1).

The truth is that we are not in a position to prove that (1) is true. We cannot know with certainty that instances of suffering of the sort described in (1) do occur in our world. But it is one thing to know or prove that (1) is true and quite another thing to have rational grounds for believing (1) to be true. We are often in the position where in the light of our experience and knowledge it is rational to believe that a certain statement is true, even though we are not in a position to prove or to know with certainty that the statement is true. In the light of our past experience and knowledge it is, for example, very reasonable to believe that neither Goldwater nor McGovern will ever be elected President, but we are scarcely in the position of knowing with certainty that neither will ever be elected President. So, too, with (1), although we cannot know with certainty that it is true, it perhaps can be rationally supported, shown to be a rational belief.

[5] Consider again the case of the fawn's suffering. Is it reasonable to believe that there is some greater good so intimately connected to that suffering that even an omnipotent, omniscient being could not have obtained that good without permitting that suffering or some evil at least as bad? It certainly does not appear reasonable to believe this. Nor does it seem reasonable to believe that there is some evil at least as bad as the fawn's suffering such that an omnipotent being simply could not have prevented it without permitting the fawn's suffering. But even if it should somehow be reasonable to believe either of these things of the fawn's suffering, we must then ask whether it is reasonable to believe either of these things of *all* the instances of seemingly pointless human and animal suffering that occur daily in our world. And surely the answer to this more general question must be no. It seems quite unlikely that *all* the instances of intense suffering occurring daily in our world are intimately related to the occurrence

of greater goods or the prevention of evils at least as bad; and even more unlikely, should they somehow all be so related, than an omnipotent, omniscient being could not have achieved at least some of those goods (or prevented some of those evils) without permitting the instances of intense suffering that are supposedly related to them. In the light of our experience and knowledge of the variety and scale of human and animal suffering in our world, the idea that none of this suffering could have been prevented by an omnipotent being without thereby losing a greater good or permitting an evil at least as bad seems an extraordinary absurd idea, quite beyond our belief. It seems then that although we cannot prove that (1) is true, it is, nevertheless, altogether reasonable to believe that (1) is true, that (1) is a rational belief.[4]

Returning now to our argument for atheism, we've seen that the second premise expresses a basic belief common to many theists and non-theists. We've also seen that our experience and knowledge of the variety and profusion of suffering in our world provides *rational support* for the first premise. Seeing that the conclusion, 'There does not exist an omnipotent, omniscient, wholly good being' follows from these two premises, it does seem that we have *rational support* for atheism, that it is reasonable for us to believe that the theistic God does not exist.

Commentary on Rowe

Rowe presents the core of his argument at [a]→. As Rowe observes, the conclusion of this argument is logically entailed by its premises. Thus, any objection to the argument must focus on the acceptability of the premises.

[4] One might object that the conclusion of this paragraph is stronger than the reasons given warrant. For it is one thing to argue that it is unreasonable to think that (1) is false and another thing to conclude that we are therefore justified in accepting (1) as true. There are propositions such that believing them is much more reasonable than disbelieving them, and yet are such that withholding judgment about them is more reasonable than believing them. To take an example of Chisholm's: it is more reasonable to believe that the Pope will be in Rome (on some arbitrarily picked future date) than to believe that he won't; but it is perhaps more reasonable to suspend judgment on the question of the Pope's whereabouts on that particular date, than to believe that he will be in Rome. Thus, it might be objected, that while we've shown that believing (1) is more reasonable than disbelieving (1), we haven't shown that believing (1) is more reasonable than withholding belief. My answer to this objection is that there are things we know which render (1) probable to the degree that it is more reasonable to believe (1) than to suspend judgment on (1). What are these things we know? First, I think, is the fact that there is an enormous variety and profusion of intense human and animal suffering in our world. Second, is the fact that much of this suffering seems quite unrelated to any greater goods (or the absence of equal or greater evils) that might justify it. And, finally, there is the fact that such suffering as is related to greater goods (or the absence of equal or greater evils) does not, in many cases, seem so intimately related as require its permission by an omnipotent bring bent on securing those goods (or the absence of those evils). These facts, I am claiming, make it more reasonable to accept (1) than to withhold judgment on (1).

1. Explain Rowe's distinction between narrow and broad senses of 'theist', 'atheist' and 'agnostic'. Why does Rowe introduce this distinction? Why does he restrict his discussion to 'theism' and 'atheism' in the narrow sense?

2. Read through Rowe's introduction to the argument at [a]↦. What point is he making in distinguishing intense suffering and the good to which suffering might sometimes contribute? Is this point correct? Why is it important for the argument at [a]↦?

3. Explain in your own words Rowe's three conditions at [b]↦ under which God would allow intense suffering. Do you agree with them? Are there other conditions that he has missed?

Consider Rowe's claim at [c]↦ that the second premise 'is held in common by many theists and many atheists'. While that seems right – and while it also seems right to say that it seems quite proper for this premise to be 'held in common by many theists and many atheists' – it is not entirely obvious that the second premise is true. Suppose, for example, that it is true that there must be *sufficiently many* instances of intense suffering in order for there to be certain greater goods or in order for there not to be certain evils equally bad or worse, but that there are *no particular* instances of intense suffering that are required in order for there to be these greater goods or in order for there not to be those evils equally bad or worse. Suppose, further, that there is some indeterminacy in what here constitutes *sufficiently many* instances of intense suffering: while having N instances of intense suffering would certainly suffice to obtain the greater goods or to ward off the evils equally bad or worse, and while having M instances of intense suffering certainly would not suffice to obtain the greater goods or to ward off the evils equally bad or worse, there is a (not determinately specifiable) range of values between N and M concerning which there simply is no fact of the matter whether having that number of instances of intense suffering *would* suffice to obtain the greater goods or to ward off the evils equally bad or worse. In those circumstances, it seems that an omniscient, wholly good being might not prevent the occurrence of some instances of intense suffering, even knowing that *some* (not determinately specifiable) number of instances of suffering could be prevented without losing the relevant greater goods or bringing about the relevant evils equally bad or worse.

Even if the case described in the last paragraph is possible – and that could certainly be questioned – it has to be said that it is not particularly intuitive. Moreover – though we shall not explore this question further here – the same seems to be true for other attempts to show that the second premise in Rowe's argument is not true. It is perhaps for this reason that most attention has been focused on the first premise in Rowe's argument.

Rowe concedes at [e]↦ that he cannot 'prove' that the first premise of his argument is true and that we cannot 'know with certainty' that the first premise of his argument is true. Rather, what Rowe claims is that we can have 'rational grounds' for believing that the first premise of his argument is true. In particular, Rowe offers a two-part argument for the conclusion that we *may* reasonably believe that the first premise of his argument is true.

First, Rowe describes in [3] a particular case of intense suffering: the case of the trapped fawn that is horribly burned in a forest fire and that lies in terrible agony for several days before it dies. Rowe's general point is given at [d]→. Since it is obvious – and conceded on all sides – that an omnipotent and omniscient being could intervene to prevent the suffering of the fawn, Rowe concludes that this is a case in which it *seems* that there is suffering that could have been prevented by an omnipotent and omniscient being without losing any greater good, or bringing about any evil equally bad or worse. That is, it seems that premise (1) is true.

4. Is the example of intense suffering that Rowe describes one both that God could prevent and that fails to satisfy any of the three conditions given at [b]→? If not, why not, and can we modify the example so that it does? If so, are there other examples of evils that God could prevent and that fail to satisfy the conditions at [b]→?

Second, Rowe goes on to note in [4] and [5] that, even though it is clear that, just because we have a case in which it *seems* that premise (1) is true, it does not follow that we have a case in which premise (1) is true, i.e. a case in which *there is* suffering that could have been prevented by an omnipotent and omniscient being without losing any greater good, or bringing about any evil equally bad or worse, we also have to take into account the fact that there are *countless* cases like that of the fawn that occur everyday. That is, the world is replete with instances of intense suffering that seem to be described by premise (1). Even if we can reasonably believe, of any individual instance of intense suffering, that it might be the case that *that* suffering could not have been prevented by an omnipotent and omniscient being without losing any greater good, or bringing about any evil equally bad or worse, surely – Rowe suggests – we can reasonably refuse to believe that it is true, of *the sum of* instances of intense suffering, that *not one of them* could have been prevented by an omnipotent and omniscient being without losing some greater good, or bringing about some evil equally bad or worse.

In the presentation of the first part of this two-step argument, Rowe *seems* to move from the claim

(*a*) there does not appear to be a greater good that would be lost, or an evil equally bad or worse that would be brought about, by the prevention of the suffering of the fawn on the part of an omnipotent and omniscient being

to the claim

(*b*) it appears that there is no greater good that would be lost, or evil equally bad or worse that would be brought about, by the prevention of the suffering of the fawn on the part of an omnipotent and omniscient being.

If Rowe is arguing in this way, then one might be tempted to think that there is a mistake in Rowe's reasoning: at the very least, the claim that it is not the case that things appear to be a certain way does not obviously support the claim that it appears that things are not that way.

Perhaps the core issue to be addressed in assessing Rowe's two-step argument is this. It certainly seems to be true that, if there is an omnipotent, omniscient and perfectly good being, then there are lots of instances of intense suffering concerning which we are unable to point to the outweighing goods that would be lost, or the countervailing evils that would occur, were the omnipotent, omniscient and perfectly good being to intervene to prevent those instances of intense suffering. Should we suppose that this fact *can* provide a good reason for thinking that there is no omnipotent, omniscient and perfectly good being?

We can do no more here than indicate some of the important issues that now arise. Plainly, one central question to ask is this: Is it reasonable to suppose that, if there are outweighing goods that would be lost, or countervailing evils that would occur, were an omnipotent, omniscient and perfectly good being to intervene to prevent certain instances of intense suffering, we are capable of identifying those outweighing goods and countervailing evils? If Rowe is not entitled to make this assumption, then he would surely not be entitled to move from (*a*) to (*b*).

5. Could Rowe support his argument with the following kind of inference: because none of the goods that we are aware of could justify God in permitting the event described in [3] (and many similar kinds of intense suffering), it is reasonable to suppose that there is no good that could permit God to allow evils of that type. Is this a defensible argument?

Another important question to ask is this: If it is not reasonable to suppose that, if there are outweighing goods that would be lost, or countervailing evils that would occur, were an omnipotent, omniscient and perfectly good being to intervene to prevent certain instances of intense suffering, we are capable of identifying those outweighing goods and countervailing evils, then what *does* fall within the realm of reasonable supposition when it comes to the assessment of claims that concern an omnipotent, omniscient and perfectly good being? Is it reasonable to suppose, for example, that, if there were an omnipotent, omniscient and perfectly good being, it would likely make a world much like the world that we inhabit? If so, how is the reasonableness of this supposition consonant with our presumed ignorance of the goods and evils that would enter into the deliberations that an omnipotent, omniscient and perfectly good being would undertake in determining what kind of world to create?

Although Rowe presents himself as constructing an argument for the non-existence of God, he goes on – in the second and third sections of his paper – to claim that reasonable theists can reasonably reject his argument. Consequently, there is some reason to suspect that the main concern of Rowe's paper is not so much with the construction of an evidential argument against the existence of God, but rather with the exploration of the suggestion that atheists might find a *ground* for their non-belief in the observation that there are instances of intense suffering which an omnipotent, omniscient being could have prevented without thereby losing some greater good or permitting some evil equally bad or worse. Clearly, Rowe does *not* suppose that his argument gives theists a reason to accept the conclusion that there is no omnipotent, omniscient, perfectly good creator of the universe: hence, at least on the account of argumentation sketched in the introduction to this section of our book, Rowe himself does not suppose that he has a successful evidential argument from evil.

6. Can Rowe's evidential argument be improved?

7. Compare Rowe's 'evidential' argument with Mackie's 'deductive' argument? Which type of argument is the stronger?

As we have already indicated, the foregoing discussion does little more than scratch the surface of recent discussions of evidential arguments from evil, and, in particular, of recent discussions of Rowe's evidential argument from evil. If you are interested in further discussion of Rowe's evidential argument from evil, or of evidential arguments from evil more generally, then you might like to look at:

Draper, P., 'Pain and Pleasure: An Evidential Problem for Theists', *Noûs*, 23 (1989): 331–50.

Howard-Snyder, D. (ed.), *The Evidential Argument from Evil*, Bloomington, Ind.: Indiana University Press, 1996.

Trakakis, N., *The God beyond Belief: In Defense of William Rowe's Evidential Argument from Evil*, Berlin: Springer, 2007.

3

Evidence, Argument and Belief in God

Introduction

In this section, we focus our attention on important considerations about the role of evidence and argument in religious belief – and, in particular, on the place of evidence and argument in connection with the particular belief that God exists. We shall consider a range of views that might be taken in connection with the claim that there is insufficient evidence and argument to support belief in God – all based on the assumption that it is at least appropriate to ask the question whether there is sufficient evidence and argument to support belief in God. As we know from the discussion in the first section of this book, there are philosophers who deny that it is appropriate even to ask the question whether there is sufficient evidence and argument to support belief in God: on their view, roughly speaking, believing in God is not a kind of believing for which it is appropriate to ask questions about supporting evidence and argument. Those who are convinced that it is not appropriate even to ask the question whether there is sufficient evidence and argument to support belief in God should suppose that the following investigation is conditional in nature: supposing that it were appropriate to ask the question whether there is sufficient evidence and argument to support belief in God, what would be the best answer to give?

Our first article – by Christopher New – sets out one kind of argument for the conclusion that there is insufficient evidence and argument for the existence of God. New argues, roughly, that there is no evidence or argument that favours the hypothesis that God exists above the hypothesis that there is an omnipotent, omniscient and perfectly *evil* creator of the world. But, suggests New, if it is true that there is no evidence or argument that favours the hypothesis that God exists above the hypothesis that there is an omnipotent, omniscient and perfectly *evil* creator of the world, surely it cannot be reasonable to believe that God exists.

Our second article – by William Clifford – can be taken to supply an essential premise in the argument that is at least implicit in New's article. In order to argue that it cannot be reasonable to believe that God exists if there is no evidence or argument that favours the hypothesis that God exists above the hypothesis that there is an omnipotent, omniscient and perfectly *evil* creator of the world, it seems that one needs to be making some more general assumption about the relationship between reason, evidence and argument. Famously, in his article, Clifford supplies a verbal formulation that might be taken to articulate the requisite general assumption: *it is wrong, always, everywhere, and for anyone, to believe anything on insufficient evidence (and argument).*

Our third article – by William James – directly contradicts the general assumption that is embodied in Clifford's verbal formulation: James denies that it is wrong, always, everywhere, and for anyone, to believe anything on insufficient evidence (and argument). Further, James insists that it can be perfectly appropriate to believe some things for which one has insufficient evidence or argument on the basis of 'passional decision', i.e., roughly, because one *wants* the things believed to be true: 'our passional nature not only lawfully may, but must, decide an option between propositions, whenever it is a genuine option that cannot by its nature be decided on intellectual grounds'. Finally, James insists that religious belief is the kind of belief that our passional nature may lawfully decide: one can believe that God exists simply because, very roughly speaking, one wants it to be the case that God exists.

Our fourth article – by Alvin Plantinga – also directly contradicts the general assumption that is embodied in Clifford's verbal formulation. However, Plantinga does not accept James's claim that it can be perfectly acceptable to believe some things for which one has insufficient evidence or argument on the basis that one wants the things believed to be true. Rather, Plantinga rejects Clifford's verbal formulation on the ground that it is self-defeating: it must be that one has some beliefs that one accepts without basing those beliefs in other beliefs that one accepts, and hence that one accepts without having sufficient evidence and argument to justify that acceptance. Moreover, Plantinga insists that the claim that God exists is an easy inference from claims about God that can be rationally accepted in the absence of sufficient evidence and argument, i.e. from claims that, by Plantinga's lights, can be 'properly basic beliefs'.

Our fifth article – by Georges Rey – accepts the claim that there is insufficient evidence and argument to justify acceptance of the claim that God exists, and uses this consideration as one part of a case for the ostensibly outrageous claim that, really, no one believes that God exists. In the extract from Rey's article that we include, Rey advances eleven considerations that he takes to support his contention that those who maintain that they believe that God exists are victims of a kind of self-deception. One reason for including this paper in the present section is to emphasise the potential importance of questions about the connections between reasonable belief, evidence and argument: if we do accept both that it is unreasonable to believe things for which one has insufficient evidence and argument and that there is insufficient evidence and argument to support belief in God, then clearly, unless we take the kind of line that is followed by Rey, we shall need to find an *explanation* of why it is that so many people unreasonably believe that God exists. This may not be an easy task.

Of course, it should not be supposed that these five articles exhaust the range of positions that can be taken on the question whether belief in God can be reasonable if there is insufficient evidence and argument to support the claim that God exists, or the range of possible responses that one might make to the prevalence of religious belief if one accepts that there is insufficient evidence and argument to render it reasonable to believe that God exists. Moreover, it should not be supposed without further argument that the questions under discussion here are *necessarily* central to religious epistemology. In particular, if New's argument is unsuccessful for reasons that have nothing to do with the deficiencies of the principle that Clifford formulates, then, at the very least, it seems that we need to be given some *other* reasons for thinking that there is insufficient evidence and argument for the belief that God exists. However, even if the questions under discussion here are not necessarily central to religious epistemology, it is surely right to claim that these questions are of considerable importance and concern.

If you are interested in pursuing further questions about the epistemology of religious belief, you might like to have a look at some of the following works:

Alston, W., *Perceiving God*, Ithaca NY: Cornell University Press, 1991.
Plantinga, A., *Warranted Christian Belief*, Oxford: Oxford University Press, 2000.
Swinburne, R., *Faith and Reason*, Oxford: Clarendon Press, 1981.

Introduction to New

Christopher New is a contemporary philosopher and novelist. He founded the department of philosophy at the University of Hong Kong in 1969, and was a member of that department in 1993 when 'Antitheism: A Reflection' appeared. Subsequently, he left academic philosophy in order to become a full-time writer. His major philosophical publications include his book *The Philosophy of Literature: An Introduction* (1993); and his major novels include his China Coast Trilogy: *Shanghai* (1988), *The Chinese Box* (2002) and *A Change of Flag* (2002).

In 'Antitheism: A Reflection', New sketches a case for 'antitheism', i.e. a case for the existence of a perfectly *evil* being that has the kind of supremacy – power over the universe and its inhabitants – that theists typically attribute to God. At least implicitly, the key claim in New's article is that the case for 'antitheism' is no less strong than the case for traditional theism: for each argument that has been given on behalf of traditional theism, there is an argument equally good or better in support of 'antitheism'. Of course, it need be no part of this case that the arguments in support of 'antitheism' are *good* or *strong*: indeed, New is certainly *not* meaning to argue that we have good reason to be 'antitheists'. Rather, the point that New wishes to make is that, since we have no better reason to be theists than we have reason to be 'antitheists', we have – in this consideration alone – compelling reason not to be theists.

Christopher New, 'Antitheism: A Reflection'

I

The world might have been different, our beliefs might have been different. As well as there being theists who believe in the existence of God, there might also have been antitheists who believed equally seriously in the existence of the Devil. Not the Devil of some theologies, God's rival and inferior, but a being with the supremacy that theists attribute to God. Antitheists, like theists, would have believed in an omnipotent, omniscient eternal creator; but whereas theists in fact believe that the supreme being is also perfectly good, antitheists would have believed that he was perfectly evil.

Suppose there *had* been a tradition of antitheism as there is in fact one of theism; suppose we had antitheologians as well as theologians. What sort of arguments could they have provided for their beliefs? Arguments just like our present theistic arguments, but stood on their heads; in other words, *reflections* of our present theistic arguments. To see that this is so, we need only consider how, if things had been different, a philosopher of today might have written an encyclopedia entry on antitheism. Let us imagine, then, that there has been an antitheistic tradition which is the reflection of our actual theistic tradition, with antitheistic thinkers whose views (and whose very names) are reflections of our actual theistic thinkers. This is how the entry might run.

II

a→ 'Probably the most famous antitheistic argument is the ontological argument, first advanced by Ts Mlesna in the eleventh century, and later adapted (without acknowledgement) by the seventeenth century antitheist Setracsed. Mlesna argues in essence that it is self-contradictory to deny the Devil's existence, hence that it is necessary that he exists. As Mlesna puts it, the Devil is by definition a being than whom no worse can be conceived. Now, anyone who has the idea of such a being in his mind and simultaneously denies that the being exists in reality is in effect saying that the idea in his mind of a being than whom no worse can be conceived is not after all that idea; for in denying that that being exists in reality he is implicitly conceding that he can conceive of a being still worse – one that exists in reality. So the Devil's existence cannot intelligibly be denied.[1]

[1] Compare St. Anselm, 'Proslogion', *Medieval Logic and Metaphysics*, D. F. Henry (ed.) (London: Hutchinson, 1972), 101–7.

b→ 'The second main argument is the cosmological argument, which is originally an antitheistic adaptation by the thirteenth century thinker Saniuqa of an argument by the ancient philosopher Eltotsira. Saniuqa argues that everything in the universe is contingent, and that every contingent thing requires a cause of its existence. In order to avoid an infinite regress, and for any contingent thing to exist at all, then, there must be a non-contingent being which is itself uncaused, but causes everything in the universe. And this necessarily existing (because non-contingent) being is the omniscient, omnipotent and omni-malevolent Devil.[2]

c→ 'The third argument is the teleological argument, also known as the argument from design. Unlike the two arguments just considered, it does not attempt to *prove* the Devil exists. Rather it claims that his existence is the most rational explanation of observed features of the world.[3] It thus has considerable persuasive power, and the eighteenth century philosopher Leunammi Tnak actually held that it was one of the most convincing of all the arguments for the Devil's existence, while the contemporary philosopher Trams has declared "the argument has a fascination for us that reason cannot easily dispel."[4] The argument starts from the observation that the universe exhibits great regularity and order on the one hand, and a marvelous adaptation of organisms to the circumstances of their existence on the other. It concludes that the most rational explanation of these features is that they did not happen by chance; rather, they are the work of a supremely intelligent designer – the Devil. It has often been pointed out, particularly, since Emuh the eighteenth century skeptic, that the conclusion that there must have been a designer does not of itself allow us to infer that the designer must have been omni-malevolent, let alone omnipotent and eternal. Antitheists reply that omni-malevolence, at least, can rationally be imputed to the designer as the best explanation of what he appears to have designed. When we consider how well the universe functions to perpetrate and perpetuate evil, it is hard (perverse, antitheists say) not to attribute omni-malevolence to its designer. Who but a malevolent being, they demand to know, would arrange for the enormous sufferings caused in the world by natural calamities and human actions alike? Think of the pain and destruction wrought by earthquakes, floods, tornadoes, diseases, droughts and famines. Would a benevolent designer have planned them? Think of the daily and routine butchery practiced by animals (including man) upon their prey. Who but a malevolent being would design the

2 Compare St. Thomas Aquinas, *Summa Theologica* (London: Burns, Oates and Washburn, Ltd., 1920), Question 2, Article 3. There arc various forms of this argument, as of all antitheistic arguments. I give here only the simplest forms.

3 Some argue that the cosmological argument should also be presented as an argument of this type. Compare R. G. Swinburne, 'Faith and the Existence of God' *Key Themes in Philosophy*, A. Phillips Griffiths (ed.) (Cambridge: C.U.P., 1989), 125.

4 Compare J. J. C. Smart, 'The Existence of God', *New Essays in Philosophical Theology*, A. Flew and A. Macintyre (eds.) (London: SCM Press, Ltd., 1955), p. 44.

massive jaws of the shark and tiger, with which they so effortlessly rend and crush the infant seal or helpless cow? Who else would design the cancer virus, so beautifully adapted to ravage and kill innocent children? Who else, indeed, would design the human brain itself with its awesome capacity, so often actualized, to torture, maim and kill by the thousand and the million? As the antitheist Mailliw Yelap has observed, if we found a time-bomb in a nursery, primed and set to explode when it would wreak the maximum of death and destruction, we would reasonably assume that someone evil had designed and deliberately put it there. How much more reasonable must it be, then, for the impartial observer to attribute the world as we know it to an evil designer?[5]

[d]→ 'Let us pause to consider these arguments for a moment. Clearly, they are open to objections. The ontological argument has attracted both criticisms and defense ever since it was put forward, and it remains controversial. It has been claimed by many, for instance, following a slightly different objection of Nolinuag (a contemporary of Mlesna) that the same form of argument could be used to prove the existence of God – i.e. a being than whom no better could be conceived – or, indeed, the existence of the worst or best conceivable instantiation of *any* concept. And this, it is alleged, is so absurd that we must conclude the argument form is invalid. Antitheists attempt to meet this objection, but their replies have not been universally accepted.

'The cosmological argument has been criticized on the ground that it does not explain why there could not be an infinite series of causes without beginning, in which case there would be no need to posit a first uncaused cause. The teleological argument has the defect, as we have seen, that it does not establish that the designer is eternal, nor that he is omnipotent, and some even claim there are indications that he might be good, not evil. Besides, it is claimed by many that evolution can explain the adaptation of organisms to their environment without recourse to the hypothesis of an intelligent designer.

[e]→ 'Defenders of the arguments attempt to answer these objections, or to meet them by modifying the arguments themselves. It is perhaps correct to say that, while none of the arguments proves the Devil exists, the objections to them are not in every case decisive. And antitheists hold that, taken together with the next two arguments, antitheistic arguments do at least present a reasonable case. Let us turn, then, to the argument from antimiracles and the argument from antireligious experience. First, the argument from antimiracles. Antimiracles are harmful or evil events which cannot be explained scientifically. Such events are attributed by antitheists to the supernatural agency of the Devil. Antimiracles are not reported as frequently now as in earlier times, but many have heard of them, and there are numerous documented instances of their alleged occurrence. Sudden deaths

5 Compare St. Thomas Aquinas, *op. cit.*, and R. G. Swinburne, *op. cit.* 127–30.

and physical or mental injuries, for instance, which occur to apparently normal and healthy people often defy scientific explanation, and are therefore attributed by antitheists to the supernatural agency of the Devil, whose intervention, they claim, is the most rational explanation of such phenomena. Of course, some skeptics reply that even if one is not available now, a scientific explanation which "naturalizes" these events will eventually be found. But the fact is, antitheists argue, none has been found so far, or not for all of them, so it is an at least equally plausible hypothesis that they are antimiracles performed by the Devil; and sometimes this is actually *more* plausible. As Enrubniws, the contemporary antitheist, has observed: "If today's evidence shows that probably a violation of natural law occurred, we ought so to believe and to seek the best explanation we can of it."[6]

[f]→ 'The second argument concerns antireligious experience. To many people, whom we have no independent reason to believe were deluded, it has seemed at different moments of their lives that they were aware of the Devil and his influence on them. (Literary representations of this appear in the traditional Tsuaf story, dramatized effectively by the poets Ewolram and Ehteog – although these posit also the existence of God.) These reports, it is claimed, cannot be discounted. Enrubniws has pointed out that, unless there are countervailing reasons, a person's sincere assertions should be taken at face value. "We ought to believe that things are as they seem to be unless and until we have evidence that we are mistaken." When I sincerely assert that I communicated with someone yesterday, my assertion has a probability of being true, unless there is some evidence against it. The same holds, he claims, for sincere assertions of communications with the Devil.[7]

'When we consider all these arguments for antitheism, how convincing a case do they seem to make? Philosophical opinion is of course divided on its answer to this question. Different authors give different weight to different arguments. While most antitheists agree that no argument is conclusive, they all claim that they do at least establish antitheism as a coherent hypothesis with rational grounds to support it. Some antitheists, of course,
[g]→ go further and claim that no other hypothesis is as well-supported.

'There is, however, one serious objection to antitheism, one that is often considered decisive by theistic or agnostic opponents, and it is that objection that I shall address in the rest of this brief article. The objection is known as the problem of good. If the Devil is omniscient, omnipotent and omni-malevolent, it is asked, why does he allow the existence of good in the world? Either he can't prevent it, in which case he is not omnipotent, or else he chooses to allow it, in which case he is not omni-malevolent. While peculiarly relevant (as briefly noted above) to the teleological argument,

6 Compare R. G. Swinburne, *op. cit.* 131.

7 Compare R. G. Swinburne, *op. cit.* 131–2.

this objection is of wider import. If it is correct, a being with all the characteristics which antitheists attribute to the Devil cannot exist. What answer can antitheists give here?

'Let us first of all distinguish between natural and moral good. Natural good comprises events and states like health, good harvests, good weather, the non-occurrence of earthquakes and tornadoes etc. which are the results of natural causes. Moral good arises from human actions – those that promote happiness rather than suffering. Let me deal with the antitheists' view on natural good first. Natural good occurs, they argue, as an inevitable result of the laws of nature that are necessary for the production of evil. If we are to cause harm, we must know how to do so, and this requires the regularities described by laws of nature. Thus, if we are to be able to drown unwanted girl-children, we must know that human beings cannot breathe under water. If we could not rely on this fact, and millions like it, which instantiate various laws of nature, our efforts to do wrong would be chaotic and ineffective. But, as Enrubniws has remarked,[8] a corollary of this fact about human beings and water, for instance, is that they will be able to breathe happily and healthily on land. So the good of easy respiration on land is a necessary consequence of the operation of laws of nature without which evil and suffering would be seriously reduced. The same point can be made, of course, with regard to other laws of nature. And it is no derogation from the Devil's omnipotence, omni-malevolence or omniscience that he does not do what will in the long run fail to maximize evil. Besides, the existence of good is necessary in another way for the production of evil. If nobody was sound or happy, how could we perform the evil acts of maiming and infecting them, or making them miserable? If the environment was filthy already, there would be no scope for us to exercise our malice or sloth in polluting it. If nobody possessed food or shelter or riches, how could we develop the evil motives necessary for pillage and theft?

'It is sometimes conceded that these arguments have force, but objected that the Devil did not need to allow so *much* good in order to obtain these evil results. He ought never to have allowed such natural goods as years of plenty, for instance, or peace or good health, goods which are not uncommon in the world. This is admittedly a difficult objection to meet, but antitheists have a reply. It is that the fewer natural goods the Devil provides, the less opportunity he provides for men to exercise responsibility. If there are great goods which we can, through our knowledge of nature, choose to produce or preserve, and we choose, rather, to prevent or destroy them, we exercise our free will in a serious, not a trivial way; and the evil we do is not toy-evil, it is serious.[9]

8 Compare R. G. Swinburne, *The Existence of God* (Oxford: O.U.P., 1979), 202–14.
9 Compare R. G. Swinburne, *The Existence of God* (Oxford: O.U.P., 1979), 218–21.

'Whether or not what appears to be superfluous good is in reality the minimum necessary for the production of the maximum of evil, it should be noted that the antitheists' reply here, by appealing to the notion of responsibility, has brought us to the problem of *moral* good and the so-called free will defense. We sometimes choose to do good, and the Devil has made the world such that we have the opportunity to do massive good if we choose. Why does an evil creator permit that? The free will defense alleges that free will is an evil, for it makes sin possible and allows us to approach a little nearer to the status of our evil creator. Since it is worse for us to do evil of our own free will than to be causally determined to produce evil, the Devil gives us free will. But in creating men with free will, he has to accept that sometimes they may act for good rather than for evil. However, the greater evil that comes about from, and is comprised by, the possession of free will far outweighs the occasional good that also occurs through its existence. The world, in other words, is a worse place for the existence of free will, with its possessors' infrequent good acts, than it would be without it. This argument, of course, depends on an empirical assumption, that there is ultimately more evil than good in the world as a result of free will. While in the nature of the case this cannot be established until the end of the world, antitheists claim that the evidence of human history so far supports the hypothesis. His freely undertaken wars and massacres, his habitual indifference to others' suffering, they declare, are far more conspicuous in the records of man's progress than are his episodic lapses into mercy, peace and friendship. In large and in small, we choose sin and crime more often than their opposites.

'A particular problem is sometimes thought to be posed by the suffering of the guilty. If the Devil exists, skeptics ask, why does he allow the guilty, who have never done anything good, sometimes to suffer? But this objection is confused. Since the Devil promotes only evil, he has no interest in protecting the wicked from suffering. So it should not surprise us that the wicked suffer as well as the good; in that way greater suffering is brought about. It is worth noticing, by the way, that the counterpart problem for theists, who hold that God, not the Devil, exists, is much harder to solve; which seems, indeed, to render their position virtually untenable.[10] For it appears wholly inconsistent with the existence of an omni-benevolent, just and omnipotent being that he should allow the innocent to suffer, and suffer pointlessly, as they apparently do. But, as we have just seen, if there is an omni-malevolent being, the motive of his every action will be to promote wickedness and suffering. Whether it is the wicked or the good that suffer is indifferent to him. It is the quantity and quality of suffering that matters, not the distribution. So he allows his pain to fall upon the unjust and the just alike.

[10] See, e.g., L. Goldstein, *The Philosopher's Habitat* (London and New York: Routledge, 1990), 199–201.

'Antitheists therefore conclude with some plausibility that the problem of good is not insoluble, and that there is no compelling argument against the existence of the Devil.'

III

The world might have been different, our beliefs might have been different. And it is instructive to ask why they are *not* different. In my fictional encyclopedia entry, I have suggested that antitheism has as good arguments as theism to support it, and in some cases perhaps better ones. But if that is true, why is there in fact no antitheistic tradition? The answer lies, I am afraid, more in our hearts than in our heads. Men are inclined to believe what they would like to be true, and they would like it to be true that man is the creature of God, not the Devil, that man has a loving, not an indifferent or malevolent, creator, and that man has a leading role in the evolving drama of the universe, rather than a mere walk-on part. Hence we have a theistic, but no antitheistic, tradition of intellectual inquiry. Not because theism is rationally more plausible than antitheism, but because it is more comforting to believe. This is a sobering thought. For as Nietzsche has said in one of his less rhetorical, but therefore more telling, remarks: why should we expect the truth to be comfortable?

Commentary on New

The paper is divided into three sections. In section I, New introduces the idea that there might have been a tradition of antitheism, i.e. a tradition of belief in a perfectly evil supreme being. In the lengthy second section, New sketches an imaginative antitheology that might have stood to antitheism as theology actually stands to theism. In section III, New suggests that the reason why we have a theistic tradition but no antitheistic tradition has nothing to do with the greater plausibility of theism, but rather is due solely to the fact that it is much more comforting to believe theism than it would be to accept antitheism.

New's antitheology considers analogues of most of the arguments that we considered in the previous section of this book. First, he suggests at [a]→ that Anselm's ontological argument can be readily paralleled by an equally good argument for the existence of a being than which none worse can be conceived. Second, he claims that Aquinas' cosmological argument and Paley's teleological argument at [b]→ and [c]→ respectively can both be readily adapted by the antitheologian, since there is nothing in those arguments that turns on the moral attributes of the being whose existence is meant to be established thereby. At [e]→ and [f]→, he argues that there are considerations about 'antimiracles' and 'antireligious experience' that can be taken to have the same force as considerations about miracles and religious experience are often taken to have. Finally, he argues at [g]→ that 'the problem of good' that arises for the antitheologian admits of just the same range of responses as does the problem of evil for the familiar theologian.

1. Write out the theistic and antitheistic versions of the ontological and cosmological arguments in parallel, with each step of the theistic arguments having a corresponding step in the antitheistic arguments. Are there any points at which antitheistic versions look less plausible than the theistic ones?

2. New describes objections to the antitheistic ontological and cosmological arguments at [d]↦. Write out theistic and antitheistic versions of these objections in parallel. Are they equally plausible?

Now, of course, New's discussion only treats directly of a tiny selection from amongst all of the theistic arguments that have ever been advanced. Even if we agree with him that there are satisfactory parallels for ontological arguments, cosmological arguments, teleological arguments, arguments from miracles, and arguments from religious experience, we might none the less think that there are other arguments for theism for which there simply are not satisfactory antitheistic parallels. Similarly, New's discussion only treats directly of a tiny selection from amongst all of the objections to theism that have ever been advanced. Even if we agree with him that there is a satisfactory parallel between theistic responses to the problem of evil and antitheistic responses to the problem of good, we might none the less think that there are other objections to antitheism that cannot be met with parallels to the satisfactory responses that can be made to objections to theism. (For example, we can ask whether there can be equally satisfactory responses to the argument from scale on the part of antitheologians.) While it might be reasonable to think that New's discussion issues an interesting challenge to theologians – construct an argument for the conclusion that God exists that cannot be paralleled by an equally good argument for the conclusion that there is a perfectly evil supreme being – it could hardly be maintained that his discussion alone makes a compelling case for the conclusion that there is no such argument to be had.

3. The ontological and cosmological arguments have little to say about God's properties; the design argument, in contrast, can be used to infer that God has the properties that one would expect of a being that designed the world. How does New accommodate this difference in his antitheistic version of the argument at [c]↦?

Moreover, it is not clear that we should agree that *all* of the parts of New's case are equally compelling. Perhaps it is plausible to claim that, so long as we accept that the concept of a perfectly evil supreme being is intelligible, or coherent, or capable of rationally being believed to be instantiated, there is nothing in the traditional theological proofs – ontological arguments, cosmological arguments, teleological arguments – that favours theism over antitheism. However, it is rather less clear that there is no good reason to suppose that, while the concept of a perfectly good supreme being is intelligible, or coherent, or capable of rationally being believed to be instantiated, the concept of a perfectly evil supreme being is not intelligible, or coherent, or capable of rationally being believed to be instantiated. And it is also less clear that there is *nothing* in considerations about miracles, religious experience, religious tradition, canonical religious texts, and the like, that favours theism over antitheism.

4. Could the arguments for the existence of God also be reconstructed as arguments for an amoral God, i.e. a being that is neither good nor evil and is not guided by any moral considerations? Select one of the arguments that New considers and rewrite it as an argument for an amoral deity. Does this change make the argument any more or less plausible?

Why might we think that the concept of a perfectly evil supreme being is not intelligible, or coherent, or capable of rationally being believed to be instantiated for reasons that do not carry over to the concept of a perfectly good supreme being? Here is one set of considerations that might be taken to suppose this line of thought (you may be able to think of others): Suppose that there are such things as moral knowledge and moral belief. Suppose, further, that there is a necessary connection between moral belief and motivation: moral beliefs are necessarily motivating in such a way that one can believe that an action is good or right only if one is inclined to approve that action, other things being equal. Given these assumptions, one might think that we can rule out the possibility that there is a perfectly evil supreme being. For, in order to be supreme, a being has to know everything that it is possible for a being to know. But, if a being knows everything that it is possible to know, then, in particular – given our assumption that there is such a thing as moral knowledge – that being has all of the moral knowledge that it is possible to have. However, by our further assumption that there is a necessary connection between moral knowledge and motivation to pursue the good, it then follows that, in order to be supreme, a being has to be motivated to pursue the good – and that surely contradicts the suggestion that a supreme being might be perfectly evil.

Perhaps the line of thought that we have just sketched has some *prima facie* plausibility, but it is not clear that it is ultimately convincing. Even granted the assumption that there are such things as moral knowledge and moral belief, it is not clear that we should grant that there is a *necessary* connection between moral knowledge and motivation of the kind that entails that one cannot knowingly commit evil. In particular, there is surely something to the contrary intuition that the worst kind of evil is the evil that is committed in the full knowledge that it is evil, and that it is possible for agents to carry out evil of this sort. Clearly, there is much more to be said about these kinds of considerations, but we cannot hope to explore them here. (It is perhaps also worth noting that we can find traditions that hold that existence is, in some sense, identical with the good, and traditions that hold that existence is, in some sense, identical with evil. *Prima facie*, at least, the prospects for distinguishing between theism and antitheism by insisting on an identity between being and goodness are not overly bright.)

5. How else might New respond to the above argument? Consider whether it is plausible to say that there is a *necessary* connection between moral knowledge and motivation. Can you think of counter-examples, i.e. where someone has beliefs about what is good but is *not* suitably motivated to act on them?

Why might we think that there is *something* in considerations about miracles, religious experience, religious tradition, canonical religious texts, and the like, that favours theism over antitheism? Well, New himself makes the point that there is no antitheistic tradition: there are no canonical antireligious texts, no canonical works of antitheology and, despite New's suggestions to the contrary, no reports of antireligious experiences. If we suppose that religious experience, religious tradition, canonical religious texts, and the like, provide *some* support for theism, then it seems that they also provide some reason to prefer theism to antitheism. Moreover, it would seem to run counter to New's objectives to resort to further arguments which claim that there is absolutely no support to be found for theism in considerations about miracles, religious experience, religious tradition, canonical religious texts, and the like: the argument that New develops is supposed to be grounded just in the parallel nature of the arguments that can be marshalled by theologians and antitheologians.

Perhaps it might be suggested that New ought to have suggested *different* kinds of parallel arguments that advert to considerations about miracles, religious experience, religious tradition, canonical religious texts, and the like. Consider, again, religious experience. Rather than suggest that there is an argument from antireligious experience that runs directly from the (surely false!) contention that *many people, whom we have no independent reason to believe were deluded, have, at different moments of their lives, taken themselves to be aware of a perfectly evil supreme being and his influence on them*, why not suggest that there is an argument from religious experience that runs directly from the same data that is taken to be the starting point for familiar arguments from religious experience? Given that there is a perfectly *evil* supreme being, is it not a reasonable expectation that that being would give at least some people misleading experiences as of a perfectly good supreme being? What better way to inflict deep and serious harm on people than by deceiving them in this manner!

6. Set out an antitheist version of the argument from miracles, akin to the antitheist version of the argument from religious experience described above.

Taken on its own, the suggestion that we are now considering is apt to seem weak: surely the familiar argument from religious experience, etc., for the existence of a perfectly good supreme being is stronger than the mooted argument from religious experience, etc., for the existence of a perfectly evil supreme being. It is a familiar point in other contexts that we can always come up with alternative hypotheses that fit our data, but – in general – we have good reason to reject more complicated alternatives to the beliefs that we accept. However, in the case at hand, there is surely *something* to the intuition that, considered just with respect to the data concerning religious experience, etc., the hypothesis that there is a deceptive perfectly evil supreme being is more complicated than the theistic hypothesis, and hence one that is less worthy of acceptance. Of course, it is not a straightforward matter to explain what makes one hypothesis more complicated than another – but we expect that many readers will feel the force of the intuition that is being adverted to here.

Even if it is granted that, when we consider the data from religious experience, etc., we should suppose that the theistic hypothesis is preferable to the antitheistic hypothesis on grounds of simplicity, it is not clear that we should make the same supposition when we consider *all* of the relevant available data. Even if New is wrong to think that, when we consider the arguments for theism one by one, *each* of those arguments can be paralleled by an antitheistic argument that is at least as strong, it may yet be the case that there is good reason to think that the 'cumulative case' for antitheism is at least as strong as the 'cumulative case' for theism. New himself makes the suggestion that, when it comes to considerations about the problem of good and the problem of evil, antitheism faces a less pressing problem when confronted with the suffering of the wicked than theism faces when confronted with the suffering of the good. Even if New is wrong about this particular case, it might well be – at least for all that has been argued thus far – that there are other cases in which antitheism does fare better than its theistic rival; and hence – at least for all that has been argued thus far – it could still be the case that, all things considered, there is no overall winning argument on behalf of theism.

7. Are there any divine properties, other than benevolence, that could be changed and written into modified versions of arguments for the existence of God without making them less plausible? Consider, giving your reasons in each case, changes to: (i) omnipotence, (ii) omniscience, (iii) timelessness, (iv) immutability, (v) oneness.

Suppose that it *does* turn out that the best current argument for theism is no stronger than the best current argument for antitheism, or even that it turns out that the *ideal* best argument for theism is no stronger than the ideal best argument for antitheism. What conclusion would it be appropriate to draw in the face of either of these consequences? In particular, what conclusions would it be appropriate to draw about the *rationality* of theists, if it turned out that *arguments* for theism are deficient in either of these ways? (Perhaps we should emphasize at this point that the questions that we are asking here are hypothetical: we are not claiming that New has succeeded in showing either that the current best case for theism is no stronger than the current best case for antitheism, or that the ideal best case for theism is no stronger than the ideal best case for antitheism. Rather, we are wondering what would follow if New had successfully prosecuted his case, or if someone else is able to provide a successful extension of New's line of thought.)

At least *prima facie*, there seems to be a range of possible responses. On the one hand, one might hold that, if the current arguments for theism are no stronger than the current arguments for antitheism, or if the best-possible arguments for theism are no stronger than the best-possible arguments for antitheism, then theism cannot – or, at least, cannot now – be rationally maintained (at least by those who are sufficiently well informed about the standing of the relevant arguments). On the other hand, one might hold that, even if the current arguments for theism are no stronger than the current arguments for antitheism, and even if the best-possible arguments for theism are no stronger than the best-possible arguments for antitheism, it is none the less possible for theism to be rationally maintained, even by those who are sufficiently well informed about the standing of the relevant arguments.

One central issue that arises when we consider the range of possible responses under the supposition that New's case can be successfully prosecuted concerns the possibility of disagreement amongst doxastic peers. Can it be that two fully rational people who are fully apprised of all of the arguments – or, at any rate, of all of the good arguments – about a contested proposition none the less *reasonably* disagree about the truth-status of that proposition? In particular, can it be that one reasonable person reasonably believes that p, and another reasonable person reasonably believes that not-p, even though both of these people recognize that the best argument for p is no stronger than an argument whose conclusion entails that not-p?

8. Evaluate New's reasons in section III for thinking that there is no antitheistic tradition.

We shall give some further attention to these difficult questions in the remaining parts of the present section; however, we should say here that there is no current consensus about how these questions should be answered. Some philosophers maintain that you are not entitled to believe unless you are in possession of arguments that *ought* to bring all other rational agents to share your beliefs. Other philosophers maintain that you are perfectly entitled to believe even if you think that there are no arguments that ought to bring all other rational agents to share your beliefs. If you are interested in pursuing these matters further, you might like to have a look at:

Feldman, R., 'Reasonable Religious Disagreements', in L. Antony (ed.), *Philosophers without Gods: Meditations on Atheism and Secular Life*, Oxford: Oxford University Press, 2007.

Gutting, G., *Religious Belief and Religious Skepticism*, South Bend, Ind.: University of Notre Dame Press, 1982.

Moffett, M., 'Reasonable Disagreement and Rational Group Inquiry', *Episteme*, 4 (2007): 352–67.

Introduction to Clifford

William Kingdon Clifford (1845–79) was a British mathematician and philosopher. Educated at King's College, London, and Trinity College, Cambridge, Clifford began giving public lectures when he was appointed Fellow of Trinity in 1868. Clifford was then appointed professor of applied mathematics at University College, London, in 1870, but his academic career ended prematurely when he died from tuberculosis.

There are two pieces of work for which Clifford is primarily remembered: (i) a discussion of the nature of space and time that seems to anticipate Einstein's general theory of relativity in some respects, and (ii) his short paper on the ethics of belief, which was published after his death in a very interesting pamphlet that brings together his main philosophical essays. The following section is from the first part of Clifford's paper on the ethics of belief.

In the material that we consider, Clifford argues for the claim that *it is wrong always, everywhere, and for anyone, to believe anything upon insufficient evidence (and argument)*. More broadly, Clifford aims to support the cause of those free-thinkers who suppose that religious believers have an obligation to answer the charge that there is insufficient evidence to support their beliefs:

> If a man, holding a belief which he was taught in childhood or persuaded of afterwards, keeps down and pushes away any doubts which arise about it in his mind, purposely avoids the reading of books and the company of men that call in question or discuss it, and regards as impious those questions which cannot easily be asked without disturbing it – the life of that man is one long sin against mankind.

It is at least worth asking the question whether Clifford supports the views of those who would say that there can be no reasonable disagreement between reasonable and well-informed believers: perhaps Clifford thinks – at least implicitly – that the proper application of reason to evidence is bound to lead to convergence of opinion.

William Clifford, 'The Ethics of Belief'

[1] A ship-owner was about to send to sea an emigrant-ship. He knew that she was old, and not over-well built at the first; that she had seen many seas and climes, and often had needed repairs. Doubts had been suggested to him that possibly she was not seaworthy. These doubts preyed upon his mind and made him unhappy; he thought that perhaps he ought to have her thoroughly overhauled and refitted, even though this should put him to great expense. Before the ship sailed, however, he succeeded in overcoming these melancholy reflections. He said to himself that she had gone safely through so many voyages and weathered so many storms that it was idle to suppose she would not come safely home from this trip also. He would put his trust in Providence, which could hardly fail to protect all these unhappy families that were leaving their fatherland to seek for better times elsewhere. He would dismiss from his mind all ungenerous suspicions about the honesty of builders and contractors. In such ways he

acquired a sincere and comfortable conviction that his vessel was thoroughly safe and seaworthy; he watched her departure with a light heart, and benevolent wishes for the success of the exiles in their strange new home that was to be; and he got his insurance-money when she went down in mid-ocean and told no tales.

[a]→ What shall we say of him? Surely this, that he was verily guilty of the death of those men. It is admitted that he did sincerely believe in the soundness of his ship; but the sincerity of his conviction can in no wise help him, because *he had no right to believe on such evidence as was before him.* He had acquired his belief not by honestly earning it in patient investigation, but by stifling his doubts. And although in the end he may have felt so sure about it that he could not think otherwise, yet inasmuch as he had knowingly and willingly worked himself into that frame of mind, he must be held responsible for it.

[b]→ Let us alter the case a little, and suppose that the ship was not unsound after all; that she made her voyage safely, and many others after it. Will that diminish the guilt of her owner? Not one jot. When an action is once done, it is right or wrong for ever; no accidental failure of its good or evil fruits can possibly alter that. The man would not have been innocent, he would only have been not found out. The question of right or wrong has to do with the origin of his belief, not the matter of it; not what it was, but how he got it; not whether it turned out to be true or false, but whether he had a right to believe on such evidence as was before him.

[2] There was once an island in which some of the inhabitants professed a religion teaching neither the doctrine of original sin nor that of eternal punishment. A suspicion got abroad that the professors of this religion had made use of unfair means to get their doctrines taught to children. They were accused of wresting the laws of their country in such a way as to remove children from the care of their natural and legal guardians; and even of stealing them away and keeping them concealed from their friends and relations. A certain number of men formed themselves into a society for the purpose of agitating the public about this matter. They published grave accusations against individual citizens of the highest position and character, and did all in their power to injure these citizens in their exercise of their professions. So great was the noise they made, that a Commission was appointed to investigate the facts; but after the Commission had carefully inquired into all the evidence that could be got, it appeared that the accused were innocent. Not only had they been accused on insufficient evidence, but the evidence of their innocence was such as the agitators might easily have obtained, if they had attempted a fair inquiry. After these disclosures the inhabitants of that country looked upon the members of the agitating society, not only as persons whose judgment was to be distrusted, but also as no longer to be counted honorable men. For although they had sincerely and conscientiously believed in the charges they had made, *yet they had no right to believe on such evidence as was before them.* Their

sincere convictions, instead of being honestly earned by patient inquiring, were stolen by listening to the voice of prejudice and passion.

[c]→ Let us vary this case also, and suppose, other things remaining as before, that a still more accurate investigation proved the accused to have been really guilty. Would this make any difference in the guilt of the accusers? Clearly not; the question is not whether their belief was true or false, but whether they entertained it on wrong grounds. They would no doubt say, 'Now you see that we were right after all; next time perhaps you will believe us.' And they might be believed, but they would not thereby become honorable men. They would not be innocent, they would only be not found out. Every one of them, if he chose to examine himself *in foro conscientiæ*, would know that he had acquired and nourished a belief, when he had no right to believe on such evidence as was before him; and therein he would know that he had done a wrong thing.

[d]→ [3] It may be said, however, that in both of these supposed cases it is not the belief which is judged to be wrong, but the action following upon it. The ship-owner might say, 'I am perfectly certain that my ship is sound, but still I feel it my duty to have her examined, before trusting the lives of so many people to her.' And it might be said to the agitator, 'However convinced you were of the justice of your cause and the truth of your convictions, you ought not to have made a public attack upon any man's character until you had examined the evidence on both sides with the utmost patience and care.'

[e]→ In the first place, let us admit that, so far as it goes, this view of the case is right and necessary; right, because even when a man's belief is so fixed that he cannot think otherwise, he still has a choice in regard to the action suggested by it, and so cannot escape the duty of investigating on the ground of the strength of his convictions; and necessary, because those who are not yet capable of controlling their feelings and thoughts must have a plain rule dealing with overt acts.

But this being premised as necessary, it becomes clear that it is not sufficient, and that our previous judgment is required to supplement it. For it is not possible so to sever the belief from the action it suggests as to condemn the one without condemning the other. No man holding a strong belief on one side of a question, or even wishing to hold a belief on one side, can investigate it with such fairness and completeness as if he were really in doubt and unbiased; so that the existence of a belief not founded on fair inquiry unfits a man for the performance of this necessary duty. . . .

[4] In the two supposed cases which have been considered, it has been judged wrong to believe on insufficient evidence, or to nourish belief by suppressing doubts and avoiding investigation. The reason of this judgment is not far to seek: it is that in both these cases the belief held by one man
[f]→ was of great importance to other men. But forasmuch as no belief held by one man, however seemingly trivial the belief, and however obscure the believer, is ever actually insignificant or without its effect on the fate of

mankind, we have no choice but to extend our judgment to all cases of belief whatever. Belief, that sacred faculty which prompts the decisions of our will, and knits into harmonious working all the compacted energies of our being, is ours not for ourselves, but for humanity. It is rightly used on truths which have been established by long experience and waiting toil, and which have stood in the fierce light of free and fearless questioning. Then it helps to bind men together, and to strengthen and direct their common action. It is desecrated when given to unproved and unquestioned statements, for the solace and private pleasure of the believer; to add a tinsel splendor to the plain straight road of our life and display a bright mirage beyond it; or even to drown the common sorrows of our kind by a self-deception which allows them not only to cast down, but also to degrade us. Whoso would deserve well of his fellows in this matter will guard the purity of his belief with a very fanaticism of jealous care, lest at any time it should rest on an unworthy object, and catch a stain which can never be wiped away.

It is not only the leader of men, statesmen, philosopher, or poet, that owes this bounden duty to mankind. Every rustic who delivers in the village ale-house his slow, infrequent sentences, may help to kill or keep alive the fatal superstitions which clog his race. Every hard-worked wife of an artisan may transmit to her children beliefs which shall knit society together, or rend it in pieces. No simplicity of mind, no obscurity of station, can escape the universal duty of questioning all that we believe.

It is true that this duty is a hard one, and the doubt which comes out of it is often a very bitter thing. It leaves us bare and powerless where we thought that we were safe and strong. To know all about anything is to know how to deal with it under all circumstances. We feel much happier and more secure when we think we know precisely what to do, no matter what happens, than when we have lost our way and do not know where to turn. And if we have supposed ourselves to know all about anything, and to be capable of doing what is fit in regard to it, we naturally do not like to find that we are really ignorant and powerless, that we have to begin again at the beginning, and try to learn what the thing is and how it is to be dealt with – if indeed anything can be learnt about it. It is the sense of power attached to a sense of knowledge that makes men desirous of believing, and afraid of doubting.

This sense of power is the highest and best of pleasures when the belief on which it is founded is a true belief, and has been fairly earned by investigation. For then we may justly feel that it is common property, and holds good for others as well as for ourselves. Then we may be glad, not that I have learned secrets by which I am safer and stronger, but that *we men* have got mastery over more of the world; and we shall be strong, not for ourselves, but in the name of Man and his strength. But if the belief has been accepted on insufficient evidence, the pleasure is a stolen one. Not only does it deceive ourselves by giving us a sense of power which we do not really possess, but it is sinful, because it is stolen in defiance of our duty to mankind. That duty is to guard ourselves from such beliefs as from a pestilence, which may shortly master our own body and then spread to the rest of the town. What would be thought of one who, for the sake of a sweet fruit, should deliberately run the risk of bringing a plague upon his family and his neighbors?

And, as in other such cases, it is not the risk only which has to be considered; for a bad action is always bad at the time when it is done, no matter what happens afterwards. Every time we let ourselves believe for unworthy reasons, we weaken our powers of self-control, of doubting, of judicially and fairly weighing evidence. We all suffer severely enough from the maintenance and support of false beliefs and the fatally wrong actions which they lead to, and the evil born when one such belief is entertained is great and wide. But a greater and wider evil arises when the credulous character is maintained and supported, when a habit of believing for unworthy reasons is fostered and made permanent. If I steal money from any person, there may be no harm done by the mere transfer of possession; he may not feel the loss, or it may prevent him from using the money badly. But I cannot help doing this great wrong towards Man, that I make myself dishonest. What hurts society is not that it should lose its property, but that it should become a den of thieves; for then it must cease to be society. This is why we ought not to do evil that good may come; for at any rate this great evil has come, that we have done evil and are made wicked thereby. In like manner, if I let myself believe anything on insufficient evidence, there may be no great harm done by the mere belief; it may be true after all, or I may never have occasion to exhibit it in outward acts. But I cannot help doing this great wrong towards Man, that I make myself credulous. The danger to society is not merely that it should believe wrong things, though that is great enough; but that it should become credulous, and lose the habit of testing things and inquiring into them; for then it must sink back into savagery. . . .

g → [5] To sum up: it is wrong always, everywhere, and for anyone, to believe anything upon insufficient evidence.

If a man, holding a belief which he was taught in childhood or persuaded of afterwards, keeps down and pushes away any doubts which arise about it in his mind, purposely avoids the reading of books and the company of men that call in question or discuss it, and regards as impious those questions which cannot easily be asked without disturbing it – the life of that man is one long sin against mankind.

Commentary on Clifford

We have divided Clifford's text into five sections. The first two sections – from [1] to [2], and from [2] to [3] – introduce two cases in which Clifford supposes that people go wrong because they fail to proportion their beliefs to the evidence that they possess. The third section – from [3] to [4] – argues against the suggestion that the wrong attaches not to the beliefs, but only to the actions of the protagonists of the two cases. The fourth section – from [4] to [5] – generalises the conclusions drawn from the study of the two cases, and sets out what Clifford takes to be the grounds for the universal human obligation to proportion all of our beliefs to the available evidence. The final section – from [5] – summarises Clifford's conclusions.

On Clifford's own account, his examples are intended to make vivid to us our intuitive judgement that it is wrong to 'stifle doubts' and to 'knowingly and willingly work oneself into a frame of mind' in which one holds certain beliefs only because one has managed to 'stifle doubts'. Moreover, it is important to Clifford that the intuitive judgement that he takes to be made vivid in these examples is a general judgement: it is *always* wrong to 'stifle doubts' and to 'knowingly and willingly work oneself into a frame of mind' in which one holds certain beliefs only because one has managed to 'stifle doubts'.

1. Examine Clifford's ship-owner example and state, giving reasons, for what (if anything) you think the owner is morally culpable. Do you agree with Clifford's assessment at [a]↦. If not, why not?

2. Consider Clifford's example of the agitators and explain in what way you think they are morally culpable. Is the case morally different from the example of the ship-owner?

At least *prima facie*, there does seem to be something correct about Clifford's discussion of his cases. For instance, given that the ship-owner has good reasons for thinking that the ship may not be seaworthy – since he is aware that it is old, much repaired, and not well constructed in the first place – it is clear that the ship-owner does have good reasons for thinking that the ship is in need of a thorough overhaul and refit. Moreover, since there is a time at which the ship-owner recognises that the ship should 'perhaps' be thoroughly overhauled and refitted, and yet he does not act on this recognition, there is clearly a case to be answered that he bears responsibility for the death of the passengers when the ship goes down. In order to disavow this responsibility, the ship-owner would need to have had a good reason for failing to act on his recognition that the ship should 'perhaps' be thoroughly overhauled and refitted. But, on Clifford's account, we are given to suppose that the ship-owner has no such good reasons. If this much is right, then we should certainly be happy to join with Clifford in holding that the ship-owner bears some responsibility for the death of his passengers.

3. Explain why Clifford gives variants of the two examples at [b]↦ and [c]↦. Is Clifford correct in thinking that these variants do not change our moral evaluation of the ship-owner or the agitators?

But there is more to Clifford's account than we have considered thus far. For Clifford provides an account of how it is that the ship-owner fails to act on his recognition that the ship should perhaps be thoroughly overhauled and refitted. First, Clifford says that the ship-owner 'says to himself' that the ship has not gone down on any of its numerous previous voyages. Second, Clifford says that the ship-owner 'would put his trust in Providence'. And, third, Clifford says that the ship-owner 'would dismiss from his mind all ungenerous suspicions about the honesty of builders and contractors'. On Clifford's account, 'in such ways' the ship-owner acquires 'a sincere and comfortable conviction' that his vessel is safe and seaworthy.

It is not clear that Clifford's account of the ship-owner's 'overcoming' of his 'melancholy reflections' rings true. Is it really *possible* that a person attain 'a sincere and comfortable conviction' simply by unwarrantedly 'dismissing from his mind' the reasons that he has for believing otherwise? (True enough, the observation that the ship has not gone down on any of its previous voyages does count as *a* reason for thinking that it will not go down on its current voyage – but this is not a very strong consideration, particularly when set against the suspicion that it is now time for a thorough overhaul and refit.) Merely *hoping* that the ship will complete its voyage safely – 'putting one's trust in Providence' – surely cannot conduce at all to 'sincere and comfortable conviction' in the face of the reasons that the ship-owner has for suspecting that the ship is not seaworthy.

Suppose that I am unsure whether I need to put in a tax return. So long as I put off consulting the relevant legislation, I can remain unsure about whether I need to put in a tax return. Moreover, if I put off consulting the relevant legislation, I may end up forgetting about my uncertainty: if I do not attend to the question whether I need to put in a tax return, then I may end up not thinking at all about whether I need to put in a tax return. However, if this is how things go, then it is not right to say that I end up acquiring a 'sincere and comfortable conviction' that I do not need to put in a tax return; rather, what happens is that the question of whether I need to put in a tax return simply gets buried. And, in this case, if the tax office eventually comes calling, it is clear that my failure to put in a tax return is culpable: for I should not have buried the question whether I needed to put in a tax return.

One thing that makes the case of the ship-owner different from the case of the tax return is that Clifford supposes that the ship-owner is made unhappy by the doubts that prey on his mind: it is not clear that it is psychologically plausible that the ship-owner could succeed in burying the question of the seaworthiness of his vessel simply by postponing an investigation of the seaworthiness of his vessel. But, in any case, even if the ship-owner could succeed in burying the question of the seaworthiness of his vessel simply by postponing an investigation of the seaworthiness of his vessel, that would not count as a case in which the ship-owner secures 'a sincere and comfortable conviction' in the seaworthiness of his vessel; rather, it would be a case in which the ship-owner simply stops paying any attention to questions about the seaworthiness of his vessel.

If there is something to these worries about the psychological plausibility of Clifford's account of the case of the ship-owner, then there is reason to worry about the bearing of this case on the conclusion that Clifford wishes to establish. Clifford takes it to be clear that the ship-owner does sincerely believe in the soundness of his ship, but criticises him on the grounds that he had no right to this belief given the evidence that was before him. However, if more psychologically plausible renderings of the case would leave it unclear whether the ship-owner really does *believe* in the soundness of his ship, then it is not clear that we can suppose that Clifford's example makes vivid our commitment to the claim that it is wrong always and everywhere to hold beliefs on insufficient evidence and argument. (Perhaps it is worth noting that we have not discussed all of the psychological complexities that arise in the case of the ship-owner. When Clifford adds the words 'even though this should put him to great expense', he is clearly pointing to the profit-making desires of the ship-owner. Since actions are always the product of both beliefs and desires, it is worth noting that a fully realistic account of the actions of the ship-owner might better indict him on the grounds that his desire to make a profit trumped his doubts about the seaworthiness of the vessel.)

4. State in your own words the counter-argument that Clifford proposes at [d]→ and his response to it at [e]→. Is his response satisfactory?

5. At [f]→ Clifford extends the principle that it is wrong to believe on insufficient evidence to all beliefs and to all believers. State in your own words and evaluate the arguments he uses through the course of [4] for the extension of his principle.

Even if it is agreed that it is not clear that Clifford's examples really do make vivid our commitment to the claim that it is wrong always and everywhere to hold beliefs on insufficient evidence and argument, it may yet be true that it *is* wrong always, everywhere, and for anyone, to believe anything upon insufficient evidence and argument. In particular, it might be thought that there is surely something to the idea that it is *irrational* to fail to proportion beliefs to evidence and argument (quite apart from Clifford's further suggestion that 'stifling doubts' can never excuse beliefs that are not proportionate to evidence and argument). Can we formulate a cogent principle to this effect?

It seems that it would be a mistake to claim that:

(1) It is irrational, always, everywhere, and for anyone, to believe anything for which *there is* insufficient evidence or argument.

When Clifford first introduces considerations about evidence, he makes it clear that he is talking about evidence that is available to the subject in question. We should not want to insist that it is irrational, always, everywhere, and for anyone, to believe anything that is not true (or not known to be true, or not known to be true by the subject), because we think that one might be blamelessly unaware of relevant considerations: lack of information is not necessarily a crime against reason.

It seems that it would be a different kind of mistake to claim that:

(2) It is irrational, always, everywhere, and for anyone, to believe anything for which *one takes himself or herself to have* insufficient evidence or argument.

Here the difficulty is that the proposed claim seems trivial, not least because it is doubtful that it is really possible to believe something for which one takes oneself to have insufficient evidence and argument. Clearly, there is something rather odd about claims of the form 'I believe that p, but of course I have no good argument or evidence that supports my doing so'. And even if there are pathological cases of belief that are ruled out by this formulation of the principle – so that it is not trivial – it none the less seems quite clear that Clifford was not aiming to defend this version of the principle.

Perhaps the principle that Clifford means to defend is something like this:

(3) It is irrational, always, everywhere, and for anyone, to believe anything for which *one has* insufficient evidence or argument.

However, if this is the claim that Clifford means to defend, then it is open to a range of objections. First, it seems plausible to hold that one must already have beliefs before one can recognise and assess evidence and arguments. But, if that is right, then it can hardly be a constraint on the rationality of one's earliest beliefs that they be proportioned to the evidence and arguments that one possesses. Second, it seems implausible to suppose that there is a rationality constraint requiring one to keep track of the grounds that one had for adopting beliefs: but, if that is right, then it is unclear whether one can be expected to be able to determine whether any given belief does fully conform to Clifford's principle. Third, there is a problem of self-application: is it true that Clifford had sufficient evidence or argument to support the belief that his principle is true? Unless we can point to the evidence or argument which is supposed to be sufficient to establish Clifford's principle, then it seems that, by its own lights, that principle is not worthy of our belief!

6. Suppose we modify Clifford's principle to: (3*) It is irrational, always, everywhere, and for anyone, to believe anything for which *one has* insufficient evidence or argument, *except* for those beliefs required in assessing the evidence and arguments that one has. Does (3*) counter the objections to (3)? Evaluate (3*).

In the light of the above objections, we might try a further modification. Perhaps the principle for which Clifford *ought* to have aimed was something like this:

(4) It is irrational, always, everywhere, and for anyone, to take on a new belief that is not appropriately proportioned to the arguments or evidence already possessed by that one.

Even this version of the principle has been taken to be subject to counter-examples. Consider, for example, the case of the footballers who play better if they believe that they will win even though their arguments and evidence do not support the proposition that they will win; or the case of young children who believe things 'because Mummy said so', even though neither their arguments nor their evidence supports the belief that what Mummy says is true; or William James's case of the mountaineer who will die unless he forms the belief that he can leap the crevasse that blocks his descent, even though neither his arguments nor his evidence supports the claim that he can leap the crevasse. While it is controversial whether these really are counter-examples to the proposed principle – since desires are also involved in the production of action, the connections between belief and the will are at best obscure, and often the most important thing is merely that one should act in a certain way quite apart from the beliefs that one is able to form – they do perhaps suffice to show that it is not *obvious* that even our quite modest reformulation of Clifford's principle is worthy of belief.

Even if we *can't* arrive at a satisfying version of Clifford's principle – i.e. a principle which ties rational belief to some kind of proportionality to possessed evidence and reasons – we may none the less be able to preserve part of Clifford's claim that it is wrong to ignore doubts that one has about received beliefs. Even if Clifford exaggerates in his comments at [g]→, one might suppose that there is surely something right in the suggestion that one should not always 'purposely avoid the reading of books and the company of men that call in question or discuss' beliefs to which one is deeply attached. At the very least, there are prudential considerations here: it is very likely that other people will be able to detect weaknesses in your system of belief that you are not yourself able to see, and it seems plausible to think that one ought to want to work on the weaknesses in one's doxastic system. Moreover, and perhaps more importantly, it is not implausible to think that one has doxastic obligations to the world at large: if you are to benefit from the work that other people do in detecting weaknesses in your system of belief, then plainly you have an obligation to return the favour, helping other people to detect weaknesses in their systems of belief. Clifford's Victorian homilies about our doxastic duties surely strike us as being rather over the top; but that is not to say that there is not some more modest range of doxastic duties that we do properly incur.

7. Clifford presents not just epistemic but also *moral* objections to believing on insufficient evidence. Evaluate his arguments for this in [4].

Even if it is agreed that there is a satisfying version of Clifford's principle, or that there is something right in the suggestion that one should not always 'purposely avoid the reading of books and the company of men that call in question or discuss' beliefs to which one is deeply attached, it is not clear that this agreement has *any* interesting implications for religious belief. While there is a clear sub-text to our extract from Clifford's essay, we need to be given some further reason for thinking that, say, belief in the existence of God is threatened by a version of Clifford's principle, or that religious believers are constitutionally incapable of keeping the company of those who call in question or discuss their religious beliefs.

Perhaps it is true that *some* religious believers – like some of those who are not religious believers – are constitutionally incapable of keeping the company of those who call in question or discuss their beliefs about religion. But it is surely beyond question that, even if some religious believers are deficient in this way, there are religious believers who are capable of keeping the company of those who call in question or discuss their religious beliefs. The prospects for developing an argument against religious belief on the basis of considerations about the virtues of open-mindedness seem utterly negligible. Thus, if there is any threat to religious belief in the considerations that are raised in Clifford's essay, they must flow from the principle that beliefs should always be proportioned to evidence and argument.

While Clifford does not indicate how one might argue that, say, one cannot come to belief in God if one is properly proportioning one's beliefs to argument and evidence, we can make one suggestion about how one might *try* to develop such a case. If New were able to establish that there is no evidence or argument that favours theism over antitheism, then – by version (4) of Clifford's principle – it seems that we could draw the conclusion that it can never be rational to take on belief in theism. Even if there were a successful argument of this kind, it would not show that one cannot be rational in persisting in one's belief in theism, given that one has this belief; at best, it shows that one cannot be rational in one's acquisition of the belief in the first instance. Perhaps, though, that would be enough to make serious difficulties for religious belief.

Even if there is some *prima facie* plausibility to the argument that we have just sketched, it is important to consider what would be the consequences of the claim that it is a successful argument. In particular, it is important to think about the ways in which this kind of argument might be deployed in other contexts, i.e. outside the philosophy of religion. If this argument is good, then so is any similar argument about cases in which we consider hypotheses that cannot be separated on grounds of evidence and argument. Consider, for example, the hypothesis that you are a brain in a vat, wired up to a computer programmed by an evil scientist to produce in you the illusion that you are a regular human subject in the world. Do you have evidence or arguments that discriminate between the hypothesis that you are such a brain in a vat and the hypothesis that you are a regular human subject in the world? If not, should you *really* draw the conclusion that you would not be rationally entitled to come to believe that you are a regular human subject in the world if you did not already hold this belief? At the very least, it seems that the proponent of the argument that we have sketched still has some work to do, to explain why the consistent deployment of this argument would not lead to widescale acceptance of rather sceptical claims.

8. Suppose that version (4) of Clifford's principle is true. Explain its implications for: (i) moral beliefs, (ii) beliefs about the past, (iii) beliefs about one's own mental states. Would the principle require us to change the way in which we usually form these beliefs?

Our discussion of Clifford's paper has been very compressed. There are many other discussions of Clifford's work in the philosophy of religion literature. For instance, you might be interested in having a look at:

Haack, S., '"The Ethics of Belief" Reconsidered', in L. Hahn (ed.), *The Philosophy of Roderick M. Chisholm*, LaSalle, Ill.: Open Court, 1997.

Mavrodes, G., 'James and Clifford on "The Will to Believe"', *The Personalist*, 44 (1963).

van Inwagen, P., 'It Is Wrong, Everywhere, Always, and for Anyone, to Believe Anything upon Insufficient Evidence', in J. Jordan and D. Howard-Snyder (eds), *Faith, Freedom and Rationality: Philosophy of Religion Today*, London: Rowman & Littlefield, 1996.

Introduction to James

William James (1842–1910) – brother of the novelist Henry James – is one of the giants of American philosophy and psychology. After completing a medical degree at Harvard in 1869, and having previously spent some years in Europe preparing to be an artist, James entered into a career as a lecturer at Harvard initially teaching anatomy and physiology and in the late 1870s philosophy and psychology. His first major work was the two-volume *Principles of Psychology* (1890); perhaps his best-known major work, *The Varieties of Religious Experience: A Study in Human Nature*, arose from his Gifford Lectures of 1901–2. His pragmatist conception of philosophy was developed in *Pragmatism: A New Name for Some Old Ways of Thinking* (1907), *The Meaning of Truth* (1909) and *Essays in Radical Empiricism* (1912). The essay that we examine here is taken from the eponymous *The Will to Believe* (1897).

In many ways, James was an empiricist and a humanist. However, he also wanted to preserve a place for religious belief, even though he doubted that religious belief could be integrated into a scientific worldview. 'The Will to Believe' is the essay in which James tries to explain how someone who is both an empiricist and a humanist can none the less be a religious believer.

It is worth noting from the beginning that 'The Will to Believe' is, in part, a response to Clifford's 'The Ethics of Belief'. Against Clifford's claim that it is wrong, always, everywhere, and for anyone, to believe anything upon insufficient evidence and argument, James insists that each of us is *required* to believe some things upon insufficient evidence and argument merely because we *want* those things to be true: 'our passional nature not only lawfully may, but must, decide an option between propositions, whenever it is a genuine option that cannot by its nature be decided on intellectual grounds'. Moreover – also against Clifford – James supposes that religious beliefs, such as the belief that God exists, belong to the class of beliefs that *can* be believed upon insufficient evidence and argument merely because we *want* those religious beliefs to be true.

William James, 'The Will to Believe'

I

Let us give the name of *hypothesis* to anything that may be proposed to our belief; and just as the electricians speak of live and dead wires, let us speak of any hypothesis as either *live* or *dead*. A live hypothesis is one which appeals as a real possibility to him to whom it is proposed. If I ask you to believe in the Mahdi, the notion makes no electric connection with your nature – it refuses to scintillate with any credibility at all. As an hypothesis it is completely dead. To an Arab, however (even if he be not one of the Mahdi's followers), the hypothesis is among the mind's possibilities: it is alive. This shows that deadness and liveness in an hypothesis are not intrinsic properties, but relations to the individual thinker. They are measured by his willingness to act. The maximum of liveness in an hypothesis means willingness to act irrevocably. Practically, that means belief; but there is some believing tendency wherever there is willingness to act at all.

Next, let us call the decision between two hypotheses an *option*. Options may be of several kinds. They may be – 1, *living* or *dead*; 2, *forced* or *avoidable*; 3, *momentous* or *trivial*; and for our purposes we may call an option a *genuine* option when it is of the forced, living, and momentous kind.

1. A living option is one in which both hypotheses are live ones. If I say to you: 'Be a theosophist or be a Mohammedan,' it is probably a dead option, because for you neither hypothesis is likely to be alive. But if I say: 'Be an agnostic or be a Christian,' it is otherwise: trained as you are, each hypothesis makes some appeal, however small, to your belief.
2. Next, if I say to you: 'Choose between going out with your umbrella or without it,' I do not offer you a genuine option, for it is not forced. You can easily avoid it by not going out at all. Similarly, if I say, 'Either love me or hate me,' 'Either call my theory true or call it false,' your option is avoidable. You may remain indifferent to me, neither loving nor hating, and you may decline to offer any judgment as to my theory. But if I say, 'Either accept this truth or go without it,' I put on you a forced option, for there is no standing place outside of the alternative. Every dilemma based on a complete logical disjunction, with no possibility of not choosing, is an option of this forced kind.
3. Finally, if I were Dr. Nansen and proposed to you to join my North Pole expedition, your option would be momentous; for this would probably be your only similar opportunity, and your choice now would either exclude you from the North Pole sort of immortality altogether or put at least the chance of it into your hands. He who refuses to embrace a unique opportunity loses the prize as surely as if he tried and failed. *Per contra*, the option is trivial when the opportunity is not unique, when the stake is insignificant, or when the decision is reversible if it later prove unwise. Such trivial options abound in the scientific life. A chemist finds an hypothesis live enough to spend a year in its verification: he believes in it to that extent. But if his experiments prove inconclusive either way, he is quit for his loss of time, no vital harm being done.

It will facilitate our discussion if we keep all these distinctions well in mind.

II

The next matter to consider is the actual psychology of human opinion. When we look at certain facts, it seems as if our passional and volitional nature lay at the root of all our convictions. When we look at others, it seems as if they could do nothing when the intellect had once said its say. Let us take the latter facts up first.

Does it not seem preposterous on the very face of it to talk of our opinions being modifiable at will? Can our will either help or hinder our intellect in its perceptions of truth? Can we, by just willing it, believe that Abraham Lincoln's existence is a myth, and that the portraits of him in McClure's Magazine are all of some one else? Can we, by any effort of our will, or by any strength of wish that it were true, believe ourselves well and about when we are roaring with rheumatism in bed, or feel certain that the sum of the two one-dollar bills in our pocket must be a hundred dollars? We can *say* any of these things, but we are absolutely impotent to believe them; and of just such things is the whole fabric of the truths that we do believe in made up – matters of fact, immediate or remote, as Hume said, and relations between ideas, which are either there or not there for us if we see them so, and which if not there cannot be put there by any action of our own.

In Pascal's Thoughts there is a celebrated passage known in literature as Pascal's wager. In it he tries to force us into Christianity by reasoning as if our concern with truth resembled our concern with the stakes in a game of chance. Translated freely his words are these: You must either believe or not believe that God is – which will you do? Your human reason cannot say. A game is going on between you and the nature of things which at the Day of Judgment will bring out either heads or tails. Weigh what your gains and your losses would be if you should stake all you have on heads, or God's existence: if you win in such case, you gain eternal beatitude; if you lose, you lose nothing at all. If there were an infinity of chances, and only one for God in this wager, still you ought to stake your all on God; for though you surely risk a finite loss by this procedure, any finite loss is reasonable, even a certain one is reasonable, if there is but the possibility of infinite gain. Go, then, and take holy water, and have masses said; belief will come and stupefy your scruples – *Cela vous fera croire et vous abêtira.* Why should you not? At bottom, what have you to lose?

You probably feel that when religious faith expresses itself thus, in the language of the gaming-table, it is put to its last trumps. Surely Pascal's own personal belief in masses and holy water had far other springs; and this celebrated page of his is but an argument for others, a last desperate snatch at a weapon against the hardness of the unbelieving heart. We feel that a faith in masses and holy water adopted wilfully after such a mechanical calculation would lack the inner soul of faith's reality; and if we were ourselves in the place of the Deity, we should probably take particular pleasure in cutting off believers of this pattern from their infinite reward. It is evident that unless there be some pre-existing tendency to believe in masses and holy water, the option offered to the will by Pascal is not a living option. Certainly no Turk ever took to masses and holy water on its account; and even to us Protestants these means of salvation seem such foregone impossibilities that Pascal's logic, invoked for them specifically, leaves us unmoved. As well might the Mahdi write to us, saying, 'I am the Expected One whom God has created in his effulgence. You shall be infinitely happy if you confess me; otherwise you shall be cut off from the light of the sun. Weigh, then, your infinite gain if I am genuine against your finite sacrifice if I am not!' His logic would be that of Pascal; but he would vainly use it on us, for the hypothesis he offers us is dead. No tendency to act on it exists in us to any degree.

The talk of believing by our volition seems, then, from one point of view, simply silly. From another point of view it is worse than silly, it is vile. When one turns to the magnificent edifice of the physical sciences, and sees how it was reared; what thousands of disinterested moral lives of men lie buried in its mere foundations; what patience and postponement, what choking down of preference, what submission to the icy laws of outer fact are wrought into its very stones and mortar; how absolutely impersonal it stands in its vast augustness, – then how besotted and contemptible seems every little sentimentalist who comes blowing his voluntary smoke-wreaths, and pretending to decide things from out of his private dream! Can we wonder if those bred in the rugged and manly school of science should feel like spewing such subjectivism out of their mouths? The whole system of loyalties which grow up in the schools of science go dead against its toleration; so that it is only natural that those who have caught the scientific fever should pass over to the opposite extreme, and write sometimes as if the incorruptibly truthful intellect ought positively to prefer bitterness and unacceptableness to the heart in its cup.

> It fortifies my soul to know
> That, though I perish, Truth is so –

sings Clough, while Huxley exclaims: 'My only consolation lies in the reflection that, however bad our posterity may become, so far as they hold by the plain rule of not pretending to believe what they have no reason to believe, because it may be to their advantage so to pretend [the word 'pretend' is surely here redundant], they will not have reached the lowest depth of immorality.' And that delicious *enfant terrible* Clifford writes: 'Belief is desecrated when given to unproved and unquestioned statements for the solace and private pleasure of the believer. . . . Whoso would deserve well of his fellows in this matter will guard the purity of his belief with a very fanaticism of jealous care, lest at any time it should rest on an unworthy
[a]→ object, and catch a stain which can never be wiped away. . . . If belief has

been accepted on insufficient evidence [even though the belief be true, as Clifford on the same page explains] the pleasure is a stolen one. . . . It is sinful because it is stolen in defiance of our duty to mankind. That duty is to guard ourselves from such beliefs as from a pestilence which may shortly master our own body and then spread to the rest of the town. . . . It is wrong always, everywhere, and for every one, to believe anything upon insufficient evidence.'

III

All this strikes one as healthy, even when expressed, as by Clifford, with somewhat too much of robustious pathos in the voice. Free-will and simple wishing do seem, in the matter of our credences, to be only fifth wheels to the coach. Yet if any one should thereupon assume that intellectual insight is what remains after wish and will and sentimental preference have taken wing, or that pure reason is what then settles our opinions, he would fly quite as directly in the teeth of the facts.

It is only our already dead hypotheses that our willing nature is unable to bring to life again. But what has made them dead for us is for the most part a previous action of our willing nature of an antagonistic kind. When I say 'willing nature,' I do not mean only such deliberate volitions as may have set up habits of belief that we cannot now escape from – I mean all such factors of belief as fear and hope, prejudice and passion, imitation and partisanship, the circumpressure of our caste and set. As a matter of fact we find ourselves believing, we hardly know how or why. Mr. Balfour gives the name of 'authority' to all those influences, born of the intellectual climate, that make hypotheses possible or impossible for us, alive or dead. Here in this room, we all of us believe in molecules and the conservation of energy, in democracy and necessary progress, in Protestant Christianity and the duty of fighting for 'the doctrine of the immortal Monroe,' all for no reasons worthy of the name. We see into these matters with no more inner clearness, and probably with much less, than any disbeliever in them might possess. His unconventionality would probably have some grounds to show for its conclusions; but for us, not insight, but the *prestige* of the opinions, is what makes the spark shoot from them and light up our sleeping magazines of faith. Our reason is quite satisfied, in nine hundred and ninety-nine cases out of every thousand of us, if it can find a few arguments that will do to recite in case our credulity is criticized by some one else. Our faith is faith in some one else's faith, and in the greatest matters this is most the case. Our belief in truth itself, for instance, that there is a truth, and that our minds and it are made for each other – what is it but a passionate affirmation of desire, in which our social system backs us up? We want to have a truth; we want to believe that our experiments and studies and discussions must put us in a continually better and better position towards it; and on this line we agree to fight out our thinking lives. But if a pyrrhonistic skeptic asks us *how we know* all this, can our logic find a reply? No! certainly it cannot. It is just one volition against another – we willing to go in for life upon a trust or assumption which he, for his part, does not care to make.

As a rule we disbelieve all facts and theories for which we have no use. Clifford's cosmic emotions find no use for Christian feelings. Huxley belabors the bishops because there is no use for sacerdotalism in his scheme of life. Newman, on the contrary, goes over to Romanism, and finds all sorts of reasons good for staying there, because a priestly system is for him an organic need and delight. Why do so few 'scientists' even look at the evidence for telepathy, so-called? Because they think, as a leading biologist, now dead, once said to me, that even if such a thing were true, scientists ought to band together to keep it suppressed and concealed. It would undo the uniformity of Nature and all sorts of other things without which scientists cannot carry on their pursuits. But if this very man had been shown something which as a scientist he might *do* with telepathy, he might not only have examined the evidence, but even have found it good enough. This very law which the logicians would impose upon us – if I may give the name of logicians to those who would rule out our willing nature here – is based on nothing but their own natural wish to exclude all elements for which they, in their professional quality of logicians, can find no use.

Evidently, then, our non-intellectual nature does influence our convictions. There are passional tendencies and volitions which run before and others which come after belief, and it is only the latter that are too late for the fair; and they are not too late when the previous passional work has been already in their own direction. Pascal's argument, instead of being powerless, then seems a regular clincher, and is the last stroke needed to make our faith in masses and holy water complete. The state of things is evidently far from simple; and pure insight and logic, whatever they might do ideally, are not the only things that really do produce our creeds.

IV

Our next duty, having recognized this mixed-up state of affairs, is to ask whether it be simply reprehensible and pathological, or whether, on the contrary, we must treat it as a normal element in making up our minds. The thesis I defend is, briefly stated, this: *Our passional nature not only lawfully may, but must, decide an option between propositions, whenever it is a genuine option that cannot by its nature be decided on intellectual grounds; for to say, under such circumstances, 'Do not decide, but leave the question open,' is itself a passional decision, – just like deciding yes or no, – and is attended with the same risk of losing the truth*. The thesis thus abstractly expressed will, I trust, soon become quite clear. . . .

VIII

And now, after all this introduction, let us go straight at our question. I have said, and now repeat it, that not only as a matter of fact do we find our passional nature influencing us in our opinions, but that there are some options between opinions in which this influence must be regarded both as an inevitable and as a lawful determinant of our choice.

I fear here that some of you my hearers will begin to scent danger, and lend an inhospitable ear. Two first steps of passion you have indeed had to admit as necessary – we must think so as to avoid dupery, and we must think so as to gain truth; but the surest path to those ideal consummations, you will probably consider, is from now onwards to take no further passional step.

Well, of course, I agree as far as the facts will allow. Wherever the option between losing truth and gaining it is not momentous, we can throw the chance of *gaining truth* away, and at any rate save ourselves from any chance of *believing falsehood*, by not making up our minds at all till objective evidence has come. In scientific questions, this is almost always the case; and even in human affairs in general, the need of acting is seldom so urgent that a false belief to act on is better than no belief at all. Law courts, indeed, have to decide on the best evidence attainable for the moment, because a judge's duty is to make law as well as to ascertain it, and (as a learned judge once said to me) few cases are worth spending much time over: the great thing is to have them decided on *any* acceptable principle, and got out of the way. But in our dealings with objective nature we obviously are recorders, not makers, of the truth; and decisions for the mere sake of deciding promptly and getting on to the next business would be wholly out of place. Throughout the breadth of physical nature facts are what they are quite independently of us, and seldom is there any such hurry about them that the risks of being duped by believing a premature theory need be faced. The questions here are always trivial options, the hypotheses are hardly living (at any rate not living for us spectators), the choice between believing truth or falsehood is seldom forced. The attitude of skeptical balance is therefore the absolutely wise one if we would escape mistakes. What difference, indeed, does it make to most of us whether we have or have not a theory of the Röntgen rays, whether we believe or not in mind-stuff, or have a conviction about the causality of conscious states? It makes no difference. Such options are not forced on us. On every account it is better not to make them, but still keep weighing reasons *pro et contra* with an indifferent hand. . . .

The question next arises: Are there not somewhere forced options in our speculative questions, and can we (as men who may be interested at least as much in positively gaining truth as in merely escaping dupery) always wait with impunity till the coercive evidence shall have arrived? It seems *a priori* improbable that the truth should be so nicely adjusted to our needs and powers as that. In the great boarding-house of nature, the cakes and the butter and the syrup seldom come out so even and leave the plates so clean. Indeed, we should view them with scientific suspicion if they did.

IX

Moral questions immediately present themselves as questions whose solution cannot wait for sensible proof. A moral question is a question not of what sensibly exists, but of what is good, or would be good if it did exist. Science can tell us what exists; but to compare the *worths*, both of what exists and of what does not exist, we must consult not science, but what Pascal calls our heart. Science herself consults her heart when she lays it down that the infinite ascertainment of fact and correction of false belief are the supreme goods for man. Challenge the statement, and science can only repeat it oracularly, or else prove it by showing that such ascertainment and correction bring man all sorts of other goods which man's heart in turn declares. The question of having moral beliefs at all or not having them is decided by our will. Are our moral preferences true or false, or are they only odd biological phenomena, making things good or bad for *us*, but in themselves indifferent? How can your pure intellect decide? If your heart does not *want* a world of moral reality, your head will assuredly never make you believe in one. Mephistophelian skepticism, indeed, will satisfy the head's play-instincts much better than any rigorous idealism can. Some men (even at the student age) are so naturally cool-hearted that the moralistic hypothesis never has for them any pungent life, and in their supercilious presence the hot young moralist always feels strangely ill at ease. The appearance of knowingness is on their side, of *naïveté* and gullibility on his. Yet, in the inarticulate heart of him, he clings to it that he is not a dupe, and that there is a realm in which (as Emerson says) all their wit and intellectual superiority is no better than the cunning of a fox. Moral skepticism can no more be refuted or proved by logic than intellectual skepticism can. When we stick to it that there *is* truth (be it of either kind), we do so with our whole nature, and resolve to stand or fall by the results. The skeptic with his whole nature adopts the doubting attitude; but which of us is the wiser, Omniscience only knows.

Turn now from these wide questions of good to a certain class of questions of fact, questions concerning personal relations, states of mind between one man and another. *Do you like me or not?* – for example. Whether you do or not depends, in countless instances, on whether I meet you half-way, am willing to assume that you must like me, and show you trust and expectation. The previous faith on my part in your liking's existence is in such cases what makes your liking come. But if I stand aloof, and refuse to budge an inch until I have objective evidence, until you shall have done something apt, as the absolutists say, *ad extorquendum assensum meum*, ten to one your liking never comes. How many women's hearts are vanquished by the mere sanguine insistence of some man that they *must* love him! he will not consent to the hypothesis that they cannot. The desire for a certain kind of truth here brings about that special truth's existence; and so it is in innumerable cases of other sorts. Who gains promotions, boons, appointments, but the man in whose life they are seen to play the part of live hypotheses, who discounts them, sacrifices other things for their sake before they have come, and takes risks for them in advance? His faith acts on the powers above him as a claim, and creates its own verification.

A social organism of any sort whatever, large or small, is what it is because each member proceeds to his own duty with a trust that the other members will simultaneously do theirs. Wherever a desired result is achieved by the co-operation of many independent persons, its existence as a fact is a pure consequence of the precursive faith in one another of those immediately concerned. A government, an army, a commercial system, a ship, a college, an athletic team, all exist on this condition, without which not only is nothing achieved, but nothing is even attempted. A whole train of passengers (individually brave enough) will be looted by a few highwaymen, simply because the latter can count on one another, while each passenger fears that if he makes a movement of resistance, he will be shot before any one else backs him up. If we believed that the whole car-full would rise at once with us, we should each severally rise, and train-robbing would never even be attempted. There are, then, cases where a fact cannot come at all unless a preliminary faith exists in its coming. *And where faith in a fact can help create the fact*, that would be an insane logic which should say that faith running ahead of scientific evidence is the 'lowest kind of immorality' into which a thinking being can fall. Yet such is the logic by which our scientific absolutists pretend to regulate our lives!

X

In truths dependent on our personal action, then, faith based on desire is certainly a lawful and possibly an indispensable thing.

But now, it will be said, these are all childish human cases, and have nothing to do with great cosmical matters, like the question of religious faith. Let us then pass on to that. Religions differ so much in their accidents that in discussing the religious question we must make it very generic and broad. What then do we now mean by the religious hypothesis? Science says things are; morality says some things are better than other things; and religion says essentially two things.

First, she says that the best things are the more eternal things, the overlapping things, the things in the universe that throw the last stone, so to speak, and say the final word. 'Perfection is eternal' – this phrase of Charles

Secrétan seems a good way of putting this first affirmation of religion, an affirmation which obviously cannot yet be verified scientifically at all.

The second affirmation of religion is that we are better off even now if we believe her first affirmation to be true.

Now, let us consider what the logical elements of this situation are *in case the religious hypothesis in both its branches be really true*. (Of course, we must admit that possibility at the outset. If we are to discuss the question at all, it must involve a living option. If for any of you religion be a hypothesis that cannot, by any living possibility be true, then you need go no farther. I speak to the 'saving remnant' alone.) So proceeding, we see, first, that religion offers itself as a *momentous* option. We are supposed to gain, even now, by our belief, and to lose by our non-belief, a certain vital good. Secondly, religion is a *forced* option, so far as that good goes. We cannot escape the issue by remaining skeptical and waiting for more light, because, although we do avoid error in that way *if religion be untrue*, we lose the good, *if it be true*, just as certainly as if we positively chose to disbelieve. It is as if a man should hesitate indefinitely to ask a certain woman to marry him because he was not perfectly sure that she would prove an angel after he brought her home. Would he not cut himself off from that particular angel-possibility as decisively as if he went and married some one else? Skepticism, then, is not avoidance of option; it is option of a certain particular kind of risk. *Better risk loss of truth than chance of error* – that is your faith-vetoer's exact position. He is actively playing his stake as much as the believer is; he is backing the field against the religious hypothesis, just as the believer is backing the religious hypothesis against the field. To preach skepticism to us as a duty until 'sufficient evidence' for religion be found, is tantamount therefore to telling us, when in presence of the religious hypothesis, that to yield to our fear of its being error is wiser and better than to yield to our hope that it may be true. It is not intellect against all passions, then; it is only intellect with one passion laying down its law. And by what, forsooth, is the supreme wisdom of this passion warranted? Dupery for dupery, what proof is there that dupery through hope is so much worse than dupery through fear? I, for one, can see no proof; and I simply refuse obedience to the scientist's command to imitate his kind of option, in a case where my own stake is important enough to give me the right to choose my own form of risk. If religion be true and the evidence for it be still insufficient, I do not wish, by putting your extinguisher upon my nature (which feels to me as if it had after all some business in this matter), to forfeit my sole chance in life of getting upon the winning side – that chance depending, of course, on my willingness to run the risk of acting as if my passional need of taking the world religiously might be prophetic and right.

All this is on the supposition that it really may be prophetic and right, and that, even to us who are discussing the matter, religion is a live hypothesis which may be true. Now, to most of us religion comes in a still further way that makes a veto on our active faith even more illogical. The more perfect and more eternal aspect of the universe is represented in our religions as having personal form. The universe is no longer a mere *It* to us, but a *Thou*, if we are religious; and any relation that may be possible from person to person might be possible here. For instance, although in one sense we are passive portions of the universe, in another we show a curious autonomy, as if we were small active centres on our own account. We feel, too, as if the appeal of religion to us were made to our own active good-will, as if evidence might be forever withheld from us unless we met the hypothesis half-way. To take a trivial illustration: just as a man who in a company of gentlemen made no advances, asked a warrant for every concession, and believed no one's word without proof, would cut himself off by such churlishness from all the social rewards that a more trusting spirit would earn – so here, one who should shut himself up in snarling logicality and try to make the gods extort his recognition willy-nilly, or not get it at all, might cut himself off forever from his only opportunity of making the gods' acquaintance. This feeling, forced on us we know not whence, that by obstinately believing that there are gods (although not to do so would be so easy both for our logic and our life) we are doing the universe the deepest service we can, seems part of the living essence of the religious hypothesis. If the hypothesis *were* true in all its parts, including this one, then pure intellectualism, with its veto on our making willing advances, would be an absurdity; and some participation of our sympathetic nature would be logically required. I, therefore, for one, cannot see my way to accepting the agnostic rules for truth-seeking, or wilfully agree to keep my willing nature out of the game. I cannot do so for this plain reason, that *a rule of thinking which would absolutely prevent me from acknowledging certain kinds of truth if those kinds of truth were really there, would be an irrational rule.* That for me is the long and short of the formal logic of the situation, no matter what the kinds of truth might materially be.

I confess I do not see how this logic can be escaped. But sad experience makes me fear that some of you may still shrink from radically saying with me, *in abstracto*, that we have the right to believe at our own risk any hypothesis that is live enough to tempt our will. I suspect, however, that if this is so, it is because you have got away from the abstract logical point of view altogether, and are thinking (perhaps without realizing it) of some particular religious hypothesis which for you is dead. The freedom to 'believe what we will' you apply to the case of some patent superstition; and the faith you think of is the faith defined by the schoolboy when he said, 'Faith is when you believe something that you know ain't true.' I can only repeat that this is misapprehension. *In concreto*, the freedom to believe can only cover living options which the intellect of the individual cannot by itself resolve; and living options never seem absurdities to him who has them to consider. When I look at the religious question as it really puts itself to concrete men, and when I think of all the possibilities which both

> practically and theoretically it involves, then this command that we shall put a stopper on our heart, instincts, and courage, and *wait* – acting of course meanwhile more or less as if religion were *not* true – till doomsday, or till such time as our intellect and senses working together may have raked in evidence enough – this command, I say, seems to me the queerest idol ever manufactured in the philosophic cave.

Commentary on James

James divides his text into ten sections (plus an introduction) from which we have selected seven. In the first section, James defines some key technical terms: 'hypothesis', 'live hypothesis', 'option', 'live option', 'forced option', 'momentous option', 'genuine option'. In the second section, James argues that it is absurd to suppose that beliefs of science and common sense are subject to the will. In the third section, James argues that our *other* beliefs – i.e. those that lie outside the realm of science and 'human affairs in general' – are often influenced by will: there are many things that we claim to believe for which we can adduce neither evidence nor argument. In the fourth section, James states his key thesis: it is perfectly proper for the will to influence belief where there is a 'genuine option' at issue. With all of these preliminaries behind him, James then turns to the main business of the paper. In the eighth section, James argues that, in cases in which there is no 'forced option' and where intellectual considerations are not decisive, we ought to suspend judgement. In the ninth section, James argues that there are moral questions that can give rise to legitimate 'passional decisions'; and he also argues that, in cases in which believing that something will be so can help to make it so, it can be legitimate to make 'passional decisions'. Finally, in the tenth section, James turns his attention to the case of religious belief, arguing that here, too, it can be legitimate to make 'passional decisions', i.e. to believe even though belief is not mandated by evidence and argument.

1. Working through section I, state in your own words the definitions of the following terms: hypothesis, live hypothesis, option, living option, forced option, momentous option. Which of these terms relies in their definition on other technical terms that James introduces?

The technical terms which James introduces are not unproblematic. In particular, it is quite unclear how we are supposed to distinguish between live hypotheses and dead hypotheses. Given that I hold a ticket, it is surely a live possibility that I shall win the state lottery next weekend. However, given only that I hold a ticket, the claim that I shall win the state lottery next weekend is not plausibly a serious candidate for my belief. Given what James says about live and dead hypotheses, we do not think that we are able to determine whether the claim that I shall win the state lottery next weekend should be classified as a live hypothesis. Moreover, given the ultimate direction of James's argument, it is not clear that he really needs to consider the case in which an option is a choice between two hypotheses. For, ultimately, it seems that the case that is really of interest to James is one in which there is a choice between two different attitudes towards a single hypothesis: either one believes that God exists, or one does not believe that God exists.

2. Evaluate the description and assessment James gives of Pascal's Wager in section II.

At the risk of putting words into James's mouth, we might say that he would have done better to take a 'genuine option' to be a choice between two mutually exclusive doxastic attitudes towards a proposition, where the proposition in question is one that lies outside the realm of science and 'common sense', but which is none the less recognised to be a serious candidate for belief. If he had framed the notion of 'genuine option' in this way, then his key claim would be that our passional nature must decide genuine options wherever those options cannot be decided on purely intellectual grounds.

3. Explain James's reasons in section III for thinking that some beliefs are influenced by the will. Which beliefs does James think are influenced by the will?

4. Explain the position that James considers in section VIII. What does James think is its main weakness?

The suggestion that questions about moral reality furnish us with genuine options that can be decided only on passional grounds depends upon the assumption that there really are moral propositions and moral beliefs. Some non-cognitivists, whose views were briefly considered in the chapters on Ayer and Berkeley, deny this assumption: they say that, properly speaking, there are neither moral propositions nor moral beliefs. If we suppose that there really are moral propositions and moral beliefs, then the suggestion that morality furnishes us with genuine options that can be decided only on passional grounds depends upon the assumption that these options cannot be decided on purely intellectual grounds. This assumption can also be denied: some philosophers who think that there really are moral propositions and moral beliefs also suppose that moral questions can be decided on the grounds of moral arguments. (Of course, it is not very common for philosophers to hold that moral questions can be decided on the grounds of evidence: but, as we have explicitly flagged from the beginning of our discussion of Clifford's paper, 'intellectual considerations' must be supposed to take in both evidence and argument.) Moreover, putting together the two points that we have just noted, we expect that rather more philosophers would agree that the question whether moral questions can be decided only on passional grounds is on all fours with the question whether there really are moral propositions and moral beliefs. But, if it is true that the question whether moral questions can be decided only on passional grounds is on all fours with the question whether there really are moral propositions and moral beliefs, then the case of morality does not provide support for the principle that James wishes to endorse.

5. Suppose that James instead gave cases of specific moral dilemmas facing individuals. Would these have provided better examples of genuine options that can be decided only on passional grounds?

The suggestion that cases in which believing that something is so can help to make it so furnish us with genuine options that can only be decided on passional grounds depends upon the assumption that possession of appropriate beliefs is central to the described cases. When we look at the cases closely, it is not obvious that this is so. Consider, first, the case of friendship. When I begin to interact with you, it would be absurd for me to *believe* that you like me: you do not yet know me. Moreover, it would be presumptuous of me to *believe* that you will like me: I do not yet know you, so I do not know whether you are the kind of person who typically does like me.

However, even though it would clearly be wrong for me to believe that you do like me, or that you will like me, it seems that it would be perfectly reasonable for me to *believe* that you might like me: and my believing that you might like me may well be enough to 'make your liking come'. Of course, it may also be true that, if I do not desire that you come to like me, then your liking will not come: but desire is not belief, and I can desire that you like me without believing that you do. If all of this is right, then the facts about the formation of friendships simply do not support James's claim that we have here a case in which *believing* makes something so.

Consider, next, the case in which a trainload of individually brave passengers is looted by a small number of highwaymen. In this case it may well be true, as James says, that if we believed that the whole car-full would rise at once with us we should each severally rise, and train-robbing would never even be attempted. However, one difficulty here is that we all have good reason to believe that it is not the case that the whole car-full would rise at once with us: the co-ordination of resistance in such circumstances is very difficult, and the outcome of resistance in the past has often proved disastrous. This is in stark contrast with the preceding cases that James mentions: governments, armies, commercial systems, ships, colleges, and athletic teams all function as they do partly because those who are involved all have good reason to believe that sufficiently many of the other people involved will act in sufficiently predictable and desirable ways. James is simply mistaken when he says that all of these entities function as they do only because of 'the precursive faith in one another of those immediately concerned', i.e. because the people involved have purely passional beliefs about their obligations, duties, and so forth. On the contrary, evidence and argument underwrite the beliefs that enable these kinds of entities to continue to operate; and so, again, the facts about these cases do not support James's claim that these are cases in which *believing* makes something so.

Even if our discussion of the examples that James gives in section IX of his paper is correct, it may be that there are other examples in which it is plausible to say that the fact that believing may contribute to making something so can justify a decision to believe that is made on purely passional grounds. Recall the putative counter-examples to Clifford's principle that we took up in that earlier discussion. Perhaps the footballers' belief that they will win can play a role in their winning; perhaps the mountaineer's belief that he will jump the crevasse can play a role in his jumping the crevasse. More exactly: perhaps it can be true that, if the footballers do not *believe* that they will win, then they will not win; and perhaps it can be true that, if the mountaineer does not *believe* that he will leap the crevasse, then he will not leap the crevasse. Moreover, it surely can be true that, if the footballers believe that they will not win, then most likely they will not win; and if the mountaineer believes that he will not leap the crevasse, then very likely he will not leap the crevasse. But, if that is right, then there can be cases in which believing plays an important role in making something so. So the only remaining question is whether these examples could be ones in which a decision to believe is justified on purely passional grounds. Could the footballers be 'passionally' justified in *believing* that they will win because they want to win, even though they take themselves not to have evidence and arguments that support the claim that they will win? Could the mountaineer be 'passionally' justified in *believing* that he will successfully leap the chasm because he wants to leap the chasm successfully, even though he takes himself not to have evidence and arguments that support the claim that he will successfully leap the chasm? We think that it is not clear how to answer these questions. However, since the answers to these questions seem to have no bearing on the case of religious belief, since religious truths are not in general dependent on or changed by what we believe, we see no harm in declining to pursue this discussion any further.

James begins his discussion of religious belief with the claim that 'the religious hypothesis' makes two affirmations: it says that 'the best things are the more eternal things, the overlapping things, the things in the universe that throw the last stone, so to speak, and say the final word' and it says that 'we are better off even now if we believe her first affirmation to be true'. This is a highly idiosyncratic account of the core content of religious belief, and it issues in a claim that is not obviously of the right form to count as the propositional content of a genuine option. However, for the purposes of the subsequent discussion, the precise formulation of 'the religious hypothesis' is not relevant: we could equally well take it to be the claim that God exists.

6. After introducing the religious hypothesis in section X, James contends that religion is a *forced* option. Restate his argument for this in your own words. Is the argument persuasive?

In order for it to be the case that James's principle – that there are genuine options that can only be decided on passional grounds – applies to the claim that God exists, it must be the case that the question of God's existence cannot be decided on intellectual grounds: that is, there cannot be sufficient intellectual grounds either for believing that God exists, or for failing to believe that God exists. But, someone might suppose, if there are not sufficient intellectual grounds for believing that God exists, and there are not sufficient intellectual grounds for believing that God does not exist, then there are sufficient intellectual grounds for suspending judgement on the question whether God exists – and hence sufficient intellectual grounds for failing to believe that God exists. That is, it cannot be the case that we here face a genuine option that cannot be decided on intellectual grounds.

We think that the objection that we have just rehearsed is unfair to James. The view to which he wishes to *object* is the view that, where evidence and theoretical argument do not provide sufficient support for either belief that p or belief that not-p, one should always suspend judgement about whether that p. The view that James wishes to *defend*, therefore, is the view that, at least sometimes, when evidence and theoretical argument do not provide sufficient support for either the belief that p or the belief that not-p, it may none the less be perfectly intellectually respectable to believe that p or to believe that not-p – and, moreover, it may be perfectly intellectually respectable to believe that p or to believe that not-p as the result of a 'passional decision'.

It could be that James is *right* to think that, at least sometimes, when evidence and theoretical argument do not provide sufficient support for either the belief that p or the belief that not-p, it may none the less be perfectly intellectually respectable to believe that p or to believe that not-p, but *wrong* to think it may be perfectly intellectually respectable to believe that p or to believe that not-p as the result of a 'passional decision'. Perhaps, for example, it is true that we sometimes have rational entitlements to beliefs even though we cannot provide either evidence or argument in support of those beliefs. (Some philosophers have thought that this is the right way to respond to some kinds of sceptical challenges: for instance, we are rationally entitled to believe that we are not brains in vats, even though we have no evidence that we are not brains in vats, and even though we can give no non-question-begging argument in defence of that claim.) But it is consistent with the suggestion that we sometimes have these kinds of rational entitlements to beliefs that it is never intellectually respectable to believe that p or to believe that not-p as the result of a 'passional decision'.

James does sketch arguments in defence of the claim that it can be perfectly proper to hold religious beliefs as the result of 'passional decisions'. In particular, he makes appeal to the claim that 'a rule of thinking which would absolutely prevent one from acknowledging certain kinds of truth if those kinds of truth were really there, would be an irrational rule'. For instance, if there is truth in religious belief, and if, consequently, there are great goods that are forgone if one does not take on religious belief, even though there is no sufficient evidence or argument for the truth of religious belief, then it is clear that the application of Clifford's principle *will* lead to the forsaking of great goods. But is James right to claim that these considerations somehow show that the adoption of Clifford's principle would be irrational?

From the context, it is clear that the 'certain kinds of truth' to which James adverts in the claim quoted in the previous paragraph are those that would arise if the world accorded with 'my passional need of taking the world' a certain way, e.g. religiously. James is not here taking back his commitment to the application of Clifford's principle in the case of science and common sense, and just as well: it is easy to see that proper rules for the assessment of evidence will prevent one from acknowledging truths when one lacks sufficient evidence in support of those truths. Rather, James is proposing that, in the absence of evidence and argument sufficient to decide a claim, if great goods would flow from belief in that claim in circumstances in which the claim were true, then, even now, it can be perfectly intellectually respectable for one to believe that claim.

7. James rejects Clifford's principle and other 'rules of thinking' because they prevent access to the truth of some propositions. For example, if evidence for the truth of some religious propositions is only available to religious believers, then Clifford's principle blocks access to the truth of those propositions by requiring that evidence should be available prior to believing them. But does not *every* epistemic rule that sets a standard on what it is permissible to believe also potentially block access to some truths? How could James respond to the objection that his argument is not against Clifford but against any epistemic principle?

One oft-made objection to James's proposal is that it allows that almost any superstitious belief can be counted intellectually respectable. While that objection goes too far – as James himself insists, many superstitious beliefs can be ruled out by evidence and argument – it does seem that there is a legitimate worry about the range of hypotheses that are not ruled out by evidence and argument, but which satisfy the condition that great goods would flow from belief in these hypotheses in circumstances in which they were true. Consider the hypothesis that there are shy and intuitive protective fairies living at the bottom of my garden. Because these fairies are shy and intuitive, there is no evidence of their existence. However, these fairies do watch over all of those who believe in them, ensuring that their life goes much better than it would otherwise go. On James's account, it seems that he has to allow that belief in these fairies can be perfectly intellectually respectable – a result that surely we should not be too eager to accept. (Perhaps it might be objected that James also insists that religious believers profit simply from having their religious beliefs: their having those beliefs makes their lives go better. However, we can suppose that the same is true for those who believe in our fairies: why should it not be the case that belief in protective fairies provides the same kinds of *immediate* benefits as belief in God?)

8. Briefly summarise the position of Clifford and James on what is required for reasonable religious beliefs. On what specific issues do they disagree? State what you take to be the best argument for each account.

Again, the discussion in this section has been very compressed: we have opened up a number of questions, but we have not made much progress towards answering them. If you are interested in further discussion of James's views, you might like to look at:

Feldman, R., 'Clifford's Principle and James's Options', *Social Epistemology*, 20 (2006): 19–33.
Gale, M., *The Divided Self of William James*, Cambridge: Cambridge University Press, 1999.
Suckiel, E., *Heaven's Champion: William James's Philosophy of Religion*, Notre Dame, Ind.: University of Notre Dame Press, 1996.

Introduction to Plantinga

Alvin Plantinga is perhaps the best-known, and certainly the most influential, contemporary philosopher of religion. Born into an academic family in 1932, Plantinga completed his PhD at Yale in 1957. After that, he taught for five years at Wayne State University, and then for twenty years at Calvin College. Since 1983, Plantinga has been a member of the department of philosophy at the University of Notre Dame.

Plantinga has made significant contributions to contemporary debates in metaphysics and epistemology, as well as to a wide range of metaphysical and epistemological problems in the philosophy of religion. He is known, among other things, for his defence of a modal ontological argument, for his development of a free-will defence against logical arguments from evil, for his attempts to show that evolutionary naturalism is a self-defeating philosophical position, and for his refinements of the Reformed epistemology initiated by the works of John Calvin and other Protestant Reformation theologians.

Plantinga is the author of many important books, including *God and Other Minds* (1967), *The Nature of Necessity* (1974), *God, Freedom and Evil* (1974), *Does God Have a Nature?* (1980), *Warrant: The Current Debate* (1993), *Warrant and Proper Function* (1993) and *Warranted Christian Belief* (2000).

In this chapter, we examine a piece of Plantinga's earliest work in the tradition of Reformed epistemology. One way of thinking about this work, in the context of the prior readings in the present section, is to take Plantinga to be arguing for a version of the claim that we must have rational entitlements to beliefs beyond those entitlements that are grounded in evidence and argument. If we take Clifford to have been claiming that all rational entitlements to belief must be grounded in evidence and argument, then Plantinga can be taken to be agreeing with James in rejecting Clifford's claim, but without taking on James's further suggestion that rational entitlements may be grounded in our 'passions'.

Alvin Plantinga, 'Is Belief in God Properly Basic?'

a →

[1] Many philosophers have urged the evidentialist objection to theistic belief; they have argued that belief in God is irrational or unreasonable or not rationally acceptable or intellectually irresponsible or noetically

substandard, because, as they say, there is insufficient evidence for it.[1] Many other philosophers and theologians – in particular, those in the great tradition of natural theology – have claimed that belief in God is intellectually acceptable, but only because the fact is that there is sufficient evidence for it. These two groups unite in holding that theistic belief is rationally acceptable only if there is sufficient evidence for it. More exactly, they hold that a person is rational or reasonable in accepting theistic belief only if she has sufficient evidence for it – only if, that is, she knows or rationally
b→ believes some other propositions which support the one in question. In [4] I argued that the evidentialist objection is rooted in classical foundationalism, an enormously popular picture or total way of looking as faith, knowledge, justified belief, rationality, and allied topics. This picture has been widely accepted ever since the days of Plato and Aristotle; its near relatives, perhaps, remain the dominant ways of thinking about these topics. We may think of the classical foundationalist as beginning with the observation that some of one's beliefs may be *based upon* others; it may be that there are a pair of propositions A and B such that I believed A on the basis of B. Although this relation isn't easy to characterise in a revealing and non-trivial fashion, it is nonetheless familiar. I believe that the word 'unbrageous' is spelled u-m-b-r-a-g-e-o-u-s-: this belief is based on another belief of mine: the belief that that's how the dictionary says it's spelled. I believe that 72 × 71 = 5,112. This belief is based on several other beliefs I hold: that 1 × 72 = 72, 7 × 2 = 14, 7 × 7 = 49, 49 + 1 = 50; and others. Some of my beliefs, however, I accept but don't accept on the basis of any other beliefs. Call these beliefs basic. I believe that 2 + 1 = 3, for example, and don't believe it on the basis of any other propositions. I also believe that I am seated at my desk, and that there is a mild pain in my right knee. These too are basic to me; I don't believe them on the basis of any other propositions. According to the classical foundationalist, some propositions are properly or rightly basic for a person and some are not. Those that are not, are rationally accepted only on the basis of evidence, where the evidence must trace back, ultimately, to what is properly basic. The existence of God, furthermore, is not among the propositions that are properly basic; hence a person is rational in accepting theistic belief only if he has evidence for it.

c→ Now many Reformed thinkers and theologians[2] have rejected natural theology (though of as the attempt to provide proofs or arguments for the existence of God). They have held not merely that the proffered arguments are unsuccessful, but that the whole enterprise is in some way radically

[1] See, for example [1], pp. 400 ff, [2] pp. 345 ff. [3], p. 22, [6], pp. 3ff, and [7], pp. 87 ff. In [4], I consider and reject the evidentialist objection to theistic belief.

[2] A Reformed thinker or theologian is one whose intellectual sympathies lie with the Protestant tradition going back to John Calvin (not someone who was formerly a theologian and has since seen the light).

misguided. In [5], I argue that the reformed objection of natural theology is best construed as an inchoate and unfocused rejection of classical foundationalism. What these Reformed thinkers really mean to hold, I think, is that belief in God need not be based on argument or evidence from other propositions at all. They mean to hold that the believer is entirely within his intellectual rights in believing as he does even if he doesn't know of any good theistic argument (deductive or inductive), even if he doesn't believe that there is any such argument, and even if in fact no such argument exists. They hold that it is perfectly rational to accept belief in God without accepting it on the basis of any other beliefs or propositions at all. In a word, they hold that belief in God is properly basic. In this paper, I shall try to develop and defend this position.

[2] But first we must achieve a deeper understanding of the evidentialist objection. It is important to see that this contention is a *normative* contention. The evidentialist objector holds that one who accepts theistic belief is in some way irrational or noetically substandard. Here 'rational' and 'irrational' are to be taken as normative or evaluative terms; according to the objector, the theist fails to measure up to a standard he ought to conform to. There is a right way and a wrong way with respect to belief as with respect to actions; we have duties, responsibilities, obligations with respect to the former just as with respect to the latter. So Professor Blanchard:

> . . . everywhere and always belief has an ethical aspect. There is such a thing as a general ethics of the intellect. The main principle of that ethic I hold to be the same inside and outside religion. This principle is simple and sweeping: Equate your assent to the evidence. [1] p. 401.

This 'ethics of the intellect' can be construed variously; many fascinating issues – issues we must here forbear to enter – arise when we try to state more exactly the various options the evidentialist may mean to adopt. Initially it looks as if he holds that there is a duty or obligation of some sort not to accept without evidence such propositions as that God exists – a duty flouted by the theist who has no evidence. If he has no evidence, then it is his duty to cease believing. But there is an oft remarked difficulty: one's beliefs, for the most part, are not directly under one's control. Most of those who believe in God could not divest themselves of that belief just by trying to do so, just as they could not in that way rid themselves of the belief that the world has existed for a very long time. So perhaps the relevant obligation is not that of divesting myself of theistic belief if I have no evidence (that is beyond my power), but to try to cultivate the sorts of intellectual habits that will tend (we hope) to issue in my accepting as basic only propositions that are properly basic.

d→ The evidentialist objection, therefore, presupposes some view as to what sorts of propositions are correctly, or rightly, or justifiably taken as basic;

it presupposes a view as to what is *properly* basic. And the minimally relevant view for the evidentialist objector is that belief in God is not properly basic. Typically this objection has been rooted in some form of *classical foundationalism*, according to which a proposition p is properly basic for a person S if and only if p is either self-evident or incorrigible for S (modern foundationlism) or either self-evident or 'evident to the senses' for S (ancient and medieval foundationlism). In [4], I argued that both forms of foundationalism are self referentially incoherent and must therefore be rejected.

Insofar as the evidentialist objection is rooted in classical foundationlism, it is poorly rooted indeed: and so far as I know, no one has developed and articulated any other reason for supposing that belief in God is not properly basic. Of course, it doesn't follow that it is properly basic; perhaps the class of properly basic propositions is broader than classical foundationalists think, but still not broad enough to admit belief in God. But why think so? What might be the objections to the Reformed view that belief in God is properly basic?

[3] I've heard it argued that if I have no evidence for the existence of God, then if I accept that proposition, my belief will be groundless, or gratuitous, or arbitrary. I think this is an error; let me explain.

e → Suppose we consider perceptual beliefs, memory beliefs, and beliefs which ascribe mental states to other persons: such beliefs as:

1. I see a tree
2. I had breakfast this morning

and

3. That person is angry

Although beliefs of this sort are typically and properly taken as basic, it would be a mistake to describe them as groundless. Upon having experience of a certain sort, I believe that I am perceiving a tree. In the typical case I do not hold this belief on the basis of other beliefs; it is nonetheless not groundless. My having that characteristic sort of experience – to use Professor Chisholm's language, my being appeared to treely – plays a crucial role in the formation and justification of that belief. We might say this experience, together, perhaps, with other circumstances, is what justifies me in holding it; this is the ground of my justification, and, by extension, the ground of the belief itself.

If I see someone displaying typical pain behaviour, I take it that he or she is in pain. Again, I don't take the displayed behaviour as evidence for that belief; I don't infer that belief from others that I hold; I don't accept it on the basis of other beliefs. Still, my perceiving the pain behaviour plays a unique role in the formation and justification of that belief; as in the previous case, it forms the ground of my justification for the belief in question. The same holds for memory beliefs. I seem to remember having breakfast this morning; that is, I have an inclination to believe the proposition that I had breakfast, along with a certain past-tinged experience that is familiar to all but hard to describe. Perhaps we should say that I am appeared to pastly; but perhaps this insufficiently distinguishes the experience in question from that accompanying beliefs about the past not grounded in my own memory. The phenomenology of memory is a rich and unexplored realm; here, I have no time to explore it. In this case as in the others, however, there is a justifying circumstance present, a condition that forms the ground of my justification for accepting the memory belief in question.

In each of these cases, a belief is taken as basic, and in each case properly taken as basic. In each case there is some circumstance or condition that confers justification; there is a circumstance that serves as the ground of justification. So in each case there will be some true proposition of the sort

4. In condition C, S is justified in taking p as basic.

Of course, C will vary with p. For a perceptual judgment such as

5. I see a rose coloured wall before me

C will include my being appeared to in a certain fashion. No doubt C will include more. If I'm appeared to in the familiar fashion but know that I'm wearing rose coloured glasses, or that I am suffering from a disease that causes me to be thus appeared to, no matter what the colour of the nearby objects, then I'm not justified in taking [5] as basic. Similarly for my memory. Suppose I know that my memory is unreliable; it often plays me tricks. In particular, when I seem to remember having breakfast, then, more often than not, I *haven't* had breakfast. Under these conditions I am not justified in taking it as basic that I had breakfast, even though I seem to remember that I did.

So being appropriately appeared to, in the perceptual case, is not sufficient condition for justification; some further condition – a condition hard to state in detail – is clearly necessary. The central point, here, however, is that a belief is properly basic only in certain conditions; these conditions are, we might say, the ground of its justification and, by extension, the ground of the belief itself. In this sense, basic beliefs are not, or are not necessarily, *groundless* beliefs.

f → Now similar things may be said about belief in God. When the Reformers claim that this belief is properly basic, they do not mean to say, of course, that there are no justifying circumstances for it, or that it is in that sense groundless or gratuitous. Quite the contrary. Calvin holds that God 'reveals and daily discloses himself to the whole workmanship of the universe', and the divine art 'reveals itself in the innumerable and yet distinct and well ordered variety of the heavenly host.' God has so created us that we have a tendency or disposition to see his hand in the world about us. More precisely, there is in us a disposition to believe propositions of the sort *this flower was created by God* or *this vast and intricate universe was created by God* when we contemplate the flower or behold the starry heavens or think about the vast reaches of the universe.

Calvin recognises, at least implicitly, that other sorts of conditions may trigger this disposition. Upon reading the Bible, one may be impressed with a deep sense that God is speaking to him. Upon having done what I know is cheap, or wrong, or wicked I may feel guilty in God's sight and form the belief *God disapproves of what I've done*. Upon confession and repentance, I may feel forgiven, forming the belief *God forgives me for what I've done*. A person in grave danger may turn to God, asking for his protection and help; and of course he or she then forms the belief that God is indeed able to hear and help if he sees fit. When life is sweet and satisfying, a spontaneous sense of gratitude may well up within the soul; someone in this condition may thank and praise the Lord for his goodness, and will of course form the accompanying belief that indeed the Lord is to be thanked and praised.

There are therefore many conditions and circumstances that call forth belief in God: guilt, gratitude, danger, a sense of God's presence, a sense that he speaks, perception of various parts of the universe. A complete job would explore the phenomenology of all these conditions and of more besides. This is a large and important topic; but here I can only point to the existence of these conditions.

Of course none of the beliefs I mentioned a moment ago is the simple belief that God exists. What we have instead are such beliefs as:

6. God is speaking to me.
7. God has created all this.
8. God disapproves of what I've done.
9. God forgives me.

and

10. God is to be thanked and praised.

These propositions are properly basic in the right circumstances. But it is quite consistent with this to suppose that the proposition there is such a person as God is neither properly basic nor taken as basic by those who believe in God. Perhaps what they take as basic are such propositions as (6)–(10), each of which self-evidently entails that God exists. It isn't the relatively high level and general proposition God exists that is properly basic, but instead propositions detailing some of his attributes or actions.

Suppose we return to the analogy between belief in God and belief in the existence of perceptual objects, other persons, and the past. Here too it is relatively specific and concrete propositions rather than their more general and abstract colleagues that are properly basic. Perhaps such items as

11. There are trees.
12. There are other persons.

and

13. The world has existed for more than five minutes.

are not in fact properly basic; it is instead such propositions as

14. I see a tree.
15. That person is pleased.

and

16. I had breakfast more than an hour ago

that deserve that accolade. Of course propositions of the latter sort immediately and self-evidently entail propositions of the former sort; and perhaps there is thus no harm in speaking of the former as properly basic, even though so to speak is to speak a bit loosely.

The same must be said about belief in God. We may say, speaking loosely, that belief in God is properly basic; strictly speaking, however, it is probably not that proposition, but such propositions as (6)–(10) that enjoy that status. But the main point, here, is that belief in God or (6)–(10), are properly basic; to say so, however, is not to deny that there are justifying conditions for these beliefs, or conditions that confer justification on one who accepts them as basic. They are therefore not groundless or gratuitous.

[g]→ [4] A second objection I've often heard: if belief in God is properly basic, why can't just any belief be properly basic? Couldn't we say the same for any bizarre aberration we can think of? What about voodoo or astrology? What about the belief that the Great Pumpkin returns every Halloween? Could I properly take *that* as basic? And if I can't, why can I properly take belief in God as basic? Suppose I believe that if I flap my arms with sufficient vigour, I can take off and fly about the room; could I defend myself against the charge of irrationality by claiming this belief is basic? If we say that belief in God is properly basic, won't we be committed to holding that just anything, or nearly anything, can properly be taken as basic, thus throwing wide the gates to irrationalism and superstition?

[h]→ Certainly not. What might lead one to think the Reformed epistemologist is in this kind of trouble? The fact that he rejects the criteria for proper basicality purveyed by classical foundationalism? But why should that be

thought to commit him to such tolerance of irrationality? Consider an analogy. In the palmy days of positivism, the positivists went about confidently wielding their verifiability criterion and declaring meaningless much that was obviously meaningful. Now suppose someone rejected a formulation of that criterion – the one to be found in the second edition of A. J. Ayer's *Language, Truth and Logic*, for example. Would that mean she was committed to holding that

17. Twas brillig; and the slithy toves did gyre and gymble in the wabe

contrary to appearances, makes good sense? But then the same goes for the Reformed epistemologist; the fact that he rejects the Classical Foundationalist's criterion of proper basicality does not mean that he is committed to supposing just anything is properly basic.

[i]→ But what then is the problem? Is it that the Reformed epistemologist not only rejects those criteria for proper basicality, but seems in no hurry to produce what he takes to be a better substitute? If he has no such criterion, how can he fairly reject belief in the Great Pumpkin as properly basic?

[j]→ This objection betrays an important misconception. How do we rightly arrive at or develop criteria for meaningfulness or justified belief, or proper basicality? Where do they come from? Must one have such a criterion before one can sensibly make any judgments – positive or negative – about proper basicality? Surely not. Suppose I don't know of a satisfactory substitute for the criterion proposed by classical foundationalism; I am nevertheless entirely within my rights in holding that certain propositions are not properly basic in certain conditions. Some propositions seem self-evident when in fact they are not; that is the lesson of some of Russell's paradoxes. Nevertheless, it would be irrational to take as basic the denial of a proposition that seems self-evident to you. Similarly, suppose it seems to you that you see a tree; you would then be irrational in taking as basic the proposition that you don't see a tree, or that there aren't any trees. In the same way, even if I don't know of some illuminating criterion of meaning, I can quite properly declare (17) meaningless.

[k]→ And this raises an important question – one Roderick Chisholm has taught us to ask. What is the status of criteria for knowledge, or proper basicality, or justified belief? Typically, these are universal statements. The modern foundationalist's criterion for proper basicality, for example, is doubly universal:

18. For any proposition A and person S, A is properly basic for S iff A is incorrigible for S or self-evident for S.

[l]→ But how could one know a thing like that? What are its credentials? Clearly enough, (18) isn't self-evident or just obviously true. But if it isn't, how does one arrive at it? What sorts of arguments would be appropriate? Of

course a foundationalist might find (18) so appealing, he simply takes it to be true, neither offering argument for it, nor accepting it on the basis of other things he believes. If he does so, however, his noetic structure will be self-referentially incoherent. (18) itself is neither self-evident nor incorrigible; hence in accepting (18) as basic, the modern foundationalist violates the condition of proper basicality he himself lays down in accepting it. On the other hand, perhaps the foundationalist will try to produce some argument for it from premises that are self-evident or incorrigible: it is exceedingly hard to see, however, what such an argument might be like. And until he has produced such arguments, what shall the rest of us do – we who do not find (18) at all obvious or compelling? How could he use (18) to show us that belief in God, for example, is not properly basic? Why should we believe (18), or pay it any attention?

m→ The fact is, I think, that neither (18) nor any other revealing necessary and sufficient condition for proper basicality clearly follows from clearly self-evident premises by clearly acceptable arguments. And hence the proper way to arrive at such a criterion is, broadly speaking, inductive. We must assemble examples of beliefs and conditions such that the former are obviously properly basic in the latter, and examples of beliefs and conditions such that the former are obviously *not* properly basic in the latter. We must then frame hypotheses as to the necessary and sufficient conditions of proper basicality and test these hypotheses by reference to those examples. Under the right conditions, for example, it is clearly rational to believe that you see a human person before you: a being who has thoughts and feelings, who knows and believes things, who makes decisions and acts. It is clear, furthermore, that you are under no obligation to reason to this belief from others you hold; under those conditions that belief is properly basic for you. But then (18) must be mistaken; the belief in question, under those circumstances, is properly basic, though neither self-evident nor incorrigible for you. Similarly, you may seem to remember that you had breakfast this morning, and perhaps you know of no reason to suppose your memory is playing tricks. If so, you are entirely justified in taking that belief as basic. Of course it isn't properly basic on the criteria offered by classical foundationalists; but that fact counts not against you but against those criteria.

n→ Accordingly, criteria for proper basicality must be reached from below rather than above; they should not be presented as ex Cathedra, but argued to and tested by a relevant set of examples. But there is no reason to assume, in advance, that everyone will agree on the examples. The Christian will of course suppose that belief in God is entirely proper and rational; if he doesn't accept this belief on the basis of other propositions, he will conclude that it is basic for him and quite properly so. Followers of Bertrand Russell and Madelyn Murray O'Hare may disagree, but how is that relevant? Must my criteria, or those of the Christian community, conform to their examples? Surely not. The Christian community is responsible to its set of examples, not to theirs.

Accordingly, the Reformed epistemologist can properly hold that belief in the Great Pumpkin is not properly basic, even though he holds that belief in God is properly basic and even if he has no full fledged criterion of proper basicality. Of course he is committed to supposing that there is a relevant *difference* between belief in God and belief in the Great Pumpkin, if he holds that the former but not the latter is properly basic. But this should prove no great embarrassment; there are plenty of candidates. These candidates are to be found in the neighbourhood of the conditions I mentioned in the last section that justify and ground belief in God. Thus, for example, the Reformed epistemologist may concur with Calvin in holding that God has implanted in us a natural tendency to see his hand in the world around us; the same cannot be said for the Great Pumpkin, there being no Great Pumpkin and no natural tendency to accept beliefs about the Great Pumpkin.

[5] By way of conclusion then: being self-evident, or incorrigible, or evident to the senses is not a necessary condition of proper basicality. Furthermore, one who holds that belief in God is properly basic is not thereby committed to the idea that belief in God is gratuitous or groundless or without justifying circumstances. And even if he lacks a general criterion of proper basicality, he is not obliged to suppose that just any or nearly any belief – belief in the Great Pumpkin, for example – is properly basic. Like everyone should, he begins with examples; and he may take belief in the Great Pumpkin as a paradigm of irrational basic belief.

References

[1] Blanshard, B. (1974) *Reason and Belief*, London: Allen & Unwin.
[2] Clifford, W. K. (1879) 'The Ethics of Belief' in *Lectures and Essays*, London: Macmillan.
[3] Flew, A. G. N. (1976) *The Presumption of Atheism*, London: Pemberton Publishing Company.
[4] Plantinga, A. (1979) 'Is Belief in God Rational?' in C. Delaney (ed.) *Rationality and Religious Belief*, Notre Dame: University of Notre Dame Press.
[5] Plantinga, A. (1980) 'The Reformed Objection to Natural Theology' *Proceedings of the American Catholic Philosophical Association.*
[6] Russell, B. (1957) 'Why I am not a Christian' in *Why I am not a Christian*, New York: Simon & Schuster.
[7] Scriven, M. (1966) *Primary Philosophy*, New York: McGraw-Hill.

Commentary on Plantinga

We have divided Plantinga's article into five sections. In section [1], Plantinga introduces at [a]→ and [b]→ the distinction between basic and non-basic beliefs, the thought that the 'evidentialist' objection to theistic belief rests on the assumption that belief in God cannot be a properly basic belief, and at [c]→ the suggestion that Reformed theologians are best-understood to have been defending the claim that belief in God is properly basic. Section [2] provides some further exploration of 'the evidentialist objection to theistic belief'. In section [3], Plantinga responds to the objection that, if belief in God were basic, then it would be groundless, or gratuitous, or arbitrary. In section [4], Plantinga responds to the objection that, if belief in God could be properly basic, then belief in just about anything at all – e.g. belief in the Great Pumpkin – could be properly basic. Finally, in the concluding paragraph – section [5] – Plantinga summarises the contentions that he has argued for in the paper.

1. Carefully read through [b]↦ and define: (i) basic beliefs; (ii) properly basic beliefs; (iii) classical foundationalism. Give your own examples of a non-basic belief, a basic belief (that is not properly basic), and a properly basic belief.

2. Examine the discussion of evidentialism at [a]↦ and in section [2], particularly at [d]↦. (i) Define evidentialism. (ii) Why does Plantinga claim that evidentialism presupposes a view as to what beliefs are properly basic, and what is that view? (iii) What is the relationship between evidentialism and classical foundationalism?

Plantinga's discussion is premised upon two assumptions: first, that there is a legitimate distinction to be made between basic and non-basic beliefs; and, second, that the 'evidentialist objection' to theistic belief depends upon the claim that theistic belief cannot be properly basic. While Plantinga attributes to 'the classical foundationalist' the assumption that some but not all of one's beliefs may be *based upon* others – i.e. that, while it may be that there is at least one pair of propositions A and B such that one believes A on the basis of B, it will be that there are some propositions that one believes but that one does not believe on the basis of any other propositions – it is important to note that Plantinga does not go on to challenge this assumption. On the contrary, Plantinga's argument takes it for granted that Reformed theologians are entitled to suppose that a rational agent quite properly – and perhaps even necessarily – has some beliefs that are not believed on the basis of other beliefs.

It is not *obvious* that we should accept that rational agents properly – and perhaps even necessarily – have beliefs that are not believed on the basis of other beliefs. Of course, it is obviously true that rational agents properly – and necessarily – have beliefs that are not believed *solely* on the basis of other beliefs. However, it is at least worth considering the suggestion that anything that deserves the name 'belief' must be part of a mutually supporting network of beliefs in such a way that it can quite properly be said that every belief is believed, at least in part, on the basis of other beliefs. Consider, for example, my belief that I am seated at my desk. While Plantinga insists that I do not believe this on the basis of any other beliefs, it is clear that this belief cannot be independent of, for example, my belief that I am not a brain in a vat, and my belief that I did not recently ingest a bunch of mind-altering chemicals. (Note that Plantinga says that the relation of *being based upon* is 'not easy to characterise in a revealing and non-trivial fashion', but that it is 'nonetheless familiar'. If the previous comments are apposite, then it is not so obvious that we are familiar with cases in which a belief is *not at least partly based upon* other beliefs.)

It is also not *obvious* that those who have wished to push an 'evidentialist' objection to theistic belief have been committed to the claim that there is a certain class of beliefs that are properly basic – in Plantinga's sense – but that the claim that God exists is not among them. In particular, as we shall suggest later in our discussion, it seems that those who suppose that every belief is at least partly based on other beliefs may none the less reasonably object to theistic beliefs on the grounds that there is insufficient evidence to support those beliefs. (One issue here concerns the proper conception of evidence. If we suppose that evidence need not be propositional in form, then we cannot accept Plantinga's way of setting up the discussion of 'the evidentialist objection'.)

3. Consider the following beliefs:

(*a*) Mercury is the planet closest to the Sun
(*b*) I have a headache
(*c*) It was raining yesterday

Giving reasons in each case, say whether each of these beliefs is – in Plantinga's sense – non-basic, basic, or properly basic. Could any of them fall into more than one of these categories?

4. Explain the distinction, introduced at [e]→ and elaborated in the following paragraphs, between grounded and ungrounded beliefs. Suppose someone thought, contrary to Plantinga and on the lines described above, that beliefs form an interconnected web and that every belief can be properly based on another belief. What beliefs might the examples (1) to (3), given at [e]→, be based on?

Plantinga claims that 'the evidentialist objection' has been typically tied to either 'modern foundationalism' or to 'ancient or medieval foundationalism' – i.e. to particular claims about the kinds of beliefs that can be properly basic. On Plantinga's account, modern foundationalists hold that only 'self-evident' or 'incorrigible' beliefs can be properly basic, and ancient or medieval foundationalists hold that only 'self-evident' or 'evident to the senses' beliefs can be properly basic. Moreover, on Plantinga's account, both of these views turn out to be 'self-referentially incoherent', and hence rationally indefensible. (Although, in the paper under discussion, Plantinga does not give grounds for the claim that these views are 'self-referentially incoherent', it is not hard to see why we might think that modern foundationalism and ancient or medieval foundationalism are self-defeating: for, on the one hand, these views themselves are neither self-evident, nor incorrigible, nor evident to the senses; and, on the other hand, these views themselves seem not to be supported by claims all of which are self-evident, or incorrigible, or evident to the senses. But, if that is right, then these claims themselves are, by their own lights, not rationally believable.)

While it is true that there have been philosophers who have supposed that the beliefs of a rational believer will either be self-evident, or incorrigible, or evident to the senses, or else logically entailed by other beliefs that are self-evident, or incorrigible, or evident to the senses, it is not obvious that philosophers who wish to run an evidentialist objection against theism, and who accept some kind of foundationalism, are obliged to accept these self-defeating versions of foundationalism. Plantinga himself notes this point at [d]↦, but adds that 'so far as I know, no one has developed and articulated any other reason for supposing that belief in God is not properly basic'. We suspect that, Plantinga's claim here notwithstanding, it is not too hard to articulate the kinds of reasons that might be adduced by philosophers who wish to run an evidentialist objection against theism, but who do not wish to endorse either modern foundationalism or ancient or medieval foundationalism.

5. Plantinga claims that beliefs like

(*a*) That person is unhappy
(*b*) I slept in late this morning
(*c*) I see clouds in the sky

are basic and can be properly basic if they have a suitable grounding. For each of these beliefs, give examples of grounding circumstances.

6. Plantinga introduces the Reformed position at [c]↦ and elaborates at [f]↦. (i) Explain the position in your own words. (ii) Giving your own examples, say what conditions might give a grounding to belief in God.

Suppose that we try to develop an account of rational entitlement to belief. What classes of belief might we unproblematically suppose to belong to the class of beliefs to which a believer can have rational entitlement? At the very least, it seems that we would want to include all of the following:

1. Beliefs that are constitutively permissible for rational agents.
2. Beliefs formed appropriately on the basis of perception.
3. Beliefs formed appropriately on the basis of memory.
4. Beliefs formed appropriately on the basis of introspection.
5. Beliefs formed appropriately on the basis of testimony.
6. Beliefs appropriately inferred from other beliefs.

If we suppose that this list is exhaustive – i.e. that every belief to which one has rational entitlement falls into at least one of these classes – then we might go on to note that there is a sense in which the list can be contracted: for, while beliefs formed on the basis of memory and beliefs formed on the basis of testimony can be beliefs to which one has rational entitlement, there is a sense in which these entitlements are bound to be *derivative* upon other entitlements. In the case of memory, rational entitlement to form beliefs on the basis of memory plausibly depends upon rational entitlement to form beliefs on the basis of rational entitlements *other than* the rational entitlement to form beliefs on the basis of memory. And, in the case of testimony, rational entitlement to form beliefs on the basis of testimony depends upon the rational entitlement of others to form beliefs on the basis of rational entitlements *other than* the rational entitlement to form beliefs on the basis of testimony.

Clearly, then, we can imagine someone running an evidentialist objection against theism who claims that there are just these four classes of *non-derivative* beliefs to which we have rational entitlement: those formed on the basis of perception, those formed on the basis of introspection, those to which we have rational entitlement simply in virtue of our being rational agents, and those that are appropriately inferred from other beliefs. However, even if we suppose that we have a pretty clear understanding of rational entitlement in connection with beliefs formed on the basis of perception, introspection and inference, it is evident that we need to say something more about the class of beliefs that are constitutively permissible for rational agents.

Consider the belief that one is not a brain in a vat. It seems very doubtful that one can properly *infer* this belief just from beliefs appropriately formed on the basis of perception and beliefs appropriately formed on the basis of introspection. On the contrary, it seems that one must already have this belief in order to be able to form beliefs appropriately on the basis of perception and introspection. If we suppose that it can none the less be reasonable for one to believe that one is not a brain in a vat, then one might suppose that we have here grounds for thinking that we have here a belief to which one has immediate rational entitlement. Moreover, we might think that this is a belief to which any rational subject must have immediate rational entitlement. (That is not to say that no rational subject could rationally think that she is a brain in a vat. The point is that, other things being equal, simply in virtue of being rational subjects, we are immediately rationally *entitled* to the belief that we are not brains in vats.)

Clearly enough, anything that can be known *a priori* might be the content of a belief to which a subject has constitutive rational entitlement; however, as we have just seen, the class of beliefs to which subjects are taken to have constitutive entitlement is arguably broader than the class of beliefs that can be known *a priori*. But, we can imagine our evidentialist objector saying, while the belief that one is not a brain in a vat is plausibly taken to be a belief to which subjects have constitutive entitlement, belief in God is not in the same boat: in order for there to be rational entitlement to the belief that God exists, there needs to be entitlement to that belief on grounds of perception, introspection and inference. But to say that there needs to be entitlement to a belief on the grounds of perception, introspection and inference is precisely to say that there can only be *evidential* entitlement to that belief.

If we formulate the evidentialist objection in this way, we may be led to view in a different light Plantinga's responses to the two objections that he considers to the suggestion that belief in God might be properly basic. On the above account of the evidentialist objection, there is no question about entitlement to perceptual, memory and introspective beliefs: provided that the beliefs are formed appropriately, I can be entitled to believe that I see a tree, that I had breakfast this morning, and that some other person is angry. However, on the above account of the evidentialist objection, there does seem to be a genuine question about entitlement to belief in God: for, unless we are prepared to say that we can *literally* see or hear God or feel God, it seems that one who denies that there is sufficient evidence or argument for God's existence can only say that the belief that God exists is one to which rational agents have constitutive permission.

Following Calvin, Plantinga claims at [f]→ that we are entitled to form certain beliefs – e.g. that this flower was made by God, that God is speaking to me, that God created all this, that God disapproves of what I have done, that God forgives me, or that God is to be thanked and praised – in appropriate conditions and circumstances – e.g. when contemplating a flower, reading the Bible, beholding the starry heavens, knowingly doing what is wrong or cheap or wicked, or feeling satisfied with the state of the world and oneself. Moreover, Plantinga claims that one can then be rationally entitled to the belief that God exists by *inferring* that belief from these other beliefs to which one has rational entitlement. However, our evidentialist objector is bound to say that one could only be entitled to form the beliefs that Plantinga mentions in the conditions and circumstances that he details if one already believes that God exists. For example, unless you believe that God exists, there is no way that you can have any entitlement to the belief that a flower was made by God in circumstances in which you contemplate that flower. But, if that is right, then we do not have a satisfactory account here of the way in which a Reformed theist can gain rational entitlement to the belief that God exists.

It is important to Plantinga's position that he claims that 'God has so created us that we have a tendency or disposition to see his hand in the world about us'. Perhaps we can understand this claim in the following way: on Plantinga's account, the beliefs mentioned in the previous paragraph are formed appropriately on the basis of the related perception. Thus, for instance, we have a tendency or disposition to form the belief that a flower was made by God when we contemplate that flower – and this counts as an instance of entitlement to belief formed appropriately on the basis of perception, but not as an instance of entitlement to belief formed appropriately on the basis of inference. Against this, our evidentialist objector will surely say that there is good evidence that we – human beings, scattered across space and time – do not have any such tendency or disposition. For example, we have good reason to believe that, in ancient China, when people contemplated flowers, they had not the slightest tendency or disposition to form the belief that God made those flowers. Similarly, it seems pretty implausible to suppose that those who are convinced that flowers have evolved in a Godless universe none the less have a tendency or disposition to believe that flowers were made by God, particularly when those people are quite happy to assure you that they have no such tendency or disposition.

7. Suppose that Plantinga responded to the above argument that sin can mask the tendency or disposition to believe in God: everyone has the tendency or disposition, but those mired in sin are simply unable to recognise that they have it. Would this be a persuasive response to the evidentialist? Explain why or why not.

8. Plantinga raises one version of the Great Pumpkin objection at [g]↦ that he responds to at [h]↦, and another version at [i]↦ that he responds to at [j]↦. Explain these two objections and replies in your own words.

Even if it is granted that there is no universal human tendency or disposition to believe that flowers were made by God, might one not reasonably think that God had endowed just *some* people with a tendency or disposition to believe that flowers are made by God? Whatever else one might say about this suggestion, it seems that one might think that it is surely going to be vulnerable to the second kind of objection that Plantinga considers: namely, that there is a vast range of beliefs that could be justified in just the same kind of way, but which we should be loath to allow admit of rational justification.

Consider Linus, who believes that his pumpkin patch is sincere (and that, consequently, the Great Pumpkin will bring him a sackload of presents in the not too distant future). Suppose that, against those who say that he is not rationally entitled to the belief that his pumpkin patch is sincere, Linus says that the Great Pumpkin has endowed *some* people with the ability to discriminate between those pumpkin patches that are sincere and those pumpkin patches that are not sincere. Surely the rest of us – i.e. those of us who do not believe in the Great Pumpkin – have the best of reasons for thinking that Linus has not provided *us* with a good reason for thinking that he is rationally entitled to his belief that his pumpkin patch is sincere. But if that is right, then – by parity of reasoning – it seems that *the rest of us* would have the best of reasons for thinking that, even if Plantinga says that God has endowed just *some* people with a tendency or disposition to believe that flowers are made by God, Plantinga has not provided *the rest of us* with a good reason for thinking that he is rationally entitled to his belief that God has endowed just *some* people with a tendency or disposition to believe that flowers are made by God.

9. Plantinga raises a general question about proper basicality at [k]↦. He criticises the foundationalist position at [l]↦ and proposes his own inductivist approach at [m]↦. Briefly summarise his arguments.

Consider Plantinga's argument at [n]↦. It is not *obvious* that this kind of response is plausible when it comes to questions about rational entitlement to belief. When we are developing a theory of rational entitlement, surely we are looking for a set of principles that apply to all rational subjects, quite apart from the particular beliefs that they hold. If we thought that everyone must have some beliefs that have *no basis at all* in the other beliefs that they hold, then perhaps we could maintain that people might just differ in the beliefs that they hold that have no basis at all in the other beliefs that they hold. But, if we doubt that anyone can have reasonable beliefs that have *no basis at all* in other beliefs that that person has, then we might think that we give up the possibility of that kind of radical relativism.

On the other hand, given the discussion to this point, one might then be tempted to conclude that, if the Reformed theist is to continue to maintain her position, then what she needs to say is that the belief that God exists is constitutively permissible for rational agents. While, of course, not all rational agents believe that God exists, rational agents *can* reasonably suppose that the claim that God exists is on a par with the claim that one is not a brain in a vat. That is, rational agents can simply believe that God exists, without any supporting argument or evidence, just as rational agents can simply believe that they are not brains in vats, without any supporting argument or evidence. (Perhaps we might even think that this line of thought yields a defensible version of presuppositionalism.)

In the introduction to this chapter, we suggested that, if we take Clifford to have been claiming that all rational entitlements to belief must be grounded in evidence and argument, then Plantinga can be taken to be agreeing with James in rejecting Clifford's claim, but without taking on James's further suggestion that rational entitlements may be grounded in our 'passions'. In conclusion, we can sharpen this claim a bit further. If we think that there are constitutive rational entitlements to belief that are not grounded in evidence and argument, then we should reject Clifford's claim that all rational entitlements to belief are grounded in evidence and argument. If we think that rational entitlements to belief cannot be grounded in our 'passions', then we should reject James's suggestion that rational entitlements may be grounded in our 'passions'. If we reject the suggestions of both Clifford and James, then we still have a range of views that we might take about the claim that God exists. We might think – perhaps following Plantinga – that it is a belief appropriately formed on the basis of perception and introspection, though in that case it is not clear that we should not say that it is then formed on the basis of evidence and argument. Or we might think – perhaps, again, following Plantinga – that it is a belief to which one is rationally entitled simply in virtue of the fact that one is a rational agent. In this latter case, it would surely be right to say that the belief is not formed on the basis of evidence and argument, but there *might* be other reasons for misgivings, along the lines of the Great Pumpkin objection.

10. State the central point of disagreement between Plantinga and Clifford, and the central point of disagreement between Plantinga and James. Take a position on each of these two points of disagreement, stating in each case what you take to be the strongest argument in favour of that position.

Needless to say, the above discussion is both controversial and incomplete. So much has been written about Plantinga's thought that here we can do no more than suggest some initial starting points for further exploration:

Baker, D. (ed.), *Alvin Plantinga*, Cambridge: Cambridge University Press, 2007.
Beilby, J., *Epistemology as Theology: An Evaluation of Alvin Plantinga's Religious Epistemology*, Aldershot: Ashgate, 2006.
Tomberlin, J. and van Inwagen, P. (eds), *Alvin Plantinga*, Dordrecht: Reidel, 1985.

Introduction to Rey

Georges Rey is a contemporary philosopher of mind. Rey completed a PhD at Harvard during the 1970s, and has been for many years a professor in the department of philosophy at the University of Maryland. He is the author of *Contemporary Philosophy of Mind: A Contentiously Classical Approach* (1997) and the co-editor, with Barry Loewer, of *Meaning in Mind: Fodor and His Critics* (1991). Moreover, he has written numerous articles on different aspects of philosophy of mind.

The excerpt from the provocative piece that we examine here argues for the conclusion that there is no one who *seriously* believes that God exists. Considered in the light of history, there is some irony in the fact that there are now philosophers who are prepared to offer sober argument on behalf of a claim of this kind. For not too many years have passed since it was commonplace for philosophers to assert that there is no one who seriously believes that God does *not* exist. (For the historical evidence that supports this latter claim, see, for example, D. Berman, *A History of Atheism in Great Britain: From Hobbes to Russell* (1988), ch. 1, 'The Repression of Atheism'.)

Because we have only taken part of a larger piece of work, the excerpt that we have provided makes some reference to material that we have not included. In particular, the first reason that Rey offers for doubting that anyone subjected to a standard Anglo-European high-school education really believes that God exists – 'Obviousness of the Considerations Raised' – refers back to the discussion in the previous section of the paper, in which Rey provides background for the presentation of his 'eleven reasons'. Points upon which Rey insists in that background discussion are: (1) that God must be taken to have a mind and, hence, a psychology; (2) that the reasons for atheism are obvious, and not dependent on subtle metaphysics or sophisticated theories of knowledge; (3) that atheism is strongly justified by the absence of evidence for belief in God; (4) that the standard arguments for the existence of God fail disastrously, not least because they fail to establish the existence of a being with a mind and a psychology; (5) that problems about 'epistemic distance' undermine efforts to ground belief in God in religious experience; and (6) that it is simply a fallacy to suppose that the demand for evidence in the case of the existence of God ultimately leads to scepticism about other minds and the external world.

Georges Rey, 'Meta-atheism: Religious Avowal as Self-deception'

There seem to me to be roughly the following eleven reasons to suppose that anyone subjected to a standard Anglo-European high school education know at some level that standard theistic claims are false (some of the reasons overlap):

[1] Obviousness of the Considerations Raised Above

The kinds of considerations I raised in the previous section are ones to which, it seems to me, any moderately educated adult is readily sensitive. Perhaps non-philosophers wouldn't bother to put it the ways I have here, and doubtless most people have not really even thought very much about the standard theological arguments or about how their ordinary beliefs form a vast interlocking network. But in discussing these things I have been at pains to raise only *commonsensical* considerations, of the sort that are regularly raised in, for example, popular science, courtroom arguments, and mystery novels, where people regularly second-guess detectives, juries, and attorneys about relevant evidence and argument. Imagine a jury hearing testimony by a defendant appealing to a *sensus spiritatus* on behalf of a claim that there was someone else at the scene of the crime: is it really in the cards that they would take it seriously 'beyond a reasonable doubt'?

[2] Patent Weakness of Religious Arguments

As regards the theological arguments, I submit that *were any of the reasonings presented in any other context, their advocates would readily recognize them as unsound.* Unless one came to the arguments with a preconceived theism, few would conclude that Creationism is really a serious alternative to evolutionary biology, or, for those who accept evolution, that God was needed as a further factor, any more than they would think that angels would be needed to push the planets in addition to gravitation. Nor (along the lines of the 'ontological argument') would they think that 'perfect' islands or demons must exist, lest their nonexistence be an imperfection; nor conclude from the fact that everything had a cause that there was a *single* cause for everything – much less that that cause must have involved a mind.

[3] Tolerance of Otherwise Delusional Claims

I don't think you need to be an atheist to have the reaction I've mentioned to the content of religious claims. Were the claims about a supernatural entity who loves, commands, scolds, forgives, and so on, to be encountered in a fashion removed from the rich, 'respectable' aesthetic and cultural traditions in which they are standardly presented, they would be widely regarded as delusional, if not psychotic. As a child, a friend of mine thought the lives of the saints were the models by which one was supposed to live, and so one day proceeded to eat ashes with her breakfast, in emulation of St Thérèse of Liseux. Her otherwise quite devout mother was horrified, and admonished her never to do anything so foolish again. (Consider how much more horrified she would have been were she to be presented at communion with an actual piece of a human body and a glass of real blood!) Or, think of how most normal, even religious people react to hippies who – sometimes in emulation of Jesus – forsake their worldly goods to wander and proselytize among the poor; or to people who murder their children because 'God told them to' (just as He told Abraham!); or to the claims of the Koresh cult in Texas, or those claims about the Hale-Bopp comet mad by the recent Heaven's Gate cult – and then remember that many religions were themselves once just such 'cults' (see in this regard the work of noted biblical scholar, Elaine Pagels 1979).

It's a useful exercise in general to note people's reactions when idiosyncratic religious claims are presented to them in a way that disguises their usual religious context. I regularly begin a class casually recounting to my students a story I claim to have read about a local judge who, confronted with a confessed murderer whom he know and loved, decided to release him, and went home and shot his son to atone for the crime instead (or, alternatively, sacrificed his son as a way of *thereby* sacrificing *himself*). If I tell the story casually enough, the look of horror and incredulity is striking on the faces of many students who don't immediately see the analogy with the familiar sacrifice of Christ. In a similar vein, even the noted theistic philosopher Robert Adams (1999) writes: 'What would you think if you asked your neighbor why he was building a large stone table in his backyard, and he said, "I'm building an altar, because God has commanded me to sacrifice my son as a whole burnt offering. Won't you come to the ceremony tomorrow morning?" All agree that the neighbor should be committed to a mental hospital' (p. 284).

[4] Reliance on Texts and Authorities

Many of the otherwise outlandish religious claims derive an air of legitimacy, of course, from their reliance on a specific set of usually archaic texts or other ultimate religious authorities, whose claims are presented 'dogmatically' (indeed, the primary meaning of 'dogma' has precisely to do with religious proclamations). The texts or authorities standardly serve as the *sole* basis for various claims (e.g., that God exists, that Jesus is the son of God) that are regarded as essentially incontestable – certainly not often contested on the basis of any *non*-textual evidence.

Faith in texts and ultimate authorities, of course, raises countless theoretical and practical problems, familiar from the history of religious strife. Most obviously: how do you know which (translation or interpretation of a) text or authority to trust? Why believe one of them does and the other does not express 'the word of God'? It is common knowledge that the familiar Bible we possess is at least in part the result of the efforts of a great many ordinary mortals, as susceptible to 'sin' and error as anyone, working in very different languages, times, and conditions and embroiled in now this, now that religious and political controversy (see Pagels, 1979, 2003). One would think it would behoove someone worried about which version genuinely reflected God's word to be constantly trying to sift through the intricate historical details, anxiously ascertaining which writers really did have a main line to God, before placing their faith imprudently in the wrong ones. However, so far as I have heard, serious biblical scholarship has little effect on most people's actual religious practices. (How many Christians, for example, will worry about the admonitions against prayer and charity seriously attributed to Jesus in the recently discovered Thomas Gospel [see Pagels, 2003, 229, #14])?

This all contrasts dramatically with science and common sense, where there are patently no such sacred texts, creeds, or ultimate authorities. Of course, there are *textbooks* and *provisional* authorities, but these are quite frequently challenged, the texts revised and updated as the result of further research (Newton's classic *Principia* is seldom read outside of historical research; Einstein's specific proposals for a unified-field theory are viewed as forlorn). In general, we know very well that truths about the world are not revealed per se by the contents of some text or the revelation of some individual. Indeed, as the history of quantum physics has shown in often startling ways, there is no claim so sacrosanct that some good scientist – or scientifically minded philosopher – might not reasonably challenge it (some have proposed revising even basic logic in view of the results!). Of course, the challenge is based on other beliefs – it makes no sense to challenge *all* one's beliefs at once – but those beliefs in turn can be challenged in terms of still others, and so forth, with no particular belief having to be based upon faith or revelation. The noted philosopher W. V. Quine (1960), developing a metaphor of Otto Neurath, often compared our position in science and common sense to that of mariners on the open sea who have to repair their boat while remaining afloat in it, standing now on one plank to repair a second, and on a second to repair a third, only to stand on the third to repair the first.

[5] Detail Resistance

This continual revision and adjustment of ordinary beliefs is related to the multifarious ways I mentioned earlier in which they are interconnected, any one of them having logical or evidential relations to indefinite numbers of the others. For example, beliefs about whether O. J. Simpson murdered Nicole Simpson are connected to beliefs about cars, freeways, airports, police, and DNA – which in turn connect them to beliefs about cities, governments, history, and even cosmology. And one expects there to be in this way *indefinite numbers of details* that could be filled out in regard to these connections. If doubts are raised about the details, they can rebound to any one of the connected beliefs: thus, evidence against a particular theory of DNA would have given jurors less reason to believe that O.J. was at the scene of the crime. And if someone were to suggest that some third party murdered Nicole Simpson, then one would expect there to be further details – for example, further fingerprints, DNA – that would serve as crucial evidence. If there were *no* such details, one would be (as many were) reasonably skeptical: again, as everyone knows, absence of evidence is evidence of absence.

By contrast, literally understood, religious claims are oddly *detail-resistant*. Perhaps the most dramatic cases are the claims about creation. Whereas scientists regularly ask about the details of the 'Big Bang' – there is an entire book, for example, about what happened in the first three minutes (see Weinberg 1977) – it seems perfectly silly to inquire into similar details of just how God did it. Just how did His saying, 'Let there be light,' actually bring about light? How did He 'say' anything at all? Or, if He merely 'designed' the world or the species in it, how did He do this? Does anyone really think there is some set of truths answering these questions? Perhaps; but it is striking how there is nothing like the systematic research on them, in anything like the way that there is massive, ongoing systematic research into the indefinitely subtle details of biology, physics and cosmology. As the philosopher Philip Kitcher (1982, ch. 5) points out, even 'Creation Science' is concerned only with resisting evolutionary biology, not with seriously investigating any of the massive details that would be required for the Creation story actually to be confirmed. And even for those who regard evolution as simply the manner of God's creation, there is (so far as I know) not the slightest interest in investigating, say, radioisotopes, sedimentary layers, and the fossil record to establish precisely how, when, and where God had any role whatsoever in the creation of atoms, compounds, amino acids, DNA, and so forth that are manifestly required for the development of life, consciousness, and intelligent capacities. Despite what they claim, theists in fact treat Him as an idle wheel that does no serious explanatory work.

Of course, theologians do discuss details. I'm not a scholar of theology; however, I'm willing to wager that few of the details they discuss are of the *evidential* sort that we ordinarily expect of ordinary claims about the world, that is, claims that link the theological to *crucial data that would be better explained by the theological than by any competing hypothesis* (as I noted earlier, rendering theistic claims *compatible* with the rest of one's beliefs is not the same are rendering them *confirmed*). Mere elaborations of the theological stories without this property – mere stories about 'angels on the head of a pin' – don't constitute such details. If there really are serious attempts to narrow down the details of God's activities by, for example, reference to the fossil record, or systematic studies of the effects of prayer, then I stand corrected. But I'd also wager that most 'believers' would find such efforts silly, perhaps even 'sacrilegious.'

Some of this resistance to detail could, of course, be attributed to intellectual sloth. But not all of it. After all, if the religious stories really were true, an incredible lot would depend upon getting the details right (for many religious people, if you believe the wrong story, you could risk winding up in hell forever!). However, when I ask 'believers' these kinds of questions of detail, I am invariably met with incredulity that I even think they're relevant. Usually the questions themselves are regarded as sacrilegious.

[6] Similarity to Fiction

This resistance to detail is strikingly similar to the same resistance one encounters in dealing with fiction. It seems as silly to ask the kind of detailed questions about God as to ask for details about fictional characters; for example, What did Hamlet have for breakfast? Just how did the tornado get Dorothy and Toto to Oz? These questions are obviously silly and have no real answers – the text pretty much exhausts what can be said about the issues. In keeping with the reliance on texts and appeals to non-literality that we've already noted, religious claims seem to be understood to be fiction from the start.

Another indication that religious stories are understood as more akin to fiction than to factual claims is the aforementioned toleration of what would otherwise be patently delusional and bizarre claims. In fictions, we standardly enjoy all manner of deviation from 'naturalism' not only in matters of fact, but even in how we react. My own favorite examples in this regard are Wagner operas, which (I confess) move me terribly. But it matters a lot that it's fiction. In the first act of *Lohengrin*, for example, Elsa is accused of having murdered her brother. Instead of demanding some evidence for such an awful charge, she falls to her knees and prays that a knight in shining armor should come and vanquish her accuser; and when he shows up – on a swan! – he agrees to do so and marry her on the spot – but only on condition she never asks who he is! Were I to witness an event like this in real life, and the people were serious, I would regard them as completely out of their minds. But in the opera I am deeply moved – just as I am by the Passion story of the sacrifice of Christ, as a *story*, even though I would be thoroughly appalled and disgusted were it the history of an *actual, intentional sacrifice.*

[7] Merely Symbolic Status of the Stories

Indeed, notice that much of the power of religious claims doesn't really consist in their literal *truth*. Imagine, again, a judge in a real court, considering an appropriate punishment for the sins of man, and let's accept the idea of an innocent person being sacrificed to expiate *someone else's* sins. But, now ask if, in the specific case of Jesus, He actually did suffer *enough*? I don't mean to say that His betrayal and crucifixion weren't pretty awful; but can one afternoon on a cross (with the prospect of Sunday in heaven) really 'balance' *all* of the 'sins' of Genghis Khan, Hitler, Stalin, or what death squads routinely do to their victims in Latin America? These are crucifixions multiplied *many a million-fold*. But, of course, all of this is less relevant if we are to take the Passion story as merely symbolic fiction, that is, not as an actual rectifying of wrongs. Mere symbols, after all, needn't share the magnitudes of what they symbolize.

[8] Peculiarly Selective Perspectives

Related to detail resistance is a peculiar skewing of perspective on the world that keeps obviously disturbing details conveniently out of sight. As mentioned earlier, Alvin Plantinga (2000, 174) notes that religious feelings are often triggered by various bits of natural scenery, for example, mountains, the sea, the night sky. Such effects are quire familiar and easy to appreciate, even by a godless sinner like myself. But, of course, these bits are not really very representative of the world as a whole. Tastes may vary here, but it's not clear that on balance the majority of the devout are seriously prepared to regard most portions of the universe as suggestive of an omni-God. They know very well that most of the universe consists, overwhelmingly, of vast tracts of empty space, dotted with horrendous explosions and careening rubble, amidst most of which any living thing would be annihilated in an instant. Even sticking to the minuscule Earth, they know that a biological war of all against all likely leaves most animals starving, diseased, and scared; and that most of human life ends in humiliating misery, perfectly nice people wasting away from awful diseases and mental deteriorations, often unable to recognize family and friends, much less retain any wisdom they may have earlier acquired (Can anyone really think that Alzheimer's helps in the building of a better immortal soul?) Of course, it's perfectly fine to be selective about what one focuses upon and enjoys; it's self-deception only if it leads one to avow hypotheses that one knows to be belied by the majority of the evidence. . . .

[9] Appeals to Mystery

Confronted with many of the above problems, many theists claim God is a 'mystery' – indeed, I once heard a famous convert, Malcolm Muggeridge, claim 'mystery' as his main reason for believing! But ignorance (read: mystery) is standardly a reason to *not* believe something. Imagine the police arresting you merely because it's a 'mystery' how you could have murdered Smith! Just so: if it's really a complete mystery how God designed or created the world and permits so much pointless suffering, then obviously that's a reason to suspect it's simply not true that He did – and my point is that this is sufficiently obvious that everyone knows it and people simply pretend that religion affords some very odd exception.

Many theists are often willing to tolerate the mysteries surrounding God because they have an additional belief, which is that they also can't know about God's ways. Now, first of all, this is contradicted by all the claims they make about His omni-properties, as well as, crucially, what He likes and dislikes. Moreover, many people claim that He's responsible for when people live and die, and think He's the sort of being that will be responsive to petitionary prayer. But these then are precisely the points at which the God hypothesis is vulnerable to obvious disconfirmation: too much happens that's hard to believe is the result of an omni-being, too little that is plausibly an answer to prayer.

Of course, people do tolerate plenty of mysteries about how the world works. Most people have only the dimmest idea about how things live and grow, or how intentions actually bring about action. But in these cases the evidence for the postulated processes is overwhelming and uncontroversial: Ordinary people haven't the slightest reason to doubt that things grow, or that thought causes action, despite the mystery about how it occurs. By contrast, anyone aware of the basic ideas of contemporary science and the lack of evidence of God has plenty of reason to doubt His existence. In such a case, mystery can be no refuge.

What's particularly odd about the belief about our supposed inability to know God's ways is that the inability is so arbitrarily and inexplicably strong: why should there be no normal evidence of his existence? Why shouldn't it be possible to establish it in the same way as the existence of bacteria or the Big Bang? In any case, it's not as though the religious try to do what they might do in these other cases, namely, think of clever, indirect ways of finding out. No, the 'mystery' is supposed to be 'deeper' and far more impenetrable than that. I can't imagine what sustains such conviction – mind you, not merely about *God*, but about the *knowability* of God's ways – except perhaps an unconscious realization that there, of course, couldn't ever be serious evidence for something that doesn't actually exist.

[10] Appeals to 'Faith'

Of course, many religious people readily recognize the failure of evidence but then go on to claim that religious beliefs are matters of 'faith,' not evidence (in an extreme case, like that of Tertullian or Kierkegaard, claiming to believe precisely 'because it is absurd'). But try thinking something of the form:

p, however I don't have adequate evidence or reasons for believing it.

or

p, but it is totally absurd to believe it.

where you substitute for *p*, some non-religious claim, for example, '2 + 2 = 37,' 'the number of stars is even,' or 'Columbus sailed in 1962.' Imagine how baffling it would be if someone claimed merely to 'have faith' about these things. As Jonathan Adler (1999) points out, there seems to be something 'impossible,' even 'conceptually incoherent' about it, a little like the incoherence of thinking you know something, but being nevertheless convinced it isn't true. . . .

[11] Betrayal by Reactions and Behavior

Most people's reactions and behavior – for example, grief, mourning at a friend's death – do not seem seriously affected by the claimed prospects of a Hereafter (one wonders about the claimed exceptions). Contrast the reactions in two situations of a young, loving, 'believing' couple who are each seriously ill: In the first, the wife has to be sent off to a luxurious convalescent hospital for care for two years before the husband can come and join her for an indefinite time thereafter. In the second, the wife is about to die, and the husband has been told he will follow in two years. If, in the second case, there really were the genuine belief in a heavenly Hereafter that (let us suppose) they both avow, why shouldn't the husband feel as glad as in the first case – indeed, even gladder, given the prospect of eternal bliss! However, I bet he'd grieve and mourn 'the loss' like anyone else. Indeed, note how most religious music for the dead is deeply lugubrious, and imagine the absurdity of performing the Mozart requiem for someone you won't see for a few years because she has gone to a luxurious resort!

Or consider petitionary prayer (in contrast to a merely meditative sort): in the first place, the idea of an omni-god that would permit, for example, children to die slowly of leukemia is already pretty puzzling; but to permit this to happen unless someone *prays* to Him to prevent it – this verges on a certain sort of sadism and moral incoherence (imagine a doctor who acted in this way!), and one wonders what people have in mind in worshipping

Him. One can well understand the desperation of someone praying in such circumstances, or in a foxhole, or in the throes of unrequited love; but such desperations are just that, and do not per se manifest serious belief (as Neils Bohr is reputed to have said in being asked why he kept a horseshoe over his door, 'I've been told they work even if you don't believe they do').

Indeed, if petitionary prayer were a matter of serious belief, then why aren't those who engage in it disposed to have the National Institutes of Health do a (non-intrusive) demographic study, say, of the different sorts of prayers, as they would were they interested in the claim that soy beans prevent cancer? And why do none of them expect prayer to cure wooden legs? Or bring back Lazarus after two thousand years? I suggest that there are obvious limits to people's self-deception, and they know full well that God couldn't really intervene in such obviously impossible ways.

References

Adams, R. (1999) *Finite and Infinite Goods* Oxford: Oxford University Press.

Adler, J. (1999) 'The Ethics of Belief: Off the Wrong Track,' *Midwest Studies*, 23: *New Directions in Philosophy*, ed. P. French and H. Wettstein, 267–85.

Alston, W. (1991) *Perceiving God*, Ithaca NY: Cornell University Press.

Kitcher, Philip (1982) *Abusing Science: The Case Against Creationism*, Cambridge: MIT Press.

Pagels, E. (1979) *The Gnostic Gospels* New York: Vintage Books.

Plantinga, A. (2000) *Warranted Christian Belief*, New York: Oxford University Press.

Quine, W. (1960) *Word and Object*, Cambridge: MIT Press.

Weinberg, S. (1977) *The First Three Minutes: a Modern View of the Origin of the Universe*, New York: Basic Books.

Wittgenstein, L. (1966) *Lectures and Conversations on Religious Belief*, Berkeley: University of California Press.

Commentary on Rey

While it is not immediately obvious how the considerations that Rey advances are supposed to support his conclusion – and while it is not even clear exactly what conclusion Rey takes himself to be arguing for – it seems reasonable to suggest that Rey is advancing an argument that has something like the following form: When we examine claims that are made by intelligent and articulate religious believers – i.e. when we look closely at what intelligent and articulate religious believers *say* – we find that these claims have various properties that indicate that we ought not to be too quick to suppose that those religious believers *really* believe what they say. Perhaps there are some people who really do believe religious claims; but those people are too unintelligent, or too ill-educated, or too young to count as serious counter-examples to the thesis that Rey wishes to defend. (Rey's reference to those 'subjected to a standard Anglo-European high school education' provides at least a vague pointer to what he takes to be the relevant standards of intelligence and articulation.)

1. Work through Rey's eleven objections, distilling each one down to a sentence. Which of his points seem to you the most and the least persuasive?

2. Consider Rey's objections [8] and [9] and evaluate the arguments that he gives.

Among the questions that are prompted immediately by this rough formulation of Rey's argument, one of the most pressing concerns is what it means to affirm or deny that someone *really* believes something that she affirms with serious, careful and articulate conviction. If we have correctly represented the argument that Rey means to defend, then it is a consequence of Rey's argument that philosophers such as Richard Swinburne and Alvin Plantinga – philosophers who have written many carefully argued books defending the kinds of claims that are typically expressed by intelligent and articulate religious believers – do not *really* believe, for example, that God exists and is the sole creator of the physical universe. But, if they do not *really* believe the kinds of claims that are defended in their works, then what account can we give of the creation of those works?

3. Explain what Rey is arguing for in [3]. Do the examples he gives in [3] provide convincing support to his argument?

While there are niceties that require further attention, it seems to be a plausible rule of thumb that, when an intelligent and articulate adult human being sincerely affirms that p, part of the explanation for this sincere affirmation is that the adult human being in question believes that p. Indeed, we might think that it is pretty much constitutive of sincere affirmation that it issues from appropriate belief: if I do not have the belief that p, then I simply do not have what it takes to be able to make a sincere affirmation that p. Perhaps we might think that, if I did not have the belief that p, but I thought that I did have the belief that p, that would be enough to enable me sincerely to affirm that p. But could it genuinely turn out that, while I do not have the belief that p, I none the less *really believe* that I do have that belief?

One way in which we might try to make sense of the idea that someone might really believe that they believe that p, even though they do not believe that p, is to make use of the idea of 'partitioning' of beliefs. Perhaps it could be that someone has the belief that they believe that p, even though they do not have the belief that p, because the belief that they believe that p is somehow 'screened off' from the further body of beliefs that makes it appropriate to say that the person in question does not believe that p. Moreover, it could be – perhaps – that when this person sincerely affirms that p they do so on the basis of their belief that they believe that p, even though they have a body of beliefs that make it appropriate to say that they do not believe that p.

4. We tend to regard deception as an intentional act: if I unintentionally give you false information, I may have misled you but I have not deceived you. But is it possible intentionally to deceive yourself? Would not this be like me trying intentionally to get you to believe something I know to be false, when you already know that it is false?

Some of the things that Rey says suggest that he holds that those who sincerely affirm that God exists none the less *really* believe that God does not exist. We could also try to make sense of this idea using the idea of 'partitioning' of beliefs. Perhaps it could be that someone has the belief that they believe that God exists, even though they have the belief that God does not exist, because the belief that they believe that God exists is somehow 'screened off' from the belief that God does not exist. Moreover, it could be – perhaps – that when this person sincerely affirms that God exists they do so on the basis of their belief that they believe that God exists, even though they also have the belief that God does not exist.

One difficulty for this way of making sense of Rey's suggestion is that, if we take the idea of 'partitioning' of beliefs seriously, then it seems that it could be possible for someone to believe that p, and for them to believe that not p, and for these beliefs to be screened off from one another. However, if there is someone who believes that God exists, and who believes that God does not exist, and whose belief that God exists is 'screened off' from her belief that God does not exist, and who affirms that God exists on the basis of her belief that God exists, then it is not clear that we end up with a case in which there is someone who sincerely affirms that God exists, but who does not *really* believe that God exists. Perhaps, though, we should simply take Rey's proposal to be that someone only counts as *really* believing that God exists if it is the case that (1) they believe that God exists, and (2) they do not believe that God does not exist.

5. On the partition view, someone who is self-deceived about p also believes, at some level, that p is false. But consider the following case. A politician responsible for introducing reforms to education policy, despite ample and widely accepted evidence that they have been a disaster, believes that those reforms are a great success. He has strong political and personal motivations to want to believe that the reforms are successful, and does not believe (on any level) that they are not. Is this a genuine case of self-deception?

Suppose that we have hit upon *roughly* the right understanding of Rey's talk about 'real belief', i.e. suppose that we are *roughly* correct in thinking that what he wants to claim is that anyone who is sufficiently intelligent, well – educated and intellectually mature, and who sincerely affirms that God exists, also has the 'partitioned' belief that God does not exist. Do the various 'reasons' that Rey advances in support of his views make sense in the light of this understanding of his talk about 'real belief'?

Consider, for example, his claim that it is simply *obvious*, for example, that atheism is strongly justified by the absence of evidence for belief in God, that the standard arguments for the existence of God fail disastrously, that problems about 'epistemic distance' undermine efforts to ground belief in God in religious experience, and that the reasons for atheism are obvious, and not dependent on subtle metaphysics or sophisticated theories of knowledge. Even if these things were simply *obvious*, would that be a good reason for thinking that sufficiently intelligent, well-educated and intellectually mature people who sincerely affirm that God exists also have the 'partitioned' belief that God does not exist? Or should we rather think that there is some other, better explanation of why these things are not obvious to sufficiently intelligent, well-educated and intellectually mature people who sincerely affirm that God exists, even though they are obvious to people such as Rey?

If we are satisfied that the various 'reasons' that Rey advances in support of his view at least make sense in the light of the most plausible understanding of his talk about 'real belief', the next question to consider is whether we should suppose that these 'reasons' provide strong support for that view. Thus, for example, even if we are satisfied that, if the things that Rey takes to be obvious are obvious, then that is some kind of reason to think that sufficiently intelligent, well-educated and intellectually mature people who sincerely affirm that God exists have the 'partitioned' belief that God does not exist, we have still to ask whether the things that Rey takes to be obvious *really* are obvious.

Consider, for example, the claim that it is simply obvious that the standard arguments for the existence of God fail disastrously. Given our discussion in Section 2, we might well be happy to accept the claim that at least some of the standard arguments for the existence of God do have serious flaws. But Rey's claim is much stronger than that: Rey's claim is that it is *obvious* that *all* of the standard arguments for the existence of God have serious flaws. We think that this claim is hardly beyond dispute. Consider, for example, the ontological argument developed by Kurt Gödel: is it simply *obvious* that that argument has serious flaws? (We need not argue about whether Gödel's ontological argument is one of the standard arguments for the existence of God. If there are extant arguments for the existence of God that are not obviously flawed, then that probably suffices to undermine the suggestion that there cannot be sufficiently intelligent, well-educated and intellectually mature people who sincerely affirm that God exists but who do not also have the 'partitioned' belief that God does not exist.)

Even if we suppose that *some* of the 'reasons' that Rey offers – in defence of the claim that anyone who is sufficiently intelligent, well – educated and intellectually mature, and who sincerely affirms that God exists, also has the 'partitioned' belief that God does not exist – at least have the *potential* to support that claim, it is not clear that all of the 'reasons' that Rey offers have this standing. In particular, whenever he makes claims about 'many religious people', or 'most religious people', we have reason to worry that – regardless of the plausibility of the ensuing claims – we are not being given considerations that are strong enough to support the universal claim that Rey purports to be defending. The class of sufficiently intelligent, well-educated and intellectually mature people who sincerely affirm that God exists is a very diverse class: not everyone in the class readily recognises the failure of evidence, or tolerates appeals to mystery, or is not interested in controlled studies of petitionary prayer, even though it is true for each of these properties that some members of the class have it.

6. Rey claims at [7] that religious stories have mainly symbolic value, and at [11] that people's behaviour is not much affected by belief in the afterlife or petitionary prayer. Are either of these observations true? Do they constitute (can they be made into/used in support of) arguments for Rey's position?

Clearly, we do not have the space here to discuss all of the fine print in Rey's presentation of his eleven 'reasons'. (We leave that task to you.) However, perhaps we can provide a model for the execution of this remaining task by considering one case: Rey's discussion of the alleged 'detail resistance' of theistic claims about creation at [5]. How might a theist respond to Rey on this point? Well, at the very least, it seems that a theist might say that, yes, there is a set of truths answering to these questions but, no, there is no prospect of carrying out anything like systematic research on them, because there is no potential source of evidence to drive that research. Even if you think that scripture is a reliable source of evidence, it is no help in the present case, since it is silent on these questions. So – barring some future revelation – all we have to go on is the deliverances of sensation and reason. But sensation only informs us about matters within the universe: we cannot see or hear what happened prior to the Big Bang. And it is utterly implausible to suppose that pure reason can deliver the answers to Rey's questions. So, unless we are vouchsafed some future revelation, there is just no prospect that we can arrive at reasonable hypotheses on these points. But, if that is right, then surely the 'detail resistance' of theistic claims about creation provides no support at all for the claim that anyone who is sufficiently intelligent, well – educated and intellectually mature, and who sincerely affirms that God exists, also has the 'partitioned' belief that God does not exist.

7. Consider Rey's comparison of religious beliefs and fiction in [6]. Is the comparison plausible?

Because Rey's article has only very recently appeared, there is not yet a literature that discusses it. However, if you are interested in pursuing work that belongs to the same genre, you might like to have a look at:

Antony, L. (ed.), *Philosophers without Gods: Meditations on Atheism and the Secular Life*, Oxford: Oxford University Press, 2007.

Clark, K. (ed.), *Philosophers who Believe*, Downers Grove, Ill.: InterVarsity Press, 2003.

Morris, T. (ed.), *God and the Philosophers: The Reconciliation of Faith and Reason*, Oxford: Oxford University Press, 1994.

4

Divine Attributes

Introduction

In this section, we look at some discussions of properties (attributes) that many – or, in some cases, all – theists ascribe to God. These discussions focus on difficulties that might be taken to arise for theism by virtue of the ascription of particular attributes to God. However, before we can turn to a brief account of the kinds of difficulties that might be thought to arise, we need to give a brief account of the different kinds of properties that are often ascribed to God.

1. *Extensive modifiers:* Theists often say that God is 'perfect', or 'maximal', or 'infinite', or 'greatest', or 'supreme', or the like. In some cases, these ascriptions are paired with the very general descriptor 'being' in the construction of definite descriptions: 'the perfect being', 'the maximal being', 'Infinite being', 'the greatest being', 'the supreme being', and so on. In other cases, these ascriptions are taken to apply to a set of base properties or attributes, which record the respects in which God is 'perfect', or 'maximal', or 'infinite', or 'greatest', or 'supreme', or the like: perhaps God is 'perfectly good', or 'maximally powerful', or 'infinitely just', or 'supremely wise', and so forth. Of course, the more properties or attributes are thought to belong to the base set, the more chance that there will be conflict between the properties or attributes arrived at by extensive modification of those base properties or attributes.
2. *Metaphysical qualities:* Some of the qualities that theists ascribe to God are qualities that are not typically ascribed to the elements of God's creation. Thus, for example, at least some theists have wished to claim that, in contrast to the elements of God's creation, God is 'simple', 'indestructible', 'impassible', 'eternal', and the like. Many theists have also ascribed other fundamental categorical properties to God; thus, for example, many theists have supposed that God is a 'person', an 'agent' and a 'conscious' being, and that God acts

with 'freedom' (and, indeed, with 'perfect freedom'). The ascription of qualities from each of these categories to God is controversial. Thus, on the one hand, there are many theists who have wished to deny that God is 'simple' and 'impassible'; and, on the other hand, there are some theists who have wished to deny that God is a 'person' (preferring, instead, to say that God is a 'principle', or something of that ilk).

3. *Originative (relational) qualities:* Theists typically say that God is the 'creator', or 'ground', or 'source' of things other than God. In particular, theists typically agree that God is the 'creator' of the physical universe and everything that is contained therein. However, some theists have also claimed that God is the maker of logic and logical truth, mathematics and mathematical truth, values and truths about values, morality and truths about morality, and so forth. Of course, there are also many theists who have insisted that logic, mathematics, values and morals are importantly independent of the existence of God: there was nothing that God had to do – or to be – to make 2 + 2 = 4, or to establish the logical law of excluded middle, or to make it the case that it is wrong to sexually abuse young children.
4. *Base qualities:* Theists typically use terms that also have application to human beings in talking about God: they say that God is 'good', 'wise', 'knowing', 'powerful', 'loving', 'just', and so forth. Of course, as we noted above, the use of these terms often occurs in conjunction with the use of an extensive modifier: God is 'perfectly good', or 'maximally powerful', or 'infinitely just', or 'supremely wise', and so forth. Moreover, theists disagree about whether we should suppose that these base terms – 'good', 'wise', 'knowing', 'powerful', 'loving', 'just', and so forth – apply to God in the same sense in which they apply to human beings. Some theists think that talk of God must always be analogical, or metaphorical, or cast in terms of what God is not, or the like; other theists suppose that one need not deny the 'otherness' of God if one supposes that these base terms may be univocally predicated of God and human beings.

Of course, there are many other qualities that some theists ascribe to God. For example, Christian theists typically suppose that God is 'triune', 'incarnate', 'suffering', 'atoning', and so forth. We shall not consider these distinctively Christian attributions in the readings that we examine; if you wish to see a contemporary treatment of these properties, you might have a look at some of Richard Swinburne's more recent books: *Responsibility and Atonement* (1989), *Revelation: From Metaphor to Analogy* (1992), *The Christian God* (1994) and *The Resurrection of God Incarnate* (2003).

One further point that should be noted concerns the *modality* of the qualities that we have mentioned. Many theists suppose that God's existence is *necessary* – i.e. that it is alethically, or metaphysically, or logically impossible that God fail to exist. Moreover, many theists suppose that the qualities that we have been discussing are *essential* properties of God, that is, properties that it is impossible for God to fail to possess given that God exists. Thus, for example, many theists suppose that God is an essentially perfect being who is essentially maximally powerful, essentially infinitely loving, essentially perfectly good, and so forth. Questions about the consistency of qualities ascribed to God typically become more urgent when the qualities in question are taken to be essential to God.

5. *O-qualities:* Given our earlier discussion of extensive modifiers and base qualities, we can infer that many theists suppose that God possesses various 'omni'-properties: many theists suppose that God is 'omnipotent', 'omniscient', 'omnibenevolent', 'omnipresent', and so forth. However, the introduction of these terms raises new questions: for there are hard questions to be asked about exactly what we should take these terms to mean. Much recent discussion of divine attributes has focused on the proper analysis of these O-terms: what are necessary and sufficient conditions for omnipotence, omniscience, omnibenevolence, and the like? While these questions about necessary and sufficient conditions might not be the best questions to ask – after all, the recent history of philosophy suggests that it is very hard to provide necessary and sufficient conditions for any interesting concept – it is true that there are various interesting puzzles that are thrown up by the use of these terms.

The first paper that we shall be looking at – by C. Wade Savage – is a response to the suggestion that the concept of omnipotence is incoherent, i.e. a response to the suggestion that it is logically impossible for there to be an omnipotent being. Thus, our first paper is an instance of worries that might be raised about the coherence of individual qualities that are often ascribed to God.

The second paper that we shall be looking at – by Nelson Pike – sets up an alleged problem about the consistency of divine omniscience and human freedom: on Pike's account, there is a good *prima facie* argument for the conclusion that it is logically impossible for there to be free human action if there is an omniscient God. Thus, this second paper is an instance of worries that might be raised about the compatibility of individual qualities often ascribed to God with what we might suppose are non-negotiable facts about the world. (Perhaps some might be happy to deny that there is free human action – but those people are typically not theists.)

The third paper that we shall be looking at – by Norman Kretzmann – attempts to defend the idea that God is the ultimate source of moral value by appeal to the doctrine of divine simplicity. There is a strong *prima facie* argument – first set out in Plato's *Euthyphro* – which suggests that values and morals must be importantly independent of the existence of God. Kretzmann claims that this argument might be defeated by appeal to the doctrine of divine simplicity. Thus, this third paper is an instance of attempts to address worries concerning the idea that God might be the 'ground' or 'source' of things other than the physical universe and its contents by appeal to other qualities that at least some theists have wished to ascribe to God.

The final work that we shall be examining – by Boethius – addresses some questions concerning the proper way to think of God's relationship to time.

Given our earlier account, it is clear that we do not suppose that we are providing a systematic treatment of the divine attributes. Rather, we shall be introducing ourselves to some fragments from a much larger discussion. If you are interested in pursuing a wider investigation of the divine attributes, you might like to consider some of the following works:

Hoffmann, J. and Rosenkrantz, G., *The Divine Attributes*, Oxford: Blackwell, 2002.
Morris, T., *Our Idea of God*, Notre Dame, Ind.: University of Notre Dame Press, 1992.
Swinburne, R., *The Coherence of Theism*, Oxford: Clarendon Press, 1977.
Wierenga, E., *The Nature of God: An Inquiry into Divine Attributes*, Ithaca, NY: Cornell University Press, 1989.

Introduction to Savage

C. Wade Savage is a contemporary philosopher of science. Since 1971, he has been Professor of Philosophy at the University of Minnesota; for some of that time, he was also Director of the UM Center for Philosophy of Science. Savage completed an MA at the University of Iowa and a PhD at Cornell, and held other academic appointments – e.g. at UCLA – prior to his arrival at the University of Minnesota. He is the author of *The Measurement of Sensation: A Critique of Perceptual Psychophysics* (1970), and has edited or co-edited many books, including: *Scientific Theories* (1990), *Philosophical and Foundational Issues in Measurement Theory* (1991) and *Between Positivism and Relativism: New Perspectives in Philosophy of Science* (1993).

In 'The Paradox of the Stone', written in 1964, Savage provides discussion of an argument that is intended to show that omnipotence is a 'paradoxical' – or 'self-contradictory', or 'necessarily empty' – notion, and hence is intended to show that it is impossible for anything to be omnipotent. Savage's article is partly a response to an earlier attempt to respond to that 'paradoxical' argument (in a paper by George Mavrodes), and partly the development of a novel response to the argument. We shall not be concerned with the accuracy of Savage's portrayal of Mavrodes' views; if you are interested in *that* question, you should have a look at Mavrodes' article, and then make up your own mind. In the main part, our focus is on the question whether Savage himself provides an adequate response to the 'paradoxical' argument.

C. Wade Savage, 'The Paradox of the Stone'

a → [1] A (1) Either God can create a stone which He cannot lift, or He cannot create a stone which He cannot lift.

(2) If God can create a stone which He cannot lift, then He is not omnipotent (since He cannot lift the stone in question).

(3) If God cannot create a stone which He cannot lift, then He is not omnipotent (since He cannot create the stone in question).
(4) Therefore, God is not omnipotent.

[b]→ Mr. Mavrodes has offered a solution to the familiar paradox above,[1] but it is erroneous. Mavrodes states that he assumes the existence of God,[2] and then reasons (in pseudo-dilemma fashion) as follows. God is either omnipotent or He is not. If we assume that He is not omnipotent, the task of creating a stone which He cannot lift is not self-contradictory. And we can conclude that God is not omnipotent on the grounds that both His ability and His inability to perform this task imply that He is not omnipotent. But to prove His non-omnipotence in this way is trivial. 'To be significant [the paradoxical argument] must derive this same conclusion *from the assumption that God is omnipotent*; that is, it must show that the assumption of the omnipotence of God leads to a *reductio*.' However, on the assumption that God is omnipotent, the task of creating a stone which God cannot lift is self-contradictory. Since inability to perform a self-contradictory task does not imply a limitation on the agent, one of the premises of the paradoxical argument – premise A(3) – is false. The argument is, in consequence, either insignificant or unsound.

There are many objections to this solution. First, the paradoxical argument need not be represented as a reductio; in A it is a dilemma. Mavrodes' reasoning implies that the paradoxical argument must either assume that God is omnipotent or assume that He is not omnipotent. This is simply [c]→ false: neither assumption need be made, and neither is made in A. Second, 'a stone which God cannot lift' is self-contradictory – on the assumption that God is omnipotent – only if 'God is omnipotent' is necessarily true. 'Russell can lift any stone' is a contingent statement. Consequently, if we assume that Russell can lift any stone we are thereby committed only to saying that creating a stone which Russell cannot lift is a task which in fact cannot be performed by Russell or anyone else. Third, if 'God is omnipotent' is necessarily true – as Mavrodes must claim for his solution to work – then his assumption that God exists begs the question of the paradoxical argument. For what the argument really tries to establish is that the existence of an omnipotent being is logically impossible. Fourth, the claim that inability to perform a self-contradictory task is no limitation on the agent is not entirely uncontroversial. Descartes suggested that an omnipotent God must be able to perform such self-contradictory tasks as making a mountain without a valley and arranging that the sum of one and two

[1] George I. Mavrodes, 'Some Puzzles Concerning Omnipotence', *Philosophical Review*, LXXII (1963), 221–223. The heart of his solution is contained in paragraphs 6, 7, and 11.
[2] See n. 2, p. 221.

is not three.[3] No doubt Mavrodes and Descartes have different theories about the nature of contradictions; but that is part of the controversy.

Mavrodes has been led astray by version A of the paradox, which apparently seeks to prove that *God is not omnipotent*. Concentration on this version, together with the inclination to say that God is by definition omnipotent, leads straight to the conclusion that the paradox is specious. For if God is by definition omnipotent, then, obviously, creating a stone which God (an omnipotent being who can lift any stone) cannot lift is a task whose description is self-contradictory. What the paradox of the stone really seeks to prove is that the notion of an omnipotent being is logically inconsistent – that is, that *the existence of an omnipotent being, God or any other, is logically impossible*. It tries to do this by focusing on the perfectly consistent task of creating a stone which the creator cannot lift. The essence of the argument is that an omnipotent being must be able to perform this task and yet cannot perform the task.

Stated in its clearest form, the paradoxical argument of the stone is as follows. Where x is any being:

d → [2] B (1) Either x can create a stone which x cannot lift, or x cannot create a stone which x cannot lift.

(2) If x can create a stone which x cannot lift, then, necessarily, there is at least one task which x cannot perform (namely, lift the stone in question).

(3) If x cannot create a stone which x cannot lift, then, necessarily, there is at least one task which x cannot perform (namely, create the stone in question).

(4) Hence, there is at least one task which x cannot perform.

(5) If x is an omnipotent being, then x can perform any task.

(6) Therefore, x is not omnipotent. Since x is any being, this argument proves that the existence of an omnipotent being, God or any other, is logically impossible.

[3] Harry G. Frankfurt, 'The Logic of Omnipotence', *Philosophical Review*, LXXIII (1964), 262–263. The relevant passage from Descartes is quoted by Frankfurt in a long footnote. Mavrodes assumes (on his 'significant' interpretation of the paradox) that creating a stone which God cannot lift is a self-contradictory task, and contends that God therefore cannot perform it. This forces him onto the second horn of dilemma A, which he tries to break by arguing that inability to perform a self-contradictory task does not imply a limitation on the agent. Frankfurt also assumes that creating a stone which God cannot lift is a self-contradictory task, but contends with Descartes (for the sake of argument) that God can nevertheless perform it. This forces him onto the first horn of the dilemma, which he tries to break with the following argument. If God can perform the self-contradictory task of creating a stone which He cannot lift, then He can just as easily perform the additional self-contradictory task of lifting the stone which He (creates and) cannot lift. Frankfurt's fundamental error is the same as Mavrodes': both suppose that on any significant interpretation the paradox sets for God the self-contradictory task of creating a stone which God (an omnipotent being who can lift any stone) cannot lift.

It is immediately clear that Mavrodes' solution will not apply to this version of the paradox. B is obviously a significant, nontrivial argument. But since it does not contain the word 'God', no critic can maintain that B assumes that God is omnipotent. For the same reason, the point that 'a stone which God cannot lift' is self-contradictory is simply irrelevant. Notice also that B is neutral on the question of whether inability to perform a self-contradictory task is a limitation on the agent's power. We can, however, replace every occurrence of 'task' with 'task whose description is not self-contradictory' without damaging the argument in any way.

[e]→ The paradox does have a correct solution, though a different one from that offered by Mavrodes. The two solutions are similar in that both consist in arguing that an agent's inability to create a stone which he cannot lift does not entail a limitation on his power. But here the similarity ends. For, as we shall see presently, the basis of the correct solution is not that creating a stone which the creator cannot lift is a self-contradictory task (which it is not). Consequently, the correct solution side-steps the question of whether an agent's inability to perform a self-contradictory task is a limitation on his power.

[3] The fallacy in the paradox of the stone lies in the falsity of the second horn – B(3) – of its dilemma: '*x* can create a stone which *x* cannot lift' does indeed entail that there is a task which *x* cannot perform and, consequently, does entail that *x* is not omnipotent. However, '*x* cannot create a stone which *x* cannot lift' does not entail that there is a task which *x* cannot perform and, consequently, does not entail that *x* is not omnipotent. That the entailment seems to hold is explained by the misleading character of the statement '*x* cannot create a stone which *x* cannot lift'. The phrase 'cannot create a stone' seems to imply that there is a task which *x* cannot perform and, consequently, seems to imply that *x* is limited in
[f]→ power. But this illusion vanishes on analysis: '*x* cannot create a stone which *x* cannot lift' can only mean 'If *x* can create a stone, then *x* can lift it'. It is obvious that the latter statement does not entail that *x* is limited in power.

A schematic representation of B(1)–B(3) will bring our point into sharper focus. Let S = stone, C = can create, and L = can lift; let *x* be any being; and let the universe of discourse be conceivable entities. Then we obtain:

C (1) (∃*y*) (Sy & Cxy & ~Lxy) v ~(∃*y*) (Sy & Cxy & ~Lxy)
(2) (∃*y*) (Sy & Cxy & ~Lxy) – (∃*y*) (Sy & ~Lxy)
(3) ~(∃*y*) (Sy & Cxy & ~Lxy) – (∃*y*) (Sy & ~Cxy)

That the second alternative in C(1) is equivalent to '(∀y) [(Sy & ~Cxy) – Lxy]' schematically explains our interpretation of '*x* cannot create a stone which *x* cannot lift' as meaning 'If *x* can create a stone, then *x* can lift it.' It is now quite clear where the fallacy in the paradoxical argument lies. Although C(2) is logically true, C(3) is not. '(∃*y*) (Sy & ~Cxy & ~Lxy)' logically implies '(∃*y*) (Sy & ~Lxy)'. But '~(∃*y*) (Sy & ~Cxy & ~Lxy)' does not logically imply '$(\exists y)$ (Sy & ~Cxy)'; nor does it logically imply '$(\exists y)$ (Sy & ~Lxy)'. In general, 'x cannot create a stone which x cannot lift' does not logically imply 'There is a task which x cannot perform'.

[4] For some reason the above analysis does not completely remove the inclination to think that an agent's inability to create a stone which he himself cannot lift does entail his inability to perform some task, does entail a limitation on his power. The reason becomes clear when we consider the task of creating a stone which someone *other than* the creator cannot lift. Suppose that y cannot lift any stone heavier than seventy pounds. Now if x cannot create a stone which y cannot lift, then x cannot create a stone heavier than seventy pounds, and is indeed limited in power. But suppose that y is omnipotent and can lift stones of any poundage. Then x's inability to create a stone which y cannot lift does not necessarily constitute a limitation on x's power. For x may be able to create stones of any poundage, although y can lift any stone which x creates. If y can lift stones of any poundage, and x cannot create a stone heavier than seventy pounds, then x cannot create a stone which y cannot lift, and x is limited in power. But if x can create stones of any poundage, and y can lift stones of any poundage, then x cannot create a stone which y cannot lift, and yet x is not thereby limited in power. Now it is easy to see that precisely parallel considerations obtain where x is both stone-creator and stone-lifter.

g → The logical facts above may be summarized as follows. Whether $x = y$ or $x \neq y$, x's inability to create a stone which y cannot lift constitutes a limitation on x's power only if (i) x is unable to create stones of any poundage, or (ii) y is unable to lift stones of any poundage. And, since either (i) or (ii) may be false, 'x cannot create a stone which y cannot lift' does not entail 'x is limited in power'. This logical point is obscured, however, by the normal context of our discussions of abilities and inabilities. Since such discussions are normally restricted to beings who are limited in their stone-creating, stone-lifting, and other abilities, the inability of a being to create a stone which he himself or some other being cannot lift normally constitutes a limitation on his power. And this produces the illusion that a being's inability to create a stone which he himself or some other being cannot lift necessarily constitutes a limitation on his power, the illusion that 'x cannot create a stone which y cannot lift' (where either $x = y$ or $x \neq y$) entails 'x is limited in power'.

Since our discussions normally concern beings of limited power, the erroneous belief that 'x cannot create a stone which x cannot lift' entails 'x is limited in power' will normally cause no difficulty. But we must beware when the discussion turns to God – a being who is presumably unlimited in power. God's inability to create a stone which He cannot lift is a limitation on His power only if (i) He is unable to create stones of any poundage, or (ii) He is unable to lift stones of any poundage – that is, only if He is limited in His power of stone-creating or His power of stone-lifting. But until it has been proved otherwise – and it is difficult to see how this could be done – we are free to suppose that God suffers neither of these limitations. On this supposition God's inability to create a stone which He cannot lift is nothing more nor less than a necessary consequence of two facets of His omnipotence.[4] For if God is omnipotent, then He can create stones of any poundage and lift stones of any poundage. And 'God can create stones of any poundage, and God can lift stones of any poundage' entails 'God cannot create a stone which He cannot lift'.

Commentary on Savage

We have divided Savage's text into four sections. Section [1] presents the version of the 'paradoxical' argument that Mavrodes discusses, and offers criticisms of Mavrodes' discussion of that argument. Section [2] presents Savage's preferred formulation of the 'paradoxical' argument, and explains why this formulation of the argument evades Mavrodes' criticisms. Section [3] gives Savage's preferred response to the 'paradoxical' argument. Finally, section [4] tries to explain away residual disquiet that one might have about Savage's preferred response.

1. Explain in your own words Savage's account at b→ of Mavrodes' solution to the paradox.

2. Explain Savage's remark at c→ that '"a stone which God cannot lift" is self-contradictory'. Why would this undermine Mavrodes' argument, as expressed at b→? Which of the four arguments against Mavrodes given in this paragraph is most persuasive?

Savage's formulation of the 'paradoxical' argument differs from Mavrodes' formulation in three significant ways. First, Savage replaces all of the occurrences of the name 'God' (and all of the occurrences of the anaphoric pronoun 'He' that refer back to uses of the name 'God') in Mavrodes' formulation with occurrences of the symbol '*x*'. Second, Savage amends the second and third premises of Mavrodes' formulation, replacing the expression '*x* is not omnipotent' with the expression 'necessarily, there is at least one task that *x* cannot perform'. Third, Savage introduces an intermediate conclusion ('There is at least one task that *x* cannot perform') and a further premise ('If *x* is an omnipotent being, then *x* can perform any task'). Thus, in place of the argument at a→, Savage proposes instead to discuss the argument at d→.

[4] Mavrodes apparently sees this point in the last three paragraphs of his article. But his insight is vitiated by his earlier mistaken attempt to solve the paradox.

3. How is the formulation of the paradox at d→ intended to improve on the formulation at a→?

There is an important sense in which both of these formulations are infelicitous. Consider this claim: 'If *x* cannot create a stone that *x* cannot lift, then *x* cannot create the stone in question.' Surely this claim is not well formed: 'the stone in question' must refer back to some particular, identified entity, and yet there is no particular stone that is identified in the sentence '*x* cannot create a stone that *x* cannot lift'. We could rephrase this sentence as follows: '*x* is unable to make it the case that there is a stone that *x* is unable to lift'. That makes it clear that the sentence makes use of a quantificational device – 'there is a stone' – that, because it is embedded within the scope of the modal modifier 'cannot', is not a suitable target for the kind of back reference that might be secured using the expression 'the stone in question'.

4. Rewrite Savage's argument at d→ using this new formulation. How does it improve on his version?

The point registered in the preceding paragraph is not idle carping. Mavrodes and Savage are agreed that the following claim is true: *if God can create a stone that He cannot lift, then God cannot lift the stone in question*. But a natural way of making the point that this claim is not even well formed would be to say something like the following: even if God *can* create a stone that He cannot lift, *until* he *does* make a stone that He cannot lift we are in no position to conclude that there *is* something that God cannot do. At best, we can conclude that, *were* God to make a stone that He cannot lift, then there *would be* something that he could not do, namely lift the stone that he had made.

Perhaps it might be replied that, while it is clear that God's ability to create a stone that He cannot lift does not threaten the claim that there is *presently* nothing that he cannot do, God's ability to create a stone that He cannot lift does threaten the claim that, *no matter how events unfold, it will always be the case* that there is nothing that God cannot do. If we amend premise (5) in Savage's argument to something like the following claim

(5′) If *x* is an omnipotent being, then it is not possible that there is a time at which *x* exists and yet is unable to perform some task

then there would be at least *pro tanto* reason to say that God's ability to create a stone that He cannot lift would threaten the claim that God is omnipotent. However, at least at first sight, this response seems to require a conflation of omnipotence with essential omnipotence: why should it not be the case that a merely omnipotent being is able to do things that bring it about that that being is no longer omnipotent?

5. If God is essentially omnipotent, then it is impossible that he could be non-omnipotent. Suppose that God is accidentally omnipotent, i.e. that it is possible that he should be non-omnipotent. In this case, God could create a stone too heavy for God to lift and in so doing make himself non-omnipotent. Does this provide a satisfactory solution to the paradox?

6. Look at Savage's discussion of Frankfurt in note 3. How does Frankfurt's solution differ from Mavrodes'? Is it an improvement?

Savage and Mavrodes are agreed that the weak point in these arguments is the falsity of the following claim: *if God cannot create a stone which God cannot lift, then God is not omnipotent*. Moreover, as Savage makes clear at [e]→, they also agree that the key to the resolution of the 'paradox' is the observation that 'an agent's inability to create a stone that he cannot lift does not entail a limitation on his power'. However, given Savage's formulation of the argument, it seems quite implausible to suppose that this observation could have any bearing on the 'paradoxical' argument: for, of course, on his formulation of that argument, there is no connection that is established between omnipotence and limitations on power. On the contrary, Savage's formulation of the argument only makes an explicit connection between omnipotence and 'the ability to perform any task'.

Indeed, getting a grip on Savage's proposed solution to the 'paradox' is no easy matter. In particular, it should be noted that Savage makes the following two claims:

1. Creating a stone which the creator of that stone cannot lift is a perfectly consistent task (whence it follows, *a fortiori*, that creating a stone which the creator of that stone cannot lift is a task).
2. 'x cannot create a stone that x cannot lift' does not entail that there is a task that x cannot perform.

It seems natural to say that, if x cannot create a stone that x cannot lift, then x cannot carry out the task of creating a stone which the creator of that stone cannot lift. As we have noted in 1, Savage himself allows that creating a stone which the creator of that stone cannot lift is a task. So it seems that Savage is committed to saying that, if x cannot create a stone that x cannot lift, then there is a task that x cannot carry out. Yet Savage's 'solution' to the 'paradox' turns on denial that this is so at [f]→.

Setting aside questions about the relevance of claims concerning limitations of power, the obvious problem with this denial is that, since 'x cannot create a stone that x cannot lift' plainly does entail that there is a task that x cannot carry out, any meaning-preserving equivalent to this claim must have the same entailment. It seems plausible to suppose that 'x cannot create a stone that x cannot lift' is equivalent to the claim 'Necessarily, if x makes a stone, then x can lift it'. ('x cannot create a stone that x cannot lift' is equivalent to: 'It is not possible that

x makes a stone that x cannot lift' – and that's equivalent to 'Necessarily, if x makes a stone, then x can lift it'.) But that claim – 'Necessarily, if x makes a stone, then x can lift it' – also entails that x cannot carry out the task of creating a stone that its creator cannot lift. In other words, Savage's central argument collapses because his claim about meaning-preserving equivalence is mistaken.

In his assessment of the advantages of his solution to the 'paradox' over the solution that is offered by Mavrodes, Savage makes the following observation:

3. The correct solution to the 'paradox' side-steps the question of whether an agent's inability to perform a self-contradictory task is a limitation of his power.

It is not obvious that Savage is right about this. In particular, it should be noted that his formulation of the 'paradoxical' argument includes premise 5: 'If x is an omnipotent being, then x can perform any task'. If we suppose that there are self-contradictory tasks, then acceptance of this premise would commit us to the claim that an omnipotent being can perform self-contradictory tasks. Thus, one might think, whether we should accept premise 5 in Savage's formulation of the 'paradoxical' argument plausibly does turn upon whether one thinks that it is appropriate to suppose that an inability to perform self-contradictory tasks is a limitation on a being's power. Of course, whether one should draw this conclusion depends upon whether one ought to think that there is close connection between omnipotence and the absence of limitations on one's power.

7. Suppose we analyse omnipotence as 'able to perform any task that is not self-contradictory'. Consider the following tasks: (1) Make it the case that 2 + 2 = 4; (2) Make it true *now* that in 2008 Hillary Clinton won the nomination of the Democratic Party; (3) Get divorced; (4) Bring about something evil for no good reason. Are these counter-examples to the analysis? Can you revise the analysis to get round them?

Suppose we did think that x is omnipotent iff it is impossible for there to be limitation of x's power. Then we might recast the 'paradoxical' argument as follows:

C (1) Either x can create a stone that x cannot lift, or x cannot create a stone that x cannot lift.
(2) If x can create a stone that x cannot lift, then it is possible for there to be a limitation of x's power: for, if x creates a stone that x cannot lift, then there will be a stone that x cannot lift, and that would be a limitation of x's power.
(3) If x cannot create a stone that x cannot lift, then that is a limitation of x's power: there is something that x cannot do – create a stone that cannot be lifted by its creator – that countless other beings can do; whence, of course, it follows that it is possible for there to be a limitation of x's power.
(4) (Hence) it is possible for there to be a limitation of x's power.
(5) x is omnipotent iff it is impossible for there to be a limitation of x's power.
(6) (Hence) x is not omnipotent.

If we accept that x is omnipotent iff it is impossible for there to be a limitation of x's power, then we might follow Savage in thinking that the key question to ask is whether premise 3 is true: if x cannot create a stone that x cannot lift, does that count as a limitation of x's power?

Savage offers an analysis at [g]→ that issues in the conclusion that x's inability to create a stone that x cannot lift does not count as a limitation of x's power. Applied to the case of God, this analysis entails that God's inability to create a stone He cannot lift is a limitation on His power only if (i) He is unable to create stones of some poundage (i.e. He is limited in his powers of stone-creation), or (ii) He is unable to lift stones of some poundage (i.e. He is limited in his powers of stone-lifting). But, on the hypothesis that God is not limited in His powers of either stone-creation or stone-lifting, it then follows that God's inability to create a stone He cannot lift is no limitation on His power. Indeed, as Savage points out, the claim 'God can create stones of any poundage and God can lift stones of any poundage' entails 'God cannot create a stone that God cannot lift'.

Should we be satisfied with Savage's analysis? That is not clear. The intuition behind the 'paradoxical' argument is that powers can conflict: having the power to do X can be inconsistent with having the power to do Y. If powers can conflict, then there can be no such thing as a being that has all possible powers, i.e. that has no limitations on its power. However, if we suppose that being able to create a stone that its creator cannot lift is a power, then what Savage's analysis shows is that possession of that power is inconsistent with possession of the power to create stones of any poundage and the power to lift stones of any poundage. So, before we can claim to be content with Savage's analysis, we need to decide whether having the ability to create a stone that its creator cannot lift counts as possession of a power. (Just to be clear: We can all agree with Savage that *lacking* the ability to create a stone that its creator cannot lift entails no limitations on either your power to create stones or your power to lift stones. But if it is appropriate to say that you lack the *power* to create a stone that its creator cannot lift, then it still follows that lacking the ability to create a stone that its creator cannot lift constitutes an abridgement of your power.)

Apart from these worries about whether lacking the ability to create a stone that its creator cannot lift constitutes an abridgement of your power, one might have other reasons to worry about Savage's analysis. Here is one such worry. Suppose that God could have bequeathed universe-making powers to other beings, and that some being other than God could have made a universe that consisted of nothing but a single stone. Suppose further that God was unable to make a universe that consisted of nothing but a single stone (perhaps because His goodness requires that, if He makes a universe, He makes a universe that contains sentient creatures). If the universe consisted of nothing but a single stone, then it could not be lifted – because lifting requires displacement relative to a suitable background and, in the envisaged scenario, there is no suitable background. Suppose, further, that it is true that both God and the other being with universe-making powers can create and lift stones of any poundage. It seems to us that, on this scenario, we ought to say that there is a limitation on God's power (of stone creation), even though Savage's analysis *entails* that there is no limitation on God's power here. (Perhaps you might think that a minor amendment to Savage's analysis will be able to cope with this counter-example. But there will doubtless be other counter-examples to that amended analysis. . . .)

8. Is it possible for two omnipotent beings to exist at the same time? What would happen if one of the omnipotent beings tried to move a stone that the other omnipotent being was trying to keep motionless?

There is much more to be said about whether the concept of omnipotence is truly paradoxical. We have only considered one kind of argument that has been advanced on behalf of that conclusion. Moreover, we have barely scratched the surface of attempts to analyse the concept of omnipotence (and, in particular, of attempts to give necessary and sufficient conditions for possession of the property of being omnipotent). Finally, we have made no serious attempt to investigate the notions of power and ability, and hence have made little progress on the question whether lacking the ability to create a stone that its creator cannot lift constitutes an abridgement of your power. If you are interested in pursuing any of these matters further, you might like to look at:

Flint, T. and Freddoso, A., 'Maximal Power', in A. Freddoso (ed.), *The Existence and Nature of God*, Notre Dame, Ind.: Notre Dame University Press, 1983.

Oppy, G., 'Omnipotence', *Philosophy and Phenomenological Research*, 71 (2005): 58–84.

Sobel, J., *Logic and Theism*, Cambridge: Cambridge University Press, 2004. Ch. 9, 'Romancing the Stone'.

Introduction to Pike

Nelson Pike is a contemporary American philosopher of religion. After completing a PhD at Harvard in 1963 (on 'Hume on Personal Identity'), Pike held positions at a number of US universities, including Cornell and the University of California at Irvine. He is the author of *God and Timelessness* (1970) and *Mystic Union: An Essay in the Phenomenology of Mysticism* (1992). The piece that you are about to read is an extract from his best-known article, 'Divine Omniscience and Voluntary Action', *Philosophical Review*, 74, 1 (1965), 27–46.

Pike's paper divides into four parts. The first part provides background to the formulation of Pike's argument for incompatibility between divine foreknowledge and voluntary human action. The second part provides a careful formulation of Pike's argument for incompatibility between divine foreknowledge and voluntary human action. The third part briefly notes that Pike's argument makes no mention of the *causes* of human action. Finally, the fourth part provides critical discussion of comments on 'the problem of divine foreknowledge' found in the works of Leibniz, Luis de Molina, Friedrich Schleiermacher and St Augustine. We have reproduced *only* the second of the four parts of Pike's paper below.

Nelson Pike, 'Divine Omniscience and Voluntary Action'

[1] Last Saturday afternoon, Jones mowed his lawn. Assuming that God exists and is (essentially) omniscient, it follows that (let us say) eighty years prior to last Saturday afternoon, God knew (and thus believed) that Jones would mow his lawn at that time. But from this it follows, I think, that at the time of action (last Saturday afternoon) Jones was not able – that is, it was not within Jones's power – to refrain from mowing his lawn. If at the time of action, Jones had been able to refrain from mowing his lawn, then (the most obvious conclusion would seem to be) at the time of action, Jones was able to do something which would have brought it about that God held a false belief eighty years earlier. But God cannot in anything be mistaken. It is not possible that some belief of His was false. Thus, last Saturday afternoon, Jones was not able to do something which would have brought it about that God held a false belief eighty years ago. To suppose that it was would be to suppose that, at the time of action, Jones was able to do something having a conceptually incoherent description, namely something that would have brought it about that one of God's beliefs was false. Hence, given that God believed eighty years ago that Jones would mow his lawn on Saturday, if we are to assign Jones the power on Saturday to refrain from mowing his lawn, this power must not be described as the power to do something that would have rendered one of God's beliefs false. How then should we describe it vis-à-vis God and His belief? So far as I can see, there are only two other alternatives. First, we might try describing it as the power to do something that would have brought it about that God believed otherwise than He did eighty years ago; or, secondly, we might try describing it as the power to do something that would have brought it about that God (Who, by hypothesis, existed eighty years earlier) did not exist eighty years earlier – that is, as the power to do something that would have brought it about that any person who believed eighty years ago that Jones would mow his lawn on Saturday (one of whom was, by hypothesis, God) held a false belief, and thus was not God. But again, neither of these latter can be accepted. Last Saturday afternoon, Jones was not able to do something that would have brought it about that God believed otherwise than He did eighty years ago. Even if we suppose (as was suggested by Calvin) that eighty years ago God knew Jones would mow his lawn on Saturday in the sense that He 'saw' Jones mowing his lawn as if this action were occurring before Him, the fact remains that God knew (and thus believed) eighty years prior to Saturday that Jones would mow his lawn. And if God held such a belief eighty years prior to Saturday, Jones did not have the power on Saturday to do something that would have made

it the case that God did not hold this belief eighty years earlier. No action performed at a given time can alter the fact that a given person held a certain belief at a time prior to the time in question. This last seems to be an *a priori* truth. For similar reasons, the last of the above alternatives must also be rejected. On the assumption that God existed eighty years prior to Saturday, Jones on Saturday was not able to do something that would have brought it about that God did not exist eighty years prior to that time. No action performed at a given time can alter the fact that a certain person existed at a time prior to the time in question. This, too, seems to me to be an *a priori* truth. But if these observations are correct, then, given that Jones mowed his lawn on Saturday, and given that God exists and is (essentially) omniscient, it seems to follow that at the time of action, Jones did not have the power to refrain from mowing his lawn. The upshot of these reflections would appear to be that Jones's mowing his lawn last Saturday cannot be counted as a voluntary action. Although I do not have an analysis of what it is for an action to be voluntary, it seems to me that a situation in which it would be wrong to assign Jones the ability or power to do other than he did would be a situation in which it would also be wrong to speak of his action as voluntary. As a general remark, if God exists and is (essentially) omniscient in the sense specified above, no human action is voluntary.[1]

[2] As the argument just presented is somewhat complex, perhaps the following schematic representation of it will be of some use.

1. 'God existed at T1' entails 'If Jones did X at T2, God believed at T1 that Jones would do X at T2'.
2. 'God believes X' entails '"X" is true'.
3. It is not within one's power at a given time to do something having a description that is logically contradictory.
4. It is not within one's power at a given time to do something that would bring it about that someone who held a certain belief at a time prior to the time in question did not hold that belief at the time prior to the time in question.
5. It is not within one's power at a given time to do something that would bring it about that a person who existed at an earlier time did not exist at that earlier time.
6. If God existed at T, and if God believed at T1 that Jones would do X at T2, then if it was within Jones's power at T2 to refrain from

[1] In Bk. II, Ch xxi, Secs. 8–11 of the *Essay*, John Locke says that an agent is not free with respect to a given action (i.e., that an action is done 'under necessity') when it is not within the agent's power to do otherwise. Locke allows a special kind of case, however, in which an action may be voluntary though done under necessity. If a man chooses to do something without knowing that it is not within his power to do otherwise (e.g., if a man chooses to stay in a room without knowing that the room is locked), his action may be voluntary though he is not free to forbear it. If Locke is right in this (and I shall not argue the point one way or the other), replace 'voluntary' with (let us say) 'free' in the above paragraph and throughout the remainder of this paper.

doing X, then (1) it was within Jones's power at T2 to do something that would have brought it about that God held a false belief at TI,
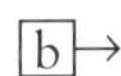 or (2) it was within Jones's power at T2 to do something which would have brought it about that God did not hold the belief He held at T, or (3) it was within Jones's power at T2 to do something that would have brought it about that any person who believed at T1 that Jones would do X at T2 (one of whom was, by hypothesis, God) held a false belief and thus was not God – that is, that God (who by hypothesis existed at T1) did not exist at T1.

7. Alternative 1 in the consequent of item 6 is false (from 2 and 3).
8. Alternative 2 in the consequent of item 6 is false (from 4).
9. Alternative 3 in the consequent of item 6 is false (from 5).
10. Therefore, if God existed at T1 and if God believed at T1 that Jones would do X at T2, then it was not within Jones's power at T2 to refrain from doing X (from 6 through 9).
11. Therefore, if God existed at T1, and if Jones did X at T2, it was not within Jones's power at T2 to refrain from doing X (from 1 and 10).

[3] In this argument, items 1 and 2 make explicit the doctrine of God's (essential) omniscience with which I am working. Items 3, 4, and 5 express what I take to be part of the logic of the concept of ability or power as it applies to human beings. Item 6 is offered as an analytic truth. If one assigns Jones the power to refrain from doing X at T2 (given that God believed at T1 that he would do X at T2), so far as I can see, one would have to describe this power in one of the three ways listed in the consequent of item 6. I do not know how to argue that these are the only alternatives, but I have been unable to find another. Item 11, when generalized for all agents and actions, and when taken together with what seems to me to be a minimal condition for the application of 'voluntary action,' yields the conclusion that if God exists (and is essentially omniscient in the way I have described) no human action is voluntary.

Commentary on Pike

We have divided our extract from Pike's text into three sections. Section [1] gives an informal – 'ordinary language' – formulation of Pike's argument. Section [2] provides a more structured – 'semi-formal' – presentation of Pike's argument, in which the various premises and inferential moves are carefully identified. The final section [3] provides a comment on the roles of the numbered sentences that appear in the more structured presentation of Pike's argument.

1. Carefully read through section [1] and briefly state in your own words why, according to Pike, no human action is voluntary if God is omniscient.

Our approach to Pike's argument will be indirect. We start with some considerations of sources of uncertainty in our thinking about the future, and then move on to an exploration of intuitions about connections between knowledge of the future and free human action. We then return to an assessment of Pike's argument in the light of our preliminary discussion.

It seems uncontroversial to observe that future states of the world depend upon (1) laws governing the evolution of states of the world over time, and (2) current (and past) states of the world. It may be that future states of the world depend *only* upon the laws and current (and past) states; however, for the purposes of this discussion, we need not inquire whether there is anything else upon which future states of the world depend.

Given that future states of the world depend upon the laws and current (and past) states, there are at least two clear sources of uncertainty in our thinking about the future: we may be ignorant of the laws that govern the evolution of states of the world; and we may lack information about current (and past) states of the world. Moreover, our lack of information about current (and past) states of the world may well not be *accidental*. On the one hand, the fact that there is an upper limit to the speed at which information can be transmitted may entail that we cannot access all of the current (and past) information that bears on our future states. And, on the other hand, the fact that there are non-accidental limits to the accuracy of the data that we can obtain also may entail that we cannot access all of the current (and past) information that bears on our future states.

2. The theory that each state of the universe is wholly necessitated by antecedent states and the laws of nature is called *determinism*. If determinism is true, then it seems that all of your actions are necessitated by states of the universe prior to your birth. Does this seem to you compatible with your actions being free? Justify your answer.

None the less, across a wide range of domains, we can make reasonably accurate predictions of the future, though, in many domains, accuracy falls off pretty steeply as the distance into the future increases. In particular, across a wide range of circumstances, we can make reasonably accurate predictions of the future behaviour of human beings, both individually and collectively. When predicting the future behaviour of individual human beings, our modelling is typically heuristic: we try to figure out what a reasonable person would do in the predicted circumstances, or what one would do if one were in the other person's shoes in the predicted circumstances, or the like. In some cases, we have good grounds for thinking that we *know* what a particular person will do, given our confidence (*a*) that the person in question will act rationally – or will do what we would do – in the predicted circumstances, and (*b*) that there is a particular action that any rational person – or, at any rate, anyone suitably like us – would perform in the predicted circumstances.

In typical cases in which we have good grounds for thinking that we know what a particular person will do, we do not suppose that our knowledge of what that person will do conflicts with that person's freedom of action: the rational person who opts for the evidently most rational course of action ought not to be classified as acting unfreely merely on that account. Of course, there will be cases in which knowledge of what a person will do depends upon factors that do undermine or cancel that person's freedom of action – e.g. knowledge that the reluctant prisoner will appear in the dock next week does not depend upon any knowledge of the unconstrained preferences of the prisoner. But, in the general case, it seems that there ought to be an alignment between freedom of action and in-principle predictability: freedom and reason both require that one act on one's appropriately acquired beliefs, desires, intentions, and so forth, in accordance with relevant norms, even though so acting makes one's behaviour predictable in the light of one's beliefs, desires, intentions, etc.

Even if one accepts that there is a general connection between freedom of action and in-principle predictability of behaviour, one might none the less hold that there are cases in which, as a matter of principle, human action is not predictable in advance. If one supposes that the world is deterministic – i.e. if one supposes that the current (and past) states of the world, together with the laws, uniquely prescribe the future – then, plausibly, one will suppose that there are no cases in which human behaviour is not predictable in principle. However, if one supposes that the evolution of the state of the world is objectively chancy – i.e. if one supposes that there are different futures that could evolve from the current (and past) states of the world, given the laws – then one can think that there are cases of (free) human action that are not predictable, even in principle, from perfect information concerning current (and past) states and the laws.

3. Suppose that determinism is true and that a supercomputer, with information about antecedent states and the laws of nature, predicts how you are going to decide some issue. Could you decide differently? Could you choose to act differently if you were told what the computer predicted?

Suppose, for example, that X is a two-state chance mechanism: when activated, X has two possible end-states, each of which has a 50 per cent chance of obtaining in any given case of activation. Suppose, further, that an agent A decides to use X in order to make a decision: perhaps, for example, A is Buridan's Ass, confronted with two equidistant and equally delectable bales of hay. If A uses X to make a decision, then, in the nature of the case, there is nothing in the current and past states of the world and the laws that enables an onlooker to figure out what A will do in advance of X's reaching one or other of its possible end-states. In this case, A's decision is, in principle, not predictable prior to X's reaching one or other of its possible end-states.

Suppose that, each Saturday, Jones uses a two-state chance mechanism to decide whether or not to mow his lawn. Suppose, in particular, that Jones will be using his two-state chance mechanism to decide whether or not to mow his lawn next Saturday. What should we say in answer to someone who asks whether Jones will mow his lawn next Saturday?

Given the way that we have set up the case, the key point is that what Jones will do *depends upon* the end-state into which his two-state choice mechanism settles after he sets it going next weekend. In order for us to know what Jones will do next weekend, we would need to know the outcome of an objectively chancy future event. A *minimum* requirement for us to have knowledge of the outcome of an objectively chancy future event is something like backwards causation – we need flow of information from that future event to our current spatio-temporal location. Unless the outcome of that objectively chancy future event can register with us here and now, there is no way that we can know what its consequences will be.

Moreover, the key part of this claim – viz. that knowledge of the outcome of an objectively chancy event requires a flow of information from the event to the knower – is perfectly general: it is simply *impossible* for an agent to have knowledge of the outcome of an objectively chancy event if there is no flow of information from the event to the agent. In other words, what goes for us would also go for God: even an omniscient being can only know the outcomes of objectively chancy events if there is a flow of information from these events to the omniscient being.

4. The theory that some states of the universe happen without necessitating antecedent causes – some states occur without any prior states accounting for them – is called *indeterminism*. If free actions have an indeterministic component, can we be responsible for them?

Does this mean that there is so much as *prima facie* difficulty in reconciling God's existence with the occurrence of objectively chancy events? It is hard to see how. True enough, if we suppose that there is only physical information, and if we suppose that agents must occupy particular spatio-temporal locations, then, for example, the finite speed of actual signal transmission will entail that there is no omniscient being. However, if we are prepared to suppose that there can be non-physical transmission of information – and which theists would wish to deny this? – then, whether or not we suppose that God is located in time, we can suppose that, at any time, we can truly say that God knows the outcomes of objectively chancy events that lie in our future.

That is not to say that theists might not prefer to deny that God knows the outcomes of objectively chancy future events. For example, if you suppose that God is located in time, and you suppose that the future does not exist, then you can hold that there is no knowledge to be had of the outcomes of objectively chancy future events. However, as far as we can see, you need next to nothing by way of controversial metaphysical assumptions in order to reconcile divine omniscience with human freedom. At the very least, there is a challenge here for those who would defend Pike's argument: how could the argument be repaired so as to accommodate the considerations that have been advanced in the preceding discussion?

5. Explain the distinction between 'free' and 'voluntary' that Pike discusses in note 1 on Locke. (i) What does it mean to say that the choice of a person who chooses to stay in a locked room, without knowing that it is locked, is 'voluntary'? (ii) Suppose that all of our free actions became only voluntary. Would we notice the difference? Would we have lost anything important?

Consider the fourth premise in Pike's argument at [a]↦. Now, of course, this premise is true: it is, we think, impossible to make sense of the idea that one might *change* the past. However, that it is impossible to change the past does not entail that it is impossible to *bring about* the past. In particular, if it is true that what someone believes at an earlier time is causally dependent upon what you do at a later time, then it is within your power to do something that brings it about that the person in question holds a particular belief at that earlier time. Strange as it may sound, if Jones's objectively chancy decision whether to mow takes place next Saturday, then it is Jones's decision at that future time that determines what it is now correct to say about God's beliefs about Jones's future decision. If, next week, Jones decides to mow, then we can now say truly that God believes that Jones will mow next Saturday; however, if, next week, Jones decides not to mow, then we can now say truly that God believes that Jones will not mow next Saturday. What God believes now imposes no constraint on Jones's free decision next Saturday because what God believes now *depends upon* the upshot of the free decision that Jones makes next Saturday.

Consider the second sub-clause of the sixth premise of Pike's argument at [b]↦. Pike claims that it follows from premise 4 that this sub-clause is false. But Pike is wrong about this: the statement at [b]↦ is actually true. For, as we have just argued, it *was* within Jones's power at T_2 to do something that *would have* brought it about that God did not hold the belief that he in fact held at T_1. *Had* Jones chosen not to mow the lawn at T_2, then it *would not have been* the case at T_1 that God believed that Jones would mow the lawn at T_2. But, of course, the statement at [b]↦ is not contradicted by the statements at [a]↦: for it is simply not true that, had Jones chosen not to mow the lawn, that would have made it the case that, at T_1, God both believed that Jones would mow the lawn at T_2 and that Jones would not mow the lawn at T_2.

Even though we think that there is a straightforward answer to Pike's argument – there is no conflict between divine omniscience and human freedom of the kind that Pike supposes there to be – it is none the less plausible to think that there is at least a *prima facie* conflict between the existence of objectively chancy events, divine omniscience and another property that has often been attributed to God, namely the attribute of impassibility. If we suppose that God is unchangeable, and hence, in particular, that nothing can have a causal effect on God, then it seems to us that it is plausible to suppose that, if there are any objectively chancy events in the world, God can have no knowledge of them. In particular, then, if we suppose – as many theists do – that genuinely free actions would be objectively chancy, we think that there is a tension between divine omniscience, human freedom, and divine impassibility.

Some theists have thought that it is not necessary to deny that God is impassible in order to account for God's knowledge of objectively chancy events on the grounds that God is the *ultimate* cause of everything that happens. The picture is something like this. Prior to creation, God surveys all possible worlds, including all of the worlds in which there are objectively chancy events. God then decides to instantiate a particular possible world, knowing the outcomes of all of the objectively chancy events in that world. Because God has decided to instantiate a particular possible world, there is no need for any 'feedback' from the world to inform God of the outcomes of objectively chancy events: knowledge of the outcome of objectively chancy events is built into the act of instantiating a possible world.

We think this picture is incoherent. We are supposing that God – an omniscient being – has beliefs about the outcomes of putatively objectively chancy events in the world that are causally prior to the occurrences of those events. In particular, we are supposing that the particular outcomes of those putatively objectively chancy events occur as they do precisely because God chooses that they should so occur – part of the reason why God chooses to instantiate this particular possible world is the pattern of outcomes of putatively objectively chancy events that occurs within it. But, given that God has beliefs about the outcomes of these putatively objectively chancy events in advance of their occurrence, it turns out that these putatively objectively chancy events cannot be chancy. Consider a particular event E. By a close cousin of Pike's argument, there is no alternative to E that could occur, since, in advance of E, there is an omniscient and omnipotent being who not only believes that E will occur, but who has also chosen to actualise our world in part because it is a world in which E occurs. In order for E to fail to occur, it would have to be the case that God chose to instantiate a different possible world; but, in the causal order, E's occurrence is downstream from God's decision about which possible world to instantiate.

6. Suppose that, while all events in the past or present are settled, the future is, to some degree, unsettled. So God, even though he knows everything there is to know about reality, will also know that some future events are 'open' – and even he will not know how they are settled until they actually occur. Is this theory coherent? Could it be used to show that human freedom, divine impassibility and omniscience are consistent?

Of course, a conflict between human freedom, divine omniscience and divine impassibility would be a quite different thing from a conflict between human freedom and divine omniscience. Few philosophers and theologians have wished to deny that God is omniscient; but many philosophers and theologians have wished to deny that God is impassible. In particular, many philosophers and theologians have thought that an impassible God could not be loving, or capable of undergoing suffering – and, hence, that an impassible God could not be the God of, say, the New Testament. This kind of dispute about the nature of God is often couched in terms of a distinction between 'the God of the philosophers' ('the God of Athens') and 'the God of everyday faith' ('the God of Jerusalem'); it remains a live dispute amongst philosophers of religion.

It might, perhaps, be worth noting here that those who believe that God is impassible do not need to deny that God acts in the world in a way that takes account of the outcomes of objectively chancy events. In particular, those who believe that God is impassible can suppose that, prior to creation, God was able to survey all of the possible worlds that could result from a particular initial state – i.e. to survey all of the possible worlds that could result from the playing out of objective chance – and, for each of these possible worlds, to schedule appropriate actions that would be carried out should that world happen to be the one that is actualised by the playing out of objective chance. On this way of thinking about things, God does not need to *register* the outcomes of objectively chancy events in order to bring it about that God's actions are appropriately co-ordinated with those outcomes: rather, God's initial – single – creative act includes a vast number of 'conditional actions' that can be 'triggered' by subsequent events. Moreover, on this way of thinking about things, it seems to turn out that there is a sense in which God can be described as 'loving', 'caring', and so forth: for we can suppose that God so orders things that his actions are always 'loving', 'caring', and so forth. (No matter which possible individuals are actualised under the playing out of objective chance, those individuals will receive providential treatment, and so forth.)

7. If God is impassible in the way described above, is it possible for human beings to have a 'personal relationship' with God?

As ever, we have only made a first few faltering steps in our investigation of the compatibility of freedom of action with collections of divine attributes that include omniscience and omnipotence. In particular, we have focused here on questions about the compatibility of human freedom of action with divine omniscience. But there are also questions about the compatibility of divine freedom of action with divine omniscience, as well as questions about the compatibility of divine freedom of action with divine perfect goodness. If you are interested in further exploration of these topics, you might wish to look at:

Pike, N., 'Omnipotence and God's Ability to Sin', *American Philosophical Quarterly*, 6 (1969): 208–16.
Rowe, W., *Can God Be Free?*, Oxford: Clarendon Press, 2004.
Zagzebski, L., *The Dilemma of Freedom and Foreknowledge*, New York: Oxford University Press, 1991.

Introduction to Kretzmann

Norman J. Kretzmann (1928–98) held an appointment in the department of philosophy at Cornell from 1966 until his death, at which time he was a Susan Linn Sage Emeritus Professor. He specialised in the history of medieval philosophy, and in philosophy of religion. Kretzmann came from a line of Lutheran pastors, but became an atheist while a university student, though he returned to belief in the existence of God towards the end of his life. Kretzmann obtained his BA from Valparaiso University in 1949, and his PhD from Johns Hopkins University in 1953.

Kretzmann's important contributions to the history of medieval philosophy included editing *The Cambridge History of Later Medieval Philosophy* (1982), and his authorship of studies of the first three volumes of Aquinas' *Summa contra Gentiles*: *The Metaphysics of Theism* (1997), *The Metaphysics of Creation* (1998) and *The Metaphysics of Providence* (2001). Important contributions to philosophy of religion include his early paper 'Omniscience and Immutability', which argues against the coherence of perfect-being theism, and his two later papers with Eleonore Stump, 'Eternity' (1981) and 'Absolute Simplicity' (1985), which are elaborations and defences of perfect-being theism. The paper that we have included in this collection is another contribution to the defence of perfect-being theism.

In the work that you are about to read, Kretzmann sets out to defend the suggestion that God is the basis of morality. In particular, Kretzmann aims to defend this suggestion against a famous objection raised by Plato (*c.*429–347 BCE) in his dialogue *Euthyphro*. Kretzmann's intriguing suggestion is that one can appeal to the standard medieval view – espoused, for example, by Aquinas (*c.*1225–74) – that God is a perfect being who possesses the attribute of being absolutely simple in order to make out the claim that God is the basis of morality. Of course, this appeal relies on the assumption that we can make sense of the claim that God is absolutely simple – and that, in turn, leads Kretzmann to consider some foundational work in the philosophy of language originally carried out by the great nineteenth-century German philosopher Gottlob Frege (1848–1925). However, before he gets to this chronologically diverse range of philosophers, Kretzmann begins with a careful reading of the biblical story of Abraham and Isaac.

Norman J. Kretzmann, 'Abraham, Isaac and Euthyphro: God and the Basis of Morality'

There are good philosophical reasons for rejecting (TS) – [the claim that right actions are right just because God approves of them, and wrong actions are wrong just because God disapproves of them] – as a basis for morality, two of which I will be mentioning shortly. But it would be a shame to permit (TS) to perish peacefully of refutation alone when it richly deserves execration. For taking (TS) seriously means taking seriously the possibility that absolutely any action could be made morally right simply in virtue of God's commanding or approving of it. If a father's killing his innocent son, whom he loves, is not an example horrible enough for you, you may be left to your darkest imaginings. But do not suppose that the adherent of (TS) can extricate himself from this terminal embarrassment with the pious rejoinder that God is good and so can be relied on not to approve of moral evil. The only standard of moral goodness supplied by (TS) is God's approval; and so to say within the context of (TS) that God is good comes to nothing more than that God approves of himself – which is easy to grant but impossible to derive any reassurance from.

For present purposes I will have to content myself with simply mentioning two of the more important, more obvious failings of (TS) as a putative basis
[a]→ for morality. In the first place, and most importantly, morality rests on

objectivity. Part of what that means is that if an individual action is really right at some time or other, then it always was and will be right. But (TS) does not preserve objectivity, as can be seen from the (TS)-interpretation of the Abraham story. In my view, this consideration alone is enough to disqualify (TS) as a theory of religious morality. In the second place, if (TS) is conjoined with a doctrine of divine rewards and punishments, as theories of religious morality usually are, it will be difficult or impossible to distinguish morality from prudence in the context of (TS). If God's command is all that makes the action right and I believe that God will punish me for disobedience, how can I convince myself that I perform the action because it is right rather than simply out of fear?

By this point (TS) should look disintegrated in disgrace, and the keenness of the reader's anticipation of (TO) – [the claim that God approves of right actions just because they are right, and disapproves of wrong actions just because they are wrong] – must be almost painful; so I will delay the consideration of (TO) no longer than it takes to announce that, incredible as it seems, (TS) will rise again.

(TO), the theory which does seem to fit the story of Abraham, obviously has the strengths corresponding to the shortcomings of (TS): (TO) does provide the objectivity necessary for morality, and it does preserve the possibility of drawing a clear distinction between morality and prudence. According to (TO), God disapproves of treachery just because it is really wrong to betray someone who trusts you. According to (TS), on the other hand, if it is wrong to betray someone who trusts you, it is so only because and only as long as God disapproves of treachery; and if we should learn tomorrow that it is approved of by God, then tomorrow it will have become *right* to betray someone who trusts you. And so it looks as if every self-respecting theist should, with a clear mind and an easy heart, repudiate (TS) and embrace (TO) with the sense that a danger to religious morality has been averted and a firm foundation for it has been secured.

But now consider (TS) and (TO) in the light of our main question: What does God have to do with morality? These two theories offer two radically different answers to that question, and those answers are 'Nothing essential' and 'Absolutely everything.' But 'Absolutely everything' is the answer provided by the just-repudiated (TS), and 'Nothing essential' is the answer entailed by (TO), which has been looking like the theory that would explain how morality could be based on religion.

Think of the story of Moses and the Ten Commandments. Moses is often called the law-giver, but since the story has him receiving the Commandments from God, that epithet is misleading; Moses was only the law-*transmitter*. God is the one who is properly described as the law-*giver*. But is he? According to (TS) he is, but according to (TO) God himself is really only a law-transmitter. For according to (TO) certain actions are really wrong and God knows which they are; and so, when he tells Moses to tell the people not to steal, he's not *legislating*, he's *teaching*. Of course such teaching on the basis of divinely expert authority may well have been [c]→ invaluable at an early stage in the moral development of mankind, but if (TO) is right, there is every reason to suppose that the objective truth about morality is there to be discovered in more and more depth and detail by human beings using their reason, without the aid of further revelation. If (TO) is right, God's 'giving' the Ten Commandments to the people through Moses is just what it would have been for God to have 'given' them the principles of arithmetic – not to disclose to them his sovereign will, but to provide them with a starter-kit for the discovery of great truths. And so, if (TO) is right, the answer to the question 'What does God have to do with morality?' is 'Nothing essential.' Of course, nothing essential need not be nothing at all. The person who first taught you arithmetic certainly has something to do with arithmetic, but nothing essential; there would be arithmetic even if that person had never existed. And, even more obviously, your first arithmetic teacher has something to do with your knowing arithmetic but, again, nothing essential; you could have learned arithmetic from someone else, and you could even have figured out quite a lot of it by yourself as you grew older and discovered the need for it. And so, if (TO) is right, it is just as absurd to consider God to be even a part of the basis for morality as it would be for you to expect to find a discussion of your first arithmetic teacher in a book entitled *Foundations of mathematics*.

(TO), which made its entrance into this discussion looking like the overwhelmingly preferable theory of religious morality, turns out to be not really a theory of *religious* morality at all, evidently cutting off any need morality might have been thought to have for a foundation in religion. And (TS), its only rival on the scene, has already proved not to be a theory of *morality* at all. At this stage of our investigation reasonable people might be excused for thinking that, since the one theory of religious morality gives God everything to do with what turns out not to be morality, while the other theory preserves the essence of morality at the cost of giving God a walk-on part that could easily be written out of the play, religious morality has been shown to be, at best, not worth any further serious thought. But even such reasonable people ought to be at least vaguely worried by the fact that the concept of God, which I began by describing as an essential ingredient in this discussion, has so far been given no attention. Of course, I have said quite a lot about God, but God as I have been talking about him is God as he appears in the stories we have been looking at and in the bit of religious-cultural background we all share. It is time now to consider the concept of God. . . .

[2] That concept of God, the one in which I am interested, is the concept of an absolutely perfect being. Among the attributes included in that concept are some that everyone has at least heard of: omniscience, omnipotence, and eternality, for instance. Perfect goodness is another familiar attribute of an absolutely perfect being, and one that will obviously be important if the concept is to have an essential role in a theory

of religious morality. But the attributes that will concern us to begin with are less familiar and less obviously relevant to our main topic, and the first of these is absolute independence.

d→ It is easy to see that nothing that could count as absolutely perfect could be dependent on anything else for anything. So anything absolutely perfect is absolutely independent; and if God is conceived of as an absolutely perfect being, then God is conceived of as absolutely independent. That line of thought, short and simple as it is, has a devastating effect on theists who might have been willing to accept (TO) after all, abandoning the project of a religious morality and settling for a religion that simply coexists with morality. For if God is an absolutely perfect being, then (TO), with its implication of moral principles on which God depends for his knowledge of good and evil, seems to be false. Even when (TO) was looking its best, it was likely to have given theists the uneasy feeling that it impugned God's majesty; but what corresponds to God's majesty in perfect-being theology is absolute independence, and absolute independence cannot be merely impugned. Like everything else about an absolutely perfect being, it's all or nothing. And so, on the basis of everything we've seen so far, no theist who conceives of God as an absolutely perfect being . . . can take refuge in the apparent safety and sanity of (TO). Perfect-being theology is incompatible with (TO) as we have been reading it. It is not incompatible with (TS), but (TS) has been shown to be so bad on other grounds that no self-respecting theist can have recourse to it at this stage of our investigation.

It may look as if the emerging conclusion is that perfect-being theology is just incompatible with morality altogether. . . . But there is one more attribute I want to introduce, one that I think will save the day. It is the hardest of all the attributes to understand, and it is called simplicity.

To say that an absolutely perfect being is absolutely simple is to say that it is altogether without components of any kind, and so simplicity can be derived from independence. For whatever has components is dependent on those components for being what it is, and so perfection entails independence, which entails simplicity. As Anselm puts it, 'everything composite needs the things it is composed of in order to *exist*. Moreover, *what* it is it owes to them, since whatever *it* is it is in virtue of them, while they are not what *they* are in virtue of *it*. And so [whatever is composite] is not completely supreme [or absolutely perfect]' *(Monologion*, XVII). Obviously an absolutely simple being cannot be a physical object, and there are other interesting implications of simplicity that are not hard to see. But the one that concerns us now might easily be overlooked in a first consideration of the concept of absolute perfection; to see it is to see how drastic a simplicity absolute simplicity has to be. . . .

[3] To say that God is absolutely simple is not merely to say that God cannot have any parts in the ordinary sense; it is also to say that God cannot be thought of as distinguishable from any of his attributes. And if God and each of his attributes are identical, then all of God's attributes

are identical with one another. Before we can make use of this notion of simplicity, we have to make sense of it.

Attribution is, of course, ordinarily expressed in subject–predicate sentences, even when the subject is God. So we would ordinarily attribute goodness and power to God by saying 'God is good' and 'God is powerful.' According to this notion of simplicity, however, such sentences are [e] imprecise. If God is conceived of as an absolutely perfect being and thus as absolutely simple, then the precise versions of such sentences will be either 'God is identical with his goodness' and 'God is identical with his power' or, even more simply, 'God is identical with goodness' and 'God is identical with power.' Let's say that the first of these pairs of more precise sentences presents *cautious* simplicity and the second pair *bold* simplicity. Since it follows from the cautious pair that God's goodness is identical with God's power and from the bold pair that goodness is identical with power, it seems fair to say that absolute simplicity presents us with a more or less dire identity crisis, one that must be resolved before we try to apply the notion to the problems of religious morality. Because cautious simplicity presents the less dire identity crisis, it is only sensible to try to make do with it as an interpretation of the notion of simplicity.

As Frege has taught us, there are two kinds of identity claims, uninformative, as in $9 = 9$, and informative, as in $9 = 3^2$. The identity crisis in the notion of simplicity (whether cautious or bold) obviously has to do with informative identity claims. There are plenty of non-mathematical examples of such claims, but we may as well stay with Frege's classic example involving the morning star, the evening star, and the planet Venus. Since the morning star is identical with Venus and the evening star is identical with Venus, it is true and informative to say that the morning star is identical with the evening star. At the same time we want not to ignore the fact that they are also different – two different ways of seeing one and the same thing. If we focus on their designations rather than on the phenomena themselves, we say that the designations 'the morning star' and 'the evening star' differ in sense although they are identical in reference. And whenever we have a true informative identity claim, we will have two expressions with one and the same referent and two different senses. What happens when these basic distinctions are applied to cautious simplicity?

As analogues to the morning star, the evening star, and Venus, we have God's goodness, God's power, and God, respectively. And so we should be able to say correctly that the designations 'God's goodness' and 'God's power' have one and the same referent – God – and differ only in sense. Putting it that way certainly satisfies the notion of cautious simplicity, but [f] can we make sense of putting it that way? If we bear in mind the analogy with Frege's paradigm, it is not hard to make sense of cautious simplicity. It might be said that, because of differing circumstances that apply only to us and not at all to that being itself, the absolutely simple being that is God is perceived by us sometimes in a way that leads us to perceive divine goodness, sometimes in a way that leads us to perceive divine power. Divine goodness and divine power are no more really distinguished from each other or from God than the morning star, the evening star, and Venus are three in reality rather than one. Obviously there is more to explain and more to worry about in connection with even cautious simplicity, but there is no point in our considering cautious simplicity any further as a possible route to a third theory of religious morality. The reason for abandoning it we have already seen in dealing with (TS) and in considering Mill's attack on Mr Mansel: as long as we are focusing on God's goodness, the question will and should always arise whether *God's* goodness is really *goodness.* And so, despite the fact that it is easier to make sense of cautious simplicity initially, we have to consider bold simplicity if the doctrine of simplicity is to provide a preferable theory of religious morality.

g→ [4] According to the small portion of perfect being theology I am presenting in this paper, perfect goodness must be an attribute of an absolutely perfect being; and in the light of the notion of simplicity in its bold form, God conceived of as an absolutely perfect being *is* perfect goodness itself. If we momentarily ignore the question whether the consequences of bold simplicity are tolerable, we can see that applying it to the difficulties in religious morality has a dramatic effect. When God is conceived of as *identical with* perfect goodness, the kind of distinction that was crucial as between (TO) and (TS) becomes a mere stylistic variation. Here are the bold-simplicity counterparts of (TO) and (TS):

(PBO) God conceived of as perfect goodness itself sanctions certain actions just because they are right and rules out certain actions just because they are wrong.

(PBS) Certain actions are right just because God conceived of as perfect goodness itself sanctions them, and certain actions are wrong just because God conceived of as perfect goodness itself rules them out.

If there is goodness itself, as there is if there is an absolutely perfect being, then obviously it is and must be the sole criterion of moral rightness and wrongness. And so (PBS) involves no subjectivity, as did our original (TS), nor does (PBO) involve principles independent of and criterial for God, as did our original (TO). (PBO) and (PBS) are just two ways of saying the same thing: actions are right if and only if goodness certifies them as such, and goodness certifies actions as right if and only if they are so.

It may look as if this third theory of religious morality transforms God from the ultimate judge of morality into no more than the abstract ultimate criterion; but, of course, God conceived of as an absolutely simple being is conceived of as the ultimate judge who is *identical with* the objective ultimate criterion itself. And so, once the crucial contribution made by bold simplicity to this third theory is taken into account, the theory could safely revert to the judgmental verbs 'approve' and 'disapprove' found in (TO) and (TS) and could even be expressed in new versions of (TO) and (TS) in which slight linguistic revisions would mark fundamental changes in interpretation. We can designate these new versions (TO') and (TS'):

[h]→ (TO') God conceived of as a moral judge identical with perfect goodness itself approves of right actions just because they are right and disapproves of wrong actions just because they are wrong.

(TS') Right actions are right just because God conceived of as a moral judge identical with perfect goodness itself approves of them and wrong actions are wrong just because God conceived of as a moral judge identical with perfect goodness itself disapproves of them.

When God in the story of Abraham swears a solemn oath, he swears by himself (what else?); when the God of perfect-being theology makes a moral judgment, he judges by the objective criterion of perfect goodness which
[i]→ is himself. And so (TO') and (TS'), unlike (TO) and (TS) but like (PBO) and (PBS), are just two ways of saying the same thing.

So far so good; but what about the fact that bold simplicity apparently requires us to say that goodness is identical with power, which means that wherever there is power there is goodness, which is blatantly false? Well, taking bold simplicity seriously requires us to recognize that the identity claim at issue is, strictly speaking, not 'Goodness is identical with power' but 'Perfect goodness is identical with perfect power,' which means that wherever there is perfect power there is perfect goodness, which is not blatantly false and may very well be true.

Such a glancing inspection is by no means enough to certify bold simplicity as free from paradox, much less to show that bold simplicity and the rest of perfect-being theology provides a basis for a theory of religious morality preferable to those ordinarily encountered. But I hope it is enough to suggest that even bold simplicity might be made sense of, with dramatic results for the association between morality and theology. God knows it needs work, but it's worth it.

Commentary on Kretzmann

We have divided Kretzmann's text into four sections. Section [1] argues that there are strong cases against both (TO) and (TS). [2] discusses the conception of God as absolutely perfect being, arguing that an absolutely perfect being would be absolutely *independent* and absolutely *simple*. [3] distinguishes two different doctrines of divine simplicity – 'cautious simplicity' and 'bold simplicity' – and then, after sketching an argument for the coherence of these doctrines based on Frege's distinction between sense and reference, goes on to argue that 'cautious simplicity' is insufficient for the purposes of the proponent of perfect-being theology. Finally, section [4] argues that, given the doctrine of bold simplicity, the theories (TO) and

(TS) morph into two different ways of making the same acceptable claim – and ends with the suggestion that, while more work needs to be done, the doctrine of 'bold simplicity' holds out hope for an acceptable understanding of the claim that God is the basis of morality.

1. Evaluate Kretzmann's objection to (TS) at [a]→. What does he mean by objectivity? Why does (TS) undermine the objectivity of morality? Is his objection persuasive?

2. Why does Kretzmann claim at [b]→ that (TS) makes it impossible to distinguish morality from prudence? Is he correct?

3. Is the inference that Kretzmann makes at [c]→ correct? Explain in your own words and evaluate Kretzmann's main concern about (TO).

Let us begin with the argument of section [2], allowing Kretzmann his contention in [1] – which seems to us in any case highly plausible – that (TS) is simply unacceptable, while (TO) entails that God cannot possibly be the ultimate foundation of morality.

The perfect-being theology that Kretzmann introduces in [2] belongs to one of the mainstream Christian theological traditions, exemplified in the writings of Anselm, Aquinas and many others. According to perfect-being theology, God is an absolutely perfect being: perfectly powerful (omnipotent), perfectly wise and knowing (omniscient), perfectly good, perfectly free, and the like. While many of these properties are uncontroversial to those who belong to other Christian theological traditions, there are some rather controversial properties that these canonical perfect-being theologians attribute to God: immutability, impassibility, absolute independence, absolute simplicity, and the like. Thinkers from other Christian theological traditions typically criticise perfect-being theology on the grounds that, because perfect-being theology attributes these controversial properties, it fails to provide a loving personal God who is causally responsive to the actions and needs of his creatures.

From Kretzmann's claim at [d]→, it is clear that he is buying into one of the controversial parts of perfect-being theology. Moreover, it is highly contentious to suppose that it is easy to see what Kretzmann here claims is easy to see. Whatever else we might suppose about absolute perfection, it seems that we should grant that an absolutely perfect being will be as perfect as it is possible for any being to be. Thus, if we suppose that independence is one of the traits that we would expect of an absolutely perfect being, the *most* that we could expect is that an absolutely perfect being will be as independent as it is possible for any being to be. But, given only that an absolutely perfect being will be as independent as it is possible for any being to be, it plainly does not follow that an absolutely perfect being will not be dependent on anything at all: that latter claim will only follow if it is possible for there to be something that does not depend upon anything at all. If, for example, logic and mathematics and morality are independent necessarily existing domains, then – *contra* Kretzmann – the absolute perfection of a being would *not* be impugned by its dependence upon these domains. (Of course, to take this line is to call in question the idea that theists need to suppose that God is the basis of morality in the way in which Kretzmann supposes that they need to do. If morality is a matter of independent necessity, then that need not be thought to be any threat at all to the idea that God is absolutely perfect – or so, at least, those who do not accept all of the assumptions of traditional perfect-being theology will be inclined to claim.)

4. Why does Kretzmann believe that (TO) is incompatible with perfect-being theology? Why is (TS) compatible with it?

The doctrine of absolute divine simplicity that Kretzmann takes up in section [3] is a very hard saying: as Kretzmann himself admits, it is a controversial question whether there is any way of making this doctrine properly intelligible. In words, at least as a first approximation, the doctrine says that 'all of God's attributes are identical with one another' and that 'God is identical to each of his attributes'. But what does this mean?

Kretzmann gives a linguistic cast to his explanation of the doctrine. Suppose that we can decompose sentences into names and predicates, where predicates are what are left of sentences when names are removed from them. (*Example*: In the sentence 'God loves Abraham', 'God' and 'Abraham' are names, and '. . . loves ___', 'God loves . . .', and '. . . loves Abraham' are predicates.) As a first approximation, we might say that the function of names is to identify or 'tag' objects: 'God' refers to God, 'Abraham' names Abraham, etc. And, at this same level of approximation, we might say that the function of predicates is to express properties: '. . . is good' expresses the property of goodness, and '. . . loves ___' expresses the lovingness relation. However, as our examples bring out, while we can use predicates to express properties, we can also use names to refer to properties: 'goodness' names the property that is expressed by the predicate '. . . is good'.

Given these basic distinctions, Kretzmann offers three different formulations of the doctrine of absolute divine simplicity. On the first version, at [e]→, the characteristic form of words used to express the doctrine looks like this: 'God is identical with his goodness' or 'God is identical with God's goodness'; on the second version, also at [e]→, the characteristic form of words used to express the doctrine looks like this: 'God is identical with goodness'; and on the third version, at [g]→, the characteristic form of words used to express the doctrine looks like this: 'God is identical with perfect goodness'. In each case, we are given words of the form 'God = F-ness', where what goes in for 'F-ness' is a name for a property. While, perhaps, we should not assume that *every* name for a property is the nominalisation of a predicate, we can note that *many* names for properties are nominalisations of predicates: 'goodness' is a nominalisation from the predicate '. . . good'. However, even in those cases where we are using names for properties that are nominalisations of predicates, we must remember that a sentence of the form 'God = F-ness' says something very different from the sentence 'God is F'. For, while the latter sentence merely attibutes the property of F-ness to God, the former sentence says that God is *identical* to the property of F-ness.

On Kretzmann's showing, the doctrine of divine simplicity says that all of God's attibutes are identical one with another, and that God is identical to each of his attributes. Thus, if we suppose that God's attributes are F-ness, G-ness, H-ness, etc., then the doctrine of divine simplicity will say that God = F-ness = G-ness = H-ness = ... Thus, it seems, on the doctrine of divine simplicity, we are committed to the claim that God is an attribute, and to the claim that the attribute that is God admits of a diverse range of linguistic formulations: F-ness, G-ness, H-ness, etc.

5. Give as good a statement as you can in your own words of the doctrine of absolute simplicity. What are the main reasons for and against it?

In order to meet the worry that it seems pretty unintuitive to suppose that there could be literal *identity* between the various divine attributes, Kretzmann appeals to Frege's explanation of how it happens that there can be true identity statements involving names. On Frege's theory, a sentence of the form 'a = b' can be true and informative because it can be that the names 'a' and 'b' refer to the very same object even though they pick out that object using very different *senses*. If, for example, we use the name 'Hesperus' to pick out the very last 'star' visible in the morning sky, and the name 'Phosphorus' to pick out the very first 'star' visible in the evening sky, and the name 'Venus' to pick out the second major planet from the sun, then it is potentially informative to be told that Phosphorus = Hesperus = Venus. In general, on Frege's theory of language, every linguistic expression has both a sense and a reference; in particular, every name has a sense which picks out the object that is denoted by the name (i.e. the referent of the name). Consider what Kretzmann says at [f]→. It is not clear that 'the analogy with Frege's paradigm' really does provide an adequate response to the worry that it is intended to address. While Frege's theory is controversial, it has at least some *prima facie* plausibility in the case of names for things that are *objects*, on a common-sense understanding of that notion. We have no trouble understanding how it could happen that people come to have multiple names for an object – a planet, a person, a city, etc. – and yet fail to realise that these multiple names are names for the very same thing. However, it is not at all clear that this understanding transfers to the case of names for attributes: it is not nearly so straightforward to suppose that we understand how it could happen that people come to have multiple names for an attribute – e.g. goodness – and yet fail to realise that these multiple names are all names for the very same attribute.

A key question to ask at this point concerns what we might call 'identity conditions' for attributes: if F-ness and G-ness are attributes, what is required in order for it to be the case that F-ness = G-ness? Consider, for example, two possible attributes of rectilinear plane figures: the attribute of *having just three equal interior angles*, and the attribute of *having just three sides of equal length*. These attributes are necessarily co-instantiated in rectilinear plane figures, since, necessarily, each of these attributes is possessed by all and only equilateral triangles. But should we conclude from this that they are *the very same* attribute? And, if we are not prepared to allow that this is a case in which we have two distinct predicates in the English language that express the same attribute, then what would be a clear, uncontroversial case of that kind?

Even if we suppose that we *can* make good sense of the idea that there might be multiple predicates in English that express – or multiple names in English that stand for – the very same attributes, it is not clear that we have a sufficient answer to worries that naturally arise in connection with the doctrine of divine simplicity. For, even on the most casual metaphysics, there seems to be something intuitively wrong with the idea that God is an attribute, the more so because it is clear that we are not to suppose that there is some other entity of which God is an attribute. If we suppose – as seems pre-theoretically plausible – that attribute-instantiations are always instantiations of attributes in distinct entities, then it just does not make any sense at all to suppose that God is an attribute – an instantiation of an attribute – even though there is no distinct entity in which God is instantiated.

6. Here is one way of developing the above objection: while we often suppose that an agent acted in some way because of its attributes, it is not clear that it even makes sense to suppose that *attributes* could be independent causal agents. When confronted with the corpse at the murder scene, we may speculate that the murderer committed the murder because he was enraged, but we will not even consider the hypothesis that the victim met his fate at the hands of the non-instantiated attribute of enragement. Is this a fair objection to Kretzmann?

There is at least one further intuitive difficulty for Kretzmann's formulation of the doctrine of divine simplicity that deserves mention. In his final formulation of the doctrine, Kretzmann holds that it requires that 'perfect power is identical with perfect goodness', but that it does not require that 'power is identical with goodness'. However, if we suppose that it is true that 'God is good', and we suppose that to say that God is good is to attribute goodness to God, then it seems that the doctrine of divine simplicity requires us to say that God is identical to goodness. Thus, it seems, either Kretzmann is committed to saying that it is not strictly speaking true that God is good, or else Kretzmann is committed to the denial of the claim that to say that God is good is to attribute goodness to God. But the former path is surely counter-intuitive for most believers; and the latter path seems to undermine understanding of exactly what Kretzmann means by the word 'attribute'.

Even on this brief discussion, it seems reasonable to suggest that it is not clear that Kretzmann has done enough to support the suggestion that 'simplicity might be made sense of'. However, even if Kretzmann has not done enough to support that suggestion, it remains an open possibility that someone else might be able to find a way to rehabilitate the doctrine of divine simplicity. So there might still be point in asking whether, given the doctrine of divine simplicity, we can make good sense of the idea that God is the basis of morality.

Kretzmann suggests that, given the doctrine of divine simplicity, the principles (TS) and (TO) collapse into two new principles – (TS') and (TO') given at [i]↦ – that are simply 'two different ways of saying the same thing', namely that perfect goodness is the ultimate arbiter of the distinction between right and wrong actions.

It is not clear that Kretzmann gives an accurate characterisation of the application of the doctrine of divine simplicity to the principles (TS) and (TO). While it seems clearly right to say – as Kretzmann does – that perfect goodness approves of right actions iff they are right and disapproves of wrong actions iff they are wrong, this claim must be distinguished from the claims (TO') and (TS'). When we come to consider the primary explanatory relation that holds between perfect goodness and right action, it seems to me that we should want to say that right actions are right *because* perfect goodness approves of them, and to deny that perfect goodness approves of right actions *because* they are right. If we accept both explanatory claims, then it seems that we could deduce the absurd conclusion that perfect goodness approves of right actions because perfect goodness approves of right actions, i.e. we would be driven to accept an explanatory solecism. But, given that we can only accept one of the explanatory claims, it seems plainly wrong to hold that perfect goodness approves of right actions because they are right: why would we think that there is any such thing as perfect goodness unless we thought that perfect goodness played the role of arbiter in the case of action?

If the argument in the previous paragraph is correct, then we can conclude that, on the assumption that it makes sense to identify God with the attribute of perfect goodness, we can identify an acceptable sense in which God is the basis of morality, since we can identify an acceptable sense in which the attribute of perfect goodness is the basis of morality. But, even if we hold out hope that there might be a way in which we can rehabilitate the doctrine of divine simplicity, it is not obvious that we can hope to rehabilitate the doctrine of divine simplicity in a way that will bear out the claim that God is the attribute of perfect goodness.

7. Explain and justify Kretzmann's remark at [i]↦.

Recall that the intuition that underlies the doctrine of divine simplicity is that God should not have any parts or components. If we suppose – as *some* theorists do – that ordinary objects have their attributes as (logical) parts, then one consequence of the doctrine of divine simplicity is that God does not have any attributes that constitute God's (logical) parts. On this view, since God is radically different in kind from all other things, there is a *prima facie* problem about how we can say anything at all about God. However, perhaps we can address this problem by postulating that a sentence of the form 'N is F' can be made true in two different ways. On the one hand, a sentence of this form can be made true by the possession of the attribute expressed by 'F' by the ordinary object denoted by 'N'. And, on the other hand, a sentence of this form can be made true by God, in the case in which 'N' denotes God. So, for examples, 'Fred is good' can be made true by Fred's possession of the attribute of goodness; whereas 'God is good' is true just because God exists.

Even if a theory of this kind were deemed acceptable, it seems doubtful that it would yield a clear sense in which God is the basis of morality. For, on this theory, it would not be the case that God is identical with perfect goodness, and it would seem to remain most plausible to claim that God approves of right actions *because* they are right, rather than the other way round. So, at the very least, we have not yet found a good reason to think that we could use a rehabilitated version of the doctrine of divine simplicity to defend the idea that God is the basis of morality. But, of course, nothing that has been said here rules out the possibility that such a good reason merely awaits discovery.

For further discussion of the doctrine of divine simplicity, you might consider:

Brower, J., 'Making Sense of Divine Simplicity', *Faith and Philosophy*, forthcoming.
Stump, E., *Aquinas*, New York: Routledge, 2003, at pp. 92–100, 127–8.
Vallicella, W., 'Divine Simplicity', *Stanford Encyclopaedia of Philosophy*, 2006: http://plato.stanford.edu/entries/divine-simplicity/

And, for further discussion of the claim that God is the basis of morality, you might choose to have a look at:

Adams, R., *Finite and Infinite Goods*, Oxford: Oxford University Press, 1999.
Quinn, P., *Divine Commands and Moral Requirements*, Oxford: Clarendon Press, 1978.
Wielenberg, E., *Value and Virtue in a Godless Universe*, Cambridge: Cambridge University Press, 2005.

Introduction to Boethius

Anicius Manlius Severinus Boethius was born into an aristocratic family in about 480 CE. Boethius excelled in studies from early childhood, and rapidly mastered the liberal arts – rhetoric, logic, astronomy, and so forth – as well as a range of languages including Greek. By the age of 30, under the patronage of the Ostrogothic king Theodoric, Boethius rose to the rank of consul without companion. Perhaps a decade later, Boethius headed the civil service, and was chief of the palace officials. In 522 CE, in a unique honour, his sons were appointed consuls together. However, soon after this, he was arrested on a charge of treason and condemned to exile and death (on what Boethius himself alleged to be false evidence). In about 524 CE, while exiled in Pavia, Boethius was horrifically tortured and then bludgeoned to death.

While in exile, during the time between his condemnation and his execution, Boethius wrote *The Consolation of Philosophy*, the final few pages of which are excerpted below. Boethius had previously translated Aristotle's works on logic – *De interpretatione*, *Topics*, *Prior Analytics*, *Posterior Analytics*, *Sophistical Fallacies* – and Porphyry's *Introduction to the Categories of Aristotle*, and had produced his own works on logic and theology. (In the introduction to the translation of Porphyry, Boethius stated that he aimed to translate *all* of the works of Aristotle and Plato that were available to him from Greek to Latin, a task that he probably would not have completed even if his life had not ended so prematurely.) Boethius' translations were very important in the transmission of the works of Aristotle and Porphyry to medieval Europe.

The excerpted section of *The Consolation of Philosophy* is concerned with the nature of eternity, and with God's relationship to time. Boethius aims to use his account of divine eternity to explain the nature of God's knowledge of free human actions, and to show that there is no problem in reconciling God's omniscience with human freedom of action. We shall be interested, in particular, in what Boethius has to say about eternity and God's relationship to time; however, you may also like to think about the ways in which Boethius' account of God's knowledge of free human actions bears on Pike's argument for the incompatibility of divine omniscience and human freedom of action.

Boethius, *The Consolation of Philosophy* (selection)

[1] 'Since, then, as we lately proved, everything that is known is cognized not in accordance with its own nature, but in accordance with the nature of the faculty that comprehends it, let us now contemplate, as far as lawful, the character of the Divine essence, that we may be able to understand also the nature of its knowledge.

[a]→ [2] 'God is eternal; in this judgment all rational beings agree. Let us, then,
consider what eternity is. For this word carries with it a revelation alike
of the Divine nature and of the Divine knowledge. Now, eternity is the
possession of endless life whole and perfect at a single moment. What this
is becomes more clear and manifest from a comparison with things tem-
[b]→ poral. For whatever lives in time is a present proceeding from the past to
the future, and there is nothing set in time which can embrace the whole
space of its life together. To-morrow's state it grasps not yet, while it has
already lost yesterday's; nay, even in the life of today ye live no longer
[c]→ than one brief transitory moment. Whatever, therefore, is subject to the
condition of time, although, as Aristotle deemed of the world, it never have
either beginning or end, and its life be stretched to the whole extent of
time's infinity, it yet is not such as rightly to be thought eternal.

For it does not include and embrace the whole space of infinite life at once, but has no present hold on things to come, not yet accomplished. Accordingly, that which includes and possesses the whole fullness of unending life at once, from which nothing future is absent, from which nothing past has escaped, this is rightly called eternal; this must of necessity be ever present to itself in full self-possession, and hold the infinity of movable time in an abiding present.

Wherefore they deem not rightly who imagine that on Plato's principles the created world is made co-eternal with the Creator, because they are told that he believed the world to have had no beginning in time, and to be destined never to come to an end. For it is one thing for existence to be endlessly prolonged, which was what Plato ascribed to the world, another for the whole of an endless life to be embraced in the present, which is manifestly a property peculiar to the Divine mind. Nor need God appear earlier in mere duration of time to created things, but only prior in the unique simplicity of His nature. For the infinite progression of things in time copies this immediate existence in the present of the changeless life, and when it cannot succeed in equaling it, declines from movelessness into motion, and falls away from the simplicity of a perpetual present to the infinite duration of the future and the past; and since it cannot possess the whole fullness of its life together, for the very reason that in a manner it never ceases to be, it seems, up to a certain point, to rival that which it cannot complete and express by attaching itself indifferently to any present moment of time, however swift and brief; and since this bears some resemblance to that ever-abiding present, it bestows on everything to which it is assigned the semblance of existence.

But since it cannot abide, it hurries along the infinite path of time, and the result has been that it continues by ceaseless movement the life the completeness of which it could not embrace while it stood still. So, if we are minded to give things their right names, we shall follow Plato in saying that God indeed is eternal, but the world everlasting.

[3] 'Since, then, every mode of judgment comprehends its objects conformably to its own nature, and since God abides for ever in an eternal present, His knowledge, also transcending all movement of time, dwells in the simplicity of its own changeless present, and, embracing the whole infinite sweep of the past and of the future, contemplates all that falls within its simple cognition as if it were now taking place. And therefore, if thou wilt carefully consider that immediate presentment whereby it discriminates all things, thou wilt more rightly deem it not foreknowledge as of something future, but knowledge of a moment that never passes. For this cause the name chosen to describe it is not prevision, but providence, because, since utterly removed in nature from things mean and trivial, its outlook embraces all things as from some lofty height.

Why, then, dost thou insist that the things which are surveyed by the Divine eye are involved in necessity, whereas clearly men impose no necessity on things which they see? Does the act of vision add any necessity to the things which thou seest before thy eyes?'

'Assuredly not.'

'And yet, if we may without unfitness compare God's present and man's, just as ye see certain things in this your temporary present, so does He see all things in His eternal present. Wherefore this Divine anticipation changes not the natures and properties of things, and it beholds things present before it, just as they will hereafter come to pass in time. Nor does it confound things in its judgment, but in the one mental view distinguishes alike what will come necessarily and what without necessity. For even as ye, when at one and the same time ye see a man walking on the earth and the sun rising in the sky, distinguish between the two, though one glance embraces both, and judge the former voluntary, the latter necessary action: so also the Divine vision in its universal range of view does in no wise confuse the characters of the things which are present to its regard, though future in respect of time. Whence it follows that when it perceives that something will come into existence, and yet is perfectly aware that this is unbound by any necessity, its apprehension is not opinion, but rather knowledge based on truth.

[4] And if to this thou sayest that what God sees to be about to come to pass cannot fail to come to pass, and that what cannot fail to come to pass happens of necessity, and wilt tie me down to this word necessity, I will acknowledge that thou affirmest a most solid truth, but one which scarcely anyone can approach to who has not made the Divine his special study. For my answer would be that the same future event is necessary from the standpoint of Divine knowledge, but when considered in its own nature it seems absolutely free and unfettered. So, then, there are two necessities – one simple, as that men are necessarily mortal; the other conditioned, as that, if you know that someone is walking, he must necessarily be walking. For that which is known cannot indeed be otherwise than as it is known to be, and yet this fact by no means carries with it that other simple necessity. For the former necessity is not imposed by the thing's own proper nature, but by the addition of a condition. No necessity compels one who is voluntarily walking to go forward, although it is necessary for him to go forward at the moment of walking.

In the same way, then, if Providence sees anything as present, that must necessarily be, though it is bound by no necessity of nature. Now, God views as present those coming events which happen of free will. These, accordingly, from the standpoint of the Divine vision are made necessary conditionally on the Divine cognizance; viewed, however, in themselves, they desist not from the absolute freedom naturally theirs. Accordingly, without doubt, all things will come to pass which God foreknows as about to happen, but of these certain proceed of free will; and though these happen, yet by the fact of their existence they do not lose their proper nature, in virtue of which before they happened it was really possible that they might not have come to pass.

'What difference, then, does the denial of necessity make, since, through their being conditioned by Divine knowledge, they come to pass as if they were in all respects under the compulsion of necessity? This difference, surely, which we saw in the case of the instances I formerly took, the sun's rising and the man's walking; which at the moment of their occurrence could not but be taking place, and yet one of them before it took place was necessarily obliged to be, while the other was not so at all. So likewise the things which to God are present without doubt exist, but some of them come from the necessity of things, others from the power of the agent. Quite rightly, then, have we said that these things are necessary if viewed from the standpoint of the Divine knowledge; but if they are considered in themselves, they are free from the bonds of necessity, even as everything which is accessible to sense, regarded from the standpoint of Thought, is universal, but viewed in its own nature particular.

d→ [5] 'But,' thou wilt say, 'if it is in my power to change my purpose, I shall make void providence, since I shall perchance change something which e→ comes within its foreknowledge.' My answer is: Thou canst indeed turn aside thy purpose; but since the truth of providence is ever at hand to see that thou canst, and whether thou dost, and whither thou turnest thyself, thou canst not avoid the Divine foreknowledge, even as thou canst not escape the sight of a present spectator, although of thy free will thou turn thyself to various actions.

[6] Wilt thou, then, say: 'Shall the Divine knowledge be changed at my discretion, so that, when I will this or that, providence changes its knowledge correspondingly?'

'Surely not.'

'True, for the Divine vision anticipates all that is coming, and transforms and reduces it to the form of its own present knowledge, and varies not, as thou deemest, in its foreknowledge, alternating to this or that, but in a f→ single flash it forestalls and includes thy mutations without altering. And this ever-present comprehension and survey of all things God has received, not from the issue of future events, but from the simplicity of His own nature. Hereby also is resolved the objection which a little while ago gave thee offence – that our doings in the future were spoken of as if supplying the cause of God's knowledge. For this faculty of knowledge, embracing all things in its immediate cognizance, has itself fixed the bounds of all things, yet itself owes nothing to what comes after.

'And all this being so, the freedom of man's will stands unshaken, and laws are not unrighteous, since their rewards and punishments are held forth to wills unbound by any necessity. God, who foreknoweth all things, still looks down from above, and the ever-present eternity of His vision concurs with the future character of all our acts, and dispenseth to the good rewards, to the bad punishments. Our hopes and prayers also are not fixed on God in vain, and when they are rightly directed cannot fail of effect. Therefore, withstand vice, practise virtue, lift up your souls to right hopes, offer humble prayers to Heaven. Great is the necessity of righteousness laid upon you if ye will not hide it from yourselves, seeing that all your actions are done before the eyes of a Judge who seeth all things.'

Commentary on Boethius

We have divided the text into six sections. The very brief section [1] establishes a context for the subsequent discussion. The key section [2] gives Boethius' account of the nature of divine eternity. Section [3] discusses the nature of divine knowledge from the standpoint of divine eternity. Section [4] considers the connection between divine knowledge and the necessity of future human action. The brief section [5] asks whether it is possible for human beings to act in ways that contradict what God knows. Finally, section [6] gives Boethius' views on the question whether God's knowledge of the world *depends* upon the world (i.e. on the question whether God's knowledge of the world is grounded in something like perception of the world).

1. At [a]→ Boethius claims that the word 'eternity' suggests something about divine nature and something about divine knowledge. What might he mean by this?

Boethius' account of divine eternity in section [2] is both gnomic and elusive. What he says – according to our chosen translation – is that 'eternity is the possession of endless life whole and perfect at a single moment. . . . [T]hat which includes and possesses the whole fullness of unending life at once, from which nothing future is absent, from which nothing past has escaped . . . must of necessity be ever present to itself in full self-possession, and hold the infinity of movable time in an abiding present.'

As a first attempt, perhaps we might try to understand these remarks in the following way. There are two quite distinct domains: the temporal domain in which we exist, and the eternal domain in which God exists. The temporal domain in which we exist has a particular kind of structure that is not shared by the eternal domain.

Consider what Boethius says about the temporal domain at [b]→. These remarks, too, are gnomic and elusive. At the very least, they seem to require a commitment to the idea that the structure of the temporal domain is something like the structure of an ordered number line: the elements of the domain are 'brief transitory moments', and these 'moments' stand in relations of 'being earlier than' and 'being later than' to one another. Furthermore, these remarks seem to require commitment to something like the thought that the temporal domain is, in some way, the sum of these 'moments', and to the idea that no single moment is an adequate reflection, or summation, or encapsulation of the entire temporal domain.

2. At [c]→, Boethius distinguishes between something that is eternal and something that exists at all times without beginning or end. Explain what you think Boethius means by this distinction.

In contemporary philosophy, there are two broadly different ways of thinking about the temporal structure of the world (though these two broadly different ways of thinking are each capable of detailed development in numerous different ways). On the one hand, there are philosophers who suppose that all of the 'moments' of time exist, and that objects exist over time by existing at different 'moments' of time. On the other hand, there are philosophers who suppose that the only 'moment' of time that exists is the 'present moment' of time, and that objects exist over time by existing at a succession of 'present moments' of time. Each of these broadly different ways of thinking about the temporal structure of the world accommodates the commitments that we claimed to discern in Boethius' remarks about the temporal domain: each allows that the structure of the temporal domain is something like the structure of an ordered number line; and each allows that no smallest part of the temporal domain is an adequate reflection of the whole. But these broadly different ways of thinking about the temporal structure of the world differ in a way that might be important for Boethius' conception of divine eternity, because they appear to differ in their implications concerning the possibility of an external vantage point from which it is possible to 'survey' the entire temporal domain.

3. There seem to be two different ways of ordering events in time. An event can be 'now', 'two days in the future', 'yesterday', 'in the distant past', etc. This is called the 'A series'. But events can also be temporally ordered by their relationship with each other: one event is 'before' another, 'after' it, or 'simultaneous with' it. This is called the 'B series'. B theorists argue that only the B series is genuine; that the B series captures everything true that can be said about temporal relations. A theorists argue that the A series is an ineliminable and essential component of a full understanding of temporal relations. Which view do you prefer and why?

Boethius' account of divine eternity appears to have two quite separate components. On the one hand, Boethius appears to tell us that divine eternity does not share the temporal structure of the world: there is no 'before and after' in the eternal domain. By way of contrast with the temporal domain, in the eternal domain there is 'possession of endless life whole and perfect at a single moment', and the eternal domain 'includes and possesses the whole fullness of unending life at once, from which nothing future is absent, from which nothing past has escaped'. On the other hand, Boethius also appears to tell us that, from the standpoint of the divine eternity, the temporal domain can be 'surveyed' in its entirety: past, present and future can be 'viewed' as a single and completed entity from the standpoint of eternity, since eternity 'hold[s] the infinity of movable time in an abiding present'.

It seems plausible to us to suppose that Boethius' account of the relationship between the eternal domain and the temporal domain – and, in particular, his proposal that the temporal domain can be 'surveyed' in its entirety from the standpoint of eternity – commits him to the view that all 'moments' of time exist, and that objects exist over time by existing at different 'moments' of time. Those who suppose that only the 'present moment' exists, and that objects exist over time by existing at a succession of 'present moments' of time, are typically committed to the idea that tense or the passage of time is a fundamental ingredient of reality; but, given that there is no tense or passage in eternity, it is simply impossible that there could be registration of tense or passage in eternity. However, if there can be no registration of tense or passage in eternity, then surely we have the strongest of grounds for denying that tense or passage is a real or genuine property of the temporal domain; for how could it be that there is a real or genuine property of the temporal domain that is simply beyond the ken of an omniscient being? (Perhaps we can also make the same point in a more picturesque way. We can only suppose that the temporal domain can be 'surveyed in its entirety' from the standpoint of eternity if the temporal domain exists 'all at once' from the standpoint of eternity. But if there is a standpoint from which the temporal domain exists 'all at once', then it can hardly be the case that there are standpoints from which it fails to be the case that the temporal domain exists 'all at once': *existence* cannot be relative to standpoints in that kind of way. To suppose otherwise is to conflate ontological considerations with evidently distinct epistemic and doxastic considerations.)

If we are right in supposing that Boethius' account of divine eternity commits him to the claim that all of the 'moments' of time exist and that objects exist over time by existing at different 'moments' of time, then we think that it is likely that many theists will not wish to accept Boethius' account of divine eternity. While Boethius himself repudiates the view that divine eternity might properly be thought of as divine everlastingness, some theists might prefer to suppose that divine eternity simply consists in existence at all times: plausibly, theists who suppose that divine eternity simply consists in existence at all times will further suppose that existence at all times includes existence at all times in an infinite past, and existence at all times in an infinite future. Alternatively, some theists might prefer to suppose that divine eternity consists in existence at all times combined with timeless existence 'beyond' the limits of the temporal domain. Theists who adopt this last view will further suppose that existence at all times requires existence at all times subsequent to divine creation of time and prior to divine annihilation of time, if there is either divine creation or divine annihilation of time. (We shall not pursue questions about the coherence of this last view here – you may well suspect that it will not be easy to give a coherent account of a domain that lies 'beyond' the limits of the temporal domain.)

4. If God created the temporal order of the universe, would it have a B series or an A series?

Of course, there is a large contemporary debate whether we should suppose that all of the 'moments' of time exist and that objects exist over time by existing at different 'moments' of time, or whether we should suppose instead that the only 'moment' of time that exists is the 'present moment' of time, and that objects exist over time by existing at a succession of 'present moments' of time. While we do not propose to take up this debate here, we think it worth noting that, on the one hand, the strongest support for the view that the only 'moment' of time that exists is the 'present moment' of time, and that objects exist over time by existing at a succession of 'present moments' of time, is typically taken to lie in common-sense intuitions about the passage of time; while, on the other hand, the strongest support for the view that all of the 'moments' of time exist, and that objects exist over time by existing at different 'moments' of time, is typically taken to lie in considerations drawn from formulations of contemporary scientific theories, including, in particular, the general theory of relativity. If you are interested in pursuing this debate, you might like to look at *Reading Metaphysics* in this series.

5. Summarise in your own words the arguments Boethius considers in [3].

Even if we suppose that Boethius' account of divine eternity is acceptable, it is not clear that it has the implications for questions about divine omniscience and human free action that Boethius himself takes it to have. We can happily grant that, if God 'sees' all of temporal reality at once from the standpoint of divine eternity, there need be no conflict between divine omniscience and human freedom; for, as Boethius points out in the section from [3] to [4], we can suppose that God simply 'sees' what we shall freely choose to do (and we can also suppose that, had we made different free choices, what God would have 'seen' would have been different from what he actually sees).

6. Explain the question posed at d→ and the answer to it given at e→.

However, consider what Boethius goes on to say at f→. In our view, what Boethius goes on to say here undoes the things that he said previously: if it is not true that the future supplies the cause of God's knowledge, then it is simply inappropriate to talk about God's 'seeing' all of temporal reality from the standpoint of divine eternity. In its ordinary sense, 'seeing' is a causal notion: when I see things in my environment, I am, *ipso facto*, in causal contact with those things: light travels from the surfaces of those things to my eyes, and triggers processes in my brain that constitute my seeing these things. If we take away the idea that the future supplies the cause of God's knowledge, then we are left with no way at all of understanding the claim that God 'sees' the future from the standpoint of eternity.

These considerations mark an interesting point of contact with Pike's argument concerning divine omniscience and human freedom (discussed above). In the introduction to his paper – not included in our excerpt – Pike says that

> In this paper, I shall argue that . . . Boethius was right in thinking that there is a selection from among the various doctrines and principles clustering about the notions of knowledge, omniscience and God which, when brought together, demand the conclusion that if God exists, no human action is voluntary. Boethius, I think, did not succeed in making explicit all of the ingredients in the problem. His suspicions were sound, but his discussion was incomplete. His argument needs to be developed.

If what we have argued above is correct, then, while Pike failed to develop an argument from among various doctrines and principles clustering about the notions of knowledge, omniscience and God which, when brought together, demand the conclusion that, if God exists, no human action is voluntary, *Boethius himself* did provide the ingredients for the development of an argument from among various doctrines and principles clustering about the notions of knowledge, omniscience, divine impassibility and God which, when brought together, demand the conclusion that, if God exists, no human action is voluntary. That is, in section [6], Boethius makes plain his commitment to divine impassibility; and, as we argued in our discussion of Pike, once you add divine impassibility to the mix, there really is a serious problem about God's knowledge of the outcomes of objectively chancy events (including, as those who suppose that human beings have libertarian freedom hold, the freely chosen actions of human beings). If God's knowledge of the outcomes of putatively objectively chancy events proceeds 'from the simplicity of his own nature', then, because 'the simplicity of his own nature' is causally prior to those putatively objectively chancy events, it follows immediately that those putatively objectively chancy events are not truly objectively chancy: if the God in whom Boethius believes exists, then no human action is voluntary (at least by the lights of those who suppose that genuine freedom is libertarian freedom).

7. Is it possible for God to have any causal relationship with the universe if he is 'outside' time and is not subject to temporal change?

If you would like to read more about questions concerning God's relationship to time, then you might choose to consider the following texts:

Leftow, B., *Time and Eternity*, Ithaca, NY: Cornell University Press, 1991.
Padgett, A., *God, Eternity and the Nature of Time*, New York: St Martin's Press, 1992.
Stump, E. and Kretzmann, N., 'Eternity', *Journal of Philosophy*, 78 (1981): 429–58.
Swinburne, R., 'The Timelessness of God', *Church Quarterly Review*, 116 (1965): 323–37, 472–86.

5

Religious Diversity

Introduction

One of the liveliest areas of discussion in philosophy of religion over the last couple of decades has concerned the problem of religious diversity. The discussion is motivated by the enormous variety of different and apparently conflicting religious beliefs. It is not simply that there are large numbers of religions that differ on almost every issue – the existence, nature, number and behaviour of gods and other supernatural beings, their histories and interactions with human beings, how human beings can interact and should behave towards them, the nature of salvation and how it can be achieved, etc. It is also that there is considerable disagreement within religious traditions. Within Christianity, for example, while there is agreement that God exists, there is a substantial diversity of opinions about God's nature (some of which were explored in the section on divine attributes) – the degree of control God exerts over human behaviour, God's knowledge of the future, whether moral truths are independent from or are determined by God's actions, etc. Add to this the historical evidence of religions that have died out – for example, the large number of different religions that were practised in the classical world.

One response to religious diversity is to argue that it provides evidence that religious claims do not address a real subject matter. According to this argument, genuinely descriptive fields of discourse such as science and mathematics admit convergence of opinion: even where there may not be agreement, a matter of science or mathematics is as least in principle resolvable with evidence and proof. Religion, by contrast, appears to have widespread and apparently irresolvable disagreement, and this – so the argument goes – is evidence for thinking that religious judgements are not objective: religious questions do not have correct answers, and there are no religious facts.

However, it is not the objectivity of religious judgements that has been the primary focus of discussion about religious diversity but rather whether it is epistemologically defensible to hold that a particular religious belief or only one religious tradition is true. Take, for example, a Christian who believes in premillennialism: that Christ will physically return to earth prior to his millennial reign. She knows that there are large numbers of religious believers who are not Christians, and also that there are large numbers of Christians who do not share her premillennial views. Moreover, she knows that many of these people are (or at least appear to be) as intelligent and informed and sincere in their religious judgements as she is. The problem, therefore, is whether she can be justified, reasonable or warranted in holding that only her religious perspective is the right one.

The problem that the evidence of widespread religious diversity presents to religious believers can be understood as a special case of a more general epistemological issue. There are many cases in which we take other people's disagreement with our judgement about something as a good reason to reconsider that judgement or to be less confident about it. For example, if I am witness to an event, and my testimony differs from that of several other people who were also witnesses, that seems a good reason to suppose that I may have misremembered; if several people average a series of numbers and each comes up with a different result, that seems a good reason for all of them to reconsider their calculations. On the other hand, for almost any political opinion you may have, you can be sure that there are a large number of people who disagree with you; but the fact that there is disagreement on political matters is not (by itself) generally taken as a reason for anyone to revise or be less confident in their political judgements. Can we say anything in general about good epistemic policy with respect to our judgements when there is evidence of widespread disagreement? And how, specifically, should a religious believer respond to religious diversity?

There are two main views. According to *exclusivists*, the beliefs of one religious tradition are true (or mostly true) and the beliefs of other religious traditions are false (at least in so far as they disagree with the one true religion). *Pluralists* claim that no one religion is superior to any other: each has a legitimate perspective. These views are represented in this section by Alvin Plantinga and John Hick respectively. In addition, there are *inclusivist* theories that occupy middle ground between exclusivism and pluralism on the issue of salvation. According to the inclusivist, although there is only one true religion, the requirements for salvation are sufficiently broad that salvation is also accessible to members of other religions.

Plantinga identifies a variety of different challenges to religious exclusivism, and helpfully distinguishes epistemic objections (that exclusivism is in some way unreasonable, unwarranted, unjustified, etc.) from moral ones (that it is arrogant or insensitive to take an exclusivist stance). Plantinga defends exclusivism by arguing that a religious believer need not concede that people with different religious views have epistemic parity with her – i.e. that they are in an equally good position to judge what is true on religious matters. He also raises what he believes to be a serious problem with the pluralist position: that *any* position that one takes on a religious issue will meet with disagreement (even if that position is to refrain from taking a position!). How can the fact that people dissent from your religious judgements be a reason to revise or withhold your opinions, Plantinga asks, if *any* religious judgement that you make will also be dissented from?

Hick argues that the right response to religious diversity is to reject religious exclusivism and recognise that there are basic ethical and metaphysical judgements that are common to all religions. For example, Hick argues that religious people believe in a mind-independent 'Real' (even if they may disagree about its nature), and that religions promote a transformational process leading believers away from a self-centred to a 'reality-centred' outlook. According to Hick, religious believers should recognise that there is no one true religion but a variety of culturally shaped perspectives on the 'Real'.

Many philosophers have taken religious diversity to present a more serious epistemological challenge than Plantinga, but without adopting pluralism. For example, some have argued that the evidence of diversity does not oblige religious believers to give up or even revise their beliefs, but that they should reassess their beliefs (McKim). According to Jerome Gellman, some of our beliefs are 'rock bottom': they have a foundational status in a believer's epistemic system, such that they do not admit reassessment. While Gellman agrees that religious diversity may oblige a believer to re-evaluate her religious beliefs, that extends only so far as those religious beliefs are not rock bottom. William Alston argues that the evidence of diversity should make one less confident in the rationality of a person's adoption of the beliefs and practices of a particular religion. Nevertheless, lacking any independent grounds for establishing which religious system is right, is it rational – in fact the only rational course that one can take – to 'sit tight' with one's own religious beliefs and practices?

This introduction has sketched only some of the main positions on a topic that has generated a substantial literature in recent years. For further investigation of the topic, the following are useful:

Basinger, D., *Religious Diversity: A Philosophical Assessment*, Burlington, Vt: Ashgate, 2002.

McKim, R., *Religious Ambiguity and Religious Diversity*, Oxford: Oxford University Press, 2001.

Meeker, K. and Quinn, P. (eds), *The Philosophical Challenge of Religious Diversity*, New York: Oxford University Press, 1999.

Introduction to Hick

John Hick (b.1922) is one of the leading contributors to philosophy of religion of the twentieth century. He is best-known for his work on the problem of evil and on religious diversity. On the former, he has advocated a soul-making theodicy in his widely read book *Evil and the God of Love* (1966, 2nd edn 1977). On the latter, he has been the most prominent advocate of religious pluralism. Hick has developed his pluralist position over numerous papers and books, giving his fullest treatment of the topic in *The Interpretation of Religion* (1989, 2nd edn 2004) from which the following selection is taken.

John Hick, *The Interpretation of Religion* (selection)

[1] I have argued that it is rational on the part of those who experience religiously to believe and to live on this basis. And I have further argued that, in so believing, they are making an affirmation about the nature of reality which will, if it is substantially true, be developed, corrected and enlarged in the course of future experience. They are thus making genuine [a]→ assertions and are making them on appropriate and acceptable grounds. If there were only one religious tradition, so that all religious experience and belief had the same intentional object, an epistemology of religion could come to rest at this point. But in fact there are a number of different such traditions and families of traditions witnessing to many different personal deities and non-personal ultimates.

[2] To recall the theistic range first, the history of religions sets before us innumerable gods, differently named and often with different characteristics. A collection of names of Mesopotamian gods made by A. Deinel in 1914 conains 3300 entries ([W. H. Romer, 'The Religion of Ancient Mesopotamia', in Claas Bleeker and Geo Widengreen (eds) *Historia religionum: Handbook for the History of Religions*, Leiden: Brill, 1969, 117–18]). In Hesiod's time there were said to be 30,000 deities ([David Hume, *Natural History of Religion* (1757), ed. H. E. Root, London: A. & C. Black, 1956, p. 28, n. 1]). And if one could list all the past and present gods and goddesses . . . they would probably form a list as bulky as the telephone directory of a large city. What are we to say, from a religious point of view, about all these gods? Do we say that they exist? And what would it be for a named god, say Balder, with his distinctive characteristics, to exist? In any straightforward sense it would at least seem to involve there being a consciousness, answering to this name, in addition to all the millions of human [b]→ consciousnesses. Are we then to say that for each name in our directory of gods there is an additional consciousness, with the further attributes specified in the description of that particular deity? In most cases this would be theoretically possible since in most cases the gods are explicitly or implicitly finite beings whose powers and spheres of operation are at least approximately known; and many of them could co-exist without contradiction. On the other hand the gods of the monotheistic faiths are thought of in each case as the one and only God, so that it is impossible for there to be more than one instantiation of this concept. It is thus not feasible to say that all the named gods, and particularly not all the most important ones, exist – at any rate not in any simple and straightforward sense.

Further, in addition to the witness of theistic religion to this multiplicity of personal deities there are yet other major forms of thought and experience which point to non-personal ultimates: Brahman, the Dharmakaya,

Nirvana, Sunyata, the Tao. . . . But if the ultimate Reality is the blissful, universal consciousness of Brahman, which at the core of our own being we all are, how can it also be the emptiness, non-being, void of Sunyata? And again, how could it also be the Tao, as the principle of cosmic order, and again, the Dharmakaya or the eternal Buddha-nature? And if it is any of these, how can it be a personal deity? Surely these reported ultimates, personal and non-personal, are mutually exclusive. Must not any final reality either be personal, with the non-personal aspect of divinity being secondary, or be impersonal, with the worship of personal deities representing a lower level of religious consciousness, destined to be left behind in the state of final enlightenment?

[3] The naturalistic response is to see all these systems of belief as factually false although perhaps as expressing the archetypal daydreams of the human mind whereby it has distracted itself from the harsh problems of life. From this point of view the luxuriant variety and the mutual incompatibility of these conceptions of the ultimate, and of the modes of experience which they inform, demonstrates that they are 'such stuff as dreams are made on'. However I have already argued (in Chapter 13) that it is entirely reasonable for the religious person, experiencing life in relation to the transcendent – whether encountered beyond oneself or in the depths of one's own being – to believe in the reality of that which is thus apparently experienced. Having reached that conclusion one cannot dismiss the realm of religious experience and belief as illusory, even though its internal plurality and diversity must preclude any simple and straightforward account of it.

c → Nor can we reasonably claim that our own form of religious experience, together with that of the tradition of which we are a part, is veridical whilst the others are not. We can of course claim this; and indeed virtually every religious tradition has done so, regarding alternative forms of religion either as false or as confused and inferior versions of itself. But the kind of rational justification set forth in Chapter 13 for treating one's own form of religious experience as a cognitive response – though always a complexly conditioned one – to a divine reality must . . . apply equally to the religious experience of others. In acknowledging this we are obeying the intellectual Golden Rule of granting to others a premise on which we rely ourselves. Persons living within other traditions, then, are equally justified in trusting their own distinctive religious experiences and in forming their beliefs on the basis of it. For the only reason for treating one's tradition differently from others is the very human, but not very cogent, reason that it is one's own! . . .

[4] Having, then, rejected . . . the sceptical view that religious experience is *in toto* delusory, and the dogmatic view that it is all delusory except that of one's own tradition, I propose to explore the third possibility that the great post-axial faiths constitute different ways of experiencing, conceiving and living in relation to an ultimate divine Reality which transcends all our varied visions of it. . . .

We now have to distinguish between the Real *an sich* and the Real as variously experienced-and-thought by different human communities. d ↦ In each of the great traditions a distinction has been drawn, though with varying degrees of emphasis between the Real (thought of as God, Brahman, the Dharmakaya . . .) in itself and the Real as manifested within e ↦ the intellectual and experiential purview of that tradition. . . . In one form or other this distinction is required by the thought that God, Brahman, the Dharmakaya, is unlimited and therefore may not be equated without remainder with anything that can be humanly experienced and defined. Unlimitedness, or infinity, is a negative concept, the denial of limitation. That this denial must be made of the Ultimate is a basic assumption of f ↦ all the great traditions. It is a natural and reasonable assumption: for an ultimate that is limited in some mode would be limited by something other than itself; and this would entail its non-ultimacy. And with the assumption of the unlimitedness of God, Brahman, the Dharmakaya, goes the equally natural and reasonable assumption that the Ultimate, in its unlimitedness, exceeds all positive characterisations in human thought and language. . . .

[5] The traditional doctrine of divine ineffability, which I want to apply to the Real *an sich*, has however been challenged.[1] In considering the challenge we need to distinguish two issues: (1) Does it make sense to say of X that our concepts do not apply to it? And (2) If this does (though in a qualified formulation) makes sense, what reason could we have to affirm it? A response to the second question will be postponed until we come to consider the relationship between the postulated Real *an sich* and its experienced *personae* and *impersonae*. But in response to the first issue: it would indeed not make sense to say of X that *none* of our concepts apply to it. (Keith Yandell (1975, 172) calls this no-concepts interpretation 'strong ineffability'.) For it is obviously impossible to refer to something that does not even have the property of 'being able to be referred to'.[2] But these are logical pedantries which need not have worried those classical thinkers who have affirmed the ultimate ineffability of the divine nature.

Such points might however usefully have prompted them to distinguish between what we might call substantial properties, such as 'being good', 'being powerful', 'having knowledge', and purely formal and logically generated properties such as 'being a referent of a term' and 'being such that our substantial concepts do not apply'. What they wanted to affirm was that the substantial characterisations do not apply to God in God's

[1] See e.g. William Alston 1956; Keith E. Yandell 1975 and 1979; Peter C. Appleby 1980; Alvin Plantinga 1980.

[2] Thus Augustine goes too far when he says that 'God is not even to be called ineffable because to say that is to make an assertion about him' (*On Christian Doctrine*, I: 6).

self-existent being, beyond the range of human experience. They often expressed this by saying that we can only make negative statements about the Ultimate. . . . This *via negativa* (or *via remotionis*) consists in applying negative concepts to the Ultimate – the concept of not being finite, and so on – as a way of saying that it lies beyond the range of all our positive substantial characterisations. It is in this qualified sense that it makes perfectly good sense to say that our substantial concepts do not apply to the Ultimate. . . .

[6] Using this distinction between the Real *an sich* and the Real as humanly [g]→ thought-and-experienced, I want to explore the pluralistic hypothesis that the great world faiths embody different perceptions and conceptions of, and correspondingly different responses to, the Real from within the major variant ways of being human; and that within each of them the transformation of human existence from self-centredness to Reality-centredness is taking place. These traditions are accordingly to be regarded as alternative soteriological 'spaces' within which, or 'ways' along which, men and women can find salvation/liberation/ultimate fulfilment. . . .

Kant distinguished between noumenon and phenomenon, or between a *Ding an sich* and that thing as it appears to human consciousness. As he explains, he is not here using the term 'noumenon' in the positive sense of that which is knowable by some faculty of non-sensible intuition (for we have no such faculty), but in the negative sense of a 'a thing in so far as it is not an object of our sensible intuition' (B307 – 1958, 268). In this strand of Kant's thought – not the only strand, but the one which I am seeking to press into service in the epistemology of religion – the noumenal world exists independently of our perception of it and the phenomenal world is that same world as it appears to our human consciousness. . . . Analogously, I want to say that the noumenal Real is experienced and thought by different human mentalities, forming and formed by different religious traditions, as the range of gods and absolutes which the phenomenology of religion reports. And these divine *personae* and metaphysical *impersonae*, as I shall call them, are not illusory but empirically, that is experientially, real as authentic manifestations of the Real. . . . I want to say that the Real *an sich* is postulated by us as a pre-supposition . . . of religious experience and the religious life, whilst the gods, as also the mystically known Brahman, Sunyata and so on, are phenomenal manifestations of the Real occurring within the realm of religious experience. . . .

But if the Real in itself is not and cannot be humanly experienced, why [h]→ postulate such an unknown and unknowable *Ding an sich*? The answer is that the divine noumenon is a necessary postulate of the pluralistic religious life of humanity. For within each tradition we regard as real the object of our worship or contemplation. If, as I have already argued, it is also proper to regard as real the objects of worship or contemplation within the other traditions, we are led to postulate the Real *an sich* as the presupposition of the veridical character of this range of forms of religious experience.[3] Without this postulate we should be left with a plurality of *personae* and *impersonae* each of which is claimed to be Ultimate, but no one of which alone can be. We should have either to regard all the reported experiences as illusory or else return to the confessional position in which we affirm the authenticity of our own stream of religious experience whilst dismissing as illusory those occurring within other traditions. But for those to whom neither of these options seems realistic the pluralistic affirmation becomes inevitable, and with it the postulation of the Real *an sich*, which is variously experienced and thought as the range of divine phenomena described by the history of religion.

Commentary on Hick

Hick introduces the problem of religious diversity in [1] and the evidence of diversity in [2]. He rejects the naturalist and exclusivist responses to the problem in [3] and introduces his own pluralist position [4]. In [5], Hick considers an objection to pluralism before further elaborating on his theory in [6].

Hick approaches the question of religious diversity on the basis, introduced in [1], that it is rational for a person who experiences religiously to form religious beliefs and to live accordingly. He goes on to propose at a↦ that if all religious believers shared the same religious tradition, then his religious epistemology would be complete. Why does he claim this? Hick's position seems to be that in so far as people respond to religious experiences by forming religious beliefs in the same god (or gods), then this is consistent with his contention that they can all do so rationally. Whereas, if there is a diversity of religious responses, Hick suggests, this presents an apparent challenge to his theory: some further explanation is required to show how all of these contrasting responses can be rational.

What precisely is it that needs explaining? We have to look ahead to c↦ to find Hick fully spelling out what the problem is. Suppose that Jane has a religious experience and forms the belief that there is one all-powerful God. This, according to Hick's epistemology, is a rational thing for Jane to do. And suppose that Jim has a religious experience and forms the belief that there are numerous gods with different properties. According to Hick's epistemology, Jim's belief is also rational. Moreover, it seems that Jane and Jim, if they agree that it is rational to form a religious belief from a religious experience, should allow not only that their own religious beliefs are rational but also that both of their beliefs are rational. But Jim's polytheism and Jane's monotheism cannot both be true. One of them, it seems, must be mistaken. So the problem that needs addressing is how religious believers can rationally form views that are in conflict. Moreover, as Hick sets out in section 2, there is widespread diversity of belief.

[3] 'If we do not postulate the ultimate Focus, the subject, the inaccessible X lying beyond the contents of belief and experience, we might consider the real Focus as it enters into lives to be a projection' (Ninian Smart 1981, 187).

1. Briefly summarise what Hick takes to be the main areas of religious disagreement.

2. Is Hick correct to say at [a]→ that his epistemology of religion could come to a rest if there was only one religion? Does religious diversity need *actually* to occur to present a problem for his theory?

Before we look at what Hick says about some of the responses to diversity, there are a couple of points in need of further clarification. First, as Hick suggests at [b]→, the central epistemological problem posed by diversity results from the inconsistency between the views held by different religious believers. Suppose that the religious beliefs that people adopt are consistent, even if they are not in agreement. For example, we could imagine that the different deities that people believe in have limited powers and distinct domains of influence, so while religious believers do not all agree on which gods exist their religious beliefs are consistent – and in principle all of their religious beliefs could be true. So a lack of consensus on religious matters would not by itself pose a problem for Hick's epistemology. Second, following from the first point, Hick's emphasis on the number of different religious traditions and the number of different gods that have been believed in throughout history is in one respect misleading. It is not the number of different religious views but rather their inconsistency that gives rise to the epistemological question described above.

3. Consider the following argument: 'In normal circumstances, different people perceiving the same object tend to agree on the properties of what they perceive. So the huge variation in the evaluation of religious experience might be seen as grounds for supposing that religious experience is not a genuinely perceptual experience of a mind-independent reality.' Evaluate this argument. How does it relate to the problem of diversity that Hick is addressing?

Hick considers two responses to diversity in section 3 before explaining his own pluralist position in the rest of the chapter. The naturalistic response, which is to reject all religious systems of belief as mistaken, is quickly dismissed by Hick on the grounds that a person is rational in forming religious beliefs on the basis of having a religious experience. Hick is perhaps a bit *too* quick. The term 'naturalism' does not have a precise meaning that is widely agreed upon in philosophy, and Hick does not assist us by providing one. However, it is often taken to involve a commitment to the theory that only 'natural' things exist and that there is nothing 'supernatural', and Hick's discussion seems to follow this usage of 'naturalism'. What counts as 'supernatural' is also a matter of debate, but a couple of possibilities are: anything that is not subject to laws of nature, or anything which is in principle inaccessible to scientific investigation. Now, it is clear that naturalists will regard religious beliefs as false. What is not clear is why Hick thinks that they must also regard religious beliefs as unreasonable. Consider the belief, widespread in some regions of the world in ancient and medieval times, that the Earth is flat. Now, we can imagine people who do not have access to evidence from astronomy, seafarers, etc., that the surface of the Earth is curved, and who believe that the Earth is flat. Certainly, their belief is false, but is it also unreasonable or irrational? They do not have evidence for believing that the Earth is (approximately) spherical and may lack a plausible explanation for why one would not fall off a curved surface. Moreover, they might take the evidence available to them that hills and valleys tend to be uneven changes in an averagely flat plane and make the plausible, if mistaken, inference that the Earth as a whole is flat. Whatever one's views of this example, it is clear that in general the truth and the reasonableness of a belief are distinct questions, and we cannot infer from the falsity of a belief that it is unreasonable. To assume otherwise is to confuse a metaphysical issue – what is actually true – with an epistemological issue – what someone can reasonably believe to be true.

The problem that Hick is considering is that if it is reasonable for one to form religious beliefs on the basis of religious experience, then it seems that one must also concede that it is reasonable that the beliefs of those in other religious traditions are also reasonable even if those beliefs are inconsistent with one's own. So why should not one say that one's own religion is uniquely correct? This is the second 'dogmatic' response that Hick rejects. His reason for dismissing this option is that someone claiming that their religion is uniquely justified is only doing so because it happens to be their own religion. Hick elaborates on this point in another paper as follows:

> in perhaps 99 percent of cases the religion to which one adheres (or against which one reacts) is selected by the accident of birth. Someone born to devout Muslim parents in Iran or Indonesia is very likely to be a Muslim; someone born to devout Buddhist parents in Thailand or Sri Lanka is very likely to be a Buddhist; someone born to devout Christian parents in Italy or Mexico is very likely to be a Catholic Christian; and so on. Thus there is a certain non-rational arbitrariness in the claim that the particular tradition within which one happens to have been born is the one and only true religion. And if the conviction is added that salvation and eternal life depend upon accepting the truths of one's own religion, it may well seem unfair that this saving truth is known only to one group, into which only a minority of the human race have had the good fortune to be born.
>
> (Hick 1999)

As Hick points out quite forcefully here, the religion into which one is born seems to be a matter of luck. So, given that religious believers in different traditions seem to be in the same epistemic situation, with regard to having religious experiences and forming religious beliefs, the dogmatic response unreasonably privileges the views of one religion over another.

> 4. Could a similar line of argument be advanced for moral beliefs? Set out what such an argument would look like. What are its implications?

As we shall see in the following chapter on Plantinga, this last point is highly contentious; and, again, Hick does not clearly distinguish the questions of whether we should say that religious-belief formation is reasonable or rational, and whether we should say that the religious beliefs in questions are true. However, let us now look at Hick's preferred solution to the problem: pluralism. Hick has rejected the naturalist position on diversity that all religious beliefs are false, and the dogmatic view that only one's own religious beliefs are true. Hick adopts the pluralist option that all religious responses to religious experience are justified and – in some to-be-specified way – true. On the face of it, this is not a promising position to take: if there is widespread inconsistency between religious beliefs, how can many religious traditions be true?

The pluralist account that Hick introduces in section 4 (and develops in section 6) needs some unpacking. It has three main components. First, he posits the 'Real', which he describes as the common ground for different religious experiences. Second, he uses at d→ a distinction inspired by Kant between the Real as it is in itself and the Real as it is experienced by religious believers and thought about in different religious traditions. Third, Hick proposes at e→ that the Real is *ineffable*: we are unable to conceive of any property of the Real. On this third point, Hick appears to argue as follows:

1. Different religious traditions have understood the Real (in whatever form it is construed in that religion) as unlimited,
2. No human experiences or thoughts can be of unlimited things; therefore,
3. The Real cannot be conceived of by humans.

Steps (1) and (2) are at e→ and step (3) is at f→. So Hick's position in outline is this: There is the Real, which is the source of religious experiences, but the properties of the Real are unknowable. So the different ideas about the Real found in different religious traditions are brought about by the Real but do not correspond to any of the Real's actual properties.

5. Hick implies at f→ that a property is limited merely by one's being able to conceive of it. Is this correct?

One obvious line of objection to Hick's proposals he quickly addresses in section 5. If Hick's view is that we cannot form any positive conception of the Real, how is it possible to discuss the topic – in Hick's own work as selected in this chapter, for example? However, he denies that one cannot make *any* reference to the Real. This would be self-defeating, because the theory that it is not possible to refer to the Real itself requires that the Real can be referred to, i.e. that it has the property of being something that cannot be referred to. So Hick needs to moderate his position. He presents two proposals. The first is that, while 'substantial' properties cannot be attributed to the Real, we can correctly say that the Real possesses certain 'purely formal' or 'logically generated' properties. Hick does not state exactly what the distinction between substantive and formal properties is, but his examples suggest that formal properties are (at least) those that an object must have merely by virtue of our being able to refer to it. Possibly he also has in mind properties that are necessarily possessed by anything, such as 'is identical with itself'. Substantial properties, presumably, are any properties that are not formal. Hick's second point is that we can refer to substantial properties in our characterisation of the Real provided we use negative theology: while no statement of the form 'The Real is *x*' is true, where *x* is a substantial property, we can truly say 'The Real is not *x*'.

6. Should Hick support the irreducible metaphor theory, discussed in the chapter on Alston?

So Hick's position is this: It follows from the ineffability of the Real that we cannot truly claim that the Real possesses any particular substantive property. However, we can ascribe purely formal properties to the Real and we can also truly say that for any particular substantial property the Real *does not* have that property. Has Hick kept to these guidelines himself? Let us consider some of the properties that Hick claims, or seems committed to claiming, are possessed by the Real.

1. The Real *exists*. Existence is clearly not a formal property, and to say that something exists also seems to be saying something positive and informative about that thing. So, in claiming that the Real exists, Hick seems to be going beyond what he thinks can truthfully be said about the Real (and on the basis of his endorsement of negative theology would presumably agree 'The Real does *not* exist'!). However, given Hick's sympathy with Kant, it is possible that he would approve of the theory that 'exists' is not a predicate, which is sometimes presented as an objection to the ontological argument for the existence of God. For example, if one says 'The tree is green, tall and deciduous', the terms like 'green', 'tall' and 'deciduous' are predicate expressions – they are used to pick out properties of the tree. Whereas if one says 'The tree is green, tall, deciduous and exists' the term 'exists', according to the Kantian theory, does not refer to an additional property that the tree might have; it posits that there is a tree with the properties of being green, tall and deciduous. Possibly, therefore, Hick would argue that 'exists' is not a predicate and therefore existence is not a substantive property.
2. The Real is *infinite*. Hick contends in section 4 that infinity and unlimitedness are negative concepts – the denial of limitation. So his view is presumably that 'The Real is infinite' does not assign a substantial property to the Real but is rather a legitimate piece of negative theology meaning 'The Real is not finite' or 'The Real is not limited'. Here are a couple of problems with this answer. The first is that, while something being infinite implies that it is not finite, it might also mean that the thing is *actually infinite*. Perhaps Hick would argue that, if 'infinite' is taken to have this latter meaning, the term cannot be truly ascribed to the Real. But Hick also wants to say that the Real is *ultimate*, and it is not clear how calling the Real 'ultimate' could count as negative theology. Or would Hick take this to mean 'The Real is not non-ultimate'? This leads

to the second problem. Hick distinguishes positive attributions of the Real from statements of negative theology primarily on the basis of whether they appear to be saying that the Real has a certain property or lacks a certain property. But looks can be deceiving. Take the sentence 'James is not married', apparently saying that James lacks a certain property. But the sentence 'James is a bachelor', which has the same content, apparently attributes a substantial property to James. If a substantial property attribution can masquerade as a claim of negative theology, and a piece of negative theology can be dressed up to look like a substantial property attribution, we require from Hick a more clearly stated criterion for how to distinguish cases.

3. The Real is 'the postulated ground of the different forms of religious experience'. This poses the most serious challenge to Hick because it is part of Hick's own definition of the Real, and seems fairly clearly to involve some positive characterisation of the Real rather than a merely formal description. Moreover, if the Real is to stand in this relationship to human beings, it must presumably have some causal impact on human experiences – again, a substantive feature of it.

7. Summarise in your own words Hick's argument in the first two paragraphs of section 6.

Notwithstanding problems with Hick's characterisation of the Real, we can see how his theory sets the scene for his pluralism. As Hick explains in e↦, the deities and absolutes of different traditions are different manifestations of the Real, and this allows him to reject both the naturalist and dogmatic options. So, on the one hand, there is a reality backing up religious experience and belief; and, on the other hand, no particular religious tradition is privileged over any other. How satisfactory is Hick's pluralism? Here are three problems.

First, is not the upshot of Hick's pluralism that religious believers have got everything wrong? Christians, for example, believe in an omnipotent, benevolent and omniscient God. As Hick says at h↦, 'within each tradition we regard as real the object of our worship or contemplation'. But, according to Hick, the *real* God is one that (following his negative theology) is *not* omnipotent, not benevolent and not omniscient. All religious traditions will be similarly mistaken except those that embrace the Real.

Second, following from this first point, while many religious believers would concede that the god, gods or absolutes in which they believe exceed human understanding, they also believe that they can be positively characterised. Moreover, the characteristics of what is believed in distinguish different religious traditions. So many Christians believe not only that God is omnipotent, benevolent and omniscient, but also that the God in which they believe essentially has those properties, and that there is no other god. In positing the Real, which lacks these properties, Hick seems to be introducing an entity in which Christians and other religious believers do not believe and which they would presumably regard as a fiction. This would be disastrous for Hick's pluralist cause, because if he is effectively advancing a distinct religion, then, far from providing an answer to the problem of religious diversity, he is instead adding yet another religious theory to the variety that are already available.

8. Could Hick argue that attributions of omnipotence, perfect benevolence and omniscience, etc., are actually denials of the possession of substantial properties? For example, could he argue that to attribute omnipotence is simply to deny limitation of power? Or would taking that line – in the context of his other views – commit him to the further claim that something can be omnipotent even if it has no power? And, even if the offered case can be sustained, could it plausibly be extended to cover *essential* omnipotence, *essential* perfect benevolence, *essential* omniscience, and the like?

9. Hick claims at [g]→ that the Real is manifested in religions that promote the transformation of human existence from self-centredness to Reality-centredness. Why does he make this claim? Are there any religious views that will be excluded from his pluralist theory because they do not promote reality-centredness? If so, what are the implications of this?

For anyone persuaded that religious experience is caused by a religious reality but that we are not in a position to say which religious tradition is right, Hick's pluralism has an initial appeal. However, as we have seen, it faces some serious problems. There remain serious doubts about whether there is a defensible form of pluralism that is both coherent and religiously acceptable.

For further discussion of Hick's pluralism, see:

Plantinga, A., *Warranted Christian Belief*, New York: Oxford University Press, 2000.

D'Costa, G., 'The Impossibility of a Pluralist Point of View', *Religious Studies*, 32 (1996): 223–32.

Hick, J., 'The Possibility of Religious Pluralism: A Reply to Gavin D'Costa', *Religious Studies*, 33 (1997): 161–6.

Hick, J., 'Religious Pluralism', in Philip L. Quinn and Charles Taliaferro (eds), *A Companion to Philosophy of Religion*, Oxford: Blackwell, 1999.

Introduction to Plantinga

In addition to Alvin Plantinga's major contributions to religious epistemology and metaphysics noted earlier, he is also known as the leading proponent of religious exclusivism. His views on the topic are developed at length in *Warranted Christian Belief*. The following paper sets out his principal arguments: it is a forceful defence of exclusivism against the pluralist critique. Plantinga considers a variety of objections to exclusivism: that the position is intellectually arrogant, egotistical, arbitrary, unjustified, irrational or unwarranted. The following selection takes Plantinga's responses to the first four of these challenges.

Alvin Plantinga, 'Pluralism: A Defense of Religious Exclusivism' (selection)

[1] There are theistic religions but also at least some non-theistic religions (or perhaps non-theistic strands of religion) among the enormous variety of religions going under the names 'Hinduism' and 'Buddhism'; among the theistic religions, there are strands of Hinduism and Buddhism and American Indian religion as well as Islam, Judaism, and Christianity; and all these differ significantly from one another. Isn't it somehow arbitrary, or irrational, or unjustified, or unwarranted, or even oppressive and imperialistic to endorse one of these as opposed to all the others? According to Jean Bodin, 'each is refuted by all';[1] must we not agree? It is in this neighbourhood that the so-called problem of pluralism arises. Of course, many concerns and problems can come under this rubric; the specific problem I mean to discuss can be thought of as follows. To put it in an internal and personal way, I find myself with religious beliefs, and religious beliefs that I realize aren't shared by nearly everyone else. For example, I believe both

(1) The world was created by God, an almighty, all-knowing, and perfectly good personal being (one that holds beliefs; has aims, plans, and intentions; and can act to accomplish these aims)

And

(2) Human beings require salvation, and God has provided a unique way of salvation through the incarnation, life, sacrificial death, and resurrection of his divine son.

Now there are many who do not believe these things. First, there are those who agree with me on (1) but not (2): there are non-Christian theistic religions. Second, there are those who don't accept either (1) or (2) but nonetheless do believe that there is something beyond the natural worlds, a something such that human well-being and salvation depend on standing in a right relation to it. And third, in the West and since the Enlightenment, anyway, there are people – *naturalists*, we may call them – who don't believe any of these three things. And my problem is this: when I become really aware of these other ways of looking at the world, what must or should I do? What is the right sort of attitude to take? What sort of impact should

[1] *Colloquium Heptaplomeres de rerum sublimium arcanis abditis*, written by 1593 but first published in 1857. English translation by Marion Kuntz (Princeton: Princeton University Press, 1975). The quotation is from the Kuntz translation, p. 256.

this awareness have on the beliefs I hold and the strength with which I hold them? My question is this: how should I think about the great diversity the world in fact displays? Can I sensibly remain an adherent to just one of these religions, rejecting the others? And here I am thinking specifically of *beliefs*. Of course, there is a great deal more to any religion or religious practice than just belief, and I don't for a moment mean to deny it. But belief is a crucially important part of most religions; it is a crucially important part of *my* religion; and the question I mean to ask here is what the awareness of religious diversity means or should mean for my religious beliefs. . . .

There are several possible reactions to awareness of religious diversity. One is to continue to believe what you have all along believed; you learn about this diversity but continue to believe, that is, take to be true, such propositions as (1) and (2) above, consequently taking to be false any beliefs, religious or otherwise, that are incompatible with (1) and (2). Following current practice, I call this *exclusivism*; the exclusivist holds that the tenets or some of the tenets of *one* religion – Christianity, let's say – are in fact true; he adds, naturally enough, that any propositions, including other religious beliefs, that are incompatible with those tenets are false. Now there is a fairly widespread belief that there is something seriously wrong with exclusivism. It is irrational, or egotistical and unjustified,[2] or intellectually arrogant[3] . . . The claim is that exclusivism as such is or involves a vice of some sort: it is wrong or deplorable; and it is this claim that I want to examine. I propose to argue that exclusivism need not involve either epistemic or moral failure and that furthermore something like it is wholly unavoidable, given our human condition.

These objections are not to the *truth* of (1) or (2) or any other proposition someone might accept in this exclusivist way (although, of course, objections of that sort are also put forward); they are instead directed to the [a]→ *propriety* or *rightness* of exclusivism. And there are initially two different kinds of indictments of exclusivism: broadly moral or ethical indictments and broadly intellectual or epistemic indictments. These overlap in interesting ways, as we shall see below. But initially, anyway, we can take some of the complaints about exclusivism and *intellectual* criticisms: it is *irrational* or *unjustified* to think in an exclusivistic way. And the other large body of

2 Thus Gary Gutting: 'Applying these considerations to religious belief, we seem led to the conclusion that, because believers have many epistemic peers who do not share their belief in God . . . , they have no right to maintain their belief without a justification. If they do so, they are guilty of epistemic egoism.' *Religious Belief and Religious Skepticism* (Notre Dame: University of Notre Dame Press, 1982), p. 90 (but see the following pages for an important qualification).

3 'Here my submission is that on this front the traditional doctrinal position of the Church has in fact militated against its traditional moral position, and has in fact encouraged Christians to approach other men immorally. Christ has taught us humility, but we have approached them with arrogance. . . . This charge of arrogance is a serious one.' Wilfred Cantwell Smith, *Religious Diversity* (New York: Harper and Row, 1976), p. 13.

complaint is moral: there is something *morally* suspect about exclusivism: it is arbitrary, or intellectually arrogant, or imperialistic. . . .

[2] Moral Objections to Exclusivism

I first turn to the moral complaints: that the exclusivist is intellectually arrogant, or egotistical, or self-servingly arbitrary, or dishonest, or imperialistic, or oppressive. But first three qualifications. An exclusivist, like anyone else, will probably be guilty of some or all of these things to at least some degree, perhaps particularly the first two; the question is, however, whether she is guilty of these things just by virtue of being an exclusivist.
b→ Second, I shall use the term 'exclusivism' in such a way that you don't count as exclusivist unless you are rather fully aware of other faiths, have had their existence and their claims called to your attention with some force and perhaps fairly frequently, and have to some degree reflected on the problem of pluralism, asking yourself such questions as whether it is or could be really true that the Lord has revealed himself and his programs to us Christians, say, in a way in which he hasn't revealed himself to those of other faiths. Thus my grandmother, for example, would not have counted as an exclusivist. She had, of course, *heard* of the heathen, as she called them, but the idea that perhaps Christians could learn from them, and learn from them with respect to religious matters, had not so much as entered her head; and the fact that it *hadn't* entered her head, I take it, was not a matter of moral dereliction on her part. The same would go for a Buddhist or Hindu peasant. These people are not, I think, plausibly charged with arrogance or other moral flaws in believing as they do.

Third, suppose I am exclusivist with respect to (1), for example, but nonculpably believe, like Thomas Aquinas, say, that I have a knock-down, drag-out argument, a demonstration or conclusive proof of the proposition that there is such a person as God; and suppose I think further (and nonculpably) that if those who don't believe (1) were to be apprised of this argument (and had the ability and training necessary to grasp it, and were to think about the argument fairly and reflectively), they too would come to believe (1). Then I could hardly be charged with these moral faults. My condition would be like that of Gödel, let's say, upon having recognized that he had a proof for the incompleteness of arithmetic. True, many of his colleagues and peers didn't believe that arithmetic was incomplete, and some believed that it *was* complete; but presumably Gödel wasn't arbitrary or egotistical in believing that arithmetic is in fact incomplete. Furthermore, he would not have been at fault had he nonculpably but *mistakenly* believed that he had found such a proof. Accordingly, I shall use the term 'exclusivist' in such a way that you don't count as an exclusivist if you nonculpably think you know of a demonstration or conclusive argument for the beliefs with respect to which you are exclusivist, or even if you nonculpably think you know of an argument that would convince all or most intelligent and honest people of the truth of that proposition. So an exclusivist, as I use the term, not only believes something like (1) or (2) and thinks false any proposition incompatible with it; she also meets a further condition C that is hard to state precisely and in detail (and in fact any attempt to do so would involve a long and at present irrelevant discussion of ceteris paribus clauses). Suffice it to say that C includes (1) being rather fully aware of other religions, (2) knowing that there is much that at least looks like genuine piety and devoutness to them, and (3) believing that you know of no arguments that would necessarily convince all or most honest and intelligent dissenters of your own religious allegiances. . . .

[3] The important moral charge is that there is a sort of self-serving arbitrariness, an arrogance or egotism, in accepting such propositions as (1) or (2) under condition C; exclusivism is guilty of some serious moral fault or flaw. According to Wilfred Cantwell Smith, 'except at the cost of insensitivity or delinquency, it is morally not possible actually to go out into the world and say to devout, intelligent, fellow human beings: ". . . we believe that we know God and we are right; you believe that you know God, and you are totally wrong." '[4]

So what can the exclusivist have to say for herself? Well, it must be conceded immediately that if she believes (1) or (2), then she must also believe that those who believe something incompatible with them are mistaken and believe what is false. That's no more than simple logic. Furthermore, she must also believe that those who do not believe as she does – those who believe neither (1) nor (2), whether or not they believe their negations – *fail* to believe something that is true, deep, and important, and that she *does* believe. She must therefore see herself as *privileged* with respect to those others – those others of both kinds. There is something of great value, she must think, that *she* has and *they* lack. They are ignorant of something – something of great importance – of which she has knowledge. But does this make her properly subject to the above censure?

I think that the answer must be no. Or if the answer is yes, then I think we have here a genuine moral dilemma; for in our earthly life here below, as my Sunday School teacher used to say, there is no real alternative; there is no reflective attitude that is not open to the same strictures. These charges of arrogance are a philosophical tar baby: get close enough to them to use them against the exclusivist, and you are likely to find them stuck fast to yourself. How so? Well, as an exclusivist, I realize I can't convince others that they should believe as I do, but I nonetheless continue to believe as I do: and the charge is that I am as a result arrogant or egotistical,

arbitrarily preferring my way of doing things to other ways.[5] But what are

[4] Smith, *Religious Diversity*, p. 14. . . .

[5] 'The only reason for treating one's tradition differently from others is the very human but not very cogent reason that it's one's own!' Hick, *An Interpretation of Religion*, p. 235.

my alternatives with respect to a proposition like (1)? There seem to be three choices.[6] I can continue to hold it; I can withhold it, in Roderick Chisholm's sense, believing neither it nor its denial; and I can accept its denial. Consider the third way, a way taken by those pluralists who, like John Hick, hold that such propositions as (1) and (2) and their colleagues from other faiths are literally false although in some way still valid responses to the Real. This seems to me to be no advance at all with respect to the arrogance or egotism problem; this is not a way out. For if I do this, I will then be in the very same condition as I am now: I will believe many propositions others don't believe and will be in condition C with respect to those propositions. For I will then believe the denials of (1) and (2) (as well as the denials of many other propositions explicitly accepted by those of other faiths). Many others, of course, do not believe the denials of (1) and (2), and in fact believe (1) and (2). Further, I will not know of any arguments that can be counted on to persuade those who do believe (1) and (2) (or propositions accepted by the adherent of other religions). I am therefore in the condition of believing propositions that many others do not believe and furthermore am in condition C. If, in the case of those who believe (1) and (2), that is sufficient for intellectual arrogance or egotism, the same goes for those who believe their denials.

So consider the second option: I can instead *withhold* the proposition in question. I can say to myself: 'The right course here, given that I can't or couldn't convince those others of what *I* believe, is to believe neither these [d]→ propositions nor their denials.' The pluralist objector to exclusivism can say that the right course under condition C is to *abstain* from believing the offending proposition and also abstain from believing its denial; call him, therefore, 'the abstemious pluralist.' But does he thus really avoid the condition that, on the part of the exclusivist, leads to the charges of egotism and arrogance? Think, for a moment, about disagreement. Disagreement, fundamentally, is a matter of adopting conflicting propositional attitudes with respect to a given proposition. In the simplest and most familiar case, I disagree with you if there is some proposition p such that I believe p and you believe $-p$. But that's just the simplest case: I believe p and you withhold it, fail to believe it. Call the first kind of disagreement 'contradicting'; call the second 'dissenting.'

My claim is that if contradicting others (under condition C spelled out above) is arrogant and egotistical, so is dissenting (under that same condition). For supposing you believe some proposition p but I don't: perhaps

[6] To speak of a choice here suggests that I can simply choose which of these three attitudes to adopt; but is that at all realistic? Are my beliefs to that degree within my control? Here I shall set aside the question of whether and to what degree my beliefs are subject to my control and within my power. Perhaps we have very little control over them; then the moral critic of exclusivism can't properly accuse the exclusivist of dereliction of moral duty, but he could still argue that the exclusivist's stance is unhappy, bad, a miserable state of affairs. Even if I can't help it that I am overbearing and conceited, my being that way is a bad state of affairs.

you believe it is wrong to discriminate against people simply on the grounds of race, but I, recognizing that there are many people who disagree with you, do not believe this proposition. I don't disbelieve it either, of course, but in the circumstances I think the right thing to do is to abstain from belief. Then am I not implicitly condemning your attitude, your *believing* the proposition, as somehow improper – naïve, perhaps, or unjustified, or in some other way less than optimal? I am implicitly saying that my attitude is the superior one; I think my course of action here is the right one and yours somehow wrong, inadequate, improper, in the circumstances at best second-rate. Also, I realize that there is no question, here, of *showing* you that your attitude is wrong or improper or naïve; so am I not guilty of intellectual arrogance? Of a sort of egotism, thinking I know better than you, arrogating to myself a privileged status with respect to you? The problem for the exclusivist was that she was obliged to think she possessed a truth missed by many others; the problem for the abstemious pluralist is that he is obliged to think he possesses a virtue others don't, or acts rightly where others don't. If, in condition C, one is arrogant by way of believing a proposition others don't, isn't one equally, under those reflective conditions, arrogant by way of withholding a proposition others don't?

e → Perhaps you will respond by saying that the abstemious pluralist gets into trouble, falls into arrogance, by way of implicitly saying or believing that his way of proceeding is *better* or *wiser* than other ways pursued by other people, and perhaps he can escape by abstaining from *that* view as well. Can't he escape the problem by refraining from believing that racial bigotry is wrong, and also refraining from holding the view that it is *better*, under the conditions that obtain, to withhold that proposition than to assert and believe it? Well, yes, he can; then he has no *reason* for his abstention; he doesn't believe that abstention is better or more appropriate; he simply does abstain. Does this get him off the egotistical hook? Perhaps. But then, of course, he can't, in consistency, also hold that there is something wrong with *not* abstaining, with coming right out and *believing* that bigotry is wrong; he loses his objection to the exclusivist. Accordingly, this way out is not available for the abstemious pluralist who accuses the exclusivist of arrogance and egotism.

Indeed, I think we can show that the abstemious pluralist who brings charges of intellectual arrogance against exclusivism is hoist with his own petard, holds a position that in a certain way is self-referentially inconsistent in the circumstances. For he believes

(3) If *S* knows that others don't believe *p* and that he is in condition C with respect to *p*, then *S* should not believe *p*;

this or something like it is the ground of the charges he brings against the exclusivist. But, the abstemious pluralist realizes that many do not accept (3); and I suppose he also realizes that it is unlikely that he can find arguments for (3) that will convince them; hence, he knows that he is in condition C. Given his acceptance of (3), therefore, the right course for him is to abstain from believing (3). Under the conditions that do in fact obtain – namely, his knowledge that others don't accept it and that condition C obtains – he can't properly accept it.

I am therefore inclined to think that one can't, in the circumstances, properly hold (3) or any other proposition that will do the job. One can't find here some principle on the basis of which to hold that the exclusivist is doing the wrong thing, suffers from some moral fault – that is, one can't find such a principle that doesn't, as we might put it, fall victim to itself.

So the abstemious pluralist is hoist with his own petard; but even apart from this dialectical argument (which in any event some will think unduly cute), aren't the charges unconvincing and implausible? I must concede that there are a variety of ways in which I can be and have been intellectually arrogant and egotistic; I have certainly fallen into this vice in the past and no doubt am not free of it now. But am I really arrogant and egotistic just by virtue of believing that I know others don't believe, where I can't show them that I am right? Suppose I think the matter over, consider the objections as carefully as I can, realize that I am finite and furthermore a sinner, certainly no better than those with whom I disagree, and indeed inferior both morally and intellectually to many who do not believe what I do; but suppose it *still* seems clear to me that the proposition in question is true. Can I really be behaving immorally in continuing to believe it? I am dead sure that it is wrong to try to advance my career by telling lies about my colleagues; I realize there are those who disagree; I also realize that in all likelihood there is no way I can find to show them that they are wrong; nonetheless I think they *are* wrong. If I think this after careful reflection – if I consider the claims of those who disagree as sympathetically as I can, if I try my level best to ascertain the truth here – and it *still* seems to me sleazy, wrong, and despicable to lie about my colleagues to advance my career, could I really be doing what is immoral by continuing to believe as before? I can't see how. If, after careful reflection and thought, you find yourself convinced that the right propositional attitude to take to (1) and (2) in the face of the facts of religious pluralism is belief or abstention from belief, how could you properly be taxed with egotism, either for so believing or for so abstaining? Even if you knew others did not agree with you? . . .

[4] Epistemic Objections to Exclusivism

I turn now to *epistemic* objections to exclusivism. There are many different specifically epistemic virtues and a corresponding plethora of epistemic vices; the ones with which the exclusivist is most frequently charged, however, are *irrationality* and *lack of justification* in holding his exclusivist beliefs. The claim is that as an exclusivist he holds unjustified beliefs and/or irrational beliefs. Better, *he* is unjustified or irrational in holding these beliefs. I shall therefore consider these two claims, and I shall argue that the exclusivist views need not be either unjustified or irrational. I will then turn to the question whether his beliefs could have *warrant* – that property, whatever precisely it is, that distinguishes knowledge from mere true belief – and whether they could have enough warrant for knowledge.

A. JUSTIFICATION

The pluralist objector sometimes claims that to hold exclusivist views, in condition C, is *unjustified* – *epistemically* unjustified. Is this true? And what does he mean when he makes this claim? As even a brief glance at the contemporary epistemological literature shows, justification is a protean and multifarious notion.[7] There are, I think, substantially two possibilities as to what he means. The central core of the notion, its beating heart, the paradigmatic centre to which most of the myriad contemporary variations are related by way of analogical extension and family resemblance, is the notion of *being within one's intellectual rights*, having violated no intellectual or cognitive duties or obligations in the formation and sustenance of the belief in question. . . .

The duties involved, naturally enough, would be specifically *epistemic* duties: perhaps a duty to proportion degree of belief to (propositional) evidence from what is *certain*, that is, self-evident and incorrigible, as with Locke, or perhaps to try one's best to get into and stay in the right relation to the truth, as with Roderick Chisholm,[8] the leading contemporary champion of the justificationist tradition with respect to knowledge. But at present there is widespread (and, as I see it, correct) agreement that there is no duty of the Lockean kind. Perhaps there is one of the Chisholmian kind, but isn't the exclusivist conforming to that duty if, after the sort of careful, indeed prayerful, consideration I mentioned in the response to the moral objection, it still seems to him strongly that (1), say, is true and accordingly still believes it? It is therefore hard to see that the exclusivist is necessarily unjustified in this way.

The second possibility for understanding the charge – the charge that exclusivism is epistemically unjustified – has to do with the oft-repeated claim that exclusivism is intellectually *arbitrary*. Perhaps the idea is that

[7] See my 'Justification in the Twentieth Century,' *Philosophical and Phenomenological Research* 50, supplement (Fall 1990), 45 ff., and see Chapter 1 of my *Warrant The Current Debate* (New York: Oxford University Press, 1993).

[8] See the three editions of *Theory of Knowledge* [(New Jersey: Prentice Hall, 1st ed., 1966; 2nd ed., 1977; 3rd ed., 1989)].

there is an intellectual duty to treat similar cases similarly; the exclusivist violates this duty by arbitrarily choosing to believe (for the moment going along with the fiction that we *choose* beliefs of this sort) (1) and (2) in the face of the plurality of conflicting religious beliefs the world presents. But suppose there is such a duty. Clearly, you do not violate it if you nonculpably think the beliefs in question are *not* on a par. And, as an exclusivist, I *do* think (nonculpably, I hope) that they are not on a par: I think (1) and (2) *true* and those incompatible with either of them *false*.

The rejoinder, of course, will be that it is not *alethic* parity (their having the same truth value) that is at issue: it is *epistemic* parity that counts. What kind of epistemic parity? What would be relevant here, I should think, would be *internal* or internalist epistemic parity: parity with respect to what is internally available to the believer. What is internally available to the believer includes, for example, detectable relationships between the belief in question and other beliefs you hold; so internal parity would include parity of propositional evidence. What is internally available to the believer also includes the *phenomenology* that goes with the beliefs in question: the *sensuous* phenomenology, but also the non-sensuous phenomenology involved, for example, in the belief's having the feel of being *right*. But once more, then, (1) and (2) are not on an internal par, for the exclusivist, with beliefs that are incompatible with them. (1) and (2), after all, seem to be true; they have for me the phenomenology that accompanies that seeming. The same cannot be said for propositions incompatible with them. If, furthermore, John Calvin is right in thinking that there is such a thing as the Sensus Divinitatis and the Internal Testimony of the Holy Spirit, then perhaps (1) and (2) are produced in me by those belief-producing processes, and have for me the phenomenology that goes with them; the same is not true for propositions incompatible with them.

But then the next rejoinder: isn't it probably true that those who reject (1) and (2) in favour of other beliefs have propositional evidence for their beliefs that is on a par with mine for my beliefs; and isn't it also probably true that the same or similar phenomenology accompanies their beliefs as accompanies mine? So that those beliefs really are epistemically and internally on a par with (1) and (2), and the exclusivist is still treating like cases differently? I don't think so: I think there really are arguments available for (1), at least, that are not available for its competitors. And as for similar phenomenology, that is not easy to say; it is not easy to look into the breast of another; the secrets of the human heart are hard to fathom; it is hard indeed to discover this sort of thing even with respect to someone you know really well. But I am prepared to stipulate both sorts of parity. Let's agree for purposes of argument that these beliefs are on an epistemic par in the sense that those of a different religious tradition have the same sort of internally available markers – evidence, phenomenology, and the like – for their beliefs as I have for (1) and (2). What follows?

Return to the case of moral belief. King David took Bathsheba, made her pregnant, and then, after the failure of various stratagems to get her husband Uriah to think the baby was his, arranged for Uriah to be killed. The prophet Nathan came to David and told him a story about a rich man and a poor man. The rich man had many flocks and herds; the poor man had only a single ewe lamb, which grew up with his children, 'ate at his table, drank from his cup, lay in his bosom, and was like a daughter to him.' The rich man had unexpected guests. Instead of slaughtering one of his own sheep, he took the poor man's single ewe lamb, slaughtered it, and served it to his guests. David exploded in anger: 'The man who did this deserves to die!' Then, in one of the most riveting passages in all the Bible, Nathan turns to David, stretches out his arm and points to him, and declares, '*You are that man!*' And David sees what he has done.

My interest here is in David's reaction to the story. I agree with David: such injustice is utterly and despicably wrong; there are really no words for it. I believe that such an action is wrong, and I believe that the proposition that it *isn't* wrong – either because really *nothing* is wrong, or because even if *some* things are wrong, *this* isn't – is false. As a matter of fact, there isn't a lot I believe more strongly. I recognize, however, that there are those who disagree with me; and once more, I doubt that I could find an argument to show them that I am right and they wrong. Further, for all I know, their conflicting beliefs have for them the same internally available epistemic markers, the same phenomenology, as mine have for me. Am I then being arbitrary, treating similar cases differently in continuing to hold, as I do, that in fact that kind of behaviour *is* dreadfully wrong? I don't think so. Am I wrong in thinking racial bigotry despicable, even though I know there are others who disagree, and even if I think they have the same internal markers for their beliefs as I have for mine? I don't think so. I believe in Serious Actualism, the view that no objects have properties in worlds in which they do not exist, not even nonexistence. Others do not believe this, and perhaps the internal markers of their dissenting views have for them the same quality as my views have for me. Am I being arbitrary in continuing to think as I do? I can't see how.

f→ And the reason here is: in each of these cases, the believer in question doesn't really think the beliefs in question *are* on a relevant epistemic par. She may agree that she and those who dissent are equally convinced of the truth of their belief, and even that they are internally on a par, that the internally available markers are similar, or relevantly similar. But she must still think that there is an important epistemic difference: she thinks that somehow the other person has *made a mistake*, or *has a blind spot*, or hasn't been wholly attentive, or hasn't received some grace she has, or is
g→ in some way epistemically less fortunate. And, of course, the pluralist critic is in no better case. He thinks the thing to do when there is internal epistemic parity is to withhold judgement; he knows that there are others who don't think so, and for all he knows, that belief has internal parity with his; if he continues in that belief, therefore, he will be in the same condition as the exclusivist; and if he doesn't continue in this belief, he no longer has an objection to the exclusivist.

But couldn't I be wrong? Of course I could! But I don't avoid the risk by withholding all religious (or philosophical or moral) beliefs; I can go wrong that way as well as any other, treating all religions, or all philosophical thoughts, or all moral views, on a par. Again, there is no safe haven here, no way to avoid risk. In particular, you won't reach safe haven by trying to take the same attitude towards all the historically available patterns of belief and withholding: for in doing so, you adopt a particular pattern of belief and withholding, one incompatible with some adopted by others. You pays your money and you takes your choice, realising that you, like anyone else, can be desperately wrong. But what else can you do? You don't really have an alternative. And how can you do better than believe and withhold according to what, after serious and responsible consideration, seems to you to be the right pattern of belief and withholding?

Commentary on Plantinga

We have split the paper into four sections. [1] defines terms and introduces two objections to exclusivism motivated by the evidence of religious diversity: moral and epistemological. Some qualifications are introduced in [2]; the moral and epistemological objections are then evaluated and rejected in [3] and [4].

Plantinga's understanding of the challenges to religious exclusivism presented by religious diversity, set out in section 1, is broadly similar to Hick's. In a→, however, Plantinga detects two different types of problem that are not clearly distinguished by Hick. On the one hand, it could be objected that to remain an exclusivist in the light of religious diversity exhibits a *moral* failing: it is intellectually arrogant, egotistical, etc. This strand of the argument is evaluated in section 3. On the other hand, exclusivism might be thought to exhibit an *epistemic* failing: it is unreasonable or *unjustifiable* to claim that the beliefs of just one religious tradition are true. Plantinga tackles this line of objection in the rest of the paper.

1. Work through [1] and (*a*) explain what Plantinga takes the problem of religious diversity to be, (*b*) concisely state his definition of exclusivism.

2. Are the moral and epistemic challenges to exclusivism independent issues? For example, could someone plausibly argue that exclusivism is morally unacceptable *because* of its epistemic failings? If so, is Plantinga right to treat the issues separately?

Section [2], on the moral objection to exclusivism, is introduced with three qualifications. These are presented as scene-setting comments that clarify the subject matter under debate and the definition of 'exclusivism'. Certainly, the first falls into this category: exclusivists, just as pluralists, can exhibit moral failings; what is of interest to us is whether there are moral failings that are the upshot of being an exclusivist. Also, it is usually taken for granted that there is epistemic parity between (at least a good number of) religious believers in different religious traditions: nobody has a knock-down argument for the truth of their personal religious beliefs. So Plantinga's third qualification looks in order. However, the second qualification needs some comment. Plantinga proposes at [b]→ modifications to the definition of exclusivism given in [1]:

(E) The exclusivist holds that the tenets of just one religion are true, and that any religious beliefs incompatible with those tenets are false,

so that we do *not* count a particular class of religious believers (that includes elderly grandmothers and Buddhist peasants) as exclusivists. To make this clearer, let us distinguish the following categories of religious believer:

(R1) Someone who believes that the tenets of just one religion are true, but is unaware of the existence of any beliefs that are inconsistent with this religion;
(R2) Someone who believes that the tenets of just one religion are true, and is aware of other religions but has not given serious consideration to them;
(R3) Someone who believes that the tenets of just one religion are true and is fully aware of the beliefs of other religions.

Since nobody who falls into category (R1) is aware of any beliefs contrary to their own religion, let us allow that (R1) is not exclusivist. But (R2) and (R3) are clearly exclusivist on the criterion specified by (E). Plantinga proposes to use the term 'exclusivist' so that no religious believers in (R2) and many in (R3) – those who have not had their attention called 'with some force' to the facts of religious diversity, etc. – will count as exclusivists. He appears to motivate this modification on the grounds that we should not regard these classes of religious believer as morally culpable for their seeming exclusivism. But the question of whether religious exclusivism is morally culpable is the issue up for debate! Moreover, even if Plantinga is correct that members of (R2) and some of (R3) are not morally culpable, might they not be epistemically culpable? Why should the discussion of the epistemic argument later in the paper be restricted to 'exclusivists' who are not morally culpable for their beliefs? Plantinga can, of course, use the expression 'exclusivism' in any way he wants. But, given that he is engaging in a debate with pluralists about the moral and epistemic obligations of exclusivists, the restrictions he imposes on the meaning of 'exclusivism' look surprising.

3. Explain Plantinga's comparison with Gödel in the third qualification in section [2]. What point is he making here? Do you agree with him?

How does Plantinga respond to the challenge that religious exclusivism is intellectually arrogant? His main argument, which is in section 3, begins by assuming that the complaint about intellectual arrogance is correct with the aim of showing that if the pluralist's charge against the exclusivist is correct, then it equally applies to *any* belief – including the belief in pluralism. If Plantinga's argument works, then he has undermined the pluralist's contention that pluralism is a morally better position (i.e. less arrogant or egotistical) than exclusivism.

So suppose it is intellectually arrogant to believe in (1). There seem to be three available options, given in [c]→:

(*a*) Keep believing in (1);
(*b*) Withhold from believing that (1) is true or believing that (1) is false;
(*c*) Believe that (1) is false.

Now, if the moral objection makes position (*a*) unacceptable, then it seems that it should also make position (*c*) unacceptable. If it is intellectually arrogant to believe that (1) is true and that those who disagree are wrong, then it is equally arrogant to believe that (1) is false and that those to disagree are wrong. This leaves option (*b*).

4. Carefully read through the fourth and fifth paragraphs of section 3 and explain: Plantinga's definition of 'abstemious pluralist', his account of disagreement, and the distinction between contradicting and dissenting.

Suppose you opt for (*b*) on the grounds that abstention is the best belief policy with regard to (1) and (2). This is the position Plantinga describes at [d]→. Are you not now at least implicitly disagreeing with – and therefore being intellectually arrogant with respect to – anyone who takes either option (*a*) or option (*b*) and believes that they are entitled to do so? Suppose, instead, you just remain coolly neutral about (1) and (2), without believing that abstention is a better belief policy. This is the position Plantinga considers at [e]→. The pluralist will now no longer disagree with supporters of (1) but at the cost of giving up on the claim that where there is disagreement abstention is a morally superior belief policy. So Plantinga's argument, in summary, is that if the charge of intellectual arrogance sticks at all it sticks to *any* position that can be taken on (1).

5. A further point indicated in section 3 is that if the moral challenge to religious exclusivism is successful it will similarly apply to *moral* exclusivism. What would be the upshot of this for moral exclusivism? Is this a persuasive response to the moral objection to religious exclusivism?

6. Explain Plantinga's argument that abstemious pluralism is 'self-referentially inconsistent'. Does the argument show that the theory is untenable?

Plantinga addresses the epistemic objection to exclusivism in [4]. He focuses on what he takes to be the most promising version of this line of argument against the exclusivist: that it is intellectually arbitrary. This was certainly a central component of Hick's arguments against exclusivism. For example, Hick's observation that the religious beliefs that a person adopts are a matter of historical and geographical accident was intended to point up the arbitrariness of having a particular religious belief system, or being religious at all.

7. Explain Plantinga's distinction between *alethic* parity and *epistemic* parity. What is its relevance in his argument in section 3?

Plantinga allows, for the sake of argument – though makes rather heavy weather of it – that non-Christian religious believers may have the same degree of confidence and evidence and internal perspective on their religious beliefs as he does on his. So does it follow that exclusivism about religious belief is intellectually arbitrary and, in this respect, unjustified? Not so, says Plantinga in [f]↦, for just consider any deeply held moral belief that you have: are you prepared to concede on this issue to someone who holds a contrary belief that you deem immoral, because that person appears confident in their opposing moral belief? In general, for moral and other types of belief, Plantinga argues, we take those who disagree with us to have failed to recognise the truth of what we believe. Now, perhaps the pluralist could argue that we are wrong to think that we have this epistemic advantage in conditions C. But Plantinga responds in [g]↦: the pluralist must believe that *he* has an epistemic advantage with respect to pluralism, i.e. that pluralism is correct and exclusivism mistaken. If it is all right for the pluralist to think he is right about pluralism, then why is it not all right for Plantinga to think he is right about exclusivism? The pluralist seems hoist by his own petard.

As we found in the preceding chapter, there are some serious difficulties facing religious pluralism, at least in the form that it has been developed by Hick. Has Plantinga shown that the arguments levelled against religious exclusivism by the pluralist are without merit? Here are some responses that the pluralist might consider. We shall leave it to the reader to evaluate their effectiveness.

a. Look at Plantinga's quotation from Wilfred Cantwell Smith at the beginning of [3]. Smith does not argue – in this quotation at least – that it is the belief in exclusivism *per se* that is morally questionable. Rather, he objects to the behaviour that is prompted by the belief in exclusivism. So would the pluralist be better-placed, with respect to Plantinga's counter-argument, by proposing that what is intellectually arrogant about exclusivism is the behaviour, specifically the overconfidence, of those who believe in it?
b. Plantinga indicates that if the charge of intellectual arrogance works against religious exclusivism, then it will also work against moral exclusivism – with the unhappy result that we should concede on moral beliefs such as the wrongness of racial bigotry. However, consider the following argument: Ethical exclusivism on some issues is not as vulnerable to the charge of intellectual arrogance as religious exclusivism precisely because it involves an ethical evaluation. Although intellectual arrogance is an ethical failing, it is not one so serious that it is impermissible under any circumstances. Since taking a position on a matter like racial bigotry is itself of ethical importance, it can

trump the ethical concern that one is being intellectually arrogant in doing so. Plantinga is wrong, therefore, in thinking that the pluralist's charge of intellectual arrogance against religious exclusivism will similarly apply to moral exclusivism. Is this a good counter-argument to Plantinga?

c. Suppose the pluralist argues as follows: 'Intellectual arrogance is an undesirable feature of a belief that it is better to avoid. But it only makes for an ethical objection to having a belief if it is reasonable to expect that you could avoid having that belief. You are not obliged to do something that you cannot achieve. By showing that the charge of intellectual arrogance is a "tar baby" that can be levelled at every belief that we have, and given that we cannot withhold all our beliefs, Plantinga shows that the charge is not an effective moral objection against *every* belief. What he does not show is that it is not an effective moral objection to *some* beliefs – specifically, those beliefs that we can reasonably be expected to modify. Religious exclusivism is one of those beliefs.' Is this a persuasive response to Plantinga?

d. There are circumstances in which it seems epistemically (and maybe also morally) good policy to modify one's beliefs in the face of apparently reasonable and confident disagreement. If at a school reunion I confidently remember winning a gold medal in high jump, while everyone else (including other competitors) recall me winning bronze, would it not be intellectually arbitrary and arrogant for me to insist that only I remembered correctly? If at an examiners' meeting half the members of staff calculate a student's annual score at 69.7 and the other half at 70.1, should not they all be uncertain about the correct result? So can the pluralist successfully argue that the religious believer, who is informed about religious diversity, is relevantly similar to the people in these examples and so should abandon exclusivism?

e. Following [C]→, Plantinga claims that since the pluralist objects to someone believing (1), and since the same objections apply to someone believing that (1) is false, then the only other option is to withhold from believing (1). And in the discussion of both the moral and the epistemic objections to exclusivism he takes the pluralist to advocate one's abstaining from religious belief. But is there not a fourth option, namely to seek *accommodation* of our beliefs with people who disagree (where the disagreement is under condition C)? Hick, for example, does not claim that Christians should withhold from their core religious beliefs, but rather proposes additional beliefs (about the Real, etc.) and reinterpretation of existing beliefs to allow for accommodation between Christianity and other religions. Putting aside the question of whether Hick's specific proposals for accommodation are good ones, would the pluralist's moral and epistemic complaints against the exclusivist be more persuasive if directed against the exclusivist's failure to accommodate?

For further discussion of religious exclusivism, you might wish to look at:

Alston, W., 'Religious Diversity and the Perceptual Knowledge of God', *Faith and Philosophy*, 5: 433–48. Reprinted in K. Meeker and P. Quinn (eds), *The Philosophical Challenge of Religious Diversity*, New York: Oxford University Press, 1988.

Feldman, R., 'Plantinga on Exclusivism', *Faith and Philosophy*, 20 (2003): 85–90.
Plantinga, A., 'Ad Hick', *Faith and Philosophy*, 14 (1997): 295–8. Reprinted in J. Hick (ed.), *Dialogues in the Philosophy of Religion*, New York: Palgrave Macmillan, 2001.

For some more general work on the epistemology of disagreement, see:

Christensen, D., 'Epistemology of Disagreement: The Good News', *The Philosophical Review*, 116 (2007): 187–217.
Kelly, T., 'The Epistemic Significance of Disagreement', in T. S. Gendler and J. Hawthorne (eds), *Oxford Studies in Epistemology*, New York: Oxford University Press, 2005.

Index